P9-AFQ-506

RED LINE

RED LINE

American Foreign Policy in a Time of Fractured Politics and Failing States

P. J. Crowley

ROWMAN & LITTLEFIELD
Lanham • Boulder • New York • London

Published by Rowman & Littlefield
A wholly owned subsidiary of The Rowman & Littlefield Publishing Group, Inc.
4501 Forbes Boulevard, Suite 200, Lanham, Maryland 20706
www.rowman.com

Unit A, Whitacre Mews, 26–34 Stannary Street, London SE11 4AB

Distributed by NATIONAL BOOK NETWORK

British Library Cataloguing in Publication Information Available

Library of Congress Cataloging-in-Publication Data Available

ISBN: 978-1-4422-5570-8 (cloth : alk. paper)
ISBN: 978-1-4422-5571-5 (electronic)

♾ ™ The paper used in this publication meets the minimum requirements of American National Standard for Information Sciences—Permanence of Paper for Printed Library Materials, ANSI/NISO Z39.48-1992.

Printed in the United States of America

To Paula, Mary, and Chris
With All My Love

CONTENTS

FOREWORD

On the twelfth anniversary of the attacks of September 11, Russian president Vladimir Putin wrote in the *New York Times*, "It is extremely dangerous to encourage people to see themselves as exceptional, whatever the motivation."[1]

Putin was reacting to comments U.S. president Barack Obama made the day before, defending his decision to take military action to hold Bashar al-Assad accountable for the use of chemical weapons in the deepening Syrian civil war.

While pledging not to become "the world's policeman," Obama believed the willingness of the United States to serve for nearly seven decades as "the anchor of global security" and enforce international norms is "what makes us exceptional."[2] He still hoped Congress would agree to support limited air strikes against Syria.

Putin linked Obama's assertion of exceptionalism with Bush's narrative from the war on terror—you're either with us or against us—and asked why the United States would want to make the same mistake in Syria that it did in Iraq, intervening without the approval of the United Nations and increasing the risk the conflict would spread beyond Syria's borders.

Five months later, with no small irony, Putin would make a much different argument regarding Russia's prerogatives in Ukraine. Later, he would also intervene in Syria to save the Assad regime from collapse.

Obama did believe in American exceptionalism—the liberal international system that the United States largely constructed and sustained has made the world more stable, peaceful, and prosperous even with the vexing challenges it confronts today. What Obama questioned was American indispensability—

that the United States has the responsibility, the ability, or the resources to right global wrongs not linked to vital U.S. national interests.

Late in his presidency, Obama told cadets at the Air Force Academy that "oftentimes the greatest damage to American credibility comes when we over-reach." He believed it was important "to learn from our history."[3]

During his two terms, Obama narrowed what he considered vital. After the overreach in Iraq, he sought to preserve American power by employing it more judiciously and, given his reliance on drones, less overtly. But the president would also learn that American credibility can be affected not just from aiming too high, but also too low.

Obama was elected as an idealist but operated far more as a realist, strongly identifying with Presidents Dwight Eisenhower and George H. W. Bush. Like Eisenhower, he feared how the use of overt force could draw the United States into escalating and costly military adventures and preferred covert action. Like Bush, he was prepared to use decisive force for a limited purpose, preferably with international support and allies.

Of course, such comparisons are always imperfect. In the early stages of the Cold War, Eisenhower counterbalanced a rising Soviet adversary with a broad array of security alliances. He also supported the overthrow of a populist government in Iran, blocked a prospective national election in Vietnam, and chose not to intervene to defend a popular revolt in Hungary.

In the early stages of the post–Cold War "new world order," Bush deftly managed the Soviet collapse and began the restructuring of America's global military posture. He fought a war over international principle and oil—specifically who controlled the supply—and in the process deepened the U.S. presence in the Middle East. He used military force to overthrow a government in Panama, but not Iraq, although he launched an open-ended air campaign to preserve a safe haven for the Iraqi Kurds.

Obama came to office seven years into a war on terror that he thought—and a clear majority of American voters agreed—had veered off course. Like Eisenhower with Korea and Bush with Vietnam, Obama had to deal with the legacy and politics of an unpopular war. What he lacked was the national sense of urgency that accompanied the Cold War—the world did seem on the precipice during the 1950s—or the sense of possibility that accompanied its end—the world could be reshaped less by our fears and more by our hopes.

Obama may have been elected with the mantra of the "audacity of hope," but he was caught between the noble aspirations of what the United States could do in the world at a strategic level—the exceptional nation that had supported a more integrated, market-oriented, and democratic world over decades—and the sober history of how it had consistently become ensnared in costly and intractable local conflicts along the way. While his rhetoric spoke to a world as it should be, his policies struggled with the world as it is and the limited politics of the moment.

Putin's criticism notwithstanding, Obama was actually not contemplating an expansive or transformative mission in Syria. He had a policy—Assad needed to step down to end the conflict that had resulted in the deaths of hundreds of thousands of people and the displacement of millions—but he wrestled with its implications. What did it obligate the United States to do?

In the aftermath of September 11, President George W. Bush advanced a strategy of preventive war—the United States reserved the right to take decisive military action to preempt dangers before they matured—that despite high-level denials seemed a lot like the role of global cop. It also appeared that way to much of the world. Having warned about the dangers of weapons of mass destruction, the legitimacy of the U.S. invasion and the credibility of the United States were destroyed when it became apparent that Saddam Hussein, thug that he was, did not pose the clear and present danger that was claimed, and Iraq descended into a sectarian-fueled morass.

Obama was determined to repair the credibility and legitimacy of American power. As the most powerful country in the world, if America was expected to protect the existing international order, it would also live by accepted norms. While the United States reserved the right to act in self-defense, it preferred to act in partnership with others, with clear international authority and shared purpose.

While Obama resisted direct involvement in Syria even with the relentless suffering and devastation the country endured, he nonetheless drew a red line over the use of chemical weapons in the grinding civil war. Assad not only ignored Obama's call to step down, but his red line as well, demonstrating a willingness to use any weapon at his disposal to stay in power.

Two years earlier, confronting a potential humanitarian crisis in Libya as Muammar Qaddafi threatened to hunt down his political opponents "like rats," Obama said the United States could not turn a blind eye to such a threat and pushed for authorization from the United Nations to allow NATO to intervene to protect the Libyan people from their predatory leader. While Obama ruled out regime change in public, he privately concluded together with his counterparts from Great Britain and France that the Libyan people would not be safe as long as Qaddafi remained in power. Even though Libyan rebels toppled Qaddafi's regime, it's highly unlikely the National Transitional Council could have succeeded without NATO's direct support.

As a result, Putin would take no chances with Syria. There would be no resolution authorizing the use of force in Syria, not even one sanctioning Assad for using chemical weapons.

Libya weighed on Obama as he considered what to do about the red line. In his own lawyerly way, Obama did not view Libya as a precedent. He said correctly that the United States did not have the capacity to right every wrong in the world. But his rhetoric—the United States could not turn a blind eye as a dictator threatened his own people—raised expectations of greater U.S. involvement.[4] But by the time the United States took significant military action in Syria, the conflict had fundamentally changed.

While Obama continued to speak to American exceptionalism, he was actually focused on the limits of American power, policy, and politics. He feared a slippery slope to another costly nation-building project that, given Iraq, he did not believe was necessary, affordable, or supported by the American people.

Obama eventually achieved an important result—ironically with Putin's help. His claim that the diplomatic initiative to force the Assad regime to surrender its chemical weapons stocks achieved more than the planned military strikes is fair. But the highly improvised policy process and mismanaged public presentation—threatening military action that he knew would not be decisive and asking Congress for authorization that would not be forthcoming—was costly. It undermined the credibility of American power and political resolve, a reality that Obama declined to acknowledge but nonetheless looms as a prominent global perception that confronts the new president.

When assessing the Obama administration's foreign policy, the current political environment, and the implications for the new administration, the president's red line moment in the Rose Garden stands out as one bookend. To paraphrase Reinhold Niebuhr, notwithstanding Obama's "dreams of managing history," he never bridged the gap between an expansive strategic narrative of American exceptionalism and its demonstrated limits.[5] The sharp rhetoric of the 2016 presidential campaign aside, the tension was still evident between the perceived imperative of American internationalism and the perils of interventionism.

But there is another bookend to the Obama foreign policy, Obama's politically risky yet strategically compelling nuclear deal with Iran. Far-sighted arms control agreements were completed periodically with America's Soviet adversary. They shaped the strategic environment for a generation, aimed at managing conflict below the threshold of war. The Iran nuclear agreement has that same potential. It was also the stuff of significant political legacies, a reality of which Obama was quite conscious. Whatever happens years from now, his name is on the agreement.

With respect to Iran, he attempted to do exactly what he advertised during the 2008 presidential campaign—constructively engage America's adversaries; find common ground where possible; manage divisions where it wasn't; and pursue the national interest but avoid another war, especially one in the Middle East.

Such coercive diplomacy certainly fits within the concept of American exceptionalism. But Obama's engagement with Iran collided with other long-standing and complex American policies, politics, and narratives. The Bush administration had declined to negotiate with Iran—evil should be confronted, not appeased, a lesson learned with Munich.

To even get to a negotiation, much less to an actual agreement, both the United States and Iran had to overcome significant political opposition and deep mutual distrust embodied in competing strategic narratives—the United States as the Great Satan and the Islamic Republic as an international pariah. Even with the agreement, those narratives linger and will constrain further cooperation for the foreseeable future.

Republicans could not prevent the Obama administration from implementing the nuclear agreement, even after enlisting the prime minister of Israel as part of the opposition. So instead, they ran against it during the 2016 campaign. Even though a clear majority of Americans supported the agreement, or at least preferred to resolve the problem without taking military action, there were pledges to "rip up" the agreement and negotiate a better deal, whether or not one was actually available.

It is an abiding myth that when it comes to the formation and execution of American foreign policy, politics should stop at the water's edge. In truth, it never has. Modern presidents from Truman to Obama have been excoriated for doing too much or not enough, for seeking foreign monsters to destroy or failing to slay them as they emerge.

In reality, it never will. Foreign policy and politics are joined at the hip. Whether the focus is at home or abroad, in functioning democracies, politics are the means through which governments gain support for what they are trying to do.

In the most dramatic intersection of foreign policy and politics in recent years, in 2016, the British people voted to leave the European Union—a movement known as BREXIT—instantly transforming the United Kingdom's relationship with the world. And the American people elected Donald Trump, whose divisive rhetoric about walls, bans, trade, and alliances suggested a similarly disruptive shift.

As I. M. Destler suggests, "U.S. politics no longer stops at the water's edge—it continues right on into the mainstream of foreign affairs."[6]

At home, while there's strong bipartisan support for American global leadership and military strength, national security has always been subject to partisanship.

Politics also affect the use of American military force. Wars today are limited, which means their outcome is political—dealing with a specific leader, group, problem, or ideology rather than vanquishing an opponent.

Not surprisingly, given the experience in Afghanistan and Iraq, the American people have been wary of being drawn into another open-ended military campaign in the heart of the Middle East that is less likely to produce something called victory than a murky outcome with lots of unforeseen consequences, risks, and costs. That skepticism—call it the Iraq Syndrome—shaped the policy choices Obama made, the strategic narratives he employed, and the rhetoric of the 2016 presidential contenders who sought to succeed him.

One can't understand U.S. foreign policy without taking into account the dramatic challenges of the past fifteen years—from the attacks of September 11 to Iraq and back again—and the rancorous American national security politics that surrounded those events. Fred Hiatt of the *Washington Post* criticizing what he viewed as Obama's strategic disengagement from the world, attributed the White House policy to the "anesthetization of U.S. opinion."[7] But with a couple of exceptions, Obama's foreign policy choices were not based on an evasion of public opinion, but reflected the political boundaries of the time.

Hiatt and others can reasonably argue that the United States needed a different foreign policy—or that the world needed a United States with a different foreign policy. But to a great extent, Obama delivered the foreign policy for which he was elected. It wasn't rooted in weakness as several of the candidates in the 2016 race suggested. It was rooted in politics. This is why, as George W. Bush once suggested, elections matter.

"Strategy," suggest Steven Weber and Bruce Jentleson, "is a coherent story about the world and what you hope to achieve in it."[8]

For a brief period, between 2009 and 2011, I was the assistant secretary for public affairs and spokesman for the U.S. Department of State. In that role, I was one of the Obama administration's narrators, attempting to explain to the American people and international publics what the United States was trying to achieve in the world. As such, given the trajectory of a thirty-year career in the military and government, I was part of the American foreign policy establishment, what the Obama inner circle considered "the Blob."[9]

This book attempts to place into historical context the key strategic narratives of the Bush and Obama administrations, particularly around what we initially termed the war on terror; their impact on American foreign policy and politics; and some key insights that should guide the new administration in 2017.

The Bush administration conceptualized the war on terror appropriately—it is even today far more a war of ideas than a war of attrition—but then became sidetracked by the war in Iraq. It failed to see how the invasion in 2003 walked straight into Osama bin Laden's narrative of the occupation of sacred Muslim lands by a crusader force. We are still dealing with the ripple effects of that decision, particularly the emergence of the Islamic State.[10]

Barack Obama was elected because of his opposition to Bush's war of choice in Iraq. He made American foreign policy more legitimate and sustainable, applying American power more judiciously, recognizing the limits of what American power can achieve at an acceptable cost, focusing greater effort where the United States can have a meaningful impact while staying within the boundaries of what the American people and international publics would support.

Obama believed he could end America's wars during his time in office, but in the aftermath of the 2011 Arab uprisings these conflicts evolved in important ways, largely beyond the ability of the United States to influence. Obama was too slow to recognize the shift. He believed that war was receding even as it was intensifying. The new administration must act on the premise that the United States will remain in a state of emergency—it is a war—for the indefinite future.

That said, the war that began in 2001 has fundamentally changed. The United States is a protagonist, but is no longer central to why it is being waged or how it will end. This is primarily a war within Islam. The conflict itself is no longer primarily about us, and we should avoid making it so.

While Obama was unable to end what he feared was perpetual war, he did extract the vast majority of U.S. ground forces from the middle of conflicts that they cannot resolve at an acceptable cost and in a sustainable time frame. But in doing so, U.S. foreign policy became too ad hoc. Despite his efforts to reset relations with the world and rebuild trust in American leadership, much of the world does not view American power as credible.

The world does not know what to expect from the United States today. Notwithstanding Donald Trump's suggestion that the United States should be more unpredictable and less transparent about its true intentions, in fact, the new administration needs to narrow the gap between what it says and what it does. Much of this requires being far more transparent as it seeks to gain international support for what it is trying to achieve in the world.

This book explores the tension among a global American foreign policy backed by an expansive set of strategic narratives that project the importance of U.S. leadership to peace, stability, and security around the world, and the restrictive domestic politics of the time and emerging international environment that speak to the limits of what America can or should do to solve global challenges and shape a world that is consistent with its interests and values.

THE BOOK'S STRUCTURE

In the Rose Garden on August 31, 2013, Barack Obama feared initiating military action that would put the United States on a slippery slope to another trillion-dollar quagmire in Syria, one that lacked a reasonable assurance of congressional and public support. The historical context for America's enduring national security narratives is covered in chapter 1.

The political boundaries from the 2000 presidential campaign evaporated on September 11. That evening, President Bush enunciated a strategic narrative around the war on terror—with us or against us—and then built a strategy around that narrative. Chapter 2 details how Barack Obama viewed Bush's war on terror as perpetual war, reconstituted and rebranded it as a war against al Qaeda, but from the outset imposed limits on how it would be waged.

Strategic narratives matter. Bush was clear that the war on terror began with al Qaeda but did not end there. He did not distinguish between those who committed acts of terror and those who supported them. That frame illuminated the path from Afghanistan to Iraq. On the campaign trail, Obama said that Iraq was not the central front in the war on terror and pledged to bring the war to a responsible end. He turned out to be wrong on both counts. The policy and politics surrounding Iraq are the subject of chapter 3.

Obama worked hard to deliver the foreign policy he described during the 2008 election. Nowhere is that more true than his pledge to engage America's antagonists, particularly Iran. The combination of engagement and pressure eventually yielded an opportunity for negotiations regarding Iran's nuclear program, although four years later than initially anticipated. Chapter 4 details the struggles to overcome decades of mistrust and potent strategic narratives on both sides.

Since September 11, the United States has believed democracy, or at least representative government, is part of the answer to violent political extremism.

The Obama administration hoped that the 2011 Arab Spring would work to the advantage of U.S. policy in the region and against al Qaeda. In fact, it enabled al Qaeda to make a comeback in the Middle East and opened the door to the Islamic State. The Obama administration's struggles with the Arab uprisings, especially Egypt, are covered in chapter 5.

Humanitarian interventions undertaken (Somalia, Bosnia, and Kosovo) and avoided (Rwanda) during the 1990s produced a potent narrative of never again—that the international community had a responsibility to intervene to stop extreme violence that risked significant regional instability. As the Arab Spring unfolded, Obama wanted to be on the right side of history but did not want to put the United States back into the nation-building business that he ultimately believed did not work. His contradictory approach to Libya— leading from behind—is reviewed in chapter 6. It would have enormous implications for Syria.

One of the significant achievements of the Obama administration was the elimination of Osama bin Laden in 2011. The White House convinced itself that bin Laden's demise and its relentless drone campaign placed al Qaeda on a path to strategic defeat. Given the Arab uprisings, that judgment would be premature. As the Obama administration would discover, described in chapter 7, the tide of war can shift dramatically.

The Obama administration believed it was overinvested in the Middle East and underinvested in the Asia-Pacific region. Given the importance of the U.S.-China relationship in the twenty-first century—the most consequential bilateral relationship in the world—the United States attempted a policy rebalance (see chapter 8) but struggled to describe it and to manage it implications. Then again, so has China.

In 2011, President Obama called for Syrian president Bashar al-Assad to step down as he used force to put down a peaceful revolution. The Syrian conflict morphed into one of the most brutal and complex conflicts in modern history. Obama viewed Syria as someone else's civil war, but it would increasingly become America's to solve after the emergence of the Islamic State. The administration's policy struggle around Syria is the subject of chapter 9.

The Obama administration's global engagement strategy included an attempted reset in relations with Russia. It worked during the presidency of Dmitri Medvedev, but was reversed under Putin. Russia's interventions in Ukraine in 2014 and Syria in 2015 did not mark a new Cold War but did signal a strategically significant disagreement over how the international system should function in the twenty-first century. Its implications are discussed in chapter 10.

The Obama administration's signature achievement is the nuclear agreement with Iran, despite hard-line opposition both in Washington and Tehran. The administration's political opponents, which included the prime minister of Israel, could not stop implementation of the deal. So they campaigned against it. Chapter 11 covers the strategic implications of the deal and the politics around it.

Throughout his presidency, Barack Obama struggled with the importance of Afghanistan to American national security. While he determined in 2009 that American security did not require the defeat of the Taliban, Obama found that even with clear limits it was difficult to bring America's longest war to a responsible end. Obama's unexpected U-turn in Afghanistan is covered in chapter 12.

The Bush administration's conception of the war on terror—with us or against us—was overly broad. The Obama administration's strategic adjustment—a war against al Qaeda—turned out to be too narrow. The next administration should view the ongoing conflict as a war within Islam that is now far more about them than about us. The evolution of the struggle and its implications for American security and politics are detailed in chapter 13.

National security played a far more prominent role in the 2016 campaign than anticipated, not only the Iran nuclear deal, the crisis in Ukraine, China, trade, and climate change, but also the war in Syria, immigration, and significant terror attacks in Europe and the United States. But the national security policy differences between the parties are not as wide as the heated rhetoric suggests. The predominant national security narrative in the 2016 campaign was no boots on the ground—meaning the region must take the lead to defeat the Islamic State, supported by the United States. Policy and politics converged (see chapter 14), even though there are still meaningful differences over tactics that should be employed going forward, from surveillance to interrogation to detention.

Politics do not stop at the water's edge. Domestic politics play a far greater role in foreign policy than is understood. That is only going to intensify in the future. Going forward, global public opinion will play an even greater role in future wars. The book concludes with some thoughts about the importance of legitimacy, transparency, and sustainability (chapter 15) and the need to alter America's national security metanarrative to restore the credibility of American power (chapter 16). The United States is exceptional. It is a global power. It is not, however, indispensable. The world is too complex.

INTRODUCTION

Red Lines and Political Boundaries

On August 31, 2013, in the midst of a Labor Day weekend, President Barack Obama stepped from the Oval Office and strode toward the familiar blue presidential podium in the White House Rose Garden. Vice President Joe Biden walked a pace or two behind. The president was about to announce the U.S. response to the almost certain use of chemical weapons by the government of Bashar al-Assad, a dangerous escalation in the grinding two-year-old Syrian civil war.

Obama had kept Syria at arm's length despite its growing impact, with hundreds of thousands killed and millions displaced. He did not see where the use of American military force could have a decisive impact on such a multilayered conflict at an acceptable cost. The United States provided light weaponry to the Syrian opposition and humanitarian assistance to refugees who spilled over to neighboring countries such as Jordan, Turkey, and Lebanon. Syria lay in the heart of a region that was vital to U.S. security, but Syria itself was not—at least not yet.

But dramatic online videos from the outskirts of Damascus strongly suggested exposure to some kind of nerve agent. The deliberate use of chemical weapons involving hundreds of deaths and thousands of casualties violated both international law and a "red line" that Obama had drawn a year earlier.

Until August 20, Syria was not even on the front page of America's newspapers. The international headlines in the Middle East were primarily about Egypt and Iran.

1

The Egyptian military had recently deposed the ineffective government of President Mohamed Morsi. Morsi had been elected freely and fairly to succeed Hosni Mubarak, who stepped down in 2011 in the midst of historic and inspiring demonstrations in Cairo's Tahrir Square during the early stages of what was thought to be an Arab Spring. At the time, Obama had identified with the aspirations of the people for change. But now Egyptian aspirations had shifted dramatically. Lacking a sitting parliament and thus a means of removing Morsi democratically, the military, Egypt's strongest and most respected institution, but with its own vested interest in Egyptian politics, stepped in.

The same day as the chemical weapons attack, the president chaired a National Security Council meeting to review U.S. aid to Egypt in light of Morsi's removal and the subsequent crackdown on the Muslim Brotherhood and other political opponents. Defenders of Egypt's old guard called it a popular impeachment. While it did appear to reflect majority sentiment in the country, by any reasonable definition, it was a coup.

After 9/11, successive U.S. governments viewed democracy as part of the solution to violent political extremism. Nonetheless, hoping to retain leverage over a key Middle East ally, the Obama administration chose not to attach a label to the military's action, avoiding a cutoff of defense assistance. Instead, it encouraged the formation of a new, "more inclusive" government.

That would not happen. Egypt returned to authoritarianism; the Muslim Brotherhood and most other political opponents were branded as "terrorists."

Obama was determined to be on the right side of history, but as the Arab uprisings morphed into a much more complex reality, it was increasingly hard to tell which side that was.

Meanwhile, Iran had just inaugurated a new president, Hassan Rouhani, who with the evident blessing of the Supreme Leader signaled that Tehran was prepared to renew efforts to resolve long-standing international concerns regarding its nuclear program.

In his inaugural speech, Obama offered an extended hand if Iran would unclench its fist. Obama believed the status quo was unsustainable and inching toward a military confrontation with potentially ominous regional ripple effects. Unlike the Bush administration, Obama was open to a direct negotiation, believing a nuclear agreement would reduce the potential for another Middle East war.

In light of the trillion-dollar occupation in Iraq and then the U.S. recession, the president was mindful of the potential costs of intervention. While maintaining that he had taken no option off the table, he was skeptical of overt military action that risked unforeseen consequences, slippery slopes, and another potential quagmire.

An early attempt at negotiations in 2009 failed to launch in the aftermath of the still-born Green Revolution. As demonstrators in Tehran protested apparent election irregularities, the Obama administration was surprisingly understated, not wanting to feed Iran's narrative of the Great Satan interfering in its domestic affairs. While reasonable in theory, the White House was nonetheless criticized in Tehran for advocating regime change and in Washington for failing to do so, a reflection of how difficult it is to balance domestic and international imperatives in a global political and information environment.

Believing that American leadership was most effective when rallying the international community around a common objective, the United States successfully coordinated a new round of international and domestic sanctions in 2010 that increased financial and political pressure on Iran.

Now, three years later, diplomatic pieces began to fall into place, although Washington and Tehran would disagree on the reasons why—the former believing that the mix of engagement and pressure was paying off and the latter seeing overdue recognition of long-standing Iranian interests.

Unknown to the outside world, secret negotiations had already taken place, and the stage was being set for informal talks at the United Nations in September and formal negotiations through the so-called P5 + 1 (the United States, Great Britain, France, Russia, China, Germany, and the European Union as negotiators with Iran on behalf of the international community) after that.[1]

The Obama White House had viewed itself as overinvested in the Middle East even before the crisis in Syria. The administration had unveiled a "pivot" to Asia, attempting to rebalance its regional policy focus where more vital national interests existed, particularly related to the U.S. economy and international trade. But the Middle East continued to be a preoccupation nonetheless.

On top of that, a continuing series of global news stories based on the leak of an unknown number of classified intelligence documents by Edward Snowden challenged the credibility of the United States and complicated its relations with its own citizens and with leaders and populations around the world. Snowden was granted political asylum in Russia. Following a brief "reset" in relations, President Vladimir Putin seemed determined to reprise its role as America's chief international antagonist.

On the domestic political front, a lingering budget stalemate risked a government shutdown and potential technical default at the end of the fiscal year that would have shaken international markets. The White House also confronted implementation of the president's controversial affordable health-care system, his top domestic priority.

The last thing Obama wanted or needed was another crisis.

The choice of the Rose Garden for the Syria announcement was a deliberate one. The Obama administration feared comparisons with President George W. Bush, who used the Oval Office to announce military action in Afghanistan and Iraq. Obama rarely used the Oval Office as a backdrop. He was elected to unwind America's wars, not to start new ones.

Bush handed off to Obama three wars of unprecedented length and growing unpopularity. The war in Afghanistan launched shortly after the attacks of September 11 was initially seen as a "war of necessity," although the American people (and the national security establishment) were increasingly skeptical of what could be accomplished there.

Coming into office, Obama believed this was the neglected front and surged more military and some civilian assets to Afghanistan, but for a narrower purpose and limited time. Obama declared that Afghanistan as an American war would end in 2014. But the Taliban would consistently make the line between combat and support hard to define.

Iraq was a disastrous "war of choice" that had generated skepticism at home and abroad about the legitimacy and efficacy of American power. Whatever its accomplishments, they were achieved at an enormous cost—human life, treasure, and political capital. Iraq succeeded Vietnam as the commanding national security narrative of this age and produced a formidable political headwind as Obama considered what to do about Syria.

Obama thought Iraq was in America's rearview mirror when he withdrew all remaining U.S. forces in 2011, a key electoral mandate. But as the Arab uprisings turned violent, the Middle East map was literally being redrawn in ways that would reshape American expectations, actions, and narratives.

The third war Obama inherited was the war on terror, which he recast as the war against al Qaeda. Osama bin Laden had been located and killed in Abbottabad, Pakistan, in a confrontation with Navy SEALs. Through a relentless and secret (although not invisible) drone campaign in Afghanistan, Pakistan, Somalia, and Yemen, al Qaeda's cohesion was fractured and capabilities greatly reduced.

Three months earlier, Obama suggested to senior military officers in a speech in Washington that "this war, like all wars, must end."[2] If that happened on his watch, it would be an attractive presidential legacy. Obama was fond of saying that "the tide of war is receding."[3] But he would soon be reminded that tides move in both directions.

Ultimately, the three wars he inherited would merge into one.

This was arguably the most complex and constraining strategic and political environment a U.S. president had confronted in at least four decades, with international events developing faster than even the most powerful country in the world could influence and a global political and information environment that left less time to carefully weigh policy imperatives and strategic risks.

The one military intervention he did initiate in Libya was deliberately limited. The United States and NATO, backed by a United Nations resolution and with Arab League support, launched an air campaign to protect the Libyan people from their leader, Muammar Qaddafi, who sought to head off a rebellion to his four-decade rule.

Obama and his counterparts in Britain and France decided the best way to protect the Libyan people was to help the National Transitional Council remove Qaddafi from power. But Obama was careful not to take ownership of Libya's transition. He took the United States out of the nation-building business, an understandable—and popular—policy choice given the negative return on investment in Iraq.

Like Bush in Iraq, Obama hoped Libya's development would be self-sustaining. While it successfully scheduled national elections, the new Libyan government was weak. Its inability to provide basic security and disarm dangerous militia, including groups sympathetic to al Qaeda, contributed to an attack on a U.S. diplomatic outpost in Benghazi in September 2012 that resulted in the deaths of four Americans, including the U.S. ambassador, Chris Stevens. Given election-year politics, Benghazi generated a domestic political firestorm that ensnared Obama's secretary of state, Hillary Clinton, in a series of investigations that would extend well into the 2016 presidential campaign.

The Benghazi controversy only added to Obama's skepticism regarding what military intervention could realistically accomplish. Unlike Libya, Obama considered Syria "someone else's civil war," but the use of chemical weapons suddenly made it his problem. In Syria, American interests and values, foreign policy and domestic politics, democratic consent and international legitimacy would all collide in ways that made the formulation, execution, and explanation of a coherent response particularly difficult.

In March 2011, angered by a failure of the Syrian government to respond in a meaningful way to a regional drought and rising food prices, and encouraged by remarkable protests in Tunisia and Egypt, Syrians began peaceful demonstrations in various cities. The Assad regime overreacted with a brutal campaign to suppress public dissent.

The United States responded cautiously, encouraging Assad to either "lead a democratic transition or get out of the way."[4] But as the death toll in Syria moved into the thousands, President Obama made a dramatic shift in U.S. policy.

"For the sake of the Syrian people," Obama declared in mid-August, "the time has come for President Assad to step aside."[5]

The president believed that Assad, by violently resisting a more open political process, had lost his legitimacy to lead the country. Regime change in Syria was now U.S. policy, but there was not an apparent course of action to achieve it. But given the historic changes that had already taken place across the Middle East, the administration believed Syria was at a tipping point as well.

One administration official in a background briefing expressed confidence that Assad's "days are numbered," a perspective that became a widely used public talking point.[6] Assad defied those expectations.

Instead, Syria would descend into a grinding and destructive civil war. By 2016, some 1,500 distinct groups would be engaged, making it virtually impossible to distinguish the good guys from the bad. The region's major powers—Saudi Arabia, Turkey, Qatar, Iran, the United States, and Russia—each had vastly different visions of a desirable final outcome.

Al Qaeda, which the Obama administration believed was headed for "strategic defeat," would exploit the Syrian crisis to make a significant comeback. But its franchise in Iraq would split over strategic ways and means, declare and defend a caliphate, and emerge as a long-term challenger for global jihadist preeminence. That competition ensured the existing threat of violent Islamist extremism would not recede, but intensify.

In 2012, defending his reluctance to intervene in Syria as he had in Libya despite the rising death toll and growing presence of an al Qaeda affiliate, President Obama suggested that the use of chemical weapons would alter his "calculus."[7] Syria possessed the third-largest stock of chemical weapons in the world, as much as ten times more than Iraq. Unlike the United States and Russia, it had not signed the Chemical Weapons Convention that proscribed their use. White House officials privately suggested the president issue a more aggressive warning than he had planned.[8]

Presidents do miscalculate or miscommunicate occasionally, particularly when speaking off the cuff regarding crises that are unfolding in real time. Formal remarks are carefully weighed and frequently vetted across what is termed the interagency. But speaking extemporaneously, with the media challenging the efficacy of administration actions or echoing criticism from political opponents, presidents can communicate too well and alter policy in subtle ways. They can say what they really think, which may not always reflect what they are prepared to do. Setting the right expectations or the right temperature regarding an international crisis is actually difficult to do.

Given the existing political divide, White Houses are leery of admitting mistakes, particularly in an election year. Whatever a president says, policy aides try mightily to keep subsequent actions—or at least perceptions of those actions—consistent with presidential rhetoric.

The red line was supposed to fill the gap between the Obama administration's expectations that Assad would eventually lose his grip on power and a political solution that was already mapped out, but faced resistance from Russia, China, and Iran. Obama hoped that Assad's protectors would ultimately agree to force Assad and his key lieutenants to step down while keeping the rest of the government functioning and opening up Syria's political system to broader representation.

In subsequent months, the red line became even brighter. The significant use of chemical weapons, said Obama, would be a "game changer."[9] One year to the day after he drew the line, Assad crossed it to a degree the administration could not ignore. Events moved quickly, and a White House noted for its self-control found the situation difficult to manage.

Given that the presumed white hats in the struggle, the moderate Syrian opposition, were both outnumbered and outgunned, the Obama administration's reluctance to get deeply involved in the Syrian conflict was understandable.

The White House never envisioned taking military action to dislodge Assad, but the president was under pressure to "do something" in Syria. He had many times called America an exceptional nation. He recognized that in a crisis, the world looked to Washington to lead. He had said that the United States was different and could not stand on the sidelines.

But he also confronted a clear political mandate to avoid inserting U.S. forces in yet another Middle East conflict. He did not believe the United States needed to be—or could afford to be—the "world's policeman." Given this clear contradiction, the administration struggled to find the right balance of policy and politics.

Washington demanded an international investigation—a team from the Organization for the Prohibition of Chemical Weapons (OPCW), which would eventually be awarded the Nobel Peace Prize for its work in Syria, happened to be in Damascus to investigate prior allegations of chemical weapons use—but abruptly changed course, declaring an international investigation would be too limited and too late. It was a curious move for an administration that viewed itself as "anything but Bush" and was bending over backward to convince the American people that Syria was not another Iraq.

Because of NATO's de facto coupling of regime change with the UN authorization to protect the Libyan people, Russia and China sidelined the Security Council. For ideological and geopolitical reasons, neither country would agree to a resolution that provided an international imprimatur for intervention against the Syrian government.

Seeking to strengthen international legitimacy for military action against the Assad regime, Great Britain, a prospective partner along with the French, placed a resolution before the House of Commons, but it unexpectedly failed. The British likewise saw parallels to Iraq and decided to sit this one out.

Despite this setback, and Obama's own doubts, on Friday, August 30, in remarks the White House helped craft, Secretary of State John Kerry outlined a compelling indictment of Bashar al-Assad.[10] Fighting the ghosts of the Iraq war and the weapons of mass destruction that never materialized in 2003, Kerry stressed the "facts" that linked the attack by a known Syrian chemical weapons unit to the highest levels of the Assad regime. The administration highlighted intelligence intercepts detailing its direct involvement.[11] Kerry pledged accountability for this serious violation of international norms.

As it sought to distinguish the limited and prudent use of force in this case from Bush's overreach in Iraq, the administration made clear it was not going to war in Syria. In the days after the president's announcement, Kerry went so far as to suggest the American attack would be "unbelievably small."[12]

But the more it sought to ease domestic concerns about a greater commitment in Syria, the more it undermined the credibility of the administration's efforts to hold Assad accountable. Nothing the White House seriously contemplated was likely to change the course of the Syrian civil war.

As Obama reached the podium, the credibility of the United States and his presidency were at risk, although the president would strongly refute that perception. Obama found himself trapped by a red line that he himself drew, and rhetoric that accelerated too far in front of domestic and international politics. He believed his administration had made the case for limited military action, but he recognized that he did not have "reasonable assurance" of support from an obstructionist Congress he did not trust and a skeptical public that feared another Middle East quagmire.

ENDURING NATIONAL
SECURITY NARRATIVES

When it comes to national security policy, presidents don't arrive in the Oval Office with a blank sheet of paper. Making sense of the foreign policy of the United States requires understanding the intersection of American policy and politics. Foreign policy is not disconnected from the political context that propels a president to office or shapes actions once there. In fact, foreign policy is defined by the political boundaries of the time.

As Obama himself admitted, "a president does not make decisions in a vacuum."[13]

By the time most candidates reach the White House, they have campaigned for years, tested and refined their thinking on foreign policy, and developed political narratives that represent who they are, what they think about America and its role in the world, and the instincts they bring to the job as commander-in-chief. In 2016, Donald Trump was a notable exception, describing a foreign policy approach based largely on impulse that traditional Republican leaders criticized publicly.[14]

The American people elect their presidents to do specific things, and increasingly given today's hyperpartisanship to correct perceived mistakes of the recent past. Political mandates matter. A key reason for today's gridlock is that the president and members of Congress are sent to Washington by an evenly divided electorate with conflicting imperatives. Compromise is punished, not rewarded.

As Obama suggested during the debate regarding the nuclear agreement with Iran, "we live in Washington and politics do intrude."[15]

The narratives that presidents bring into office animate not just politics in the United States, but shape perceptions abroad as well. As the leader of the most powerful country in the world, what a president or even a presidential candidate says gets noticed—for example, it was no surprise Trump's strident populist rhetoric about banning Muslims from the United States ended up in an al Shabaab recruiting video. The world has its own narratives about the United States—leader of the free world when it wants something from Washington and hyperpower when it believes America has gone too far.

Politics is the art of the possible, and narratives are mechanisms to attract and sustain public support for what a government wants to do. Narratives rhyme with the past and mobilize the present.

Narratives can reflect history—perceptions of its right and wrong sides. They form around historical turning points, strategic miscalculations, warnings missed, or opportunities lost. They do have blind spots. They can become political traps that complicate or skew the formulation and execution of American foreign policy.

The American national security narratives that inform foreign policy are remarkably enduring. Even with all the partisanship of the current age, there are consistent threads that form a tapestry, a mythology that traces the evolution of American foreign policy and politics from World War II through the Cold War to 9/11, and now to this post-9/11 age of persistent conflict.

Under a series of political banners, American military personnel have deployed across the 38th Parallel in Korea, into rice paddies in Vietnam, along the Fulda Gap in central Europe, into the Iraq desert, to the shores of Somalia, over the skies of Bosnia and Kosovo, into the mountains of Afghanistan, back to Iraq, and now Syria and other Middle East conflict states.

Franklin Delano Roosevelt was careful not to get too far in front of public opinion as he prepared for a war he knew would involve the United States at some point. The allies attempted to negotiate with Adolf Hitler, who even now remains the personification of evil and is frequently invoked when an American president contemplates military action. "Munich" has served as a powerful narrative regarding the dangers of appeasement and has inhibited American governments from negotiating with adversaries.

Pearl Harbor not only precipitated the American entry into World War II, but it was also a catalyst for a major restructuring of the country's national security architecture, with a strategic imperative never to be surprised again. Pearl Harbor has become shorthand for the danger of being unprepared for the next potential threat, its latest manifestation a "cyber Pearl Harbor" that could cripple the country's critical infrastructure or economy.[16]

Cold War politics—with both parties contesting which was stronger on national security—contributed to the gradual militarization of the strategy of containment. Nine successive administrations, from the Marshall Plan to the breaching of the Berlin Wall, were committed to "bear any burden" as the United States served as the "free world's" vanguard against communism.

Losses were perceived as undermining the credibility of American power, but that was as much about domestic politics as America's standing in the world. The "loss" of China was an influential political factor that drove five presidential administrations to defend Vietnam as a vital Cold War "domino" even though it was peripheral to the seminal struggle against the Soviet Union.

It should never have become the critical test of American power and prestige. Vietnam should have remained someone else's civil war.

Jimmy Carter elevated the importance of human rights and access to Middle East oil as central pillars of American foreign policy. His decision to allow the Shah of Iran to enter the United States for medical treatment precipitated the occupation of the American Embassy and the ensuing diplomatic hostage crisis. Over thirty-five years, potent narratives representing enduring grievances—America as a conspiratorial Great Satan and the Islamic Republic of Iran as a rogue nation and international pariah—resonate today even as relations between Washington and Tehran begin to thaw.

Even as Washington argued over painful lessons from the Vietnam withdrawal, it enabled the United States to refocus on its struggle against the Soviet Union, which Ronald Reagan famously termed the "evil empire." Whether the United States won the Cold War or the Soviet Union simply abandoned the contest, the fact that the struggle ended on such favorable terms shaped perceptions of the U.S. role in the world, its imperative to lead the global system that it largely created, and expectations regarding how the world should respond to the exercise of U.S. power.

Reagan experienced unanticipated consequences in Lebanon, where troops were inserted to preserve order, but fell victim to a new asymmetric weapon—terrorism—that would define a new age in warfare. In the aftermath, Secretary of Defense Caspar Weinberger advanced a doctrine that military force should only be employed in pursuit of vital interests and with the anticipated support of the Congress and the American people.

America's foreign policy has always had a schizophrenic strand. Notwithstanding John Quincy Adams's admonition regarding the dangers of military adventures in search of "foreign monsters," at least as many Americans identify with Thomas Paine's conception of America as an idea, with the capacity to "change the world yet again."

With the Cold War's end, the tension intensified between two competing conceptions of America's role in the world—whether there was a moral responsibility to advance American values and to combat evil wherever it was manifest, or whether protected by two oceans and blessed with peaceful neighbors, the United States should mind its own business.

President George H. W. Bush envisioned a "new world order" in the post–Cold War era. Its first test was the Gulf War, which accomplished its primary objective, restoration of the sovereignty of Kuwait. But it left in place the unpredictable strongman Saddam Hussein. Iraq would pose a regional threat that would preoccupy four American administrations—and now a fifth.

Notwithstanding the vigorous political debate that preceded the Gulf War, fears of another "quagmire" evaporated following the stunning employment of American military technology and capability. The lessons, codified in the Powell Doctrine, included the importance of overwhelming force to achieve clear military objectives and the need for a viable exit strategy once they are achieved. Bush believed he had driven a stake into the heart of the Vietnam syndrome.[17] U.S. forces returned home rapidly to ticker-tape parades and a warm embrace by the American people.

America was the unquestioned global power. America viewed itself as the indispensable nation. Freed from the constraints of the world that was, the United States imagined it could help shape a world as it should be, increasingly democratic, market oriented, and governed by shared international norms. Nations did not just exist. They could be reconstructed, working through the United Nations and other international institutions largely created, supported, and dominated by the United States.

In the initial stages of Bosnia, the first Bush administration suggested it did not have "a dog in that fight." It did intervene in Somalia, a humanitarian operation that conveyed to the Clinton administration. The subsequent "mission creep" into a nation-building exercise ended badly with "Black Hawk Down."

Somalia shaped the Clinton administration's decision not to intervene in Rwanda, which President Clinton later considered one of his greatest regrets in office. The interplay between Somalia and Rwanda would produce the counternarrative of "never again," a powerful policy logic that would influence the Obama administration's decision making in Libya.

Clinton did deploy air and ground forces in Bosnia and Kosovo. Both efforts were ultimately successful, examples of the use of military force coupled with "coercive diplomacy" to resolve humanitarian crises that were in the national interest, but not necessarily vital to U.S. national security. These "military operations other than war" renewed the debate about the proper use of military force—the same questions Weinberger and Powell highlighted. These issues would surface during the 2000 presidential campaign between George W. Bush and Al Gore.

There were notable terrorism attacks at home and abroad that began to reshape American national security policy and strategy—the World Trade Center in New York in 1993; the Alfred P. Murrah Building in Oklahoma City in 1995; the American Embassies in Nairobi, Kenya, and Dar es Salaam, Tanzania, on the same day in 1998; and the *USS Cole* in Aden, Yemen, just days before the 2000 election—but not yet its politics and narratives.

In fact, when Bill Clinton ordered cruise missile strikes against Afghanistan and Sudan in response to the East Africa embassy bombings, his political opponents claimed he was manufacturing a crisis to divert public attention from his personal scandal involving a White House intern. They drew comparisons to a contemporaneous movie, *Wag the Dog*, which advanced a remarkably coincidental plot.

REACTIVE FOREIGN POLICIES

As a candidate, George W. Bush spoke of the need for a more humble and less arrogant foreign policy. While he believed in the importance of the decisive use of military power, he questioned how the military had been employed during much of the 1990s. The military's purpose was to win wars, not reengineer failing states. He did not believe the United States could afford to be the world's policeman.

But America's national security priorities, policies, and strategic narratives changed on September 11. Gone were the political boundaries established during the 2000 election. The humble policy advanced on the campaign trail was replaced by an aggressive strategy to not only punish those responsible for the attacks on the World Trade Center towers and the Pentagon but also transform the Middle East's sclerotic political structures that enabled the terrorist threat against the United States.

That evening, President Bush declared a "war against terror." In the critical weeks and months after 9/11, the Bush administration faced little political opposition. The mass media, likewise stunned by what had occurred, did not seriously challenge the emerging narrative and the strategy built around it—at least not until critical decisions and mistakes had already been made.

Even though the president acknowledged many times that the long-term struggle against terrorism was inherently political—winning hearts and minds—the immediate focus was military victory. The Bush administration believed that the geopolitical forces that had guided American policy, strategy, and politics during the Cold War and post–Cold War period no longer applied.

For two years, the Bush administration was free to define the war and its larger context: who our adversaries were, what was at stake, and where and how the struggle would be waged. It wasn't until the 2004 election that the normal give-and-take of national security politics began to reemerge.

Despite growing public disaffection with the war in Iraq that was anything but a "cakewalk," the Bush administration was able to gain sufficient public support to undertake a "surge" of forces to Iraq in 2007 that, combined with the so-called Anbar Awakening, an Iraqi response to the extreme violence of al Qaeda in Iraq, changed the momentum of the conflict that had evolved into a bitter Iraqi civil war, with 150,000 American troops caught in the middle.

The United States went to war against al Qaeda in Afghanistan, but ended up in a lengthy conflict with the Taliban instead. The United States went to war against Saddam Hussein in Iraq, and ended up in a war against al Qaeda. The American people eventually judged both to be a mistake. That public skepticism had a profound effect on the 2008 election campaign, the policy debate that ensued, the candidate the American people elected, and the mandate the new president would receive.

For almost eight years, George W. Bush advanced a strategic narrative that presented a stark choice to all global actors—you are either with us or against us.

Barack Obama embodied a potent and popular counternarrative.

"If you were to boil it all down to a bumper sticker," suggested one White House aide, "it's 'Wind down these two wars (Afghanistan and Iraq), reestablish American standing and leadership in the world, and focus on a broader set of priorities, from Asia and the global economy to a nuclear-non-proliferation regime.' "[18]

Obama hoped to rebuild America's alliances and key partnerships, both to restore faith in American leadership and share the burden of collective security; rebalance U.S. national security strategy, concentrating more significantly in the Asia-Pacific region; and employ all dimensions of power—diplomatic, economic, information, and military. This was the foreign policy a clear majority of Americans voted for in 2008.

"If George W. Bush's foreign policy was largely a reaction to 9/11," the *New Yorker*'s David Remick suggested, Obama's was "a reaction to the reaction."[19]

The prevailing political boundaries evaporated in 2001. They were restored in 2008 and profoundly shaped Obama's foreign policy, war strategies, and political narratives. For the most part, Obama stayed within those political boundaries.

Obama's foreign policy was not timid. There were plenty of bold strokes. Obama promised a "new beginning" in relations with the Middle East, offered to engage Iran and other American antagonists, envisioned a world without nuclear weapons, and pursued a comprehensive peace agreement that would end the conflict with Israel and produce a Palestinian state. Obama was awarded the Nobel Peace Prize after only eight months in office, based largely on this agenda.

But Obama struggled with the push and pull of policy and politics—believing in the importance of American leadership, yet guided by an electorate that viewed the United States as overextended in the aftermath of the global financial crisis. The result was an ad hoc application of American power, continuing to carry a big stick, but exercising great care regarding where, how, and at what cost it is used.

Obama never squared two competing political imperatives: on the one hand, the conception of America as the exceptional nation with global interests and a strategic and indeed a moral obligation to lead an international system that it largely created and still dominates; and on the other a limited domestic political mandate to end America's costly wars and avoid being the world's policeman on far-away beats that were not tied to vital American interests.

Carefully crafted policies and political narratives collided with the real world. The dramatic revolutions in the Middle East forced difficult choices between interests and values, and security and democracy. The administration wanted the people to win and the despots to lose. Obama positioned the United States on the side of change, but overestimated the prospects of democratic reform. The Obama administration hoped for a new beginning, but instead confronted more of the same—and in the case of Syria, a grim reality that will take decades to reverse. In truth, the Middle East's revolutions, insurgencies, and counterrevolutions are beyond Washington's control.

As he approached the podium that late August day, Obama was caught between an evolving international crisis that demanded decisive American action and a domestic political environment that was skeptical of being drawn into another Middle East war. Obama found the divide too wide to bridge.

Where the American people expected to hear a decisive voice in the face of a gross violation of international norms, instead they received a tutorial on the American constitutional process.

Rather than launching the military action he suggested was warranted and for which he believed he had existing authority, Obama hit the pause button and requested the advice and consent of a Congress that had no appetite for a consequential vote.

While he followed what he viewed as his political mandate, the mismanaged process surrounding his decision damaged the credibility of American power. Even though he stumbled into a beneficial result—Syria gave up chemical weapons that risked escalation within and beyond its borders—the fact the president requested political and public support for military action and failed to receive it casts serious doubt on the steadfastness of American leadership.

Obama was right when he said in 2014 that the world looks to Washington for leadership, not Moscow or Beijing. But at the moment, there is also great uncertainty regarding what to expect from America. As the 2016 campaign shifted into high gear, an increasingly prickly Obama reiterated that there was a difference between campaigning and governing, a lesson he himself learned and one that awaits the new president.

Notwithstanding the sharp rhetoric—with Republicans excoriating Obama's failed leadership and Democrats pledging more intensified action—the vexing contradiction between an expansive view of American exceptionalism and a prevailing skepticism of what the United States can plausibly accomplish follows the new president into the Oval Office.

There is a strategically important gap between what the American people say they want from a president in the abstract, sustaining an ever bigger American stick and sounding tough on the international stage; and what they don't want in the real world, committing the United States to military adventures that are more likely to exacerbate rather than solve the leading security challenge of the age, the threat of violent political extremism and terrorist attacks against the American homeland.

American foreign policy today is profoundly shaped by this interaction between domestic and international politics and the impact on foreign policy and strategic narratives across an increasingly integrated global political and information environment. Contrary to the admonition of Senator Arthur Vandenberg at the start of the Cold War, politics never stops at the water's edge. There is no longer a meaningful divide between the domestic and foreign.

But to understand the political forces and policy choices that confront the new administration, it is important to review how American foreign policy, strategy, politics, and narratives have evolved over the past seventy years.

1

REASONABLE ASSURANCE

On November 28, 1984, Secretary of Defense Caspar W. Weinberger addressed the National Press Club in Washington, D.C. His speech was entitled "The Uses of Military Power" and set out to answer a much-debated question: "Under what circumstances, and by what means, does a great democracy such as ours reach the painful decision that the use of military force is necessary to protect our interests or to carry out our national policy?"[1] The speech had been deliberately delayed until after the 1984 presidential campaign.[2]

Weinberger's remarks came slightly more than a year after 241 Marines died in Lebanon at the hands of an emerging terrorist organization, Hezbollah. President Ronald Reagan had dispatched the Marines to Beirut as part of a well-meaning but ill-defined effort to help the Lebanese government regain control of its country.

It was also just shy of ten years after the Congress formally ended the Vietnam War, an unnecessary war of choice that became an ill-advised test of the credibility of American power.

In both cases, the United States inserted itself in the middle of someone else's civil war. In Lebanon, Reagan quickly recognized the miscalculation and carefully extracted the Marines with minimal strategic consequence.

Vietnam was impelled by a zero-sum Cold War logic that equated negotiation with appeasement; dictated that every inch of territory in the world was important; and assumed that military force could change the calculus of an opponent Washington never understood nor respected. Two presidents deepened the U.S. commitment to South Vietnam. Two others were largely defined by the war—and destroyed by it.

In his speech, Weinberger outlined a "doctrine" with six tests to guide whether the United States should intervene in a foreign crisis. Military force should be committed only as a "last resort"; when national interests of "vital" importance are at stake; with the clear intention of "winning"; in support of "clearly defined political and military objectives"; constantly reassessing and adjusting the force composition and disposition as appropriate; and with a "reasonable assurance" of popular and congressional support.[3]

Weinberger's speech was shaped in part by questionable revisionist thinking, that the Vietnam war could have been won if civilian leaders had not hindered the military effort.[4] A similar accusation would resurface in 2016 regarding Iraq and Syria.

But in particular he tried to establish a context for what had just occurred in Lebanon, where U.S. forces deployed for a peacekeeping mission were drawn into a civil war of questionable importance to American national security. This was a misguided attempt by the United States to serve as the region's "policeman."[5] Despite the tragic result, it would not be the last. General John Abizaid, the commander of U.S. Central Command, suggested in 2006 that the Hezbollah attack and not 9/11 marked the start of what the Bush administration would label the "war on terror."[6]

Notwithstanding subsequent political debates about withdrawals sending the wrong message to adversaries—Osama bin Laden would refer to the Beirut attack in his 1996 fatwa, believing mistakenly that the "American Crusaders" once bloodied would again withdraw from the Middle East[7]—Weinberger believed Reagan was right to "redeploy" U.S. forces from Lebanon as the White House characterized it at the time.

The American people evidently agreed. Ronald Reagan was easily reelected.

Weinberger was prescient when he called the line between war and peace "less clearly drawn than at any time in our history."[8] It certainly reflects what the United States has experienced in the three decades since.

Weinberger understood from Vietnam and Lebanon—in one instance where successive presidents believed politics inhibited a dramatic change of course and another where politics impelled a rapid shift—the strategic importance of public opinion to military success.

Reasonable assurance didn't mean a president needed to build public support for a military mission before taking action. Like Lebanon, and many times since, commanders-in-chief deployed forces and explained their mission simultaneously. But it was imperative that a commander-in-chief set the right expectations with the American people regarding what is at stake, how the crisis impacts U.S. national security, and the extent of the commitment involved.

That was certainly not the case with Vietnam.

WHO LOST CHINA?

Harry S. Truman, as he sought to define America's leadership role in the aftermath of World War II and restructure the government in line with its growing global responsibilities, was challenged by Senator Arthur Vandenberg to "scare the hell out of the country" in order to gain congressional and public support for the budgetary increases that would be required.[9]

He did.

"I believe that it must be the policy of the United States to support free peoples who are resisting attempted subjugation by armed minorities or by outside pressures," Truman said in a compelling address in March 1947 outlining the Truman Doctrine.[10]

Truman was able to "save" Greece, Turkey, and Europe, but not China. Communist forces under Mao Zedong defeated the Nationalist government and its charismatic leader, Chiang Kai-shek, established the People's Republic of China, and in early 1950 signed a mutual defense treaty with the Soviet Union.

A powerful political narrative decrying the "loss" of China, prompted by conservative voices such as *Time* publisher Henry Luce and columnist Joseph Alsop, would resonate politically for the next two decades.[11] It was reinforced by the destructive communist witch hunt of Senator Joseph McCarthy that marginalized many of the government's best Asia experts.

The "free world" suffered another setback in June 1950 when 100,000 North Korean soldiers invaded South Korea. The United States dispatched troops to help defend Korea under a United Nations Security Council resolution (the USSR was boycotting the Security Council due to the UN's refusal to seat Red China, as the United States labeled it at the time).

Truman did not seek a congressional declaration of war, believing that the ensuing debate would inflame partisan tensions over the question of China.[12] Instead, he waged a "police action," but as it ground on, the rally-round-the-flag effect wore off and it soon became "Truman's War."

Truman struggled to develop a sustainable strategy and tangled with his commander, General Douglas MacArthur, over its relationship to broader regional security issues. In 1951, Truman relieved MacArthur for insubordination.

In a politically charged farewell address before Congress, MacArthur said, "War's very object is victory, not prolonged indecision. In war there is no substitute for victory."[13] The challenge of defining victory in a limited war, where the result is an uncertain political outcome rather than the conquest of an opposing army, has bedeviled presidents and policy makers ever since.

The Truman Doctrine imposed an "indiscriminate globalism" on U.S. policy without regard to a country's actual relevance to American national security.[14] It created a skewed lens through which Washington viewed emerging political movements such as the Vietcong not as nationalists, but as agents of Moscow and Beijing.

Similarly, in 2016, lumping the multilayered terrorist threat under a single label—radical Islamic terrorism—Republican presidential candidates overlooked important differences that underpin the Islamic State, al Qaeda, and other malevolent actors that are fundamental to defeating them.

Truman opted for stability over self-determination, exchanging French concessions regarding the post–World War II restructuring of Europe's economy and security in return for American acquiescence to French interests in Indochina.[15]

Casting Vietnam as part of the Cold War struggle with the Soviet Union solved a contradiction within America's policy. The United States was not condoning colonialism; it was fighting communism. It was not thwarting the independence of a unified Vietnam; it was defending Vietnam against the aggression of the North.

"Just as the policy had gotten turned around, so too had the words," David Halberstam wrote in *The Best and the Brightest.*[16]

Truman chose not to run for reelection once he knew Dwight D. Eisenhower would enter the race, ensuring that an internationalist (either Eisenhower or Adlai Stevenson) and not an isolationist (Robert Taft) would succeed him, a manifestation of political pragmatism that would be almost inconceivable today.[17]

Eisenhower supported the Truman Doctrine and the assumptions behind it. He pledged never to "vacillate, to appease, to placate" totalitarianism.[18] Eisenhower electrified the 1952 campaign by promising to go to Korea if elected and develop a plan to bring Truman's war to an "honorable" end.

"If there must be war there," Ike said in October 1952 on the campaign trail, "let it be Asians against Asians, with our support on the side of freedom."[19]

Following France's defeat at Dien Bien Phu, the Geneva Conference divided Vietnam at the seventeenth parallel with the understanding that there would be elections on reunification in 1956. The United States declined to be bound by its terms, recognizing that 80 percent of the Vietnamese people would vote for Ho Chi Minh. The Eisenhower administration convinced itself that once the population understood what was at stake—"independence" from a Soviet-directed communist movement—"genuinely free elections" reflecting "the will of the people" would eventually yield a politically mature (meaning pro-Western) choice.

Eisenhower sought to prevent a falling "domino" without becoming a direct combatant in Vietnam's civil war.[20] Employing a deft hidden hand as president, Ike worked assiduously out of the public eye to avoid another Asian land war.[21] Fearing an expansion of China's regional influence, he nevertheless declared—wrongly as subsequent events revealed—that the survival of South Vietnam as an independent nation was a vital American national interest.[22] In 1957, in the aftermath of the Suez Crisis, the president advanced the Eisenhower Doctrine whereby the United States increased its commitment to the Middle East, presuming that any regional vacuum would be filled by Moscow if not by Washington.[23]

The administration provided direct military assistance to South Vietnam, based on the assumption it would undertake necessary political reforms.[24] As it worked to strengthen the legitimacy of South Vietnam's unpopular yet anti-communist government, Eisenhower in 1957 hosted a visit to the United States by President Ngo Dinh Diem. The *New York Times* called him an "Asian liberator" and the *St. Petersburg Times* saluted him for standing against "the Red tide."[25]

Of course, the tighter Washington's embrace—he was our man in Saigon—the more his legitimacy was undermined within Vietnam, an American puppet in yet another phase of the country's long colonial struggle.

As a senator, John F. Kennedy praised Diem as "the cornerstone of the Free World in Southeast Asia, the keystone of the arch, the finger in the dike."[26] As a candidate, he projected confidence "in the universality of American values, institutions and policies and the ability of the United States to control political change in the world."[27]

BEAR ANY BURDEN

As a newly elected president, Kennedy's soaring inaugural rhetoric—the United States would "pay any price, bear any burden, meet any hardship, support any friend, oppose any foe to assure the survival and the success of liberty"—inspired the country and reiterated America's sense of global purpose.[28] But it also set a high standard that would trap policy makers into a course of action driven as much by domestic politics as vital national interests.

Kennedy was wary of increasing America's military commitment to Vietnam. But after the Bay of Pigs debacle, the Berlin crisis, and Kennedy's poor performance at the Vienna summit with Soviet leader Nikita Khrushchev in 1961, he candidly admitted to Scotty Reston of the *New York Times*, "we now have a problem in trying to make our power more credible, and Vietnam looks like the place."[29]

This concern about the credibility of American power—whether the United States was viewed as reliable by its allies and resolute by its adversaries—would come to dominate policy deliberations regarding Vietnam. But these fears were rooted every bit as much in domestic politics as geopolitics, that the perception of weakness could impact the next election as much as a future superpower confrontation.

Kennedy actually sought to avoid taking responsibility for a war that he believed was Vietnam's to wage. He thought that sending military advisors rather than combat troops to Vietnam in 1962—the number increased from five hundred to sixteen thousand under his watch—would actually avoid a deeper American commitment. The expectation was they could be withdrawn within months once South Vietnamese forces became more capable, the first of many corners about to be turned or anticipated lights at the end of tunnels.

But each incremental decision raised the prospective political costs of any subsequent policy shift.

By 1963, Kennedy had successfully resolved the Cuban missile crisis—a celebrated diplomatic achievement that firmly established the president's Cold War bonafides—yet he remained anxious about Vietnam's domestic political implications.

"In the final analysis, it is their war. They are the ones who have to win it or lose it," President Kennedy told legendary CBS anchorman Walter Cronkite two months before he was assassinated.[30]

But even as it was wary of becoming overcommitted, the Kennedy administration was actively subverting the prospects of a negotiated settlement proposed by French President Charles de Gaulle. Officials in Washington, according to historian Fredrik Logevall, were "not merely skeptical of what negotiations might bring"—de Gaulle suggested Vietnamese reunification as a neutral state like Tito-led Yugoslavia—"they were downright fearful of the likely results."[31]

A negotiated settlement would have precluded the subsequent American strategic overcommitment in Vietnam, but it posed immediate political risk of perceived appeasement.

For its part, the Diem regime stubbornly resisted the political steps necessary to strengthen its support among the Vietnamese people. Instead, it became increasingly repressive in the face of recurring protests by the country's Buddhist monks. The iconic photo of the self-immolation of Buddhist monk Thich Quang Duc in June 1963 underscored how deeply unpopular the South Vietnamese government was, one of a number of cues that Americans missed regarding what was realistically achievable in Vietnam.

Eventually, the Kennedy administration gave a green light to the overthrow of the increasingly isolated and erratic Diem, a major step toward the Americanization of Vietnam's civil war.

What Kennedy would have done had he lived to see a second term remains a matter of significant debate. When presenting his defense budget to Congress in March 1961, Kennedy suggested that "the basic problems facing the world today are not susceptible to a military solution," a theme that Barack Obama would echo half a century later.[32]

His successor, President Lyndon B. Johnson, was a very different leader with a very different history. Johnson had a very ambitious domestic policy agenda in mind for the country and saw Vietnam as a threat that could divert public support away from his domestic legacy.

CREDIBILITY OF AMERICAN POWER

"I am not going to lose Vietnam," LBJ told Ambassador Henry Cabot Lodge Jr. in the days following the Kennedy assassination. "I am not going to be the President who saw Southeast Asia go the way China went."[33]

The narrative of a lost China weighed heavily on Johnson. So did the inconclusive end of the Korean war. Notwithstanding the compelling strategic success that South Korea represents today, during the 1950s, Truman was widely vilified that Korea ended not in victory, but a "tie."[34]

Johnson attempted to use military force to send a message and change North Vietnam's calculus. He launched an intensive bombing campaign to coerce Hanoi into negotiations on more advantageous terms. But he repeatedly misread the inherent imbalance of interests between the two sides. By contrast, the North Vietnamese recognized that, like the French, the Americans would eventually tire of the conflict.

To protect his domestic initiatives, the Great Society, Johnson escalated the war "by stealth" and hid his actual intentions from Congress and the public.[35] He was successful for a time, but it was ultimately unsustainable, with devastating political and economic ramifications.

Key figures in the Johnson administration spoke of the importance of the credibility of U.S. policy and power. They feared European allies would be unsure of American leadership if America withdrew prematurely. Ironically, Vietnam actually delayed progress toward detente that both the United States and Soviet Union sought—and Europe supported.[36] George Ball was a notable exception, suggesting that disengagement—"to cut our losses"—would actually reinforce American leadership.[37] But the politics of the time did not yet support such a move.

In 1964, after North Vietnam allegedly fired on American ships in the Gulf of Tonkin, Congress passed a resolution authorizing a military response to demonstrate U.S. strength and resolve. Following a largely symbolic bombing campaign, popular support for Johnson's handling of Vietnam jumped in a Louis Harris poll from 42 to 72 percent favorability.[38] The Tonkin resolution would be stretched well beyond its original intent as the legal basis for the Americanization of the Vietnam conflict.

Johnson ran for reelection as the candidate who would not escalate the war, the third consecutive president to publicly express skepticism of a deeper U.S. role in Vietnam.

"We don't want to get involved in a nation with 700 million people and get tied down in a land war in Asia," Johnson pledged in September 1964 during the stretch run of the campaign.[39] He won by a landslide.

Although he had considerable freedom of action after the election, Johnson ended up executing a plan in Vietnam that closely resembled what Senator Barry Goldwater proposed during the campaign.[40] He may have believed that politics should stop at the water's edge but in reality knew better. Even though 75 percent of Americans favored negotiations to end the war, Johnson was not confident that would translate to electoral support.[41]

The American people, he told a confidant, will "forgive you for anything but being weak."[42]

Given the Cold War, the Johnson administration became trapped in three overriding political narratives—they could not afford to lose another country to communism; they could not negotiate a U.S. departure; and they became convinced that the credibility of American power rested on success in Vietnam.

They also could not admit that their policy was almost certain to fail. "It was better to fight and lose in Vietnam," wrote Gordon Goldstein in *Lessons in Disaster*, a book that became a must-read within the Obama White House, "than not fight at all."[43]

Tragically, the Johnson administration committed American prestige in support of an extraordinarily weak partner. The counterinsurgency strategy the United States developed in Vietnam required the support of the population, which its ally clearly did not possess. The deep divisions within Vietnamese society were evident, but Washington did not adequately factor them into its policy.

The same challenges of weak governments and divided populations would plague U.S. efforts in both Afghanistan and Iraq.

In Vietnam, wrote Logevall in *Choosing War*, the United States became "more committed to this war than were their clients."[44]

"Johnson's strategy meant straddling, and often crossing, the line between savvy information management and outright dishonesty," Stephen Sestanovich wrote in *Maximalist*.[45] His lack of candor—if not outright deceit regarding the true nature of the war and growing American commitment to South Vietnam—would be costly.

By mid-1967, the war was severely impacting the U.S. economy. Three percent of its gross national product was dedicated to the war and 9 percent to defense spending.[46] The consequent rising inflation made it increasingly difficult for Johnson to fund both guns and butter. When he proposed a 10 percent surcharge on individual and corporate tax returns, a majority of Americans for the first time believed the war was a "mistake."[47]

But setbacks were viewed as a public relations problem rather than a moment to reconsider basic strategic assumptions regarding what was possible or necessary in Vietnam. Key metrics—troops deployed, bombs dropped, the enemy killed—all suggested the war was being won. All were misleading.

In the fall, Johnson launched a victory campaign, viewing public opinion as "the weakest chink in our armor."[48] General William Westmoreland, the commander of U.S. forces in Vietnam, was brought back to Washington to deliver encouraging remarks at the National Press Club in November.

Westmoreland suggested the end of the war was coming into view.[49] He was right, although for the wrong reason.

In January 1968, North Vietnam and the National Liberation Front, having infiltrated sixty-seven thousand soldiers throughout South Vietnam, launched simultaneous attacks in all of the country's major cities, including

Saigon. The timing of the attack was no coincidence, coming at the start of an election year in the United States.

Vietnam was the first television war, and as *Washington Post* reporter Don Oberdorfer wrote, "the Tet offensive was America's first television super-battle."[50]

Westmoreland accurately described the action to the press in Saigon as a significant North Vietnamese military failure. But his message was upstaged by a photograph on the front pages of America's newspapers the following day that showed the execution on a Saigon street corner of a Vietcong officer by the head of South Vietnam's National Police. Dramatic footage also appeared that evening on NBC's *Huntley-Brinkley Report* to an audience of twenty million people.

Such incidents reinforced growing public doubts about the mission. Days later, press coverage of a military operation in Ben Tre included the memorable line that came to symbolize the war itself: "It became necessary to destroy the town to save it."[51]

The Tet offensive, suggested Oberdorfer, "was the final blow to the sagging credibility of the Johnson administration."[52] It did not generate a significant shift in public opinion—support for the war had been steadily declining over the previous year—but marked the crossover point where a clear majority favored deescalation.

A subsequent proposal for a substantial increase in the number of troops in Vietnam "to regain the initiative" further undermined the Johnson administration's narrative of a path to success.[53] If the United States was winning in Vietnam, why did it require so many more troops?

More importantly, Tet fractured elite opinion of the war and legitimated opposing views, creating political room for a major change in strategy. On February 27, the influential Walter Cronkite suggested that the best the United States could hope for was a "stalemate."[54]

NBC followed with its own special report, which concluded, "The grand objective—the building of a free nation—is not nearer, but further from realization. In short, the war, as the Administration has defined it, is being lost."[55]

Shortly after Tet, former Secretary of State Dean Acheson, one of the Establishment's Wise Men, told Johnson, "We can no longer do the job we set out to do in the time we have left, and we must take steps to disengage."[56] In other words, public opinion would not support military operations for the length of time required to achieve a result that could plausibly be called a success.

Johnson tried to wage the Vietnam war so as to avoid Truman's fate in Korea, but he suffered the same one. Recognizing how divided the country was about the war, he declined to run for reelection.

DECENT INTERVAL

Well before the Tet offensive, Richard Nixon, contemplating a run for the presidency, was already focused on moving the United States out of Vietnam and the broader implications.[57] Tet was sufficiently jarring in terms of policy and politics that it enabled Nixon to advocate a dramatic change of course and narrative regarding Vietnam.

Contrary to his campaign rhetoric, President Nixon did not have a secret plan to end the war. But the public gave Nixon time to engineer an honorable exit. But Nixon's approach contained the same miscalculation as Johnson's—that decisive American bombing would somehow change North Vietnamese calculations.[58] It never did. As former Deputy Secretary of State John Negroponte, at the time a junior foreign service officer in Vietnam, remembered, "We bombed them into accepting our concessions."[59]

While Nixon bought some time politically through his "silent majority" speech in November 1969, Hanoi saw that public opinion had turned against the war and shifted to a protracted war strategy intended to wait the United States out.[60]

Forty years later, the same dynamic would play out with Afghanistan, with the Obama administration trying to manage an exit from a lengthy and unpopular war, leaving the Taliban to draw appropriate conclusions. Unlike the Vietcong, however, the Taliban have little chance of unifying Afghanistan.

Nixon, like LBJ, worried about the impact that a military defeat would have on international confidence in American leadership and thus pursued a policy of gradual Vietnamization of the war that would ensure a "decent interval" between the American withdrawal and the likely reunification of Vietnam under North Vietnamese control.[61]

The United States and North Vietnam eventually reached a peace agreement on roughly the terms that Johnson sought five years earlier. It was characterized as "peace with honor."

While the United States had long viewed the preservation of South Vietnam as a moral and strategic imperative, with Washington increasingly absorbed by Watergate, South Vietnam was essentially on its own.

Congress in March 1975 refused a Ford administration request for close to $1 billion in emergency military, humanitarian, and economic aid for South Vietnam. The South Vietnamese government, despite fifty-eight thousand American and many more Vietnamese lives lost and hundreds of billions of assistance provided over its two decades, collapsed in the face of the final North Vietnamese push, an ignominious end to a two-decade attempt at nation building.

As historian George C. Herring suggested, "Had it looked all over the world, the United States could not have chosen a less promising place for an experiment in nation-building."[62]

Within thirty years, the Bush and Obama administrations would oversee an equally challenging nation-building project in Afghanistan, one of the least integrated nations on the planet, that would prove to be equally inscrutable as the United States sought to dictate the winners and losers within an indigenous struggle driven by local rather than global agendas.

Given the iconic scene of the desperate American helicopter evacuation from Saigon, suggests James T. Patterson, "wrangling over the 'lessons of Vietnam' lay at the root of almost every significant foreign policy and military debate in the United States."[63]

The generational debate over Vietnam—it would unexpectedly resurface as a major issue in 2004 with the presidential candidacy of Massachusetts Senator (and Vietnam veteran and later Secretary of State) John Kerry—was informed to a great degree by the leak of the Pentagon Papers, a classified study of America's Vietnam policy, to the *New York Times* in 1971.

The fact that the United States (unlike the British government, which released a massive analysis in mid-2016) has only scratched the surface in its examination of lessons learned in Iraq was clearly evident during the 2016 presidential campaign, which included frequent barbs regarding lying to the public, bad congressional votes, and a premature troop withdrawal.

The prevailing public view remains that Iraq was a mistake.

Like Vietnam, it profoundly impacts the politics of the ongoing U.S. challenge across the war-torn Middle East, but there are few agreed-upon lessons learned to help shape a coherent and sustainable policy. Like Vietnam, in the aftermath of a major strategic error, the first generation is simply focused on its outsized costs and unanticipated consequences. The political imperative is simply to avoid another Iraq; understanding and applying its lessons takes longer.

POLITICS TRUMPED STRATEGY

Four consecutive chief executives sought to contain what they viewed as a monolithic communist ideology while seeking to avoid another world war. Yet each Americanized and ultimately militarized the commitment to a country that displayed few characteristics of a democratic state. A war that no one sought became the only viable policy option given the geopolitics and domestic politics of the Cold War.[64]

While American leaders spoke of "credibility" in international terms, "it mattered at least as much in domestic terms," suggested Logevall.[65]

American political narratives decreed that every global nook and cranny had geopolitical significance. Any fallen domino would be costly. History didn't apply to the United States. Any country could be transformed through American protection and know-how and successfully integrated into the free world.

The lesson of Munich was that aggression must be confronted by clear demonstrations of resolve and, if necessary, military force. Negotiations were perceived as weakness. The Eisenhower, Johnson, and Nixon administrations were unwilling to seek negotiated settlements in 1954, 1964, and 1969 that could have avoided the Americanization of the conflict. The American position was consistently that negotiations could only occur once the battlefield situation improved.

Ultimately, it was Hanoi that was actually willing to bear the disproportionate burden, had history and time on its side, and would take the necessary steps to change the American calculus, not the other way around.

The United States would repeat this mistake in Afghanistan when it failed to adequately distinguish the very different threats posed by al Qaeda and the Taliban. The White House compounded that error when it declined to pursue a political resolution when it had the greatest leverage and before battlefield setbacks and rising costs turned public opinion against the effort.

VIETNAM SYNDROME

Secretary of State George Shultz, who crossed swords repeatedly with Weinberger while in office, was critical of the Weinberger doctrine, calling it "the Vietnam Syndrome in spades, carried out to an absurd level, and the complete abdication of the duties of leadership."[66]

General Colin Powell, serving as Weinberger's military assistant at the time, helped him write the speech. Later as chairman of the Joint Chiefs, he advanced his own thinking regarding the use of military force in a 1992 article in *Foreign Affairs*, applying lessons from the Gulf War and his own experience in Vietnam.

Whereas Weinberger's doctrine reflected Cold War strategic thought, Powell's thinking reflected the changing responsibilities of the "new world order," including humanitarian missions in Turkey and Somalia. He expressed faith in the ability of the American people "to sense when and where we should draw the line" between military action and restraint.[67]

Whereas Weinberger suggested force should only be employed in support of vital national interests, Powell was less concerned with the nature of the objectives than ensuring that the appropriate level of force was used to achieve them. Powell was skeptical of using force to send a message, but rather using force to achieve a clearly defined result. Obama struggled with this very question as he responded to Syria's violation of the red line: how to hold Assad accountable while recognizing that the military operation he contemplated would have limited impact on the broader civil war.

Posed as a series of questions, Powell's doctrine asked: Is vital national security interest threatened? Is there a clear, attainable objective? Have risks and costs been fully analyzed? Have other nonviolent means been exhausted? Is there a plausible exit strategy to avoid endless entanglement? Have the consequences of our action been fully considered? Is the action supported by the American people? He also added an important addendum: once the country decides something is important enough to justify military action, employ overwhelming force to achieve the objective.[68]

Interestingly, while Powell inferred the importance of public support for the use of force within a democratic system, he did not consider it an explicit precondition to undertake a military operation. He believed that Weinberger's doctrine "went too far," particularly given the prospect that a confrontation could develop quickly, leaving insufficient time to make the case to the public or to Congress. Powell cited the U.S. incursion into Panama in 1989 as an example.[69]

As chairman of the Joint Chiefs, Powell recommended and President George H. W. Bush employed overwhelming force in 1991 to drive Iraqi forces from Kuwait. President George W. Bush failed to follow that advice when he adopted a light footprint strategy in 2003.

Powell's successor, General John Shalikashvili, sought in the Balkans to amend the Powell Doctrine to allow for the use of force where the cause was important but not necessarily vital. That thinking reflected the posture of the United States in the post–Cold War era. As the only global power in the world in the emerging 24/7 media environment, there was a greater political impetus to "do something" to solve an emerging crisis, whether or not a vital interest is involved.

But what Weinberger got right—and Powell reinforced—was the importance of political support to strategic success—what the American people want their government to do in the name of national security; the perceived urgency of the challenge; the potential costs of intervention; and the long-term implications.

Vietnam reshaped the military and its relationship with the American people, in ways that were constructive and problematic. A fundamental restructuring of the military placed critical specialties in the reserve forces to ensure that future wars would require a reserve call-up, which would require a proper political debate. That's exactly what happened prior to the Gulf War.[70]

Vietnam also led to the introduction of the all-volunteer force. On the one hand, it produced the most capable military force the world has ever seen. Since Vietnam, public respect for and support for the military has reached all-time highs. On the other hand, the burden of military service falls on a relatively narrow cross-section of the population. Given the nature of modern conflict, the military now goes to war, but society doesn't. Nonetheless, public opinion remains central to the sustainability of military campaigns.

Weinberger's construct of a "reasonable assurance" presumed that public opinion must be cultivated as part of a military campaign. It also recognized a meaningful role for Congress even as it continued to cede considerable war-making authority to the executive despite the 1973 Congressional War Powers Resolution.

Those who voted for the Gulf of Tonkin resolution in 1964 never envisioned that Johnson would use it as justification for a ground war in Vietnam. Ironically, few who voted for the Authorization of the Use of Military Force in 2001 after the attacks of September 11 imagined it would still be in force fifteen years later and used as the legal basis for military operations in Iraq and Syria.

While Vietnam did not inhibit commanders-in-chief over the succeeding four decades from deploying U.S. forces under a variety of circumstances, it did limit until 9/11 what presidents felt they could accomplish with military interventions.

As Marvin and Deborah Kalb wrote in *Haunting Legacy,* "Words such as 'Vietnam,' 'quagmire,' or 'syndrome' have become instant shorthand for the popular image of the United States getting trapped in another long, costly, and unwinnable war."[71]

General William Westmoreland suggested the war was won militarily, but lost politically. Others criticized the fact that the United States never employed its full military power on North Vietnam. The strategy of "gradualism" represented unacceptable political constraints on the employment of force. As Ronald Reagan said during the 1980 presidential campaign, the country "should never ask young men to fight and possibly die in a war our government is afraid to let them win."[72]

President George W. Bush avoided getting involved in operational details in Afghanistan and Iraq, not wanting to replicate Johnson's experience of making targeting decisions against North Vietnam. "I'll follow the advice of the generals," became a familiar refrain, even though it ignored Clausewitz's imperative that war should be guided by political and not military objectives.

In Vietnam, "the problems were political, but the response was military."[73] The military fought a war in support of an unrealistic political objective. Since then, the United States has continued to struggle to marry military objectives with desired political end states.

But defining victory in a limited war is not easy. Kennedy asked even before the U.S. escalation in Vietnam how we would know if we were winning. Donald Rumsfeld would ask a similar question forty years later, whether the United States confronted an adversary that could replenish its forces faster than they could be eliminated.

Former Secretary of Defense Robert McNamara suggested that a key lesson from Vietnam was the recognition that "external military force has limited power to restore a failed state."[74] The United States would relearn that lesson over and over in subsequent interventions.

In Vietnam, the United States did not achieve its military objectives, but strategically, America "won" the peace. All of the stated reasons for the intervention in Vietnam, the dominoes actually aligned constructively for the United States in subsequent decades.[75] But Vietnam is viewed politically as a "loss," given that Americans tend to see a military campaign as a noble crusade and as an end in itself rather than the means to a broader political outcome.

Even though its departure from Vietnam enabled a strategic reset that paved the way for a resolution of the Cold War on advantageous terms, Vietnam became a leading master narrative in American politics, and its political scars and lessons learned would dominate American strategic and political thought for a generation.

Obama viewed himself as the first president of the post-Vietnam generation and considered that war "settled history" that should not significantly impact foreign policy in the twenty-first century.[76] A *New Yorker* profile of Richard Holbrooke, who negotiated the Dayton Accords that ended the Bosnia conflict and was a long-standing Clinton confidante, highlighted unwanted comparisons between Afghanistan and Vietnam and exposed political and generational tensions that the administration never completely overcame.[77] But Vietnam remained a sufficiently potent narrative that Obama mentioned it three times in his December 2009 speech announcing his policy decisions on Afghanistan.

His approach to Afghanistan, Libya, and Syria was certainly consistent with what the United States thought it learned in Vietnam, and relearned in Iraq. He would intervene with clear limits, believing that what could be achieved was unlikely to be worth the economic, strategic, and political costs.

2

WAR AGAINST AL QAEDA

During the 2016 campaign, in response to criticism of his national security strategy from those seeking to succeed him, Barack Obama said at a press conference that there is a difference between campaigning for president and being president. The president himself went through that same transition—the reality inside the Oval Office is far more complex than the picture painted in stump speeches or campaign debates.

Between 2002 and 2008, as he campaigned for the U.S. Senate and later the presidency, Obama consistently viewed Afghanistan as the "right battle-field" and Iraq as a costly diversion that exacerbated the terrorist threat posed by al Qaeda.

At the time of Obama's election, there were roughly four times as many troops in Iraq as in Afghanistan. As Chairman of the Joint Chiefs Mike Mullen indicated in 2007, given Iraq, the United States could only do what it could in Afghanistan. Obama planned to reverse that equation.

During a briefing to Obama's transition team by Lieutenant General Doug Lute, who oversaw the war in Afghanistan on the Bush National Security Council staff and would do the same under Obama, his first slide indicated the United States did not have a strategy in Afghanistan that could either be articulated or achieved.[1]

Just days before taking office, Vice President-elect Joe Biden returned from a trip to the region and cautioned Obama, "We've got to decide why we're there. It's al Qaeda. If there was no al Qaeda, we would not be there. Period."[2]

Seven years after September 11 and its subsequent intervention, the United States still struggled to understand what it needed to accomplish in

Afghanistan. Eight years later, those same questions would persist. In his inauguration speech, Obama pledged to achieve a "hard-earned peace" in Afghanistan. It would prove to be more difficult than the new administration grasped.

As he began to wrestle with a revised strategy, there was mounting skepticism among the American people—and within Obama's national security team as well. By the summer of 2009, fewer than 50 percent of Americans viewed the war as worth fighting.[3]

While he sought to redirect greater effort against core al Qaeda, those directly responsible for the attacks of September 11, he recognized that Afghanistan was actually less important than his campaign rhetoric indicated. Al Qaeda's center of gravity, and as it turned out the location of its leader, was Pakistan. As the movement evolved, other regions, including the Gulf, Levant, and Sahel, took on greater significance.

Obama would eventually develop a hybrid approach that split the difference between what he pledged on the campaign trail, what his military commanders recommended as a new strategy, and what he believed the American people and their representatives in Congress would support.

It was a deft balancing act. He gave his military commanders almost everything they said they needed—a significant increase in forces and firepower to support a version of counterinsurgency adapted from the recent American experience in Iraq. But he established clear limits regarding what he was willing to do and for how long.

Obama questioned not only what needed to be accomplished there, but what could be achieved at a sustainable cost and in a realistic time frame. In the summer of 2009, Afghanistan experienced another disputed election with credible charges of corruption and ballot tampering that called into question the legitimacy of the incumbent government of President Hamid Karzai. While the U.S. intent was to prevent Afghanistan from again becoming a terrorist safe haven, success depended on a weak and erratic partner.

In this, Obama was applying lessons learned from Vietnam as much as Iraq.

Like Vietnam, he would gradually shift responsibility for the conflict to the government in Kabul and unwind the American combat role. The Afghanization policy was achieved, but it would fail to change the fundamental dynamic of the conflict.

But unlike Vietnam, Obama would find negotiating a peace agreement with the Taliban to be elusive. Politics would influence his decision to leave a military contingent in Afghanistan, less to reinforce success than to prevent the failure of the still fragile government in Kabul. Unlike 1975, when Congress eliminated aid to the government in Saigon over the objections of the Ford administration, Obama's strategy received bipartisan support.

In 2009, Obama recast the Bush administration's war on terror as the war on al Qaeda. While this made perfect strategic and political sense—a war on terror could not realistically be won; a war against al Qaeda could—just as Bush's original conception of the conflict was too expansive, Obama's reconceptualization proved to be too narrow.

POLITICS BOUNDARIES EVAPORATE
AFTER 9/11

Unlike Obama, George W. Bush faced few political constraints as he defined the war on terror and constructed a far-reaching policy around this concept.

During the 2000 campaign, it was Al Gore who argued for an interventionist foreign policy while Bush cautioned of being militarily overcommitted around the world.

In his first foreign policy speech of the campaign, at The Citadel in September 1999, Bush briefly mentioned the threat of biological, chemical, and nuclear terrorism, then added, "Let me be clear. Our first line of defense is a simple message: Every group or nation must know, if they sponsor such attacks, our response will be devastating."[4]

President Bush and his national security team did not think the Clinton administration was aggressive enough following the terrorist attacks on the American embassies in East Africa in August 1998, specifically timed eight years after the beginning of Desert Shield, the entry of U.S. forces into Saudi Arabia.[5]

The bombings introduced al Qaeda to the American people. The American military response, cruise missile strikes against training facilities in Afghanistan and a pharmaceutical plant in Sudan, introduced bin Laden to a global audience that had never heard of him, perversely marking a kind of "global brand launch" from which he gained popularity and supporters.[6]

But the Clinton administration did take terrorism seriously. There were meaningful policy, military, intelligence, and structural adjustments in light of the first World Trade Center bombing in 1993, the Oklahoma City bombing in 1995, the Khobar Towers explosion in 1996, the embassy attacks in Kenya and Tanzania, various plots around the Millennium in 1999, and the bombing of the *USS Cole* in Yemen just prior to the 2000 election.

CIA Director George Tenet wrote a memo to his senior staff in late 1998 entitled "We Are at War," increasing the priority for intelligence collection regarding al Qaeda.[7]

Clinton shared the concern about the potential link between terrorism and weapons of mass destruction. The threat was not abstract; in 1995, one such doomsday scenario unfolded with a sarin release within the Tokyo subway by Aum Shinrikyo.

But terrorism was not yet viewed as a priority politically. When President Clinton ordered the cruise missile attacks against targets in Afghanistan and Sudan, criticism at the time was not that the White House should do more, but that its response was a diversion given his burgeoning personal problems.

Bush felt it did not send a strong enough message. "It was clear that bin Laden felt emboldened and didn't feel threatened by the United States," he would say later.[8]

But this was a misreading of the al Qaeda strategy. Given bin Laden's experience fighting Soviet forces, he hoped to draw America into a similar quagmire in Afghanistan. Bin Laden eventually got his wish, but would lose his base of operations in the process. Bush would in turn inadvertently grant bin Laden the holy war he sought—in Iraq.

President Bush was informed of the September 11 attacks while attending an education event at the Emma Booker Elementary School in Sarasota, Florida. His first remarks were unscripted, and ironically echoed a phrase his father had used in 1990 after Iraq invaded Kuwait. "Terrorism against our nation will not stand," Bush said.[9]

With the Secret Service concerned of the possibility of follow-on attacks, Air Force One shuttled from Florida to military bases in the Midwest before transporting the president back to Washington. In Louisiana, Bush said "freedom will be defended."[10] He did not make public remarks in Nebraska but held a National Security Council meeting via videoconference, where he first introduced the frame that would dominate the remainder of his presidency. He told his war cabinet, "We are at war against terror."[11]

September 11, Bush wrote in his diary, was the "Pearl Harbor of the 21st century."[12] Like FDR before him, the attacks instantly transformed domestic politics and provided the president wide latitude to act in ways he could not envision on the campaign trail. The foreign policy parameters that were drawn during the 2000 campaign and the political expectations that flowed from it were fundamentally altered.

George W. Bush was free to craft an expansive narrative that defined the conflict, but back at the White House, as he drafted remarks for the president to deliver that evening, presidential speechwriter Michael Gerson did not have a lot of material upon which to draw. President Bush had said very little publicly about terrorism. There had been several deputies meetings on al Qaeda, but only one principals meeting.*

Using that reference in The Citadel speech, Gerson suggested language that, in responding to the attacks, the United States would make no distinction between those who planned the attacks and those who "tolerated or encouraged the terrorists."[13]

In his initial statement in the Oval Office on September 11, President Bush declared a "war against terrorism," and added a critical link between terrorists and state sponsors that would dominate American strategic thinking for the rest of the decade. "We will make no distinction between the terrorists who committed these acts and those who harbor them."[14]

These seventeen words would be the most consequential and strategically significant of the Bush presidency, creating the bridge that would lead the United States from Afghanistan to Iraq. In fact, by the time the president made his Oval Office speech, the question of striking Iraq had already been discussed among key staff.[15]

WITH US OR AGAINST US

Speaking to a joint session of Congress on September 21, arguably the most powerful address of his presidency, President Bush acknowledged that the emerging war on terror would be a lengthy struggle, and pledged al Qaeda's eventual "disruption" and "defeat," specific goals that would be embraced by the Obama administration as well.[16] But he went much further.

"Our war on terror begins with al Qaeda, but it does not end there," Bush said. "It will not end until every terrorist group of global reach has been found, stopped and defeated."[17]

It was not just about who executed the September 11 attacks. It also implicated other terrorist organizations who threatened America, its allies, and its interests.

---

*Policy options are first developed by interagency policy teams formed around all major foreign policy questions. Issues are then considered by agency deputies meeting in the White House Situation Room. Questions that require a presidential decision move to the principal or cabinet level. There was significant dysfunction within the Bush administration policy process due to an unresolved divide between Vice President Dick Cheney and Secretary of Defense Donald Rumsfeld, and Secretary of State Colin Powell and National Security Advisor Condoleezza Rice. The Obama administration would overcompensate, leading to insider charges of micromanagement.

"Not since John F. Kennedy promised in 1961 'to bear any burden' to fight the cold war had an American president made as expansive a pledge," suggested historian Timothy Naftali.[18]

Bush was careful to draw a distinction between the likes of al Qaeda— "traitors to their own faith" who had hijacked Islam—and Muslims around the world. He described bin Laden as heir to "all the murderous ideologies of the 20th century"—fascism, Nazism, and totalitarianism—and vowed he and his cohort would end up "in history's unmarked grave of discarded lies."[19]

Bush was rightfully concerned that his war on terror not be perceived as a war against Islam. During the 2016 campaign, Democrats would praise Bush for his tempered language while rightly criticizing Republican front-runner Donald Trump's demagoguery. Trump called for a temporary ban on Muslims traveling to the United States after both the San Bernardino and Orlando shootings, comments that fed the jihadist narrative of an inexorable divide between the true believers and the West.

At the same time, Bush's comparison between al Qaeda and Nazi Germany greatly inflated the threat bin Laden actually posed. Even with a few thousand adherents, al Qaeda did not represent an existential threat. Nonetheless, terminology would eventually merge—a wide range of Islamic movements would be painted as representing "Islamofascism"—feeding the very perception of a clash of civilizations Bush warned against.

Of greatest strategic consequence, Bush seemingly re-created the type of bipolar divide that characterized the Cold War. "Every nation, in every region, now has a decision to make. Either you are with us, or you are with the terrorists. From this day forward, any nation that continues to harbor or support terrorism will be regarded by the United States as a hostile regime."[20]

There was no question where NATO stood. For the first time in its history, NATO invoked Article V—an attack on one was an attack on all. It was an incredible gesture of solidarity, one the United States failed to appreciate at the time.

The with-or-against logic reflected a strong belief that a nonstate actor like al Qaeda could not have pulled off such a sophisticated plot without support from an actual state.

Some within the Bush administration would search for links between al Qaeda and Iraq, but there were well-developed ties between the Taliban, bin Laden's host, and Pakistan, the Taliban's most ardent supporter and one of only three countries (Saudi Arabia and the United Arab Emirates the others) that formally recognized Mullah Omar and his Taliban government.

A day after the attacks on the World Trade Center towers and the Pentagon, General Mahmoud Ahmad, head of Pakistan's Inter-Service Intelligence or ISI, who happened to be in Washington at the time, paid a visit to Deputy Secretary of State Richard Armitage at the State Department. His seventh-floor, mahogany-walled office provided a direct view of the still-smoldering Pentagon across the Potomac River.

Picking up the logic from President Bush's remarks the night before, Armitage pressed General Ahmad, "Are you with us or against us?"[21]

The intent was to give countries, Pakistan especially, a chance to break from the past. The Pakistani civilian government would consistently say the right things, and earn recognition as a major non-NATO ally.[22]

But Pakistan's military and intelligence services could not overcome their overriding concern about India and played a multisided game—supporting some of the very extremist forces against which the United States went to war.[23] That bin Laden was discovered in a compound in Abbottabad, not far from a prominent Pakistani military facility, and Mullah Omar died a natural death in a Pakistani hospital were not matters of happenstance.

Both the Bush and Obama administrations would eventually conclude that continued support for the Taliban was not a matter of rogue elements within Pakistan but in fact government policy.[24] Despite its black-and-white narrative regarding terrorists and state sponsors (Washington actually contemplated designating Islamabad as such during the 1990s), the United States never really confronted Pakistan's duplicity. The fact Pakistan possessed the fastest-growing nuclear arsenal in the world was undoubtedly a factor.

Nor did it seriously confront Saudi Arabia, whose export of Wahhabism, a conservative form of Islam, to countries such as Pakistan served as the wellspring of the political intolerance at the core of movements like al Qaeda and the Taliban. The importance of Saudi Arabia to global oil markets and as a regional counterweight to Iran were major factors.

What the Bush administration "with us or against us" narrative did do was conflate the danger posed by al Qaeda, those directly responsible for the attacks of September 11, and the Taliban, a regional ally that had provided Osama bin Laden shelter, but did not have a global agenda. The Taliban never represented a direct threat to the United States. But most of the American effort in Afghanistan involved fighting the Taliban, not al Qaeda. Much like the American experience in Vietnam, it would recognize belatedly that it had overmilitarized its response to 9/11 and fought a lengthy war that was far rooted in local politics and tangential to the jihadist threat to the United States.

WAR ON TERROR

The "war on terror" was a captivating political slogan, but it came with major conceptual problems: Who was the enemy? Where were they? Terrorism was a tactic, not an adversary. What does victory mean? How does it end? As former National Security Advisor Brent Scowcroft cautioned, "A 'war on terrorism' could mislead."[25]

To the extent that the war on terror, like the Cold War, was "metaphorical," Walter Russell Mead suggested it would lead to a strategy that emphasized alliances and containment, depriving the likes of al Qaeda of victories and preventing its expansion by constructing civil societies more immune from its influence.[26] But instead it became a divisive issue between the United States and its natural allies.

While there was always an understanding that the war on terror was primarily a battle of ideas, the Bush administration believed that the terrorism threat required a fundamental rethinking of the pillars of U.S. national security strategy. Deterrence and containment were no longer viable. The United States needed to go on the offensive.

The White House drafted what would become the authorization for the use of military force, the declaration of war against al Qaeda and its associates. The draft read that the president was authorized to use "all necessary and appropriate force," not just against those directly responsible, but to "preempt any related future acts of terrorism or aggression against the United States."[27]

Congress scaled back that language in the final legislation, believing it would amount to perpetual war. Nonetheless, the law set out broad parameters for the conflict consistent with the president's narrative.

"Congress declared war," wrote Ivo Daalder and James Lindsay, "and left it up to the White House to decide who the enemy was."[28]

From the outset, the Bush administration was divided regarding what it needed to achieve in Afghanistan. Undersecretary of Defense Doug Feith wrote in a memo in late 2001 that "nation-building had baggage."[29] The Bush administration was wary of the kind of long-term commitment in Afghanistan that the international community had made in Bosnia and Kosovo. It hoped for a quick exit from Afghanistan, believing that the security of the country was an Afghan responsibility.

At the same time, it understood the risk of a resumption of fighting among Afghan warlords absent some kind of international mediation. As Bob Woodward wrote in *Bush at War*, "the overriding lesson from the 1990s in Afghanistan was: Don't leave a vacuum."[30]

As it approached intervention in Afghanistan, the United States launched a sophisticated political strategy designed to gain support from Afghan tribal leaders. America was not there to fight Afghans nor did it plan a permanent presence in the country. It was there to help drive out the foreigners who placed Afghanistan in danger and overthrow the Taliban who made the wrong choice for Afghanistan.[31] The United States was helped by a communiqué from the Organization of Islamic Communities (OIC) that argued the al Qaeda attack was in contravention of the teachings of Islam.[32]

The Bush administration's fundamental goals in Afghanistan, removing the Taliban from power and eliminating the al Qaeda safe haven, were achieved in only 102 days. Working with the United Nations and the international community, the Bonn Conference near the end of 2001 identified Karzai as Afghanistan's new interim leader. His selection was ratified first by a loya jirga, working through Afghan custom to provide the new government legitimacy. Over the next four years, the country ratified a new constitution and conducted parliamentary and presidential elections.

But the political imperative that Afghanistan should never again be used as a location for terrorist attacks against the United States, combined with the Bush narrative that captured indigenous forces like the Taliban as an adversary in the war on terror, resulted in a policy that inflated the country's strategic importance.

As it became more deeply involved in the question of who and what would replace the Taliban, and committed to prevent the return of the Taliban in the absence of any peace process, the Bush administration was already engaged in nation building.[33] Robert Grenier, the CIA station chief in Islamabad, later acknowledged that the United States set out ambitious goals that "Americans could not achieve and Afghans could not sustain."[34]

AXIS OF EVIL

In the immediate aftermath of September 11, the Bush administration's expansive narrative of a war on terror seemed to be reaffirmed as a number of letters laced with anthrax were mailed to various U.S. destinations, particularly the U.S. Capitol.

"We were all convinced that it was al Qaeda's second wave," National Security Advisor and Secretary of State Condoleezza Rice wrote later in *No Higher Honor*.[35] It greatly accelerated the policy marriage of terrorism and weapons of mass destruction. That was followed in December by Richard

Reid's attempt to detonate a shoe bomb on board a civilian airliner bound from Paris to Miami.

President Bush in his State of the Union speech in January 2002 introduced the "axis of evil," each country a state sponsor of terrorism and proliferator of weapons of mass destruction. It was an inventive phrase, combining the conception of the Axis powers of World War II with Ronald Reagan's characterization of an "evil empire" that resonated politically.

One of the original versions of the speech cited an "axis of hatred," but speechwriter David Frum changed it to "axis of evil," one of Bush's favorite words. At first Iraq was the only country mentioned.[36] A later revision added Iran and North Korea and included the phrase "States like these, and their terrorist allies, constitute an axis of evil, arming to threaten the peace of the world."[37]

Linking Iraq and Iran in this fashion (the two countries were in fact bitter rivals and fought a brutal and costly war during much of the 1980s), the president overlooked how much Iran would benefit from Saddam's demise. Iran, proud of its Persian history and culture, felt disrespected by being associated with North Korea, which resembled a criminal enterprise as much as a sovereign state.

But now the three narratives that would dominate the Bush administration's rhetoric and strategy were in place. The world faced a binary choice—with us or against us. There would be no distinction between those who actually attacked the United States and those who supported global terrorism. The possibility that rogue nations with weapons of mass destruction might collude with terrorist networks like al Qaeda was viewed as an intolerable threat to the nation's security.

"Taking on tyrants, rooting out terrorists, confronting rogue states with weapons of mass destruction, and perhaps even planting a seed for democracy were missions worthy of a great president," wrote Peter Baker in *Days of Fire*.[38]

There was little political opposition as the Bush administration constructed this bridge from Afghanistan to Iraq. A poll taken before the axis of evil speech suggested 77 percent of Americans supported military action in Iraq, with just 17 percent opposed. Most Americans believed despite the lack of clear evidence that Saddam Hussein had something to do with 9/11.

Meanwhile, with the al Qaeda safe haven destroyed, Mullah Omar, bin Laden, and an estimated one thousand fighters fled into Pakistan, settling in remote sections of the country loosely governed by Islamabad but close to their strongholds in Afghanistan and among Pashtuns who were sympathetic to the Taliban.[39]

The Bush administration viewed the Taliban as a spent force. Various Taliban peace feelers were rejected or ignored. Interest in political reconciliation would only come years later, well after the Taliban had reconstituted and posed a renewed threat to the Kabul government. It was hoped that continued pressure would push the movement's commanders to break with Omar.[40] In fact, the hospitable geography provided the Taliban the opportunity to recover and "return to its roots as a guerrilla force."[41]

The Taliban began targeting the government and international aid workers. By 2006, the level of violence in Afghanistan had increased significantly—attacks by the Taliban had risen 400 percent and the number of deaths in those attacks 800 percent.[42] The lack of security gradually undermined local support.

Politically, it lent credence to Obama's critique on the campaign trail that the Bush administration's diversion to Iraq had costly ramifications in Afghanistan that needed to be reversed.

THE RIGHT WAR

Elected to unwind America's wars, Obama believed the American people would support him for two years.[43] But in its first National Security Council meeting on Afghanistan, as he evaluated a military request for more troops that was on his desk when he arrived in the Oval Office (a step that appeared consistent with Obama's campaign platform), there was a realization that the Afghan War would likely continue into a second term, beyond the window of public support he believed existed.[44]

Unclear what more troops would accomplish, Obama ordered an initial review of the existing strategy. Led by Bruce Riedel, a retired CIA regional expert and campaign advisor, a central finding was that the key to preventing Afghanistan from again becoming an extremist safe haven lay next door in Pakistan. By 2009, al Qaeda only had a relatively minor presence in Afghanistan—one hundred fighters or so. Even if the Taliban came to power again, the judgment was that al Qaeda's core leadership would stay in Pakistan.[45]

In 2001, the CIA assessed that al Qaeda and the Taliban were "joined at the hip."[46] By 2009, while the Taliban continued to support al Qaeda, Riedel did not see their interests as identical, nor did he believe they represented the same threat to U.S. national security. Core al Qaeda, those directly responsible for 9/11, needed to be destroyed. The open question was what it would take to convince the Taliban, which was fighting to return to power, to negotiate instead.

As it considered what was needed in Afghanistan, the new administration wrestled with two different strategic imperatives—counterterrorism or counterinsurgency—whether it was enough to just focus on eliminating bad guys or whether their defeat necessitated strengthening Afghan civil society. Counterinsurgency required a lot more resources and time, a heavy political and strategic lift in the eighth year of a war, even one launched for good reason.[47] At the end of the review, Obama would split the difference. Obama would build up Afghan capabilities and attack al Qaeda in Pakistan, primarily through drone strikes, a strategy that was effective but carried significant regional political costs.

In its reconceptualization of the "war on terror," Obama defined a war against al Qaeda with a much tighter purpose, to "disrupt, dismantle, and defeat" the global network directly responsible for the attacks of September 11.[48]*

The new terminology not only defined a specific adversary; it also established a realistic finish line.[49] It was impractical and unnecessary to defeat all terrorist networks with global reach, as Bush initially conceived the war on terror. As Leon Panetta wrote in his memoir *Worthy Fights*, the revised mission was a "more focused and achievable aim, and it better reflected America's interest in the region."[50]

Consistent with his campaign pledge, the president authorized an increase of twenty-one thousand troops to help secure Afghanistan's upcoming presidential election during the summer of 2009. But he soon faced the prospect of yet another request for more forces. The new commander in Afghanistan, General Stanley McChrystal, sought to implement a similar kind of counterinsurgency strategy that seemed to work in Iraq.

The White House launched yet another review. While the military still believed its objective was to defeat the Taliban in Afghanistan, the prevailing view within the Obama administration was that a fully resourced counterinsurgency strategy was neither strategically necessary nor politically sustainable.[51] The Taliban's roots within Afghanistan were ultimately too deep for the United States to affect in a realistic time frame.

"I am not going to do a ten-year, one-trillion-dollar Afghan plan," the president said clearly in one meeting.[52] As if to emphasize the point, the White House released a statement making clear to the Afghan government as well as the U.S. military that "our commitment isn't open-ended."[53]

---

*In 2008, the Center for American Progress published a homeland security strategy that I authored, entitled *Safe at Home*. In it, I recommended that the overly broad concept of a war on terror be retired in favor of a new descriptor that was more achievable. But as the threat has evolved, the frame of a war against al Qaeda turned out to be too narrow.

Another crucial factor influencing Obama's thinking was frustration with Karzai. The Obama White House grew tired of his public criticism and poor performance. Both sides developed lengthy lists of grievances. To Karzai, the American military was slow to recognize how collateral damage on the battlefield eroded support for the U.S. presence and played into the Taliban's hands. To Washington, widespread corruption undermined the perceived legitimacy of the Afghan government at home and abroad.

Ambassador Karl Eikenberry (formerly a U.S. military commander in Afghanistan as well) argued that Karzai was "not an adequate strategic partner" and questioned the degree to which the United States could overcome local factors, including the nature of the country and level of corruption, in order to enable counterinsurgency to succeed.[54] The Eikenberry cable, which was requested by the White House but not coordinated with the military in advance, was leaked to the *New York Times*. The public airing of interagency disagreements rankled the White House that much preferred a "no drama" approach to policy making.

The administration ultimately determined that success in Afghanistan depended to a significant degree on changing Pakistan's hedging strategy. Islamabad supported the Taliban because they feared potential Indian influence that might come with the kind of inclusive government the United States supported. As Vice President Biden argued convincingly, "If you don't get Pakistan right, you can't win."[55]

Pakistan feared, with justification, that the United States would turn its back on the region once it ended the Afghan war. Given the strong terrorist connections to Pakistan from various plots against the United States— Najibullah Zazi, David Headley, and Faisal Shahzad—the United States required more effort from Pakistan. In turn, Washington had to remove any uncertainty regarding its policy.

As Robert Gates reflected in his memoir *Duty*, with the White House more focused on an exit strategy than success, it did not appear that Obama was ever totally committed to his strategy.[56] In fact, Obama did not believe a counterinsurgency strategy was sustainable or would work.

Obama lowered the bar regarding what he hoped to achieve in Afghanistan. The United States would check the Taliban momentum and degrade them to a level that could reasonably be managed by a more effective Afghan government and security force. It would pursue a hybrid between counterinsurgency and counterintelligence, what James Mann described as "counterinsurgency in a hurry."[57] Just before announcing his decision, Obama summarized his policy as "in quickly, out quickly, focus on al Qaeda, and build the Afghan army."[58]

The goal was not to "try to make Afghanistan a perfect place." Rather it was getting the country "to the best possible place."[59] Seeing that the war would not end during his first term, Obama aimed instead to withdraw U.S. forces by the end of his second. That, too, would be more difficult than he expected.

AFGHANIZATION

Obama gave a thirty-four-minute speech at West Point in December 2009. There was no mention of victory. He reiterated the core objective: "to disrupt, dismantle, and defeat al Qaeda in Afghanistan and Pakistan, and to prevent its capacity to threaten America and our allies in the future."[60]

The president committed to send an additional thirty thousand troops to "seize the initiative," reverse the Taliban's momentum, preclude their ability to overthrow the Kabul government, and strengthen Afghanistan security forces and governmental institutions. In addition to military forces, Obama pledged "a civilian surge" with increased development assistance, particularly in the agricultural sector. He also hinted at a reconciliation process, saying that there would be a future in Afghanistan for former fighters who abandon violence and respect human rights. Obama viewed the challenge as a shared responsibility, saying, "This is not just America's war." He encouraged NATO allies to remain committed to the mission and offered long-term partnerships to both Afghanistan and Pakistan, committing to a strategy "that works on both sides of the border."[61]

The most controversial aspect of the president's strategy was the public declaration that the U.S. combat role in Afghanistan would be scaled back on a specific timetable. There would be a gradual transition to Afghan responsibility, beginning in July 2011. "America has no interest in fighting an endless war in Afghanistan," Obama said.[62]

In his remarks, Obama made repeated references to Vietnam, rejecting parallels that argued for alternatives that he characterized as "cutting our losses," "muddle through," or an "open-ended escalation." He distinguished between Afghanistan, where the September 11 attack originated, and Vietnam, where the United States confronted a popular insurgency.[63]

Seeing a need for rebuilding at home, he repeated in public what he had said in private, that he was not committing the United States to a decade-long "nation-building project."[64] It is telling that, as Obama suggested to Steve Kroft of *60 Minutes* a few days after his West Point speech, despite eight years of effort in Afghanistan, if he attempted a rapid drawdown of U.S. forces, "The country, I believe, would collapse."[65] That's what happened in Vietnam.

Obama's public declaration of a deadline had conflicting strategic and political implications. According to Colin Dueck, from a military standpoint, "the two halves of this announcement worked against one another"—it communicated to the Taliban that U.S. forces would leave at some point and that as an indigenous force they could simply wait the Americans out. From a domestic political standpoint, "Obama found both halves of the stated policy to be helpful," reassuring the skeptics that the war would not continue indefinitely.[66]

Obama rejected criticism that his strategy—beefing up the American troop presence but for a brief period—was confusing, saying "we don't want to be an occupying force," a clear nod to Iraq. But he acknowledged that the situation in Afghanistan did not lend itself to "simple black and white answers."[67]

In the region, it reinforced fears that the United States would again lose interest in Afghanistan and leave Pakistan to cope with an unsettled mess. For the Taliban, there was less incentive to negotiate. "You have the watches," one fighter told an American interrogator, "but we have the time."[68]

Not surprisingly, efforts to launch a political process floundered due to uncertainties on all sides. At various times, the U.S. military resisted, seeking greater progress on the battlefield as a necessary precondition for negotiations. Pakistan would arrest the Taliban's chief negotiator because it did not feel its interests were represented. Afghanistan wanted the Taliban to negotiate with Kabul, not Washington. And the Taliban was unwilling to meet America's preconditions; it never really broke with al Qaeda.

"We should have started talking in 2003," General McChrystal would say later.[69] The United States didn't when it held the best cards, embracing diplomacy only after it had lost crucial leverage.

Washington put real resources behind its offer of a strategic partnership with Pakistan—$7.5 billion over five years. American officials would expend considerable effort trying to convince the Pakistani government, particularly its military leadership, that its support for extremist groups was a double-edged sword that ultimately threatened Pakistan's own security and sovereignty. It proved to be a tough sell.

While the administration would seek to regain lost momentum in Afghanistan while continuing to build up Afghanistan's government and security forces, the United States would go after the sanctuaries in Pakistan, Yemen, and Somalia with a vengeance, although this part of the strategy would be largely covert.

If the administration's judgment was that Afghanistan was no longer central to the fight against al Qaeda, that view received indirect affirmation just days after the West Point speech when Umar Farouk Abdulmutallab, linked to an American cleric in Yemen, attempted to bring down a civilian airliner over Detroit employing an underwear bomb. The plot demonstrated that much of al Qaeda's operational capability had shifted away from the movement's core to its franchises, especially al Qaeda in the Arabian Peninsula.

The same day as the Obama inaugural, January 20, 2009, Saudi and Yemeni militants announced the formation of AQAP.[70] Now, less than a year later, they had launched an attack on the American homeland that only narrowly failed. Five months later, AQAP attempted to bring down cargo aircraft over the United States by inserting explosives into printer ink cartridges.

Abdulmutallab provided considerable intelligence (refuting a key argument about the military prison at Guantanamo) that implicated the American cleric Anwar al-Awlaki.

Immediately after 9/11, Awlaki, at the time an imam at a mosque just outside of Washington, D.C., condemned the al Qaeda attacks and envisioned himself as "a bridge" between America and the Islamic world.[71] Within a decade, he had established a very significant online profile as an inspirational figure within AQAP, evidently encouraging Major Nidal Hasan to launch his attack against soldiers at Fort Hood in November 2009. He evolved into an operational leader of the jihad against the United States with a direct role in Abdulmuttalab's attempt to blow up a civilian airliner on Christmas Day.

The drone strike that killed Awlaki in September 2011 was a controversial action that targeted an American citizen without the benefit of due process. At the time of his death, Awlaki was considered one of the most dangerous people in the world.[72] Given the Internet age, his videos encouraging violent extremism remained a potent weapon years after his demise.

Left unanswered in Obama's remarks was the nature of America's long-term strategic partnership with Afghanistan. As Henry Kissinger warned about Vietnam, once troop withdrawals begin, they take on a life of their own. In fact, Obama pursued a withdrawal strategy for much of his presidency, establishing a clear trajectory to end the Afghan war, the longest in U.S. history. He changed course only when it became clear that his Afghanization strategy required a timetable based on conditions in Kabul, not Washington.

3

CENTRAL FRONT

In a 2008 op-ed in the *New York Times,* candidate Barack Obama wrote, "Iraq is not the central front in the war on terrorism, and it never has been."[1] Like a majority of Americans five years into the war, he viewed Iraq as a disastrous mistake.

Obama believed the presence of U.S. forces was an impediment to a political resolution of Iraq's civil war. "Only by redeploying our troops," Obama wrote, "can we press the Iraqis to reach comprehensive political accommodation."[2] He would test that proposition as president.

Obama's opposition to the war—his chief primary opponents (Hillary Clinton, Joe Biden, and John Edwards) all voted in favor as sitting senators—gave him a huge electoral advantage. He was committed to rebuilding America's economy at home and its image abroad. In his view, the indefinite presence of tens of thousands of troops was not sustainable strategically, politically, or financially.

The United States did help to create a new parliamentary system of government in Iraq. Images of purple fingers when Iraqis went to the polls in 2005 were compelling. They offered a dramatic alternative to the authoritarian republics or monarchies that dominated politics in the Arab world.

"We did the most radical thing America has done in the Arab world in the post war period," said Tom Friedman of the *New York Times.* "We actually sponsored the first consensual election between the constituent communities and elements of an Arab country."[3] That said, Iraq was never going to be a model for the rest of the region; leaders in the region, including American allies, viewed democracy as an existential threat and used rising sectarianism as justification for political repression.

But the failure to locate more than a few chemical weapons in Iraq and the chaos that followed the U.S. invasion destroyed its perceived legitimacy and severely damaged America's credibility around the world. Whatever the American accomplishments in Iraq, they came at an enormous cost—human life, treasure, and political capital.

Even as Obama campaigned to replace him, President George W. Bush was doubling down on Iraq. Seeking to recover lost ground both strategically and politically, Bush ordered a surge of U.S. forces to work with Sunni tribes to stabilize key provinces in Iraq where sectarian violence was fiercest. No doubt he hoped to create a positive trajectory before leaving office, moderating an otherwise harsh verdict on his presidency.

Obama opposed the surge (former Secretary of Defense Bob Gates suggested Obama did so for political reasons[4]) as "a policy which has already been tried and a policy which has failed."[5] But it did sufficiently lower the level of violence in Iraq in 2008 to enable the Bush administration to negotiate a Status of Forces Agreement with Iraq that fixed an end date for the U.S. combat mission.

While there is little question that the presence of tens of thousands of U.S. troops intensified the violence within Iraq and exacerbated violent political extremism directed at the United States, the eventual withdrawal of American forces did little to resolve the underlying sectarian divisions that eventually tore Iraq apart at the seams, inadvertently opening a fissure that allowed the rise of the Islamic State.

Despite a good-faith negotiation to define a long-term strategic partnership between the two countries, a residual U.S. military force under conditions acceptable to both sides was simply not feasible. Politics would not support an extension here or there. A sovereign Iraq was ready to stand on its own, and a long-term U.S. military presence infringed on that prerogative. After an unexpectedly long and costly war, America was ready to put Iraq in its rearview mirror.

In 2008, the American people elected a candidate who promised to do just that. In turn, the Bush administration's surge created a "decent interval" that provided sufficient political cover for the Obama administration to withdraw U.S. forces by 2011.

Over a quarter century, four consecutive American presidents spent more time, energy, and resources devoted to Iraq than any other country on earth. In the process, Iraq became a vital national interest, although not a political one. The continued presence of the Islamic State in Iraq ensured it would preoccupy a fifth beginning in January 2017.

None of this was planned.

NEW WORLD ORDER

Despite the troublesome nature of the regime of Saddam Hussein, the Reagan administration drew closer to Iraq as a counterweight to Iran. It said little as Iraq employed chemical weapons in its war with Iran, a lesson not lost in Tehran. Given the still raw memory of the takeover of the U.S. Embassy by Iranian students, Iraq benefited consistently from being viewed as the lesser of evils.

The George H. W. Bush administration hoped that greater diplomatic and economic interaction could moderate Iraq's behavior.[6] But in August 1990 Saddam Hussein invaded Kuwait, driven by debt incurred during its war with Iran and nursing a grievance that the Gulf states had not provided enough support.

Policy, politics, and narratives were tightly aligned as President Bush drew a line in the sand. "This will not stand," he said, "this aggression against Kuwait."[7]

In a subsequent speech, he underscored four principles that would guide the American and international response: a complete Iraqi withdrawal from Kuwait; restoration of Kuwait's legitimate government; the U.S. commitment to the security of Saudi Arabia and stability of the region; and the protection of American citizens abroad.[8]

Bush and his national security team viewed the challenge as a test of the post–Cold War "new world order," an opportunity for the emerging international community to enforce appropriate standards of conduct for countries and their leaders. The administration later abandoned the term, fearing it was too idealistic and potentially costly.[9]

Pursuing a multilateral resolution, the first Bush administration built an unprecedented coalition of more than thirty countries to oppose Saddam. Thanks to effective diplomacy, the Gulf War enjoyed considerable international legitimacy. The financial and in-kind contributions of allies and supporters defrayed much of its direct costs.

There was a clear domestic political benefit as well. As Secretary of State James Baker wrote later, "The stronger the coalition, the easier it was to generate consensus at home. Likewise, the more domestic support we had, the more the President was put in a commanding position vis-a-vis other govern-ments."[10]

President Bush worked assiduously to elicit the understanding of Soviet President Mikhail Gorbachev. Iraq had been a Soviet client state. The Berlin Wall had fallen just a year earlier, and the world was evolving from zero-sum to positive-sum calculations. Bush viewed maintaining constructive relations with Moscow as crucial to the integration of the Soviet Union into the inter-national system.

Former National Security Advisor Brent Scowcroft suggested the Cold War ended not with the fall of the Berlin Wall but with the joint condemnation by the United States and Soviet Union immediately after the Iraqi invasion.[11] Despite investing significantly in a working relationship with President Dmitri Medvedev as part of policy "reset" with Russia, Obama would ignore Russian concerns regarding the NATO intervention in Libya.

The United Nations, given the Bush administration's respect for Russia's regional interests, functioned as its founders envisioned. The Security Council, exercising moral authority in ways it couldn't during the Cold War, passed twelve security council resolutions in support of Kuwait, ten before the war commenced.[12] Rather than an obstacle, Scowcroft viewed the UN as an "essential source of authority and legitimacy."[13]

The Bush administration's faith in the United Nations was not the pre-vailing view within the Republican Party. Most conservatives, including Bush's son, viewed the UN as a constraint.

The elder Bush served as U.S. ambassador to the United Nations and believed the United States needed to stay within the parameters of what the UN had approved. He committed to the liberation of Kuwait, not the transfor-mation of Iraq. The Bush administration recognized the danger of getting into a protracted occupation and the need to maintain the balance of power against Iran.[14]

"We early on decided it was not up to us to drive him from power," recalled Scowcroft. "He was still a nasty piece of work, there's no question about that, but he was not a threat in a strategic sense."[15] The United States would not "follow up Iraq's occupation with one of our own."[16]

CNN EFFECT

Operation Desert Storm was America's first major war since Vietnam. It was also the first significant test of America's All-Volunteer Force, far more effec-tive than the conscript military that fought in Vietnam.

Desert Storm shattered the Vietnam Syndrome, opening the door to the aggressive use of the military to shape the post–Cold War environment. With the president's backing, General Norman Schwarzkopf, the theater commander, and General Colin Powell, chairman of the Joint Chiefs, employed overwhelming force to achieve the military objective, explicitly avoiding the gradualist approach employed in Vietnam. Curiously, Iraq obliged. Saddam Hussein doubted Bush would actually attack.

Saudi Arabia was wary of the deployment of U.S. military forces to the Kingdom but recognized the threat that Saddam Hussein now posed. King Fahd approved stationing U.S. forces in Saudi Arabia based on the presumption that when the conflict ended, "you'll leave."[17]

Congressional and public opinion was divided sharply even as the Operation Desert Shield buildup continued. President Bush dispatched his secretary of state for a last-minute meeting in Geneva with Iraqi Foreign Minister Tariq Aziz, demonstrating a willingness to go the extra mile to avoid war. The ensuing vote in Congress authorizing military force was the closest in U.S. history, with the House voting 250 to 183 in favor of a resolution authorizing military force and the Senate by a narrower 52 to 47 margin.

Public opinion was an issue in the region as well. In all, more than a half million American service members deployed for the war, but for the most part, their operating locations were only identified as Southwest Asia, not a specific country. While there were legitimate operational security concerns, there was also a lack of confidence among the region's monarchies that their publics would be supportive if they knew the details of the American defense cooperation. Washington went along. A quarter century later, perceptions of the U.S. role in the region remain driven far more by conspiracy theory than fact.

The Bush administration did an effective job of setting expectations and then exceeding them. Public opinion turned overwhelmingly favorable with a devastatingly effective air campaign that resembled "a kind of virtual war" and a rapid ground assault that lasted a mere one hundred hours.[18] Iraq was the perfect war, an intensive, high-tech battle with an adversary that could be seen, confronted, and destroyed.

Vietnam was the first television war; Iraq was the first covered live. In an unprecedented move, Saddam Hussein allowed CNN to broadcast in real time from Baghdad, opening a direct channel to attempt to influence American perceptions. He failed, although there were some controversies over targeting and the impact on Iraqi civilians.

In Washington, while the White House was careful not to micromanage campaign tactics, it was sensitive to regional perceptions. When images from the battlefield showed the destruction of retreating Iraqi forces (dubbed by the media as the Highway of Death), the president with the concurrence of his military commanders ended the assault even though in the fog of war it left Saddam Hussein with considerable firepower still at his disposal. Scowcroft acknowledged it was "a significant aspect of the decision."[19] This was an early example of the "CNN Effect."[20]★

The Bush administration did not develop a political strategy regarding how the war would end. Despite being compared to Adolf Hitler, Saddam was left standing when the shooting stopped. Bush organized the international coalition behind the objective of driving Saddam out of Kuwait, not out of power. The National Intelligence Estimate at the time judged Saddam to be a product of Iraqi political culture and that "changing the nature of Iraqi politics is a long-term process and not likely to be achieved by the fall of Saddam Hussein."[21]

The president believed—reasonably even though events unfolded differently—that Saddam would be overthrown after such a stinging military defeat.[22] In fact, given that he easily reconstituted his military power, "Saddam actually thought that he had won."[23]

As the troops returned to a warm embrace by the American people, Bush enjoyed high approval ratings. But concerns about the economy quickly overtook the war's success. A popular bumper sticker during the 1992 presidential campaign was: "Saddam Hussein still has his job. Do you?"[24]

The war did produce constructive geopolitical benefits, most significantly the Madrid Conference, the Oslo Process, and the prospect of comprehensive Middle East peace. But twenty-five years later, despite a clear understanding on all sides of what a viable comprehensive peace agreement looks like, a two-state solution between the Israelis and Palestinians remains elusive. The real problem is not substance, but politics. The parties have not prepared their people nor the region to make the compromises necessary to end the conflict.

In many respects, the Gulf War never ended. The war's murky conclusion necessitated a decade-long protection and containment mission—Operations Provide Comfort (later renamed Northern Watch) and Southern Watch, with American military forces stationed in the region to protect the Kurds and deter Iraq from threatening its neighbors again. This led to a series of crises and confrontations over the next decade. While successful, they came at a cost.

★There has been considerable research regarding the CNN Effect. Dramatic images on cable television don't force governments to respond in ways beyond existing policy. But there is strong evidence that policy makers are forced to make more rapid decisions without time to fully assess strategic consequences.

"After Desert Storm, the United States became, in the eyes of many Muslims at least, an occupying force."[25] One of them was Osama bin Laden. Buoyed by the mujahideen victory over the Soviet Union in Afghanistan, bin Laden offered to defend the Saudi kingdom against Iraq. When the king declined, his al Qaeda movement went to war against the "far enemy," the United States.[26]

Bush expected to address the residual threat posed by Saddam Hussein during a second term. Given the unexpected electoral result in 1992, that became unfinished business to which many key figures in the Bush administration would return in 2001.

IN A BOX

Bill Clinton was critical of Bush's "ambivalence about supporting democracy" on the campaign trail in 1992.[27] The Clinton administration advocated a strategy of "enlargement," promoting a global community of democracies and market economies.[28] Yet Clinton said in the early days of his first term that "the people of Iraq would be better off if they had a different leader." But he added, "my job is not to pick their rulers for them."[29]

The Clinton administration followed a three-pronged approach: maintaining the political consensus regarding UN resolutions; finding ways to undermine Saddam's hold on power; and responding aggressively to military provocations, an approach eventually dubbed "containment plus."[30] The enforcement of the no-fly zones steadily weakened Iraq's military capability. It was war under the radar.

Given the pattern of Iraq's behavior, which American officials characterized as "cheat and retreat," the U.S. government was convinced he was hiding something.[31] If the international community lost its will regarding complete Iraqi compliance with UN resolutions, Clinton was certain Saddam would "rebuild an arsenal of devastating destruction."[32] If he had them, Clinton was sure Saddam would use them.

After Saddam expelled UN inspectors in 1998, the Clinton administration conducted a brief but intensive air campaign that it hoped would set back Iraq's programs by two years. Ugly as the policy was, it worked. Saddam remained a troublesome opponent, but was greatly weakened as a regional military threat—the Clinton administration rightly assessed that he remained "in a box." As Richard Haass acknowledged, "Saddam was in power but not in a position to do serious harm."[33]

But by the late 1990s, regional public opinion turned against the U.S.-led containment strategy and the UN-led sanctions and inspection process. Even though Saddam was responsible for the suffering—he preferred to build palaces for his cronies than tend to the needs of his people—he generated considerable sympathy, poisoning American relations with the region in the process.

The inspection regime, effective in documenting past Iraqi WMD activities, could not prove the negative—that Saddam no longer possessed weapons of mass destruction. A kind of sanctions fatigue set in, with Saddam able to evade much of the impact through oil smuggling.

During this same period, there was rising concern regarding the threat of terrorism. Everyone's worst-case scenario was the risk that a terrorist organization might acquire a weapon of mass destruction, especially some kind of nuclear device. Clinton gave voice to that danger in a speech at the Pentagon in 1998, although not with the same sense of urgency as his successor.[34]

At roughly the same time, the Project for the New American Century (PNAC) promoted the need for more assertive U.S. global leadership "to shape a new century favorable to American principles and interests." The group featured a number of conservatives who would play prominent roles in the administration of George W. Bush. Iraq became a key demonstration project, with the goal "to meet threats before they become dire."[35]

Particularly among neoconservatives—the intellectual Irving Kristol famously described the movement as "liberals mugged by reality"[36]—a primary lesson to emerge from both Vietnam and the Gulf War was a rejection of the policy of containment, despite its evident success during the Cold War. They were far more comfortable with the Manichean rhetoric that called out evil—the hallmark being Reagan's "evil empire"—and the activist foreign policy that it implied. Promoting American values and interests was an obligation. Containment was an unacceptable constraint on the employment of American power.[37]

Paul Wolfowitz, a senior defense official during both Bush presidencies, argued that Saddam Hussein was getting stronger, not weaker, and needed to be removed from power.[38] When Congress passed and President Clinton signed the Iraq Liberation Act, the policy of the United States was no longer containment, but regime change in Iraq.

"For many in the Bush administration, Iraq was unfinished business," suggested George Tenet. After the attacks of September 11, there was a psychological and political imperative, not unlike the response after Pearl Harbor. "The message was: We can never afford to be surprised again."[39]

But the policy ambition would broaden. Success in Iraq could instill democracy in the region, creating a more amenable environment for U.S. interests, including Israel.[40] Max Boot suggested it represented "the chance to right the scales, to establish the first Arab democracy, and to show the Arab people that the United States is as committed to freedom for them as it was for the people of Eastern Europe."[41]

MUSHROOM CLOUD

By July 2002, it was clear to National Security Advisor Condoleezza Rice that the United States was going to war in Iraq.[42] But the administration still had to explain why to the American people and the world.

Given that the United States and Iraq had been in a state of armed conflict for a dozen years, the American public was already predisposed in favor of military action.[43] That was not the case around the world, where publics were widely skeptical. In Brazil, for example, 96 percent of those polled were opposed. Even with regional stalwarts such as Israel and Jordan, 90 percent of those polled were opposed.[44]

Administration officials suggested later there were many reasons for the United States to remove Saddam Hussein from power—for example, Iraq's noncompliance with UN resolutions. It picked what it believed to be the most compelling argument.[45] Former Secretary of Defense Donald Rumsfeld would call the controversy "a public relations error," although it was much more than that.[46] Former CIA Director Michael Hayden acknowledged, "It was the case most easily articulated. It was just wrong."[47]★

Vice President Dick Cheney told the Veterans of Foreign Wars National Convention in August 2002, "Simply stated, there is no doubt that Saddam Hussein now has weapons of mass destruction." That statement was true— there were stocks of chemical weapons—but misrepresented the urgency surrounding Iraq's actual capabilities and the proliferation risk.[48]

As Condoleezza Rice suggested in an interview on CNN on September 8, 2002, "The problem here is that there will always be some uncertainty

---

★The Bush administration suggested that, should Saddam Hussein escape sanctions, he would reconstitute his nuclear weapons program. But given its veto power at the UN, the United States had the ability to prevent that from ever happening. Saddam committed atrocities against his own people, including the Halabja chemical weapons attack against the Kurds in 1988 and brutal suppression of the Shia rebellion in 1991. The Bush administration could have employed the same lost legitimacy argument that the Obama administration did with Qaddafi and Assad during the Arab Spring.

about how quickly he can acquire nuclear weapons. But we don't want the smoking gun to be a mushroom cloud."[49]

The National Intelligence Estimate produced by the U.S. intelligence community during the later half of 2002 projected that if unchecked, Iraq "probably will have a nuclear weapon during this decade."[50] But a British memo presented a much thinner case against Saddam Hussein. "Saddam was not threatening his neighbors, and his WMD capability was less than that of Libya, North Korea or Iran."[51]

The Bush administration, particularly the vice president, portrayed the Iraq invasion within the umbrella of the war on terror. The administration pointed to the presence of Abu Musab al-Zarqawi, who after the U.S. invasion pledged loyalty to bin Laden and formed al Qaeda in Iraq. It debated a strike on Zarqawi's operation, Ansar al-Islam, in the lead-up to Secretary of State Colin Powell's dramatic UN speech.

"That would wipe out my briefing," Powell suggested.[52]

At the UN, Powell highlighted Zarqawi by name, identifying him as an al Qaeda "collaborator." Drawing from Bush's initial conception of the war on terror—we will not distinguish between the terrorists and those who support them—he claimed that Iraq "harbors a deadly terrorist network."[53]

Yet there was no evidence the Iraqi government had anything to do with him. Saddam was the very kind of apostate leader bin Laden hoped to displace. These enemies of the United States were never destined to be friends.

Shortly before the invasion, President Bush told an audience at the American Enterprise Institute that "A new regime in Iraq would serve as a dramatic and inspiring example of freedom for other nations in the region."[54]

Inside the administration, Richard Haass, head of policy planning for the State Department, believed that, as laudable as bringing democracy to Iraq might be, it does not justify military force.[55]

Haass and his Policy Planning team at the State Department advanced a memorandum in September 2002 that highlighted the need to align resources with ambitions. "In post-conflict reconstruction," he suggested, "you usually get what you pay for." He warned of a lack of "software" in Iraq that would enable the promotion of democracy and the risk that "spoilers" could jeopardize the effort.[56]

Rice was sanguine about the rationale, admitting that "we did not go to Iraq to bring democracy any more than Roosevelt went to war against Hitler to democratize Germany, though that became American policy once the Nazis were defeated."[57]

Intriguingly, President Bush declared in his speech to the United Nations General Assembly six months before military action that Saddam Hussein's regime had lost his legitimacy, an argument that President Obama would use in the context of both Libya and Syria. The United Nations Security Council through Resolution 1441 voted 15-0 in November 2002 that Iraq was in material breach of its international obligations, which the United States ultimately used as justification for its invasion.

"The fact is, we invaded Iraq because we believed we had run out of other options," Rice reflected later. "We had come to the conclusion that it was time to deal with Saddam and believed that the world would be better off with the dictator out of power."[58]

While the Bush administration made its case for war, there were skeptics.

"Saddam was not an imminent threat," according to former Acting CIA Director Michael Morell.[59] But the CIA provides intelligence, not policy advice. Notwithstanding later claims that there was an intelligence failure, the sense of urgency that the Bush administration attached to Iraq was about policy and politics, not intelligence.[60]

"There was plenty of time to build a solid international coalition if we had more patience," said General John Abizaid, the commander of Central Command during the early postconflict phase.[61] But the White House, for both political and philosophical reasons, was unwilling to pursue the kind of coalition that existed in 1991.

Former National Security Advisor Brent Scowcroft wrote an op-ed in the *Wall Street Journal* expressing doubts about the links between Saddam Hussein and al Qaeda. Scowcroft was one of the few to look at the Iraq war in terms of potential costs.[62]

The opposition also included an Illinois state senator, planning a run for the U.S. Senate. He argued that another war in Iraq was not only a dangerous diversion, but would make the challenge of combating global terrorism more difficult.

Barack Obama anticipated the risk that an American intervention would "fan the flames of the Middle East, and encourage the worst, rather than best, impulses of the Arab world, and strengthen the recruitment arm of al Qaeda."[63] Neither Congress nor the media, given the proximity to 9/11, challenged the assumptions behind the war.[64] Arthur Schlesinger viewed it as a "failure of the political process."[65]

Congress passed a joint resolution authorizing the use of force against Iraq on October 2, 2002. Deliberately scheduled prior to midterm elections, it stated that al Qaeda was known to be in Iraq and that Iraq's ongoing support for international terrorist groups justified military action. Iraq was about to become the central front in the war on terror.

CAKEWALK

Weeks before the invasion, Iraqi dissidents told the president that "People will greet the troops with sweets and flowers."[66] Cheney told *Meet the Press* on March 16 that the troops will be "greeted as liberators."[67] The Bush administration believed that if the United States showed resolve, its key allies would fall in line. Its adversaries would fall to the wayside. There would be no need to stay long.

On March 19, 2003, in very brief remarks from the Oval Office, President George W. Bush announced the start of military operations "to disarm Iraq, to free its people and to defend the world from grave danger." The president chose to eliminate the threat posed by Saddam Hussein's "weapons of mass murder" now "so that we do not have to meet it later with armies of fire fighters and police and doctors on the streets of our cities."[68]

2004 was an election year, and the administration hoped for a rapid turnover of the country to an interim government that would enable American forces to withdraw before American voters went to the polls.[69]

Utilizing a light military footprint in Iraq, the Bush administration sought to reverse Powell's emphasis on the use of overwhelming force to achieve its stated objectives. The Bush administration did not believe it would take more troops in the postconflict phase than for the war itself. With Saddam deposed, remnants of the Iraqi government and military would quickly secure the country. A token military force would remain behind to support an interim government, secure weapons caches, deliver humanitarian assistance, and develop plans for democratic elections.

The Pentagon didn't plan for a postwar because the Bush administration didn't want a postwar. "It wasn't an oversight; it was deliberate," wrote Fred Kaplan in *The Insurgents*.[70]

No nation building. No quagmire.

The initial combat phase unfolded just as the administration hoped. A friend of the vice president, Ken Adelman, described it as a "cakewalk."[71] President Bush followed that with his own declaration of "mission accomplished" on the deck of the *USS Abraham Lincoln*. He declared an end to the Iraq War America signed up to support.

"Americans assumed the war was over when really it had only just begun," suggested Dominic Tierney in *The Right Way to Lose a War*.[72]

The Bush administration convinced itself that Iraq would be self-ordering, but then made critical mistakes—principally early declarations disbanding the Iraqi army and removing those associated with the Ba'ath Party from government service, a move ironically encouraged by Iranian officials.[73] What the Bush administration actually confronted was what the CIA would later characterize as a "catastrophic success"—the demise of Saddam Hussein, but then the rapid emergence of ethnic tensions, religious rivalries, and resentment at foreign occupation.[74]

By July 2003, Lieutenant General Ricardo Sanchez described the emerging environment in Iraq as a "terrorist magnet." But he assumed, as did much of the Bush administration, that fighting them there would reduce the threat to the American homeland.[75]

But as Andrew Bacevich wrote in *The Limits of Power*, "Between April 28, 2003 and February 22, 2006, Iraq came apart at the seams."[76] The former marked an incident when U.S. forces fired on a crowd demonstrating in Fallujah; the latter was the date terrorists blew up the Mosque of the Golden Dome in Samarra, a low point in the burgeoning Sunni-Shiite sectarian civil war.

The administration struggled to communicate around the unanticipated conflict. From the outset, the Bush administration interpreted the violent reaction to the U.S. invasion as resistance to the "advance of liberty" rather than the beginnings of a sectarian civil war among factions competing for power.[77]

The Bush administration was blind to the risk that Iraqis would misperceive American intentions. The Abu Ghraib prison had a well-justified reputation for torture and human rights abuses under the previous regime. Regrettably, the prison was the scene of notorious mistreatment of Iraqi inmates by unqualified military reservists, documented in dramatic and devastating images released by *60 Minutes II*.

"War is an inherently political act," Bacevich wrote in *America's War in the Greater Middle East*. "Abu Ghraib represented a political setback of monumental proportions."[78] The Bush administration believed Iraq was the opening chapter of the transformation of the Middle East. Instead, Abu Ghraib reinforced the worst regional perceptions of the United States. America brought chaos to the region, not democracy. Some even believed it was a deliberate effort to keep the region weak.

As the insurgency developed, talking points developed by the White House Office of Strategic Initiatives identified Iraq as the "central front" in the war on terror.[79] Al Qaeda was more than ready to accommodate. Iraq would for a time validate bin Laden's narrative of a "clash of civilizations."[80]

In his 1996 fatwa—al Qaeda's declaration of war—bin Laden accused the United States of forming a "Crusader-Zionist alliance," occupying sacred Muslim lands and threatening the Islamic world's most valuable asset, its energy reserves. Recognizing the dramatic imbalance in military capabilities, bin Laden directed the mujahideen to initiate a "guerrilla war" against the United States.[81] Iraq was tailor-made for that purpose.

The decision to invade Iraq was "a propaganda coup" for al Qaeda.[82] Suggests the CIA's Morell, it "supported the al Qaeda narrative and helped spread the group's ideology, a consequence not well understood before the war."[83] Far from making the country safer, it intensified the terrorist threat directed at the United States and its allies.

By the time American military forces attacked Zarqawi's remote camp in March 2003, a week into the campaign, he was already in Baghdad, putting in place an expanding network that would foment a sectarian civil war and destroy the Bush administration's narrative that war would be easy, quick, and inexpensive.

Zarqawi moved quickly, attacking first the Jordanian Embassy and then the United Nations mission in Baghdad. This was not the work of regime "dead-enders," as Secretary of Defense Donald Rumsfeld suggested, but a sophisticated campaign to isolate the United States, undermine its regional alliances, limit international assistance to the country, and pave the way for the establishment of an Islamic caliphate.

In 2004, Zarqawi released a five-minute, grainy video that would serve as a crude harbinger of the carefully staged videos that became a staple of the Islamic State. Zarqawi challenged fellow Muslims not to "sit idly by" or "sleep soundly" while Muslim honor was "bleeding" with the "images of shame" from the prisoner abuse at Abu Ghraib. He then beheaded American business-man Nicholas Berg, dressed in orange garb that resembled prison clothing worn both in Abu Ghraib and Guantanamo.[84]

Zarqawi's reputation and movement grew quickly, attracting legions of former Sunni Ba'athists and foreign fighters. "People were joining al Qaeda because of him," said a former associate.[85]

"Washington made him a terrorist superstar," wrote Joby Warrick in *Black Flags*.[86] Without the U.S. invasion, Zarqawi would have remained a low-level actor. Without Zarqawi, there would be no Islamic State. To the region, the United States handed a Sunni-run country to the Shia-led government. For the Shia, it was a moment of religious fulfillment. For the Sunnis, it was a clarion call for a new generation of jihadis to defend the true faith, and a lot easier to get to than Afghanistan.[87]

Zarqawi formed an uneasy alliance with bin Laden, but there soon developed an open dispute over the ways and means of al Qaeda in Iraq. Its violence against Muslims was damaging the al Qaeda brand.

Bin Laden's intention was to build popular support for the al Qaeda movement—win hearts and minds—through jihad against the United States. Only after the American infidels were driven from Muslim lands could the faithful begin to contemplate establishment of a genuine Muslim community, taking over governance from the apostate secular leaders and corrupt monarchies.

By contrast, Zarqawi and the leaders who followed him were intent to establish a caliphate much sooner. Anticipating that the United States would follow its intervention in Afghanistan with an invasion of Iraq, Zarqawi deliberately ignited a sectarian civil war against the majority Shia who were the beneficiaries of Saddam's removal.[88]

Bin Laden's second in command, Ayman al-Zawahiri, warned Zarqawi in a letter that he was losing Muslim hearts and minds in the "battlefield of the media," in the process undermining its broader appeal within the Islamic world.[89] "We don't need this," Zawahiri said.[90]

But Zarqawi ignored the advice and declared his intent to establish an Islamic State in Iraq. While he was killed before that happened, his successors did so in October 2006. Since it controlled no territory, the move represented little more than an effort to "dress up its terrorism in religious garb."[91] The new Islamic caliphate struggled to survive but would find another opening in the chaos that followed the Arab Spring.

THE SURGE

In 2005, the White House released a National Security Strategy for Victory in Iraq. It established as a long-term objective an Iraq that is "peaceful, united, stable, and secure, well integrated into the international community." It identified Iraq as the "central front in the global war on terror."[92] In his speech outlining the strategy, Bush used the word victory fifteen times.[93]

The document drew significantly from the work of Peter Feaver, a Duke professor who had long studied the intersection of war and public opinion and worked on the National Security Council staff. Feaver wrote major sections of the strategy and the president's speech outlining the administration's revised goals. The White House staff debated whether the right goal of the U.S. strategy should be "victory" or "success." Victory won out.[94]

Feaver believed sustaining public support for the U.S. presence in Iraq was less about rising costs per se, but whether the public had confidence that the investment carried a high likelihood of success.

The revised counterinsurgency strategy beneath the surge emphasized protection of the Iraqi population as the center of gravity. But by the time political and military leaders arrived at a strategy that might work, the public and congressional support that Weinberger said was vital to success had largely evaporated. Nonetheless, Bush recast his administration's narrative, presenting a plan to a skeptical Congress and public that was about "how we are going to win" rather than "how we're going to leave."[95]

The surge coincided with the so-called Anbar Awakening and helped stabilize Iraq to such a degree that both the United States and Iraq began to envision an endgame.

So did the American people, who went to the polls in November 2008 and selected a candidate who pledged to get U.S. forces out of Iraq.

Whereas Bush faced few constraints in the years after September 11, his perceived overreach narrowed the domestic political boundaries considerably. Obama's foreign policy platform reflected the political limits of the time—the United States was exceptional, but could not be everywhere, could not right every wrong, had to make careful choices that preserved power rather than squander it, and required allies to share the burden and generate legitimacy for what needed to be done.

On the campaign trail, Obama laid out his objectives for Iraq, "a functioning, sovereign country that can protect its borders, that is not a base camp for terrorists."[96] But he left no doubt regarding his foremost policy and political mandate: withdraw U.S. forces from Iraq as a key element of resetting America's relationship with the international community and repairing America's struggling economy.

In 2003, the Obama narrative was right: Iraq was a diversion that generated new recruits, exacerbated tensions in the region, and created perceptions America was "at war with Islam."[97] But by 2008, al Qaeda viewed Iraq as the "main effort" in its war with the United States. The strategic reality changed, but American politics didn't. "Iraq was not important in 2003," suggested David Fitzgerald and David Ryan, but "it was in 2010 and more so in 2014."[98]

In a July 2008 tour of America's two war zones, Obama discussed the war with military and diplomatic leaders and reiterated his belief that Afghanistan should now be the priority. That view was not shared by the then U.S.

commander in Iraq, General David Petraeus, who would serve as Obama's commander in Afghanistan and later as his director of Central Intelligence.[99]

In many ways, Iraq became the flip side of Vietnam. The longer the Vietnam war went on, the less vital it became to the broader Cold War struggle. It should never have become the test of the credibility of American power in the world. Conversely, the longer the Iraq war went on, the more important it became. Iraq should never have become the "central front" in the war on terror, but it did, allowing al Qaeda to recover, not in a fringe country like Afghanistan, but as Jordan's King Abdullah said, "in the heart of the Arab world."[100]

4

EXTENDED HAND

In a campaign debate in 2007, Barack Obama suggested he would engage America's adversaries and antagonists without precondition in pursuit of U.S. interests. He criticized the logic that a willingness to talk to countries like Iran, Syria, Venezuela, Cuba, and North Korea represented appeasement. His response elicited criticism from his chief opponent for the Democratic nomination, Senator Hillary Clinton, who accused him of being naive. She supported American leadership and vigorous diplomacy, but believed such high-stakes negotiations should be approached cautiously without undermining the interests of regional allies.[1]

There was actually not as wide a difference as was projected at the time. Obama would make engagement a hallmark of his presidency, with Clinton and her team at the State Department preparing the ground for dramatic diplomatic breakthroughs in Burma, Cuba, and Iran.

In his inaugural speech in 2009, Obama introduced multiple narratives that would guide his foreign policy across two terms in office. He considered dictators on "the wrong side of history" in a world that now judged leaders based on "what you build rather than what you destroy." Obama pledged to engage countries based on "mutual interest and mutual respect" and expressed a willingness "to extend a hand if they unclench their fist."[2]

Obama's engagement policy was a reflection of the difficult and costly U.S. experience in Iraq and the growing risk that a preemptive military confrontation between Israel and Iran over its nuclear program could drag the United States into another Middle East war. While America's European allies welcomed the Obama administration's commitment to join the so-called P5 + 1 (the major nuclear powers along with Germany and the European

Union representing the international community) without preconditions, the decision presented complicated political pressures.

The White House's interest in a diplomatic solution placed it at odds with its closest regional allies. Israeli Prime Minister Benjamin Netanyahu would actually help lead the political opposition to a deal with Iran, taking the unprecedented step of addressing the U.S. Congress and encouraging its Republican leadership to vote down the agreement.

America's Sunni allies shared this skepticism, although they expressed it in private, not public. One of the most colorful diplomatic cables released by WikiLeaks in 2010 said the Saudi king's preferred approach to the Iranian nuclear program was not negotiations but a military attack to "cut off the head of the snake."[3]

The Obama administration would make the nuclear negotiations with Iran arguably its highest foreign policy priority. But given its history and fraught politics, Iran was the regional challenge the Obama administration focused on the most and for a long time "talked about the least."[4]

THE GREAT SATAN

Jimmy Carter, the first post-Vietnam president, deepened the U.S. commitment to the Middle East. Carter helped Israel and Egypt conclude a historic peace agreement, a cornerstone of American regional policy ever since.

The Carter Doctrine recognized a vital interest in preserving the unimpeded flow of oil from the Persian Gulf to the American and global economies. The availability and price of oil was an area where foreign policy, economics, and domestic politics merged. The commitment translated to greater defense cooperation and protection for major regional energy producers, particularly Saudi Arabia and its Gulf neighbors, as well as repeated (and largely futile) attempts to impose order on the region.

Carter and his immediate predecessors relied on the Shah of Iran to help maintain stability in the Middle East. In a visit to Tehran on New Year's Eve 1977, Carter saluted the Shah as "an island of stability."[5] In fact, he was anything but. Just over a year later, the Shah, ailing both physically and politically, would leave Iran for good, just ahead of the revolution that would bring Ayatollah Ruhollah Khomeini back from exile and into power.

Initially, American diplomats in Tehran viewed Khomeini through a Cold War lens, encouraged by his staunch anticommunist rhetoric while ignoring the anti-Americanism at the heart of his worldview.[6]

In October 1979, the Carter administration agreed to allow the deposed and dying Shah of Iran to seek medical treatment in the United States. A group of university students in Tehran known as the Muslim Student Followers of the Imam's Line had already initiated planning for a brief takeover of the American Embassy. The Shah's admittance served as a catalyst.

The students planned to stay only a couple of days, but Khomeini, seeing an opportunity to consolidate power, endorsed the protest after it was launched. The embassy takeover "acquired a life of its own."[7]

To Khomeini, "domestic political calculations were paramount," suggests Ray Takeyh of the Council on Foreign Relations.[8] But the Ayatollah's support transformed what was intended as a brief protest into an international crisis that would shape policies and actions on both sides for decades.[9]

The hostage crisis, fairly or not, epitomized the "malaise" of the post-Vietnam period. It became a political and media preoccupation. ABC launched a weeknight program focused on the crisis entitled *The Iran Crisis: America Held Hostage*, later renamed *Nightline*.

In April 1980, on the cusp of a reelection campaign, Carter approved a rescue attempt. Operation Eagle Claw was aborted due to a sandstorm, but turned into a disaster when two aircraft collided at a deployment point inside Iran. Iran allowed a public viewing of the charred remains of the eight Americans who died in the inferno that resulted. Those searing images played a major role in Carter's electoral defeat.

Iran waited until the waning moments of the Carter presidency to resolve the hostage crisis. The Algiers Accord between the two countries included a pledge from the United States that it will not "intervene, directly or indirectly, politically or militarily, in Iran's internal affairs."[10]

In the ensuing years, the United States and Iran existed in a state of mutual antagonism, "suspended between war and peace."[11] Rather than accommodating the United States in the region—the choice the Shah had made—the new leadership constructed a policy that was "neither East nor West," words that adorn the entrance to its Ministry of Foreign Affairs.[12]

Both countries nursed grievances that fed a profound lack of trust.

To America, Iran was a rogue nation with a revolutionary government that refused to play by internationally accepted rules. Washington was troubled by the regime's anti-Americanism, anti-Semitism, and provocative language regarding the "export of revolution" throughout the region.

To Iran, the United States, despite its narrative of independence and self-determination, routinely interfered in the affairs of other countries.[13] The United States did plot against the government of Mohammad Mossadeq in

1953, backing Great Britain after Iran threatened to nationalize its oil industry. Iran's narrative overlooks the fact that the Shah, in accordance with his constitutional authority, actually dismissed the prime minister.[14] At the time, Iran's clerics were either indifferent to Mossadeq's fate or conspiring against him.[15] However, that history long fed Iranian fears that behind all American actions was a policy of regime change.

In 1991, the Bush administration decried Iraq's attempt to change international borders through force. But in 1980, in the midst of the hostage crisis, the Carter administration was silent as Saddam Hussein launched a war against Iran, abrogating an agreement with Tehran that had settled a territorial dispute over the province of Khuzestan.[16] Only in 1982, after Iran successfully launched a counteroffensive, did Washington express concern about the seizure of territory by force.[17]

During the ensuing Persian Gulf tanker war, as American warships patrolled the intensely narrow body of water, an Iraqi Air Force crew mistakenly targeted the *USS Stark* with two Exocet missiles. While the ship was saved only through the heroic efforts of its crew despite thirty-seven Americans killed in the incident, the Reagan administration blamed Iran for the broader conflict that it considered a threat to the flow of oil from the region.[18] Iraq was taken off the terrorism list and provided intelligence support and hundreds of millions of dollars in agricultural credits.[19] While Washington portrayed itself in public as neutral, Tehran did not see it that way.

"It baffled Iran's leaders and citizens alike how the Western bloc, with its emphasis on human rights and democratic values, had come to embrace a tyrannical Sunni leader," wrote Takeyh.[20] Tehran lost faith that it could rely on any government or international agreement to guarantee its security.

Even though the Reagan administration and its successors insisted they would never negotiate with terrorists, National Security Advisor Robert "Bud" McFarlane traveled to Tehran to engineer an exchange of sophisticated missiles for American hostages in Lebanon. McFarlane carried with him a cake and a Bible signed by President Reagan, just one indication of Washington's struggles to relate to Iran's revolutionary and religious government. Ironically, the midlevel Iranian officials he met included Hassan Rouhani, who would eventually be elected president.[21]

The Iran–Contra scandal, as it became known in America, poisoned political wells on both sides. The Reagan administration had contravened both U.S. law and stated policies against negotiating with terrorists. A number of high-level officials went to jail. Pragmatists within the Iranian government were heavily criticized for dealing with the Great Satan, which deepened the governing schism within Iranian politics.[22]

MISSED OPPORTUNITIES

On a number of occasions in subsequent years, one side seemed prepared for dialogue only to be rebuffed by the other. During the Gulf War, the Bush administration's rationale for not overthrowing Saddam Hussein was a need to maintain a regional balance of power.[23] At the same time, Iran recognized that any diminution of Iraq's military capability worked in its favor and sent signals that it would cooperate in the rescue of any allied pilots downed within Iranian territory.

After the war, the Bush administration notably excluded Iran from the Madrid conference to launch a Middle East peace process even though Tehran was willing to support any agreement that was acceptable to the Palestinians. From Washington's perspective, it was hard enough just getting the Israelis, Palestinians, Syrians, and Saudis in the same room. It didn't want Iran to play the role of the spoiler.

But the United States failed to appreciate the negative impact of Iran's exclusion.[24] In response, Tehran deepened its outreach to rejectionist groups like Hamas. It came to view the peace process and the prospective rapprochement between Israel and the Arab states as an effort to further isolate Iran.

Nonetheless, Iranian President Akbar Hashemi Rafsanjani was interested in more constructive relations with the West and attempted on multiple occasions to resolve issues with the United States.[25] President George H. W. Bush seemed to reciprocate in his inaugural address when he said that "Good will begets good will."[26] Working through indirect channels, the Bush administration suggested a willingness to respond to Iranian concerns, including the release of frozen financial assets, in return for help with the release of American hostages in Lebanon.

But even after the last Western hostage was freed in late 1991, with direct assistance from Iran, the Bush administration failed to respond despite American assurances to United Nations intermediaries that it would. Since 1992 was an election year, there was significant political risk in any approach to Iran. The initiative was deferred to a second Bush term.[27]

Rafsanjani tried again with Bill Clinton. In 1995, Iran selected Conoco over French-owned Total to develop offshore oil fields, intended as a major gesture that was approved by Ayatollah Ali Khamenei, who had succeeded Khomeini. Even though the Clinton White House was initially inclined to allow the deal to proceed, it reversed course when confronted with significant opposition by Israel, AIPAC, and Congress.[28] Congress then passed the Iran Libya Sanctions Act, specifically targeting companies that did business with Iran. While this created a policy breach with Europe, the measure passed the

House of Representatives 415–0, a strong indication of the favorable politics of supporting Israel and attacking Iran.[29]

The Clinton administration made significant overtures after the election of Mohammad Khatami, who sought better relations with Iran's neighbors and the outside world. He became the first sitting Iranian president to visit Riyadh. At the center of his outreach was a "dialogue among civilizations," a deliberate narrative refuting political scientist Samuel Huntington's theory of an irresolvable conflict between Western culture and Islam.[30]

Khatami granted an interview with CNN in January 1998, where he professed an "intellectual affinity" with American civilization, expressed regret for the hostage crisis, and offered qualified support for the peace process. He encouraged the United States to overcome the lingering "Cold War mentality" in its policies and hoped that expanded civilian exchanges could crack the "wall of mistrust" that existed between the two governments.[31]

Secretary of State Madeleine Albright reciprocated in remarks to the American-Iranian Council by wishing Iran a Happy New Year in Farsi, apologizing for the U.S. role in the Mossadeq overthrow, and admitting that support for Saddam Hussein during the Iran–Iraq war was "regrettably shortsighted." However, Tehran focused on her comments that challenged the legitimacy of the Ayatollah, which Seyed Hossein Mousavian, a former Iranian national security official and diplomat, considered a "strategic mistake."[32]

Beyond modest gestures such as sports exchanges and the relaxation of import restrictions on carpets and pistachios, the mutual outreach stalled. The Clinton administration structured much of its post–Cold War thinking around containment of the malignant effects of "rogue nations." Iran was a charter member.

In the aftermath of 9/11, Iran found ways to be helpful as the United States intervened in Afghanistan, at one point producing a map showing Taliban troop concentrations.[33] It was the Iranian delegate to the December 2001 Bonn Conference, Javad Zarif, later its foreign minister, who suggested that the final international agreement on a new Afghanistan should include a call for democratic elections. Iran offered $500 million at the Tokyo donor conference for Afghanistan in January 2002, the largest pledge of those attending, including the United States.[34]

While Iran continued to see America as hostile, there was a recognition of the need for a "more rational relationship with America."[35] But the window closed quickly. The interception by Israel of the *Karine A*, a ship carrying prohibited weapons from Iran for the Palestinian Authority, had a profound impact on the Bush administration's views of both Palestinian leader Yasser

Arafat and Iran. Even though the Khatami government professed no knowledge of the shipment and quietly asked the United States for information to aid its investigation of who was behind it, cooperation turned to antagonism.[36]

The American response was the "axis of evil." As much as the Iranian people disliked the theocracy and its isolation from the outside world, "they resented being defamed by an American politician and equated with the unsavory states of Iraq and North Korea."[37] The phrase affirmed Tehran's deepest suspicions that the United States would never reach an accommodation with Iran.

Nonetheless, only weeks after the Bush administration had invaded Iraq and toppled the government of Saddam Hussein, removing from power Iran's chief regional antagonist, the Swiss ambassador to Tehran forwarded to Washington a truly game-changing message: an offer of unconditional negotiations with the United States on all major issues between the two countries.[38]

"The proposal astonished the Americans. The Iranians put all their cards on the table," suggested Trita Parsi.[39] They expressed a willingness to sign the Additional Protocol of the Non-Proliferation Treaty and place their nuclear program under international inspection; end support for Hamas, which continued to challenge the existence of Israel and undermine the peace process; disarm Hezbollah and transform it into a political party; support the stabilization of Iraq; and help combat al Qaeda.

Parsi suggests Iran was also willing to accept Saudi Arabia's peace plan that called for the creation of a Palestinian state and normalization of relations with Israel. Tehran expected that successful negotiations would result in the end of all sanctions against Iran, war reparations from Iraq, access to dual-use technologies, and respect for Iran's legitimate regional security interests.[40]

Richard Haass, the head of the State Department's policy planning staff at the time, thought the United States had nothing to lose by testing Iran's interest in dialogue.[41] Iran's proposal was, thought Takeyh, a grand bargain "where an intractable theocracy essentially sued for peace." But the United States did not respond, a decision he termed "a gross case of diplomatic malpractice."[42] A year later, President Bush expressed interest in a comprehensive dialogue, but by that time, Tehran had stepped back.

In 2003, Britain, France, and Germany—the EU3—held extended nuclear negotiations that led to Iran's agreement to sign the Additional Protocol of the NPT, which allowed the IAEA to conduct more intrusive inspections of relevant facilities. Iran also temporarily suspended its nuclear activities, pending further negotiations that would recognize Iran's right to have a civilian nuclear program as allowed under the NPT. In return, Iran expected the Europeans to draw the United States into the talks, enabling a broader security dialogue that Tehran sought.[43] But again inertia prevailed.

With the election of Mahmoud Ahmadinejad in 2005, Iran chose a more confrontational path, believing that greater public belligerence would gain support in the region and force the United States to accommodate Iran's interests. Now it was Iran that miscalculated. Ahmadinejad vowed to wipe Israel off the map, a comment that was meant as a political metaphor and not as a military strategy. But the words were toxic and gave the United States and Israel a powerful weapon to further isolate Iran internationally.

In 2007, Secretary of State Condoleezza Rice discussed with President Bush and National Security Advisor Steve Hadley the prospect of opening a diplomatic interest section in Tehran to give policy makers a better understanding of the political dynamics of the country. Secretary Rice even floated the idea with Russian Foreign Minister Sergei Lavrov as part of an initiative to see if conditions could be created that would allow the United States to join the P5 + 1 negotiations. Russian President Vladimir Putin raised the administration's interest with the Ayatollah, but Iran was not prepared to engage.[44]

The 2007 National Intelligence Estimate concluded that the question of a nuclear weapon hinged on "an Iranian political decision." In other words, Iran deliberately created a sufficiently large nuclear program to make it harder for the West to insist that Iran give it up. According to Flynt and Hillary Mann Leverett, Iran hoped to use the nuclear program as a lever that Iran could use to gain broader acceptance of its role in the region and beyond.[45]

While the Bush administration established the two-track strategy that the Obama administration followed—the offer of negotiations but threat of sanctions if they fail to satisfy international concerns about their nuclear program—it placed significant preconditions on its willingness to participate fully in the P5 + 1 process. This required an Iranian agreement to suspend enrichment activity before negotiations begin. That was a nonstarter, since Iran viewed its nuclear activities as a right that it was unwilling to forfeit.

RIGHTS AND RESPONSIBILITIES

Two days after his inauguration, Obama received a congratulatory message from Ahmadinejad, a first for the Islamic Republic. While it contained predictable language regarding America's "warmongering, invasion, bullying, trickery, the humiliation of other countries by the imposition of biased and unfair requirements," Ahmadinejad suggested that "the path of righteousness" might reduce "the enormous damage done in the past."[46]

Ahmadinejad, even though he favored better relations with the United States under the right circumstances, had made himself an obstacle to any kind of rapprochement with his boast regarding Israel. Nonetheless, suggests Parsi, the letter's significance was the fact it was sent, indicating a willingness to engage in a spirit of "mutual respect."[47]

The White House ignored Ahmadinejad but responded creatively through multiple channels. In an interview with *Al Arabiya* only days into his first term, Obama offered "a new partnership based on mutual respect and mutual interest."[48] That was followed weeks later with a message released on the White House website and through YouTube on the occasion of Nowruz, the Iranian New Year. Speaking directly to the Iranian people, the president outlined two dimensions of the emerging narrative—the United States desired to see Iran "take its rightful place in the community of nations," but that right came with responsibilities to be a more constructive regional actor.[49]

Dennis Ross, who would be a key figure regarding the administration's developing approach to Iran, was putting the finishing touches on a book with coauthor David Makovsky about a new American strategy for the Middle East when Obama was elected. They advocated a "hybrid approach" to Iran that involved both engagement (although not open-ended) and the prospect of tougher sanctions should good-faith negotiations fail.[50] The administration's goal, they said, was *"engagement without illusion"* (emphasis in the original).[51] That's basically how Obama proceeded, choosing a different path that recognized that thirty-five years of isolation had failed to yield progress.

The change in tone in Washington yielded a cautious response from Tehran. While critical of the idea of a dual-track approach—pressure undercuts engagement—Khamenei seemed willing to judge the new administration by its actions as opposed to its words. "We'll see and judge," he said in a speech in March 2009. "You change and we will change as well."[52]

The early exchanges reflected a more realistic U.S. outlook. While believing the Iranian people deserved better, the White House viewed the government in Tehran as a reality Washington could not change.

The Bush administration was not prepared to negotiate with evil. The Obama administration did not see a choice. Obama sent two letters to Khamenei. The Ayatollah responded to the first with a long list of grievances regarding American policy to the first, but it was viewed as sufficiently constructive that Obama wrote back.

"This second letter was one of the most significant exchanges between the two capitals at the highest level of government since the Islamic Revolution," assessed Mousavian, the former Iranian diplomat. Obama offered two U.S. officials, Undersecretary of State Williams Burns and National Security Council Director Puneet Talwar, to begin a dialogue. But this time Iran would struggle to respond.

In addition to these public and private exchanges, Obama constructed a broader context for his emerging strategy regarding Iran—that a nuclear breakthrough no longer carried the international cache that it once did. His argument was that while Iran was constructing a nuclear capability, the world was moving in the opposite direction.

In Prague in April 2009, President Obama advanced a vision of "a world without nuclear weapons," although immediately adding that the goal was not likely to be achieved in his lifetime.[53] However impractical, the speech was deliberately provocative and intended to place nonproliferation and nuclear security at the center of U.S. national security policy.[54]

The narrative attempted to deal with a tacit agreement between the existing nuclear powers and the nonaligned movement when the Non-Proliferation Treaty was first negotiated. Under the NPT, superpowers pledged to eventually give up nuclear weapons. Obama's vision of a world without nuclear weapons, even if impractical, satisfied former nonaligned countries that conditioned renewal of the treaty in 2010 on a reaffirmation of the original goal of the NPT.

Obama explicitly recognized Iran's "right to peaceful nuclear energy with rigorous inspections."[55] But the president argued that nuclear weapons were not in Iran's national security interest, risking a regional arms race involving other leading regional actors—Saudi Arabia, Egypt, and Turkey—that would make Iran less safe. The Middle East was already complex enough, the administration judged, even before adding nuclear weapons to the equation.

A military strike against Iran's nuclear infrastructure would delay but not prevent Iran from building a weapon. In fact, it would increase the likelihood of an Iranian nuclear capability as the ultimate insurance policy for regime survival.[56] North Korea had already reached that conclusion. Geopolitically, Tehran also saw that a nuclear program changed how the world approached states such as India and Pakistan.

Said Ross and Makovsky, a military strike would "create all sorts of unknowns that are bound to be anything but good."[57] The Obama administration hoped to launch a new round of negotiations right after the Iranian presidential elections in June 2009.

GREEN REVOLUTION

Most analysts, and the U.S. government, expected Ahmadinejad to be reelected. Without establishing a specific timeline, Obama projected that by the end of 2009, the White House would know how serious Iran was to find a negotiated solution.

But late in the campaign, there was unexpected enthusiasm surrounding the candidacy of former Prime Minister Mir Hossein Mousavi, one of three candidates permitted to run against the incumbent. Mousavi was not considered charismatic, certainly less than former President Khatami, who had captured the imagination of reformers within Iran.

Mousavi had been an effective steward of Iran's economy and offered the prospect of a less confrontational approach to the outside world. He was prepared to negotiate with the United States under the right conditions and might be able to ease Iran's isolation abroad while fighting corruption and inefficiency at home.

Ten days before the election, the presidential candidates participated in an unprecedented televised debate, reflecting Iran's vibrant if constrained political environment. The clerical regime sought to modestly expand its political space and encouraged a high voter turnout that would provide added legitimacy for the regime.

Regardless of the actual outcome—the incumbent probably won an unexpectedly close vote—the Ahmadinejad camp took no chances. The government ordered state-controlled media to report that Ahmadinejad was leading in early returns before any actual polling results had been tabulated. Security forces disrupted the media center the Mousavi campaign had established to report on any election irregularities.[58]

The official result gave Ahmadinejad a comfortable victory—63 percent to Mousavi's 34 percent. But the regime's heavy hand on the voting scales skewed the results to such a degree that it undermined the legitimacy of the election and spawned the Green Revolution. The ensuing protests were the largest since the 1979 revolution.[59]

The Obama administration was cautious in its response to the demonstrations. The White House bent over backward not to be viewed as meddling in Iran's internal affairs. It sought to keep the focus on events in Tehran rather than statements from Washington that would allow the regime to play its Great Satan card. "It's not about us," suggested one White House official. "It's about them."[60]

While a rational choice, it backfired. The Iranian government arrested a range of political figures, including the losing candidates. Confrontations with government security forces grew more violent, culminating with the now iconic image of Neda Agha-Soltan, shot to death in Tehran by the Basij, a paramilitary militia loyal to the regime.

At one point, Jared Cohen, a member of the State Department's policy planning staff, on his own initiative asked Twitter to delay a planned service outage because protesters found social media an important source of outside information. The White House, perceiving that the action constituted "interference" in Iranian politics—contrary to the president's policy direction—was angry enough to threaten to fire him.[61]★

While the White House instincts were reasonable—the opposition needed to be viewed as a legitimate indigenous movement and a low public profile was believed to best support the relaunch of nuclear negotiations—the administration was roundly criticized by political adversaries and allies alike for its belated response.

Former Massachusetts Governor Mitt Romney, who would eventually challenge Obama in the 2012 campaign, believed the United States needed to call out Iran's repression while characterizing the administration policies as "going around the world and apologizing for America."[62]

Tehran quickly became paralyzed by its own internal divisions. Said Parsi, "the entire Iranian power establishment was literally at war with itself."[63] The Obama administration, already accused of deemphasizing human rights in its early dialogue with China, sensed it had taken another political hit. The Green Revolution was stalled in 2009, but it foreshadowed even more dramatic regional political developments. When demonstrations broke out in Egypt in 2011, the White House reaction would be very different.

CRIPPLING SANCTIONS

The Obama administration believed the Bush administration's refusal to negotiate within the P5 + 1 process was a mistake. Secretary of State Hillary Clinton told a Council on Foreign Relations audience in July 2009 that "we outsourced our policy to Iran and frankly it didn't work out very well."[64]

★To the dismay of the NSC staff, the State Department embraced the story as an indicator of how social media was changing the diplomatic practice and global politics. As the president anticipated, Iran did try to paint the demonstrations as a Western conspiracy. On the other hand, Cohen's initiative became a valuable talking point to refute charges the administration did nothing to support the Green Revolution.

Anticipating negotiations after the Iranian election, the United States was searching for a way to break the ice with Iran. The vehicle—a confidence-building measure in diplomatic parlance—became Iran's need for fuel for the Tehran Research Reactor or TRR, a forty-year-old facility that produced medical isotopes for kidney, heart, and cancer patients.

The Obama administration offered to provide fuel for the research reactor, which did not pose a proliferation risk, in exchange for roughly 1,200 kilograms of low-enriched uranium in the Iranian stockpile that did.

The White House believed it needed to put time back on "three ticking clocks"—Iran's continued march toward high enrichment of uranium; the increased potential that Israel would take military action to preempt what they viewed as an existential threat; and the possibility that Saudi Arabia would begin its own program the closer Iran got to an actual weapon.[65]

Prospects for negotiations were soon complicated by the revelation of a secret Iranian nuclear facility at Qom. To Iran, the Qom facility on top of a declared facility at Natanz ensured the survivability of its nuclear program in the event of a preemptive strike. To the West, it was further evidence of Iran's failure to cooperate with the International Atomic Energy Agency. It put Iran on the defensive and embarrassed its strongest defenders, particularly Russia, just ahead of the initial meeting of the P5 + 1.

While Iran gave positive indications when the proposal was placed on the table in Geneva in October 2009, in Tehran, no one wanted to be viewed as caving in to the West. The Ayatollah rejected the TRR deal.[66]

At the end of 2009, the Obama administration shifted from engagement to pressure. It pressed a wide range of countries, including China, that sanctions were necessary to prod Iran to negotiate.

The White House and State Department worked hard with Congress to direct the sanctions against the most onerous elements of the Iranian government, particularly the Iranian Revolutionary Guard Corps, while retaining considerable flexibility to ensure they would gain the necessary international support at the United Nations. Saudi Arabia made clear to countries that had existing oil contracts with Iran, particularly China, South Korea, and Japan, that it would boost exports to compensate for the loss of Iranian oil.

The sanctions hammered Iran's currency and spurred an increase in inflation. This would have a perverse effect—increasing the security forces' control of the economy while harming the Iranian middle class that was crucial to the reformist movement.

Just as the United States was putting the finishing touches on a new tough round of sanctions, Turkey and Brazil made one last effort at a diplomatic

breakthrough. They convinced Iran to agree to the original TRR proposal—
1,200 kilograms of low-enriched uranium in return for an assured supply of
fuel pads for the research reactor.

There were a number of agendas at work behind the initiative by Turkey
and Brazil—for the former a chance to demonstrate a stronger regional role
and the latter a chance to break through the major power stranglehold within
the United Nations Security Council. Curiously, Brazilian President Luiz Iná-
cio Lula da Silva and Turkish Prime Minister Recep Tayyip Erdogan both
received letters from President Obama clearly spelling out key concerns and
what Washington considered the ingredients of an appropriate deal. The letters
actually added confusion regarding what the United States would accept.[67] The
Turks and Brazilians felt Obama's conditions had been met. But the White
House balked. While the TRR proposal had utility through most of 2009, by
the middle of 2010, the Obama administration had reached agreement with
Russia and China regarding a new round of sanctions, and Congress was poised
to act as well. Also, since Tehran continued its enrichment program, the impact
of the swap was greatly reduced, since the LEU now represented only 50
percent of Iran's stockpile.

Iran, suggested one U.S. official, had missed the sell-by date.[68]

Domestic political limitations in both the United States and Iran contributed to the stalemate. In Washington's view, it needed a new round of sanctions—getting tough on Tehran—if it had any hope of gaining political support
for a diplomatic initiative with Iran down the road. In Tehran, it would take
another election for Iran to recognize that negotiations were the only "pathway out of a threatening cul-de-sac."[69]

Iran's ambassador to the IAEA, Ali Asghar Soltanieh, suggested in 2010
that it would be a "strategic mistake" for Iran to build nuclear weapons, that it
recognized it could not compete with the United States or other regional
countries in that space.[70] Iranian officials went to great lengths to highlight
the judgments of Khomeini and Khamenei that nuclear weapons are *haraam*,
meaning "forbidden by God," which carried considerable political and religious weight.

But Iran still had to prove it to the outside world.

5

WRONG SIDE OF HISTORY

In his first overseas trip as president, Barack Obama stopped in Turkey, a Muslim country, a democracy, an ally, and one of the fastest-growing economies in the world. In an address to the Turkish parliament, Obama said, "The United States is not, and will never be, at war with Islam."[1]

He added that America's relationship with the Muslim world should not be based solely on opposition to terrorism, but "broader engagement based on mutual interest and mutual respect."[2] He expanded that outreach with a major address in Cairo in June 2009, where he pledged a "new beginning" in relations with the people of the region.

It was an extraordinary speech in tone and substance, a cornerstone of the administration's global engagement: reaching beyond governments and taking advantage of new technologies to speak directly to the people.[3]

Unlike the second inaugural address of President George W. Bush, with its aspiration of promoting democracy and ending tyranny throughout the world, this was far more personal and concrete. Instead of characterizing international relationships in zero-sum terms—you are either with us or against us—Obama stressed how regional and global challenges are shared and spoke about a partnership, acting boldly to meet the needs of people across the region, of tolerance, equality, justice, and dignity.

He addressed several areas of tension that influence regional perceptions of the United States: the wars in Afghanistan and Iraq and the ongoing challenge posed by al Qaeda; the search for peace among Israelis, Palestinians, and Arabs; Iran and the question of nuclear weapons in the region; advocating for governments that reflect the will of their people, whether democracies or not;

and promoting religious tolerance, women's rights, education, and economic development.

For Obama, like many of his predecessors, Middle East policy reflected tension between the idealism of American values and the realism of U.S. regional interests. The administration hoped the Cairo speech and its acknowledgment of regional grievances would expand its policy options in the Middle East.[4]

The Obama administration believed in the advance of democracy but was uncertain how to best promote it, given how the Iraq invasion and the ensuing chaos had compromised regional perceptions of U.S. intentions. Unlike Bush, "democracy promotion would not be the guiding principle of our policy in the Middle East," wrote Dennis Ross in *Doomed to Succeed*.[5]

Several elements in his Cairo speech would influence his response to the 2011 Arab uprisings: that governments should "reflect the will of the people" and should rule "through consent, not coercion." Obama would not attempt to impose a system of government on any nation, a reflection of his retreat from the task of nation building that he believed was not affordable nor historically successful.[6]

Obama cautioned that "change cannot happen overnight," without knowing that eighteen months later a single act of civil disobedience in Tunisia would create a dynamic that profoundly altered the regional political landscape and turn thirty years of U.S. policy on its head.

Obama was determined to change regional perceptions of the United States. He believed the key to improving America's standing in the Middle East was resolving the Israeli-Palestinian conflict. Al Qaeda and others had consistently used the plight of the Palestinians and U.S. support for Israel as a political wedge issue. The Obama administration would make the relaunch of direct negotiations a cornerstone of his Middle East policy, only to confront uncompromising regional politics too invested in the status quo and a lack of trust among key leaders.

Early in Obama's first term, at the encouragement of Rahm Emanuel, the White House chief of staff, the administration took a public position that Israeli settlements were illegitimate and encouraged Israel to agree to a complete settlement freeze as a confidence-building measure to relaunch direct negotiations with the Palestinians.[7]

While the intention was to gain credibility within the Arab world, it went well beyond what the existing Israeli government was prepared to offer and ran counter to what was anticipated in an eventual peace agreement—that

Israel could expand West Bank settlement blocs it anticipated retaining as part of a land swap.[8]

Secretary of State Hillary Clinton, cautious of categorical statements that failed to take into account vital national interests of other countries, was skeptical of laying down a public marker on settlements that no Israeli prime minister was likely to accept. "She thought that would put us up a tree," said a Clinton aide.[9]

But having repeated the U.S. position on settlements in Cairo and having signaled a willingness to negotiate with Iran without preconditions, the White House misjudged the anxiety that the speech generated in Israel and then compounded the problem by leaving the region without stopping in Jerusalem. The relationship with Obama and Prime Minister Benjamin Netanyahu started on the wrong foot and never really recovered.

While the administration devoted significant effort to achieving a framework agreement, by November 2015, the White House acknowledged that a breakthrough to a final status agreement would not occur on Obama's watch. The challenge for the foreseeable future became managing relations between Israelis and Palestinians in the absence of direct negotiations while "preventing the emergence of a one-state solution" that would force Israel to decide between being a Jewish state or a democracy.[10]

However, by then, the Israeli-Palestinian conflict no longer drove Arab attitudes toward the United States. It would be eclipsed by other issues, including the civil war in Syria, growing regional sectarianism, and the challenge posed by a resurgent Iran.

In the end, the Cairo speech proved to be a "trap" that created high public expectations that could never be fulfilled.[11] Perceptions of the United States would remain stubbornly negative and critical, although for different reasons. Rightly or wrongly, the United States under Bush was accused of doing too much in the region; under Obama it was for not doing enough.

FREEDOM AGENDA

Security and stability had long been the pillars of U.S. policy in the Middle East. The immediate consistently trumped the long-term, even after 9/11. That was certainly true in Libya, where Muammar Qaddafi was an erratic despot but had become a useful ally in the war on terror, and Egypt, where Hosni Mubarak was a friend of the United States and a constructive actor in the peace process even as he resisted reforming the country's political system in any meaningful way.

There have always been competing historical strands in the DNA of U.S. policy. A country whose revolution changed the global order had evolved into a superpower heavily invested in the status quo. As Walter Russell Mead wrote, "We may want the system to change, but we also want it to stay the same—to be stable."[12]

President Bush in his 2005 inaugural speech set out a goal of "ending tyranny in our world,"[13] a notable if impractical goal, with little actual capacity to accomplish it. Various color revolutions offered hope, but its democratic start-up in Iraq was plagued by sectarian politics and its Afghan counterpart by corruption. Yet Bush's speech reflected how Americans view the country's unique role in the world.

Thomas Paine in *Common Sense* spoke of the "power to begin the world all over again."[14] This perceived mission to shape the world based on American ideals and values has a rich history. Andrew Jackson in his farewell address described America as a chosen people and the "guardians of freedom."[15]

For a time, this ideology was associated with territorial expansion and the belief in manifest destiny. But the United States never lost its missionary zeal, presuming early in the twentieth century it could make the world safe for democracy.

Franklin Delano Roosevelt, in a fireside chat two days after the attack on Pearl Harbor, pledged that not only was the objective of the war with Japan complete victory, it was to break "the sources of international brutality, wherever they exist."[16] Of course, to defeat the Axis powers, his temporary ally was Joseph Stalin, brutal in his own right.

The United States preached democracy during the Cold War but at times subverted it as well. The crowning achievements were in Europe, Japan, and Korea, where America invested significant effort and stayed long enough to see its democratic seeds bear fruit. After the Cold War, there was a brief period where interests and values aligned. Democratic enlargement, NATO expansion, and integrated markets were viewed as hand-and-glove policies that would make the world more stable and prosperous.[17]

The politics could still be tricky, particularly surrounding relationships where the prospects of political reform were far longer term. Bill Clinton accused the first Bush administration of coddling China's dictators in the suppression of political activists in Tiananmen Square in 1989, yet championed its inclusion in the World Trade Organization, believing that globalization would open up greater political space in the country.

In its response to September 11, there were two prominent threads in the Bush narrative: freedom was under attack and democracy was part of the solution. At the National Cathedral soon after 9/11, the president suggested, "They attacked America, because we are freedom's home and defender."[18] Later, Osama bin Laden would reject that notion when he quipped that under Bush's logic, al Qaeda should have attacked Sweden.

After 9/11, democracy came to be viewed "as the antidote to extremism," without appreciating how majority rule would complicate U.S. relations in the region.[19]

The president told Republican governors six months before the Iraq invasion, "Afghanistan and Iraq will lead that part of the world to democracy. They are going to be the catalyst to change the Middle East and the world."[20]

More than a year later later, following the invasion and capture of Saddam Hussein, President Bush expressed the hope that "All Iraqis can now come together and reject violence and build a new Iraq."[21] It didn't work out that way.

When Bush gave his inaugural speech, Iraq was days away from its own parliamentary election that would prominently feature images of purple fingers as Iraqis took their first step toward self-determination. But it was also well on its way to becoming, in the words of U.S. Ambassador John Negroponte, a "post-conflict failed state."[22]

The chaos that followed the American invasion communicated a far different message than the United States intended. Democracy was something to be avoided at all cost. Russian President Vladimir Putin chided Bush that Russia did not want the same kind of democracy the United States brought to Iraq.[23]

To his credit, democracy promotion yielded an important shift in the U.S. approach to Middle East peace. On June 24, 2002, Bush pledged support for a Palestinian state and called for Palestinians to create a functioning democracy.[24]

That said, when Hamas won a subsequent free and fair election from Fatah, the party that dominated the Palestinian Authority but was viewed as corrupt, the Bush administration refused to recognize the result.[25] For all intents and purposes, suggested David Kramer, assistant secretary of state for democracy, human rights, and labor during the Bush administration and later head of Freedom House, "the freedom agenda was over."[26]

In a speech at Cairo University in 2005, Secretary of State Condoleezza Rice declared the United States supports "the democratic aspirations of all people."[27] President Obama would largely echo the same sentiment in his own Cairo speech four years later.

Obama as a senator, speaking to the Chicago Council on Foreign Relations shortly after Rice's address, suggested, "The notion that Iraq would quickly and easily become a bulwark of flourishing democracy in the Middle East was not a plan for victory, but an ideological fantasy."[28]

However, just five years later, Obama would claim Iraq was sufficiently stable and democratic to confidently withdraw all remaining troops from the country, fulfilling a core campaign pledge. Eight years later, he would redeploy limited military forces to Iraq to combat the Islamic State, but only if the prime minister he had called a champion of inclusive democracy stepped down from office.

In his Chicago speech, Obama said a key lesson from Iraq was that, even where the United States can support indigenous democratic movements, "the institutions of democracy, free markets, a free press, a strong civil society, cannot be built overnight, and they cannot be built at the end of a barrel of a gun." Freedom, Obama said tellingly, does not come just from "deposing a tyrant and handing out ballots," but only when there is a genuinely secure environment.[29]

Obama would fail to follow his own advice in Libya.

ASPIRATIONS OF THE PEOPLE

Political, social, and economic reform was recognized as fundamental to the region's future, but American leaders tended to address the issue more conceptually in public. Specific criticism was more often delivered in private. Many in the region seemed surprised to learn from diplomatic cables released by WikiLeaks that the United States shared their concerns about repression and corruption.

Dennis Ross and David Makovsky in their 2009 book predicted, "liberalization will be more evolutionary than revolutionary."[30] That would turn out to be true, but not before the region experienced multiple revolutions and counterrevolutions. Only one fragile democracy emerged, in Tunisia.

In mid-2010, President Obama signed Presidential Study Document 11, instructing his foreign policy team to analyze how to better promote political change in the Middle East. The study, which included Ross, underscored the high costs of the status quo, the identification of the United States with authoritarian regimes, and the presumption that long-term American interests could be advanced by supporting forces of change.[31]

Entitled "Political Reform in the Middle East and North Africa," it cited "growing citizen discontent" across the region that regimes, including American allies, were failing to address. The risk was "fewer capable, credible partners who can support our regional priorities." American credibility "will be undermined if we are seen or perceived to be backing repressive regimes and ignoring the rights and aspirations of citizens."[32]

The still-secret study suggested it was difficult to predict dramatic political change or prevent ethnic or sectarian tensions that accompany revolutions.[33] It challenged the realist assumption that stability always served American interests and encouraged a "strong push by the United States for reform." It did not foresee immediate and wholesale changes. The expectation was that opportunities would arise on a country-by-country basis as they made succession plans. It acknowledged that if these transitions are not well managed, there would be "negative implications for U.S. interests."[34]

On the eve of the Arab Spring, Secretary of State Hillary Clinton gave a speech in Doha at the Forum for the Future, informed in part by that study. She suggested the foundations of the region were "sinking in the sand," that the status quo was unsustainable.[35] She was right. Within twenty-four hours, the authoritarian leader of Tunisia abdicated. Suddenly the Obama administration confronted a region that was literally changing day by day.

In his first National Security Strategy, President Obama stated the need to "face the world as it is."[36] Now he saw in the Arab Spring the opportunity to pursue "the world as it should be."[37] The Obama administration framed the Arab Spring in terms of universal rights, stressing the importance of peaceful protest, freedom of expression, freedom of assembly, freedom to determine one's own future.

The successful protest sparked by a street vendor in Tunisia inspired even more dramatic demonstrations in Egypt's Tahrir Square and then spread across the region, as people with deep-seated grievances broke through a barrier of fear and demanded change.*

---

*On January 4, 2011, when the BBC's Kim Ghattas asked about growing unrest in Tunisia, I acknowledged at the State Department podium that I had no update on Tunisia. Preparation for the daily press briefing is a lengthy process over several hours that involves identifying issues that the United States wants or needs to discuss publicly as well as anticipating areas of interest from the diverse group of journalists who regularly cover the department. That day, concern for Iran's nuclear program, efforts toward Middle East peace, and the status of the U.S. ambassador to Libya were the leading regional areas of interest. A week later, we were still viewing developments in Tunisia and Algeria as distinct. The following

Thanks to robust information networks, people across the region now could see what was happening next door. The Arab uprisings were at least partly the product of such new interconnections. Twitter helped them mobilize. YouTube added drama and emotion. Facebook helped them organize. Information is a key dimension of power, and digitization lowered the barriers of entry into what became a global conversation.

Old and new media combined into a powerful force that governments could no longer control, a "new Arab public sphere" with a shared narrative demanding change.[38]

The Internet enabled Tunisians to evade government censorship and demonstrate against regime corruption that was well documented in the diplomatic cables released by WikiLeaks. Activists created a parallel site called TuniLeaks. As Hillary Clinton said later, WikiLeaks represented "a big douse of gasoline on a smoldering fire."[39]

The vast majority of people using social media during the beginning stages of the Arab uprisings in 2011 were from outside the Middle East. But the high level of social media activity surrounding these revolutions influenced how other countries responded to what was happening. There was a greater impetus to "do something," even if that something was simply a statement of support.

These were real revolutions, based on local grievances and not, as some leaders suggested, the product of outside agitation. Every country in the region was affected in some way. Responses varied, some with limited political concessions, others with greater social investments, and a few with force and greater repression.

There was tension between America's outsized global leadership role and its practical ability to impact such unpredictable events. In the Situation Room, officials spent as much time just trying to understand what was happening as considering how to shape future events.[40] A region used to moving at a snail's pace was traveling at light speed.

From Tunisia and Egypt to Bahrain and Libya, long accused of backing tyrants over the people, lines were being drawn and the United States was being called out. Whose side are you on?

Having been blamed for a missed opportunity during Iran's Green Revolution in 2009, the uprisings gave the Obama administration a second opportu-

---

week, the State Department authorized dependents to evacuate the country as a prudent step in response to the growing unrest. By the end of the month, what had become known as the Arab Spring dominated global headlines and the daily press briefing. The United States had long encouraged reform across the Middle East and North Africa; everyone was surprised how rapidly events unfolded. The policy process struggled to keep up; so did those of us charged with explaining it.

nity to brandish its democracy credentials.[41] But there were far-reaching questions without clear answers.

Was there a Mandela-like statesman in any one of these countries to lead such a transition? In a region imbued with a zero-sum mentality, what would majority rule mean for minorities and women, both of which lost ground during Iraq's democratic transition?

If Egypt must respond to the aspirations of its people, what about Bahrain, a Shia majority country ruled by a Sunni monarchy? If the United States was prepared to protect the Libyan people, what about Syria? If everyone has a right to determine their own future, what about the Palestinians, whose demands overlapped the Arab Spring protests in meaningful ways? There were reasonable policy answers to such questions, but those answers still challenged the credibility of American actions.

The Arab Spring was a "political tornado," and the Obama administration found a consistent response elusive.[42] It had one narrative and twenty-two distinct policies among Arab countries.[43] Washington gave some countries a push and others a pass. It backed immediate change in a handful of countries, gradual change in others, and was muted where change was either not possible or where interests were still too compelling to alter. Marrying policy actions with a consistent and credible narrative became progressively harder.

Its heart and its head were not always in sync.

The United States, says David Fromkin, is a country "that does not believe in history."[44] Nonetheless, the White House struggled to identify its right side. Said one aide, "This could be 1989 or 1979."[45] It turned out to be neither one. History was not linear. In the case of Egypt, it turned out to be circular.

Unlike Tunisia, which sits on the fringe of the Middle East, Egypt is its political heart. Egypt's revolution was already under way below the surface. The April 6 Movement had orchestrated an effective Mahalla labor strike in 2008 that called attention to the economic plight of Egypt's working classes. Police beat one activist, Khaled Said, to death for publishing evidence of police abuse. The brutality was documented and posted on a Facebook page—We Are All Khaled Said—which attracted hundreds of thousands of supporters, in the process creating the makings of a political organization.

Egypt was under pressure from the United States to expand its political space.* In 2005, Mubarak had competed in a more open presidential election,

---

*In a bilateral meeting just nine months before the turmoil in Tahrir Square, the Egyptian foreign minister complained to Secretary Clinton directly after a public rebuke of the Egyptian government during a State Department press briefing for failing to adequately investigate credible claims of police violence against political opponents.

but failed to follow through with more inclusive parliamentary elections. In 2005, the Muslim Brotherhood won 88 seats in parliament, only to see that total revert to zero in 2010. Mubarak insisted on the right to dismiss parliament without the public's consent and kept in place Egypt's emergency law that curbed public dissent.[46]

Egypt embodied the tension between realism and idealism that formed the push and pull of U.S. foreign policy and political rhetoric—a government that was an ally and autocratic. Change in Egypt would have profound regional implications.

The president and his cabinet sought to use their influence to encourage a nonviolent response. Some of the president's defining statements during the Arab uprising followed this logic: leaders who resorted to violence lost their legitimacy to lead.

Washington had long hoped for political change in Egypt, but the captivating Tahrir demonstrations were disorganized, powered by a shared understanding of what they were against—the continued rule of the Mubaraks, both father and son—but not what they were for. They would fail to make the shift from protest to political movement.

In his State of the Union speech, Obama saluted the people of Tunisia and expressed support for "the democratic aspirations of all people," a line that came right out of his Cairo speech two years earlier.[47] He did not mention Egypt.

Protest leaders organized a Day of Rage on January 25—Police Day—a national holiday in honor of an institution that a significant number of Egyptians detested. It was broadcast on Al Jazeera, electrifying not just Egypt but the region as well.

Even though she had challenged the region's governments to reform just days earlier, Clinton spoke cautiously when asked about Egypt. She termed the Mubarak government "stable,"★ reflecting the administration's hope for a gradual political transition.

Mubarak told Obama in a telephone conversation that he would weather the storm. Drawing parallels to Gamal Abdel Nasser, he believed the protests would run their course within ten days. Obama followed the call with a statement urging the Egyptian government to undertake "political, social, and economic reforms that meet the aspirations of the Egyptian people."[48]

★The secretary of state was wrong when she called the Egyptian government stable, but her comments reflected an ongoing administration debate regarding the prospects for political reform and how to best encourage it. When the secretary next visited Egypt, some political activists declined to meet with her, an indication of how closely they followed Washington's response.

The administration recognized there was no going back to the status quo, but there was an internal policy debate regarding how to achieve a favorable long-term outcome. Younger advisors identified with the protesters. Older hands recalled the Iranian revolution. Regional leaders weighed in on behalf of Mubarak.

In the many conversations U.S. officials had with Mubarak through the years about the need for change, his response was consistent: it's either me or the Muslim Brotherhood. He was not entirely wrong. The Muslim Brotherhood, far more conservative and religious than the secular government, was best positioned to take advantage of any political opening. But Mubarak never made more than symbolic concessions to political reform.

If democracy was the goal, the Muslim Brotherhood could not be excluded, a fact that some presidential aspirants overlooked in their subsequent criticism of Obama's policy.[49] The administration recognized as it encouraged a peaceful transition that newly empowered Egyptian citizens, particularly those in Tahrir Square, would require time to organize to be able to compete in an evolving political environment.

But there was a hitch. If Mubarak stepped aside as the demonstrators demanded, the existing Egyptian Constitution required an election within sixty days. The administration hoped to work around that stipulation by encouraging Mubarak to appoint a vice president for the first time in his tenure. Mubarak did, naming Omar Suleiman, Egypt's head of intelligence, to oversee needed political reforms. To Washington, he was an asset; to the demonstrators in Tahrir Square, he was more of the same.*

Clinton was concerned about regional perceptions that the United States was abandoning an ally. On January 30, on *Meet the Press*, she said in public what she had said in private to her counterpart in the Egyptian government: what was needed was "a peaceful, *orderly* transition to a democratic regime" (emphasis in the original).[50]

Obama with Clinton's encouragement dispatched Frank Wisner, a retired diplomat, former U.S. ambassador to Egypt, and someone Mubarak trusted, to convince Mubarak that the status quo was unsustainable and that he should announce a timetable for his departure. After his meeting, Wisner counseled policy makers in Washington to be patient, give Mubarak time to adjust, and avoid a public push.[51]

---

*Communicating during this fluid situation was tricky. Events moved faster than the policy process. I tweeted out that merely reshuffling the deck chairs within the Egyptian government was not enough to satisfy the protesters, a reflection of the emerging U.S. policy. At the same time, senior White House officials were meeting to consider how to respond to Mubarak's latest move. I was directed to stop tweeting about Egypt.

On February 1, in the middle of a high-level White House meeting, Mubarak announced he would not run for reelection, nor would his son Gamal succeed him. But it was buried in a meandering address to the Egyptian people. Had it been better orchestrated, the demonstrators may have realized they had won. But it quickly became clear they would not disband until the government fell.[52]

In a call with Mubarak, Obama told him he did not have time to engineer a lengthy transition.[53] But the Egyptian leader still resisted. Afterward the president announced in the Grand Foyer of the White House, "An orderly transition must be meaningful, it must be peaceful, and it must begin now," one of the boldest public commitments to democratic change issued by an American president in decades.[54]

His message shocked other key regional allies, particularly Saudi Arabia and even Israel. Demanding a transition "now" was perceived as humiliating a trusted ally.[55]

The Egyptian government struck back on February 2, sending thugs to disperse the protesters, a confrontation that became known as the "Battle of the Camel."[56] The protest movement held firm. From that point forward, Mubarak's fate was sealed.[57]

Days after his not-so-secret mission, Wisner made public comments that seemed to contradict the emerging U.S. policy but in the turmoil of the moment were misunderstood. He emphasized at the Munich Security Conference that "President Mubarak's continued leadership is still critical."[58] Wisner's intent was to encourage Mubarak to lead the process, but he seemed to contradict Obama's demand for an immediate transition.★

While Mubarak held on, the White House released a written statement in the president's name. "The Egyptian people have made it clear that there is no going back to the way things were."[59]

The Egyptian military, seeing its own interests threatened, responded to the "legitimate" demands of the protesters and pushed him aside.

The Obama administration identified with the region's aspirations, but even under Obama, poll after poll underscored that its populations liked Americans, their culture, and their innovative nature, but disliked specific American policies. As one protester said after Mubarak left office, "Message to

---

★No one in the White House or State Department knew that Wisner planned to speak via teleconference to the Munich Security Conference, which included the secretary of state. His comments were a fair reflection of what the United States encouraged Mubarak to do, but by then such an ideal scenario had been overtaken by events.

the world from Egypt: We can change the world." But then he tellingly added, "We hate Israel."[60]

The U.S. push for political inclusion belied how powerful Egypt's establishment was, and the degree it would resist self-determination and political Islam.

FREE AND FAIR FAILURE

Obama told the British parliament in 2011 it was a false choice to prioritize stability over democracy or interests over ideals in U.S. foreign policy. Reflecting on lessons learned in Iraq, he suggested the United States would act with "humility," that "freedoms must be won by the people themselves, not imposed from without." But he added presciently that "power rarely gives up without a fight."[61]

While the military took responsibility for Egypt's transition, it had little experience with governance and had its own interests to protect. There were few reasons to believe it could be an effective agent of democratic change. In fact, the Egyptian military served as a "firewall" against meaningful political reform.[62]

In the first year after the Arab Spring, the Egyptian economy contracted by close to 1 percent. A million jobs were lost, and unemployment rose to 15 percent—25 percent among the young. Tourism, a staple of the Egyptian economy, was dramatically reduced. Democratic progress in Egypt depended on economic reform, but the country was not structured to open up to the rest of the world. A major obstacle was the Egyptian military's outsized role in economic affairs and its unwillingness to yield the privilege that came with it.[63] Egypt burned through money to prop up its currency.

At the same time, Egypt's governmental institutions were pulling in opposite directions. One ministry ordered the arrest of representatives of non-governmental organizations focused on democracy, which placed the Egyptian transitional government and the United States in a no-win situation. Washington demanded their release, opening itself up to claims of interference with Egypt's judiciary—biased as it was. In the end, the Americans were released on bond and tried in absentia.

In retrospect, Washington should have been firmer with the Supreme Council of the Armed Forces, which oversaw the transition. Washington sought to use billions in military aid as leverage to encourage change, but it bought far less than envisioned. Wealthy regional benefactors—including presumed American allies in the Gulf—actively worked to defeat the emerging American policy.[64]

A year after Mubarak stepped down, twenty-seven million Egyptians voted in the country's first free election. Progressives failed to mobilize viable candidates. Those most directly responsible for the Tahrir Square protest won only three of 508 seats. The Muslim Brotherhood dominated the first Egyptian parliament in a coalition with Salifists. The Brotherhood initially chose not to field a candidate for president, then reversed course.

Ideally, the election of a representative assembly would have paved the way for a new constitution and then election of a president. Egypt never got the process right. As various factions gained sway, they sought to consolidate power, not share it. The Egyptian judiciary, dominated by the country's political establishment, dissolved the first post-Tahrir parliament four months after it was seated and just days before the presidential vote, undermining the establishment of a system of checks and balances.

The eventual choice for president came down to Mubarak's "handpicked successor or his handpicked opponent."[65] Morsi's election was free and fair, but he was an ineffective leader who never tried to reach beyond his core constituency. The new constitution the Muslim Brotherhood advanced failed to provide sufficient protections for minorities and women, a clear setback for civil society.

U.S. officials encouraged Egyptians to be patient, build democratic institutions, and establish a tradition of the peaceful transfer of power through credible elections. But within months, with help from the Egyptian military, a reform initiative, Tamarod, collected more signatures in favor of Morsi's departure than initially voted for him.

The Egyptian military removed Morsi from office, a move many across Egypt's political spectrum considered a "popular impeachment." The old order had been "decapitated, not overthrown."[66]

BACK TO SQUARE ONE

For legal and policy reasons, the United States said nothing, declining to make a judgment whether the Egyptian military's action constituted a coup. Such a finding would have required a suspension of all military aid.

Using a legal framework developed during a governmental crisis in Honduras in 2009, the Obama administration decided the best course was not to decide.[67] As State Department spokesperson Jen Psaki explained, hoping to encourage the emergence of an inclusive democratic government in Egypt, "it is not in our national interest to make a determination."[68] Nonetheless, America's silence said a great deal.

In Honduras, the gambit worked. Working within the Organization of American States, the United States parlayed the crisis in Honduras to make a strong regional statement for democracy. It pushed back on populists like Hugo Chavez in Venezuela, who supported President Manuel Zalaya's effort to evade existing constitutional term limits.*

In Egypt, the opposite occurred. While Morsi's successor, General Abdel Fattah el-Sisi, was the people's choice, he formed a government that was anything but inclusive or democratic. The United States did not expect an Egyptian Jefferson, but what emerged was an Egyptian Pharaoh. Egypt's subsequent crackdown on its political opposition, journalists, and civil society took the country back to square one. Rather than the democratic hopes of Tahrir Square, Egypt re-created conditions that tend to generate violent political extremism.

In the immediate aftermath, Obama said, "We can't return to business as usual." But after a fierce internal debate over balancing values and security interests—"trench warfare" according to an unnamed aide—the administration did just that. Egypt's military aid was fully restored, along with all hardware that had been withheld. Egypt celebrated the delivery of eight contested F-16s with an air show over Cairo.[69]

In September 2013, in a speech at the United Nations, Obama failed to even mention democracy as a core objective for the United States. At times American leaders spoke of a Marshall Plan to promote self-determination and economic opportunity within a new Middle East. But absent the Cold War imperative, the United States declined to be democracy's "venture capitalist."[70]

America was actually "outgunned" by countries with competing visions—none of them democratic or pluralistic. Tunisia remains the lone new democratic outpost in the Middle East and an unlikely model that can be replicated elsewhere.[71]

The administration could not square its rhetoric surrounding the Arab Spring with its actual policies; as Secretary of State John Kerry put it, trying "to thread a needle carefully" between an ally that contributed to regional

---

*Honduras was actually a clash of governmental branches. The Honduran Congress ordered the military to depose President Manuel Zalaya. In that sense, it was not a "military coup." Because the crisis occurred as the Honduran presidential campaign was getting under way, the State Department deferred action pending the election and recognized Porfirio Lobo Sosa as Zalaya's successor.

security but not the advance of basic human rights, the very same bargain the United States tolerated prior to 2001.[72]

After pushing Mubarak from power, struggling to help the Muslim Brotherhood govern effectively, criticizing the military coup without actually calling it one, and then capitulating to the return of authoritarianism in Egypt, the United States found itself "in that sweet spot," acknowledged Deputy National Security Advisor Ben Rhodes, "where everyone is pissed off at us."[73] The Obama administration's Cairo narrative was effectively dead. Secretary of State Hillary Clinton suggested to Obama that the Arab uprisings would turn out all right, "but it would take twenty-five years."[74]

In Egypt, the destruction of the Muslim Brotherhood, problematic as it was yet a political counterweight to al Qaeda, left more space for the jihadist narrative that political rights would not come through democratic means but through force.[75]

6

LEADING FROM BEHIND

S tanding in front of a bank of American flags at the National Defense University, President Obama updated the American people on the "limited military action" undertaken by the United States and NATO with a United Nations mandate to protect the Libyan people from their vengeful if not unhinged leader, Muammar Qaddafi.[1]

Over the previous three months, President Zine El Abidine Ben Ali in Tunisia had abdicated. President Hosni Mubarak in Egypt was pushed aside by his military, encouraged by the United States.

Yet unlike his neighbors Qaddafi decided to fight to retain power. Confronted with an organized rebel movement centered in Benghazi, he vowed to hunt down political opponents like "rats" and fight to the death. It never occurred to Qaddafi that he would lose.[2]

The political awakening on display in public squares across the Middle East was mesmerizing, but Washington was uncertain of its implications.

Interests and values never align perfectly, but they seemed to converge in the Arab Spring. Replacing dictatorships with more representative governments was believed to be part of the solution to violent political extremism. What was happening in the Middle East seemed reminiscent of the end of the Cold War, an opportunity to employ American influence to help shape a world as it should be.[3]

Prompted by not just the United States and other Western powers but countries in the region as well, the United Nations Security Council passed a resolution that authorized "all necessary measures" to protect civilians under threat of attack.

While the president cautioned that the United States could not be expected to intervene everywhere people were suffering at the hands of their government, he spoke of the urgent situation in Libya, including cities shelled; targeted killings; attacks on hospitals; water, food, and fuel denied; and sexual violence employed as a weapon of war.

"Some nations may be able to turn a blind eye to atrocities in other countries. The United States of America is different," Obama said. "And as President, I refused to wait for the images of slaughter and mass graves before taking action."[4]

Fifteen months earlier, Obama suggested in his Nobel Prize speech in Oslo that the force was appropriate in pursuit of humanitarian objectives.[5] He got the chance to demonstrate that in Libya.

The president cited a "national interest" of preventing violence in Libya from spilling over and destabilizing neighboring countries. Obama's concern about instability in and around Libya was well founded; the ripple effects of the rebellion would actually add to it. Arms from Qaddafi's considerable weapons caches and from shipments to Libya by regional countries backing competing factions would contribute to intensified violence in Nigeria, Mali, Gaza, Syria, Somalia, and other countries in between. Once again, the United States would disrupt the status quo to be surprised yet again by the shock wave that followed.

Obama considered the United States the world's exceptional nation and wanted the United States to be on the right side of history. But he did not believe that external interventions, even one supported by the world's most powerful country, could reshape the internal dynamic of any country. Given the costly struggles with nation building in Afghanistan and Iraq, he was prepared to employ limited military force to prevent bad things from happening, but would not commit significant resources to construct something better in its place. He would defer to others, particularly in Europe, presumed to have a higher stake in Libya's future.

Even as he tried to apply the lessons from Iraq, Obama ended up repeating a critical error in Libya, albeit one without a trillion-dollar price tag. Unexpectedly, Libya would become another object lesson regarding the dangers of regime change without a realistic plan for the day after. Libya, like Iraq, was not self-ordering and would descend into chaos, providing violent extremists another opportunity to fill a dangerous political vacuum, gain territory, and create an extremist foothold within Europe's shadow.

Libya would generate a stubborn political crisis at home and become a significant obstacle to an effective international response to an even more dangerous and tragic conflict in Syria.

When the United States finally intervened there, it was against the Islamic State, not against the Assad regime. It was to protect the American people, not the Syrian people.

NEVER AGAIN

As the crisis heightened in Libya, a senior White House aide suggested Libya represented a potential "Srebrenica on steroids."[6]

The reference to Srebrenica was instructive, referring to the horrific episode of ethnic cleansing that marked the tragic turning point of the Bosnia conflict. Before Srebrenica, the international community's response was haphazard and ineffective. After the fact, the United States, Europe, and the United Nations applied sufficient military and diplomatic pressure to negotiate a settlement in Dayton, Ohio, that ended the conflict.

Libya was the latest manifestation of an unresolved foreign policy debate that has continued since the end of the Cold War regarding humanitarian challenges that did not trigger a vital national security interest. Each subsequent American administration approached these interventions differently.

Bosnia was at war from the moment it declared independence in March 1992. Between 1991 and the eventual end of the conflict in 1995, up to three hundred thousand people were killed as the country disintegrated. But the United States viewed it as primarily a European challenge to resolve. Bush's Secretary of State James Baker famously said, "We don't have a dog in this fight."[7]

Baker, believing that the United States should not be "the world's policeman," argued that only an early and significant intervention of ground forces would have precluded the Bosnian conflict. A consummate political operator, Baker did not see how the American people would support "the degree of force that would have been required in Bosnia."[8]

George H. W. Bush did intervene in Somalia following an unexpected election loss. Somalia was a country without a central government and wracked by a dramatic humanitarian crisis, a by-product of the ensuing political vacuum and significant clan warfare. The Bush administration dispatched troops to stabilize the situation.

Announcing the move, President Bush said that "the United States alone cannot right the world's wrongs." But employing a logic that Obama would echo, he added that "some crises in the world cannot be resolved without American involvement, that American action is often necessary as a catalyst for broader involvement in the community of nations."[9]

Bush's expectation was that the troops would be home by the time a new president was inaugurated in January 1993. But like most recent humanitarian interventions, it proved to be far more complicated than anticipated.

Under President Bill Clinton, the military experienced "mission creep" in Somalia as the military objective expanded from feeding hungry people to resolving the underlying power struggle that created the crisis. An ill-conceived military raid against the forces of clan leader Mohamed Farrah Aideed—captured in the book and film *Black Hawk Down*—resulted in eighteen American soldiers dead and another seventy-four wounded. Somalia was Clinton's Bay of Pigs.[10]

In light of Somalia, the United States avoided a significant response in Rwanda where eight hundred thousand people—10 percent of the country's population—were slaughtered in a three-month period. Clinton termed Rwanda "one of the greatest regrets of my presidency."[11] Congressional opposition to military deployments to countries not considered vital to U.S. national interests was a significant factor in his decision.

Clinton intervened in Haiti, where the United Nations for the first time authorized the use of "all necessary means" to restore a democratically elected leader expelled through a military coup. But the administration had domestic politics on its side, since the prospects of large numbers of Haitians attempting a treacherous voyage on makeshift rafts from Haiti to the U.S. mainland was far more visible to the American people, particularly in a swing state like Florida.

Despite having encouraged a more assertive policy during the 1992 presidential campaign, given the experience in Somalia, Clinton took a cautious approach to Bosnia, attempting to apply limited force without becoming deeply involved. French President Jacques Chirac complained that "the position of leader of the free world is vacant."[12]

Given the emerging 24/7 global news cycle, Clinton did feel pressure to do something—"war by CNN" as he termed it.[13] But it was only after the Bosnian Serbs attacked UN-declared safe zones in eastern Bosnia—Goradze, Zepa, and Srebrenica—that the administration moved beyond the policy and political limits of the time.

A Croatian counteroffensive changed the military equation on the ground sufficiently to enable a negotiated settlement with the leaders of Bosnia, Serbia, and Croatia in November 1995. The Dayton Accords called for a sixty-thousand-member international implementation force, one-third of them American. Even with the significant U.S. diplomatic success, public opposition to the deployment of American forces ran as high as 70 percent.[14]

While Washington committed to lead the peacekeeping mission, it also insisted on an exit deadline, which President Clinton extended twice and eventually dropped.[15] The operation was routinely extended for several years, since it involved no casualties and little risk to soldiers there.

Congress went along, with the Senate voting in favor thanks to the leadership of Robert Dole and the House voting against the policy but in favor of the troops.[16]

General John Shalikashvili, who succeeded Colin Powell as chairman of the Joint Chiefs, agreed with the Powell Doctrine, undertaking military missions with clear objectives, sufficient forces, and an exit strategy.

"What Shalikashvili wanted to change," wrote David Halberstam in *War in a Time of Peace*, "was the *Weinberger Doctrine*" (emphasis in the original).[17] He sought greater flexibility for a tailored military force to serve a humanitarian purpose.

Richard Holbrooke termed the international community's response to the crisis in the Balkans as "the greatest collective security failure of the West since the 1930s."[18] Together with Rwanda, it fueled a powerful political narrative "never again" that resurfaced during the Bush administration in Darfur and the Obama administration in Libya.

Bosnia affirmed that American power could be employed in the service of American values, not just interests. Clinton in his second inaugural address introduced an expansive conception of enlightened American power. At the apex of its unipolar moment, Clinton said, "America stands alone as the world's indispensable nation."[19]

The term was embraced by Clinton's second secretary of state, Madeleine Albright. She suggested years later that the narrative was meant to encourage the American public, concerned about the costs of humanitarian interventions and recurring military action in Iraq, that "the international system needed an engaged America."[20]

American indispensability would receive its first test in Kosovo. The Dayton Accords left many unanswered questions, including the future of a province in Serbia that had been contested for six centuries.[21] The Bush administration had issued a Christmas warning pledging to respond to Serb aggression in Kosovo.[22] The Clinton administration reaffirmed it.

Following the Racak massacre in January 1999, Serb forces pushed an estimated eight hundred thousand Kosovar Albanians out of the province and into refugee camps in Albania and Macedonia. Another five hundred thousand were internally displaced, meaning three-quarters of the total population were driven from their homes.[23]

In response, NATO launched an air campaign in March 1999 that enjoyed considerable political legitimacy even without an authorizing resolution from the United Nations, since Russia and China opposed outside intervention regarding internal disputes within sovereign states. As German Foreign Minister Joschka Fisher suggested, "If people are being massacred, you cannot mutter about having no mandate. You must act."[24] In light of Iraq, Obama would see the lack of an international mandate as an obstacle.

Kosovo was an information war, decided through a political agreement and not military conquest. NATO established three clear goals: force the Serbs out of Kosovo, deploy international forces in their place, and encourage the refugees to return home.★

While the United States underestimated its duration, Serbian president Slobodan Milosevic capitulated because he could not break NATO's solidarity and feared losing political control of his own country.

"It was a very strange war," recalled Ambassador Chris Hill, the U.S. envoy for Kosovo at the time. "Bombing to change someone's mind is a new one in the annals of war."[25] Actually, the United States tried the same tactic in Vietnam.

While the bombing campaign achieved its stated objective—Russia helped pressure the Serbs to withdraw, enabling the Kosovars to return, protected by a combined force that included Russian troops—some ten thousand people perished in the conflict.

Many observers at the time and since criticized Clinton for ruling out ground forces at the start of the NATO campaign. Military leaders believed that political factors restricted the use of significant military force.† But this ignores the inherent political nature of the conflict. The desired end result was

---

★Kosovo was NATO's first actual war. The Alliance established an information operations cell within headquarters (I was part of the U.S. deployment) to respond to events on the battlefield in real time and stay connected to European capitals to maintain political unity. NATO could not lose provided the alliance remained together.

†Presidential candidates frequently say they will follow the advice of the generals. But this ignores the key role politics should play in every conflict. The Air Force was critical of bombing restrictions directed by the White House, but the Kosovo campaign, ugly as it was, achieved its objectives without putting any boots on the ground, redeeming the beliefs of air pioneers like General Billy Mitchell.

political stability in Europe, not military victory. NATO rightly traded the intensity of the bombing campaign to preserve European political unity and promote Russian cooperation.

That said, the NATO intervention on top of the Alliance's enlargement undermined President Boris Yeltsin's policy of Western cooperation. It did not appear to Moscow that the West took Russia's legitimate interests into account. Kosovo's ensuing declaration of independence still complicates U.S.-Russia relations.[26]

Kosovo spawned the doctrine of a "responsibility to protect" that trumped traditional notions of international sovereignty when accepted international norms were egregiously violated. Military force could serve ideals, not just interests.[27] But it meant that a major power like the United States became deeply involved in the politics of small states, a circumstance that from Vietnam to Somalia did not produce anticipated outcomes.

While neoconservatives believed the United States should support democratic change, traditionalists viewed such nation-building missions as a distraction from higher military priorities. Those who signed the Republican Contract with America in 1994 were skeptical of using the military for largely humanitarian purposes, and resistant to working through the United Nations.[28]

A number of high-level policy makers in the Obama administration shared strong instincts in favor of liberal interventionism. Obama, far more a policy realist, was actually not one of them.

LOST LEGITIMACY

The Middle East was of vital importance to the United States, but Libya was not.[29] Like the politics surrounding most recent military actions, the Libyan conflict was less about the country than its leader. To idealists, Qaddafi was a serial human rights violator and poster child for what was wrong with the region. To realists, he was a fringe player who had tried to make himself useful.

For Americans, wars are easier to understand and support when there is a villain—Milosevic, bin Laden, Saddam, and now Qaddafi. But making them personal obscured the broader interests at stake and muddied what was required to achieve the desired long-term political outcome. As the United States supposedly learned in Iraq, going to war is not just about eliminating a dangerous and erratic leader.

Qaddafi was a long-standing state sponsor of terrorism with American blood on his hands. Most Americans could not find Libya on the map, but the two countries clashed repeatedly during the 1980s and they remembered the picture of the flattened cockpit of Pan Am 103 on a field near Lockerbie, Scotland. Most of the victims of the 1988 act of terror were American. The United States and the international community held Libya responsible.

After 9/11 and the U.S. invasion of Iraq, Qaddafi tried to reinvent himself. He cooperated with the United States regarding counterterrorism operations against al Qaeda, since Libyans were among the movement's senior leaders. He traded his nascent nuclear program, the major ingredients of which were shipped to the Oak Ridge Laboratories in Tennessee, for what he hoped would be a more fruitful relationship with the West.

In theory, a central pillar of the U.S. policy throughout the war on terror was preventing weapons of mass destruction from getting into the hands of extremist groups. In that respect, Qaddafi did everything the United States wanted him to do.

Ironically, in a phone conversation with President Bush after the deal, Bush suggested it marked a "new beginning" in relations between the United States and Libya, the same aspiration Obama would have for the region as a whole.[30]

In reality, Qaddafi was a megalomaniacal caricature of a modern dictator. Qaddafi had declared himself the "King of Kings of Africa" in 2008. His praetorian guard included beautiful and heavily armed women. Qaddafi craved high-level attention, and late in her tenure, Secretary of State Condoleezza Rice visited Tripoli. She came away thinking Qaddafi lived "in a kind of alternate reality."[31]

Qaddafi was ridiculed in State Department cables released by WikiLeaks in late 2010, including details of his inner circle, disdain for hotels and elevators, and insistence on pitching a tent wherever he traveled. After they were published, there were threats against the sitting U.S. ambassador, Gene Cretz, who was brought home for consultations just as the Arab Spring was stirring. For his own protection, he never returned.*

As the turmoil grew in Tripoli, the Obama administration closed its embassy and evacuated its diplomatic personnel and American citizens who lived and worked in the country. While a necessary step, it removed the clear-

---

*Qaddafi was sensitive to criticism. He declared "jihad" on Switzerland in response to what he perceived as disrespect to a family member. When asked about Qaddafi's implied threat, I harkened back to his almost incomprehensible speech at the United Nations months earlier and suggested he employed a lot of words but little common sense. Qaddafi froze billions in energy deals with U.S. firms until I expressed regret (not an apology) that the comments were perceived as a personal attack. They were.

est window the United States had into what was happening in the country.★ Once that process was complete in late February 2011, the White House took a more aggressive stand against Qaddafi.

In early March, in a press conference with President Felipe Calderon of Mexico, Obama declared that by turning state-sponsored violence against the Libyan people, "Muammar Qaddafi has lost the legitimacy to lead and he must leave."[32] He highlighted Rwanda and Bosnia and argued against repeating some of history's darkest moments.

Susan Rice, the U.S. ambassador to the UN, was the National Security Council's senior director for African affairs at the time of Rwanda. And NSC Special Assistant Samantha Power (who later succeeded Rice at the UN) wrote a Pulitzer Prize–winning book, *A Problem from Hell*, arguing that a president must have a "bias toward belief" in favor of the use of military force to prevent massacres like Srebrenica.[33] Senator John McCain, Obama's opponent in the 2008 presidential election, who supported a no-fly zone, also drew comparisons with America's experience in the Balkans.

But there were crucial differences between the American experience in the Balkans and what the Obama administration contemplated in Libya. The NATO interventions in Bosnia and Kosovo followed lengthy diplomatic engagement and negotiation. They both produced political settlements that were enforced through the deployment of peacekeeping forces.

Obama recognized the historic opportunity that the Arab uprisings represented. As the tumult cascaded from Tunisia to Egypt, from Yemen to Bahrain and now to Libya, he identified with the aspirations of the people, but earnestly believed there was a limit to what the United States could do to help them.

Obama spoke regularly about the need for "nation-building here at home," a narrative that reflected America's war-weariness. And as he said in Cairo in 2009, he had no intention of imposing solutions that were made in America.

A 51-49 CALL

As they debated an appropriate course of action, Obama's advisors were all over the map—evaluating Qaddafi's true intentions and the danger to the Lib-

---

★There was turmoil at the Libyan Embassy in Washington as well. In late February 2011, Libya's popular ambassador, Ali Aujali, broke with Qaddafi and sided with the National Transitional Council. The Libyan Foreign Ministry sent a fax indicating that Aujali no longer represented the Libyan government, which the State Department chose not to act

yan people; ascertaining the identity and capabilities of the rebel movement, the National Transitional Council; hearing urgent calls for action from key European allies and the Arab League; sensing the history of the moment; and fearing known and unknown consequences of yet another intervention in the Middle East.

At one point on the critical day of decision, March 15, 2011, Ambassador Rice told her French counterpart, Gerard Araud, "You are not going to drag us into your shitty war."[34] But after a National Security Council meeting, Rice would call back to advocate a more aggressive course of action than even France or Great Britain contemplated.

The Obama administration considered a range of options for Libya, from doing nothing to boots on the ground.[35] Rather than a symbolic no-fly zone—Qaddafi was using tanks far more than airplanes to suppress the revolution emanating from Benghazi—Obama pushed for a United Nations resolution, the first of its kind, to authorize military strikes against Libyan forces on the ground to preempt an "imminent massacre."[36]

Secretary of Defense Robert Gates termed the decision a "51–49 call."[37] Gates preferred to concentrate on the wars in Iraq and Afghanistan.

In the end, the strongest believers in the promise of humanitarian interventionism—Rice, Power, advisor and speechwriter Ben Rhodes, and Hillary Clinton—convinced the president, with the judgment of history in the balance, to act. For Clinton, given the prospect of large-scale violence, in the eyes of a senior aide, "for all the risks of acting, the risks of not acting were greater."[38] The lack of an international response would be viewed as a green light to quash the protests that were still under way across the region.

Her decisive support for the humanitarian intervention became a campaign issue in 2016. Hillary Clinton received criticism from both the left and the right that Qaddafi, while a bad guy, was cooperating in the fight against terrorism. Senator Bernie Sanders used Libya to remind voters of the unintended consequences of regime change and her support for the Iraq invasion in 2003.[39] Donald Trump would cite the Islamic State's presence in both Iraq and Libya to argue against foreign interventions involving regime change and nation building. He viewed authoritarian leaders willing to join forces against the Islamic State and al Qaeda as potential allies.[40]

---

on pending notification through a formal diplomatic route, the normal practice. For days, Aujali's status was a topic of interest in the State Department briefing. After multiple attempts to reach the Libyan government, Foreign Minister Musa Kusa called, telling Assistant Secretary Jeff Feltman, "Mr. Crowley says you're having trouble reaching me." Kusa did not bring up the issues of diplomatic representation. Feltman didn't either. Meanwhile, Aujali served as a passionate advocate in Washington for the Libyan opposition.

Having decided to employ military force, Obama chose not to seek congressional approval. Even as the crisis in Libya was developing, the House of Representatives was trying to shut down the government. The White House did not believe Congress was capable of voting on military action in a timely way. A number of key legislators agreed.[41]

Obama said later about Syria, "we cannot resolve someone else's civil war through force."[42] But this is exactly what the United States and NATO did in Libya.

On March 19, while on a trip to Brazil, the president announced to the American people that U.S. forces were "answering the call of a threatened people."[43] It happened to fall eight years to the day that the United States announced its invasion of Iraq.

"[T]he use of force is not our first choice," Obama said in a brief announcement. "But we cannot stand idly by when a tyrant tells his people that there will be no mercy, and his forces step up their assaults on cities like Benghazi and Misurata, where innocent men and women face brutality and death at the hands of their own government."[44]

After launching military operations, Obama spent as much time describing what his policy wasn't as what he hoped to achieve through military force. Libya was not Iraq. Obama viewed his mandate as ending America's existing wars, not starting new ones.

Obama used the speech at National Defense University to scale back his war of choice barely three weeks after it began. Having helped the Libyan rebel movement blunt Qaddafi's counteroffensive, the United States shifted to a "supporting role." It would provide special capabilities such as intelligence, air refueling and other logistical support, search and rescue, and electronic warfare.

Other members, including Great Britain, France, Denmark, and Sweden, would undertake the lion's share of the offensive operations over Libya, a dramatic departure from the dominating role the United States normally plays within NATO. What happened after that was up to Europe.[45]

"The United States," the president said, "has done what we said we would do."[46]

However, despite the president's rhetoric, U.S. forces were still dropping bombs using conventional aircraft and drones. To cover the gaps between what the president said, military forces did, and what the law required, administration lawyers developed a rationale that the NATO-led intervention did not represent the type of hostilities envisioned under the War Powers Act, since it involved no ground forces, no sustained exchange of fire with Libyan forces, and thus little prospect of American casualties.[47]

The United States was, in the words of an unnamed White House official, "leading from behind."[48] This meant America would not take "ownership" of the post–Qaddafi Libya.

In fact, no one did.[49] A key reason was the "hangover" from Iraq.[50]*

REGIME CHANGE

The United Nations Security Council passed Resolution 1973 on March 17, 2011. It authorized NATO and a handful of regional allies to "protect civilians and civilian populated areas under the threat of attack." The resolution imposed a no-fly zone on Libya while authorizing the delivery of humanitarian assistance to the Libyan people.

After what he perceived as the excessive unilateralism of the Bush administration, Obama was determined to work more constructively with the international community. International cooperation was an asset in Obama's eyes, not a constraint. Solving problems, especially those that did not involve vital interests, required willing partners who were prepared to share the responsibility and resource burden.

The Obama administration had rejoined the Human Rights Council in 2009 despite the fact its membership included countries with terrible records. Human Rights Watch would estimate that 350 protesters died prior to the NATO intervention, with a potential for more.[51] Clinton traveled to Geneva, where the UN condemned Qaddafi's violent response and launched a formal investigation.[52] The Security Council even referred the question of potential crimes against humanity to the International Criminal Court.[53]

Libya represented an ideal confluence of geopolitical conditions: an undeniably urgent situation; a request for intervention by a credible political force inside the country that reflected a viable alternative to Qaddafi's brutal rule; clear regional support through the Arab League; a United Nations Security Council Resolution that provided a mandate, legality, and legitimacy for military action; acceptance of the mission by NATO, along with partners from the region willing to put "skin in the game."

---

*NATO was not tasked to do any planning for a postconflict mission. There were discussions with the new interim Libyan government about a UN peacekeeping force to help provide security. The Libyans for both political and historical reasons did not feel they could accept an external force. In the 1990s and the heyday of humanitarian interventionism, Washington might have pushed for a different answer. After Iraq, it didn't.

Russia and China for geopolitical reasons normally oppose any international sanction for the interference of external forces into the sovereign affairs of a state, but the Libya crisis occurred at a fortuitous moment. Under Russian President Dmitri Medvedev, there was a "reset" in relations, albeit a temporary one. Relations with Beijing were not close, but when confronted with international crises, China was always leery about being the odd man out.

They acceded to UNSCR 1973 primarily as a gesture to the Arab and African states, hoping that a brief show of force would open the door for a political settlement. Unlike Mubarak or even Assad, Qaddafi had no friends in the region. The Arab League was happy to see him go, but the request for intervention in Libya was hardly a regional vote for democracy.

In fact, there are good reasons to view Arab concern about Libya as a deliberate diversion from other regional developments, particularly growing unrest in Bahrain. Within days of the NATO intervention in Libya, military forces from Saudi Arabia and other Gulf states intervened in Bahrain to help the government of King Hamid bin Isa Al Khalifa brutally suppress a Shia-led uprising that they viewed not as a democratic movement but rather a subversive act by neighboring Iran.

Even as the Obama administration handed off primary responsibility for the Libya mission to NATO, it was unclear in Brussels, Washington, and other national capitals what adequate protection for the Libyan people looked like.

At a meeting of foreign ministers in Berlin in mid-April, NATO attempted to answer that question, calling for the Qaddafi regime to end its attacks on civilians, withdraw deployed forces back to military bases, and allow unhindered humanitarian assistance.[54]

That same day, in a joint op-ed by President Obama, French President Nicolas Sarkozy, and British Prime Minister David Cameron published in the *International Herald Tribune*, *Le Figaro*, and *Times of London*, the leaders seemed to go farther. While acknowledging that the international mandate in Libya was not to remove Qaddafi by force, they pledged that NATO operations would continue "so long as Qaddafi is in power."[55]

Just three weeks earlier, Obama had stressed that "broadening our military mission to include regime change would be a mistake."[56] Now it appeared there was a conscious decision that "the only way to protect civilians was to bring new leadership to the country."[57] NATO stretched its mandate to accomplish that goal, becoming the de facto air force for the rebel movement.[58] The CIA quietly communicated through its Libyan intelligence contacts that Qaddafi had to go.[59]

During the 2012 presidential campaign, Republican challenger Governor Mitt Romney criticized the decision to expand the operation as "mission creep" or "mission muddle," a characterization that Obama rejected. Highlighting Qaddafi as a dictator with American blood on his hands, the president candidly said, "we were going to make sure we finished the job."[60]

In mid-July, the State Department recognized the National Transitional Council as the legitimate representative of the Libyan people. A month later, rebel forces finally broke through Qaddafi's forces and took control of Tripoli. While there was a discussion within NATO of terminating its bombing campaign when Qaddafi was pushed from power, the military mission ended only after rebels found Qaddafi hiding in a drainage ditch, killed him, and then buried him in an unmarked grave.

UN Resolution 1973 explicitly barred ground forces from entering Libya. It did not mention regime change. The Obama administration's public posture remained that it was just protecting the Libyan people, which Gates acknowledged later involved maintaining "a fiction."[61]

"The Russians felt they had been played for suckers in Libya," he told the *New York Times*. "They felt there had been a bait and switch. I said at the time we would pay hell getting them to cooperate in the future."[62]

Vladimir Putin was critical of Medvedev's acquiescence regarding the UN resolution, NATO intervention, and Qaddafi's removal from power. Once he returned to the presidency, Libya certainly influenced his subsequent intransigence over Syria.[63]

"Qaddafi is going to fall eventually," a senior administration official told *Rolling Stone* months after the NATO intervention began. "The question is: What demons are waiting that we don't yet know about?"[64]

The decision to couple a policy of regime change with the emerging concept of an international "responsibility to protect" civilians in Libya would haunt Western powers in Syria. Russia would serve as Bashar al-Assad's indispensable nation and do everything in its power, including its own military intervention, to protect him. Without a clear path to a political solution, millions of Syrians would lose hope and vote with their feet. The ensuing wave of refugees would paralyze Europe.

THE DAY AFTER

Reflecting later on lessons learned in Libya, Obama posed a rhetorical question: "Do we have an answer the day after?"[65] But despite intervening, his administration never came up with a satisfactory one.

Obama rejected as a "false choice" the option of doing nothing or becoming the world's policeman.[66] While pledging the United States would do its part, the task of building strong civil institutions of a modern and functioning state would belong to the international community and the Libyan people. While Libya had assets—$33 billion in assets were frozen through UN sanctions—what it lacked was expertise.

"Qaddafi left his countrymen with a void: no army, no police, no unions, nothing to bring them together," wrote Robert F. Worth, who covered the Libyan revolution for the *New York Times*.[67] What they did have was lots of players with lots of weapons, with enough firepower to challenge the interim government. Yet the Libyans chose to march down the path to elections largely on their own.

"They were very keen to take responsibility for their country," said Jeremy Shapiro, who worked on Libya policy at the State Department at the time. "And we were very keen to let them."[68]

For a combination of reasons, both the Libyan reticence regarding foreign interference and the American reluctance to assume another nation-building project, there was no support for an international stabilization force.[69]

Nine months after Qaddafi's death, Libya held free, fair, and surprisingly peaceful elections. But democracy was not going to take root absent security. As Clinton told the House Select Committee investigating Benghazi, "a lot of them knew what they wanted, but didn't know how to get from where they were to that goal."[70]

"We were not ready," Libya's interim prime minister, Mahmoud Jibril, acknowledged later.[71]

In the absence of a stabilizing force American diplomats confronted an increasingly dangerous environment. An attack in Benghazi on September 11, 2012, left four Americans dead, including the U.S. ambassador, Chris Stevens, which created a domestic political firestorm in Washington.

Given the timing of the attack, just two months before the 2012 presidential vote, there was a politically driven furor over the administration's initial description of what happened. UN Ambassador Susan Rice (she would later serve as National Security Advisor after the controversy derailed her candidacy to be secretary of state) suggested the attack was spontaneous, in response to a U.S.-made movie trailer critical of the prophet Muhummad that sparked an initial protest at the U.S. Embassy in Cairo.

The subsequent controversy surrounding Benghazi was, contrary to the claims of members of Congress, not about a misrepresentation of what happened at the diplomatic compound—the obscure video was one (if not the only) motivation behind the Benghazi attack. One of the perpetrators of the attack, later captured in a special operations raid, confirmed according to Clinton that Benghazi was a deliberate attack influenced by the video.[72]

But the talking points reflected White House concern regarding any connection between the Benghazi attack and its earlier decision to intervene.[73] Fairly or not, the Benghazi attack challenged the Obama administration's political narrative of al Qaeda's retreat.[74]

While Obama feared how a security vacuum in Libya could affect the stability of neighboring countries, he underestimated the degree to which it exacerbated the regional extremist threat picture. Weapons flowed to other trouble spots, complicating the cornerstone of U.S. regional counterterrorism policy, preventing the emergence of safe havens that terrorist organizations could exploit.

On the surface, the very real potential that Libya could become a failed state and extremist safe haven would have argued for a more substantial policy and resource commitment to Libya. An administration official described the campaign in Libya as a chance to "realign our interests and values."[75] While Obama avoided the costly mistakes Bush made in Iraq, he committed a similar miscalculation in failing to develop a realistic plan regarding its postconflict phase. Absent a concerted effort to ensure a stable postconflict transition, "the initial intervention made little sense strategically," wrote Colin Dueck in *The Obama Doctrine*. "In this specific sense, Libya was actually very much like Iraq."[76]

Internal rivalries within Libya led not just to renewed fighting but eventually to dueling governments in different power centers within the country, one in Tripoli and the other in Tobruk, reflecting a long-standing political fault line within Libya. A United Nations mediation effort struggled over many months to create a government of national unity.

In 2015, with competing governments, parliaments, and armies controlling different sections of the country, it is no surprise that the flag of the Islamic State would rise amid the mayhem.[77]

Both Bush and Obama focused too much attention on the danger posed by their respective leaders, Saddam Hussein and Muammar Qaddafi, and not enough on the regional implications of their removal. Bush did so for philosophical reasons—the military should not be involved in nation building; Obama for political reasons—the lack of political support because of Iraq to take ownership of another Middle East military adventure.

Given that Libya was not viewed as a vital interest and the political limitations of the moment, the Obama administration made an understandable choice, although it ran contrary to America's self-image of indispensability and its strategy of preventing the emergence of extremist safe havens.

Those political limitations were reinforced by the churn surrounding Benghazi. "The furor over Ambassador Stevens' death made it very difficult to argue for further engagement in Libya," wrote James Traub in *Foreign Policy*. "Nevertheless, there was no real plan to do so."[78]

Obama later expressed regret for not doing more to help Libya after the fall of Qaddafi, saying that the United States and Europe "underestimated the need to come in full force." But he defended his original decision, suggesting, "Had we not intervened, it's likely that Libya would be Syria."[79]

But as Marc Lynch suggested in *The New Arab Wars*, "Libya was a decisive turning point in the transformation of the Arab uprisings from domestic peaceful uprisings to a regional proxy war."[80] Given how the NATO intervention unfolded in Libya, and the unintended consequences that flowed from it, the U.S. and international community were unwilling and unable to effectively confront the far more destructive conflict in Syria.

7

ALL WARS END

In late June 2011, still buoyed by the Navy SEAL mission seven weeks earlier that killed Osama bin Laden, President Obama reiterated in an evening address from the East Room his intention to bring the wars in Iraq and Afghanistan to a "responsible end."

Recalling his West Point speech from December 2009, he believed the United States and its allies had reversed Taliban momentum and improved the capability of Afghan forces to gradually take over responsibility for their own security. As a result, he announced that the U.S. forces that surged in 2010 would be withdrawn on schedule. The elimination of Osama bin Laden made this much easier to accomplish, at least politically, although Donald Trump, during the 2016 campaign, would suggest that Obama was "reckless" to announce such moves in public.[1]

Obama was determined that Afghanistan not be "a war without end."[2] Just before his West Point speech, Obama personally produced a six-page summary of the results of the intensive months-long review and ensured that its key participants—the secretary of defense, the chairman and vice chairman of the Joint Chiefs, and commander of Central Command—were all in agreement. He had not signed up to an open-ended nation-building effort nor a full-blown counterinsurgency campaign.

Obama's announcement of the beginning of an Afghan transition reflected the prevailing political sentiment that the United States had largely achieved all it could in Afghanistan.[3] Just a month earlier, the House of Representatives narrowly rejected a motion that would have established firm deadlines for the withdrawal of U.S. forces.

While acknowledging that the path forward would be difficult, Obama said, "The tide of war is receding."[4] He repeated the phrase four months later when he announced that all U.S. forces would be withdrawn from Iraq by the end of the year.

There were favorable trends that lent credence to Obama's strategy and narrative. The Taliban appeared willing to negotiate. The Anbar Awakening continued to hold. As the president said in an important speech on the Middle East in mid-May, "al Qaeda was losing its struggle for relevance."[5]

While Obama anticipated rapid change in some places, gradual change in others, and some "fierce contests for power," he saw power shifting from the dictators to the people, that there was a "story of self-determination" unfolding that would move the region beyond its repressive status quo.[6]

Four months into the Arab Spring, Obama believed that "through the moral force of nonviolence, the people have achieved more change in six months than terrorists have accomplished in decades."[7] However, except for Tunisia, progress was ephemeral.

Across the region, the existing order was not just breaking up; countries were also breaking down. The Obama administration lent its voice to the demand for human dignity and freedom, but did not have a solution that would preserve the basic security necessary to protect the universal rights of affected populations. The lack of effective government institutions within fractured states opened the door for political extremists and scheming neighbors. Sectarian violence and proxy wars trumped local politics, providing malign actors like al Qaeda a chance to regain momentum and literally gain ground.

Even in Iraq and Afghanistan, while political leaders voiced preparedness to assume responsibility for their own security, virulent insurgencies persisted. Local government capabilities had advanced, but not far enough.

In Afghanistan, while a long-overdue conversation with the Taliban did commence, plans to end the war proceeded without regard to whether a political resolution was feasible. At the same time, the relationship with Pakistan was deteriorating rapidly.

Nonetheless, as he surveyed the strategic landscape in the fall of 2011, with the withdrawal from Iraq approaching, Afghanistan on a path to closure, and key terrorist figures removed from the battlefield, Obama could be forgiven for a furtive glance at an attractive presidential legacy, ending all three wars he inherited from George W. Bush.

Even for the most powerful leader on the planet, the world gets a vote. Obama's miscalculation was not that he gave voice to America's enduring hopes, but that he held on to that narrative as long as he did, even as multiple conflicts intensified.

STRATEGIC DEFEAT

Relatively unnoticed during the 2008 campaign, Obama stressed the importance of Pakistan and the sanctuary that al Qaeda presumably enjoyed in its tribal region. In a prophetic speech at the Woodrow Wilson Center in 2007, Obama made clear, "If we have actionable intelligence about high-value terrorist targets and President Musharraf won't act, we will."[8]

Once in office, the Obama administration waged its war against al Qaeda with significant determination and success. Al Qaeda's leadership remained under constant pressure. Successful strikes had taken many top-tier operatives off the battlefield; their replacements were not as capable. Obama considered the struggle against al Qaeda as "a just war—a war waged proportionately, in last resort, and in self-defense."[9]

In his speech accepting the Nobel Peace Prize in Oslo in December 2009, he spoke of the "relationship between war and peace, and our effort to replace one with the other." Reiterating a theme from his earlier speech in Cairo, he recognized the importance of human aspirations and that the United States and the West must support "these movements of hope and history." But given the "dizzying pace of globalization" and the "cultural leveling of modernity," he anticipated forces that would attempt to move their tribe or their religion backward.[10]

He recognized the increasing trend was toward war not between nations, but within them. Understanding that evil does exist in the world, he also anticipated the challenge of "how to prevent the slaughter of civilians by their own government, or to stop a civil war whose violence and suffering can engulf an entire region." He did not consider this to be just an American responsibility.[11]

This campaign against al Qaeda was waged largely in secret. The president reiterated regularly a desire to make the war against al Qaeda more transparent, and the military operation that eliminated bin Laden provided an irresistible opportunity.

The discovery of bin Laden in Abbottabad was one of the most closely held secrets within the U.S. government. Only a small number of high-level officials had access to the intelligence that pointed to the walled compound in Abbottabad, not far from Pakistan's version of West Point.

A number of options were considered regarding how best to conduct an operation to detain, but more realistically to eliminate him, including long-range bomber or cruise missile attacks. Obama preferred a special operations mission. He wanted proof that bin Laden was actually at the compound, recognizing how important his death would be in the political and psychological war with al Qaeda.

SEAL Team Six arrived at bin Laden's compound undetected, particularly by the Pakistani military, a fact that would greatly embarrass its leadership. While secret, the operation was not invisible. From its outset, the neighborhood, particularly through social media, began reacting to the unusual noise in the middle of the night.

The operation was well rehearsed and superbly executed, but not without incident. One of the advanced helicopters used in the raid struck a retaining wall while arriving at the compound and was left behind, a calling card that accelerated how quickly the White House would be required to acknowledge the mission.

Inside the Situation Room, once U.S. forces returned safely to Afghanistan, presumably with bin Laden's remains, there was an impulse to hold any announcement until DNA tests could confirm that the most wanted man in the world was in fact dead. "This is going to come out," CIA Director Leon Panetta interjected.[12]

Likewise, Pakistani Chief of Staff Ashraf Kayani pushed his U.S. counterpart, Admiral Michael Mullen, for a quick release. "You gotta get this out." Kayani understood he would have a tough time explaining the raid and the Pakistani military's failure to detect it. Even before receiving the DNA analysis, the Pakistanis confirmed it was bin Laden.[13]

A congressional aide scooped the president on Twitter and announced bin Laden's demise before Obama did. In the days after the raid, as the American people celebrated the end of the early twenty-first century's arch villain, the White House and national security agencies went into overdrive to provide details and texture to the operation.*

But the administration struggled in the days after the mission to get its story straight. Was the plan to detain bin Laden? Was there a firefight? Did bin

---

*In Washington parlance, this is called tick-tock, taking the reader inside the Situation Room and relating how the president came to make a tough decision, who said what as the National Security Council worked through various options, whose views ultimately carried the day, and how the group reacted when the unexpected happened. Every administration struggles to find the right balance between disclosures that put government decision making in perspective and revelations that go too far.

Laden have a weapon? Was he shielded by one of his wives? While at least some of the confusion can be attributed to the "fog of war"—first reports *do* usually get significant details wrong—far more was simply that government officials, eager to put the agencies and key individuals involved in the middle of a major win in the war against al Qaeda, quickly went beyond what they actually knew, or created a flawed picture from the pieces that were available. For all of the concern about excessive secrecy, once the faucet is turned on, the American people learn a lot about what government is doing on their behalf.

In fact, so much information came to light, particularly details regarding intelligence operations and special operations tactics, that Secretary of Defense Robert Gates felt obliged to offer the White House some public affairs advice. "Why doesn't everybody just shut the fuck up," he complained to National Security Advisor Tom Donilon.[14]

But that was never a realistic option. First of all, the death of bin Laden was the most positive development in the war since 2001. For Americans, wars become personal, and bin Laden embodied the terrorist threat against the United States. Politics played a role as well. Given the deep partisan divide over practices put in place in the aftermath of September 11, particularly so-called enhanced interrogation techniques including waterboarding the Obama administration had terminated, former Bush administration officials were anxious to position their policies and decisions as part of a decade-long effort that finally achieved success.

Beyond that, in the two decades since the Gulf War, the relationship between government and the American media had changed significantly. While still adversarial, the level of mutual understanding among journalists who specialized in national security coverage and the military, intelligence, and security agencies had deepened considerably. Media elites with years of experience covering the security beat—journalists with large contact lists and significant public profiles—knew where critical details resided within government and tapped into those sources for information.

Many within government recognized that a critical dimension of modern conflict involved information warfare. Perceptions on the modern battlefield are important, particular when the opposing force is less interested in holding territory than influencing policy.

Bin Laden's death was a big win, although it came with a very significant cost with America's putative ally, Pakistan.

The White House tried to paper over the matter by portraying the operation as "joint," highlighting the fact that information provided by the Pakistani government helped lead U.S. intelligence agencies to Abbottabad. But the cover story didn't hold.

In Washington, officials acknowledged that the Pakistanis were deliberately kept in the dark. In Islamabad, as a public furor developed over the military's failure to detect the SEAL raid, the United States was criticized for violating Pakistani sovereignty. In February 2012, Pakistan razed the bin Laden compound in Abbottabad. It had no interest in a tourist attraction that the nation considered a humiliation.

To the Islamic world more broadly, the U.S. government's communications were well crafted and effective. The administration consulted with Saudi Arabia and other Muslim authorities regarding burial plans, demonstrating respect for Islamic practices.

Utilizing information collected from the compound in Abbottabad, the U.S. government portrayed bin Laden as an isolated figure trying to manage a fractious movement that had lost favor within the Islamic world. Bin Laden himself recognized how the excessive violence perpetrated in Iraq in particular had damaged the al Qaeda brand.

Given bin Laden's demise, the Obama administration suggested that core al Qaeda was now "on a path to defeat," a premature assessment, based on subsequent developments. However, al Qaeda was far less capable of perpetrating another spectacular and complex attack on the American homeland as it did on September 11. The White House did recognize that various al Qaeda franchises and sympathizers had emerged in several countries—Yemen, Somalia, Nigeria, Libya, Mali, and others—and would pose a danger to American citizens and interests for years. Here there were positive developments as well. Anwar al-Awlaki was successfully targeted (although his son, also an American, was killed in a separate drone strike). The cooperation with the new Yemeni government was viewed as a regional model. Al Shabaab was losing ground to a nascent government supported by the U.S. and African Union. The French had decisively interceded in Mali.

The administration's optimism was rooted not just in its operational successes, but also in its belief the Arab Spring undermined the bin Laden narrative that change could only be achieved through violence.[15] A compelling video released by the State Department featured the reclusive al Qaeda leader huddled in front of a television, a sharp contrast to the vibrant political demonstrations under way in places like Tahrir Square.

As campaign season began in 2012, Vice President Joe Biden developed a powerfully simple summation of Obama's reelection platform. "If you are looking for a bumper sticker to sum up how President Obama has handled what we inherited," Biden told an audience in New York, "it's pretty simple: Osama bin Laden is dead and General Motors is alive."[16] But the evolving conflict—or more accurately conflicts—in the Middle East was anything but simple.

Awlaki had introduced to the al Qaeda movement the potential for remote radicalization—individuals could be inspired and activated without traveling or receiving any meaningful support. Nidal Hasan, encouraged by Awlaki to attack his fellow soldiers at Fort Hood, was an early example.

As U.S. forces were pulling back into main operating bases as Iraq took over its own security, al Qaeda and its erstwhile franchise were gradually getting back on their feet. Even as the Obama administration continued to celebrate bin Laden's death, Ayman al-Zawahiri, his successor, was engineering a jihadi surge in Syria that would transform the regional landscape and force dramatic U-turns in the American security policy, strategic narrative, and political expectations. Zawahiri directed AQI to organize a presence in Syria, taking advantage of the established network that had funneled fighters into Iraq. Assad's government looked the other way. Al Qaeda's presence reinforced Syria's narrative that its political opposition were terrorists.[17]

Al Qaeda was not headed for strategic defeat. In fact, as the Syrian crisis deepened, its affiliate, Jabhat al-Nusra, would become one of the most effective combatants among the complex array of opposition forces. But an internal dispute over strategic ends would fundamentally change the nature of the war the United States thought it was waging.

The war might end at some point, but not during the two terms of the Obama administration. The jihadi threat would persist indefinitely. Realistic solutions would not be measured in months or years, but would be the challenge of a generation.

NEW CHAPTER

In a 2006 speech to the Chicago Council on Foreign Affairs, then Senator Obama said that a key goal for Iraq must be "preventing Iraq from becoming what Afghanistan once was."[18]

Obama suggested greater engagement across the Middle East, including with Syria and Iran, to try to increase the regional stake in Iraq's stable development and to avoid a security vacuum "filled with chaos, terrorism, refugees, and violence, as it could have a destabilizing effect throughout the entire region."[19]

Viewing Iraq as a diversion that, like Vietnam, undermined U.S. national security, Obama believed that responsibly ending the war—or at least the American involvement in it—would "strengthen American leadership around the world."[20]

Obama's slogan was not just about politics. Reducing the cost of America's wars was fundamental to repairing the U.S. economy. With America bogged down in Iraq and Afghanistan, China was expanding its regional and global reach. Not only did it have the world's fastest-growing economy and a significant balance of trade advantage, clear majorities around the world viewed China as a rising power and America as a declining one.

The moves were seen as addition by subtraction, improving American security posture in the process. In a floor statement in the Senate in 2007, he labeled Iraq "somebody else's civil war," a theme as president he would emphasize regarding Syria.[21] The presence of U.S. forces in Iraq had certainly exacerbated the terrorist threat.

On the campaign trail, Obama expressed a desire to withdraw all troops from Iraq over a sixteen-month period. Even though he opposed the surge, as president, Obama benefited politically from its progress on the ground. In his first year in office, American casualties were reduced to 139, less than half the level of 2008. While it took longer to do, he ended the U.S. combat mission on his original timeline. A residual force remained behind to advise and assist Iraqi forces while negotiations proceeded on a follow-on presence.[22]

Subsequent criticism of Obama's decision to withdraw all forces from Iraq overlooked the fact that Iraq was sovereign. There was a genuine negotiation regarding a long-term presence, including a continual rotation of forces to Iraq that was similar to regional deployments conducted during the 1990s.[23]

Privately, many Iraqi leaders wanted U.S. forces to stay, but they were unwilling to make that case to an Iraqi public that was eager to see them leave. Given the long-standing friction between American forces and the Iraqi population, the 2007 incident in Nisour Square where Blackwater guards (one of whom was convicted later in a U.S. court of murder) killed seventeen Iraqis being emblematic, Baghdad was not going to give the Americans the legal immunity it received in other countries.[24]

As the negotiation over a new status of forces agreement reached an impasse, Iraq seemed stable. "We were victims of our own success," James Jeffrey, the U.S. ambassador to Iraq, recalled later.[25] During the first term, Afghanistan was of far greater concern than Iraq.

In the end, politics on both sides of the equation pushed for a clean break. A follow-on force was "not in the cards," according to General John Abizaid, former commander of Central Command.[26] The Iraqis wanted their country back, while the U.S. withdrawal would ameliorate al Qaeda's narrative regarding a war with Islam and the occupation of sacred Muslim lands by a foreign power.

"After nearly nine years," Obama said in remarks in the White House briefing room in late October, "America's war in Iraq will be over."[27] His announcement coincided with the death of Libyan leader Muammar Qaddafi. Obama believed that the Iraqi and Libyan people were now free to forge their own future.

Referring to Iraqi Prime Minister Nouri al-Maliki, Obama indicated that "We are in full agreement about how to move forward" to build "an Iraq that is stable, secure and self-reliant."[28]

President Obama met with Maliki at the White House right before the last U.S. forces departed Iraq in December 2011 to mark a "new chapter" in relations between the United States and Iraq. The president suggested Maliki "leads Iraq's most inclusive government yet."[29] Hyperbole (and wishful thinking) always play a role in diplomacy, but the president's comments overlooked the 2010 Iraqi election. Ayad Allawi's Iraqiyya Party, with the most pluralistic slate of candidates, actually won more parliamentary seats, but Maliki outmaneuvered him to retain control of the government.[30] The United States explored the idea of a national unity government, but it didn't take.

For his part the Iraqi prime minister talked specifically about "the dangers of a sectarian war in Iraq, in Syria, and in the region, because it will be like a snowball in that it will expand and it will be difficult to control it."[31] But without Washington as the honest broker, Maliki no longer felt he needed to act inclusively. The Shia-led Iraqi government neglected the political gains achieved through the surge in Sunni areas. Iran's influence grew without an American counterweight.[32]

Within days, Maliki moved to consolidate his position. He issued an arrest warrant for Iraq's vice president and a Sunni political rival, Tariq al-Hashemi. Maliki refused to appoint Sunnis to high-level positions, instead assuming the critical roles of minister of interior and defense. The performance of Iraqi security forces steadily declined.

AGE OF PERSISTENT CONFLICT

In a thoughtful speech to the Oxford Union shortly before leaving the Department of Defense in late 2012, General Counsel (and later Secretary of Homeland Security) Jeh Johnson discussed the struggle against violent extremism and how the war against al Qaeda, the Taliban, and associated forces might end.

Johnson projected a future tipping point where al Qaeda no longer possessed the capability to "launch a strategic attack against the United States." At that point the organization would be "effectively destroyed." The residual threat would involve individuals, organizational remnants, or other unaffiliated groups that could be confronted below the level of "armed conflict."[33] This would involve effective intelligence gathering, vigilant law enforcement, cooperation with global counterterrorism partners, and covert operations as opposed to sustained military campaigns.

Johnson's speech at Oxford reflected the administration's aspirations for a second term. The president had withdrawn all troops from Iraq and had charted out a similar game plan for Afghanistan. Regarding the war against al Qaeda, while there was still a residual threat—a number of plots had been thwarted through improved capability and luck—the president anticipated a crossover point that would mark the end of the state of emergency that America declared after September 11.

Ever the constitutional lawyer, Obama was focused on the heightened powers that had steadily flowed to the executive branch over the previous decade—the ability to wage war, order the use of lethal force based on a legal process but not due process, and collect and hold vast stores of information under legal authorities constructed in a different age and intended for a different purpose. He thought it was important to identify the circumstances under which the balance of powers across institutions of government, the essential give and take of a functioning democracy, would be restored.

In a speech at National Defense University in May 2013, Obama sounded a similar theme, vowing to "fight terrorism without keeping America on a perpetual wartime footing." In the interest of democracy, Obama said, "this war, like all wars, must end."[34]

Obama also believed that, while terrorism would continue to be the most immediate security challenge confronting America for the foreseeable future, it should not be the central organizing principle of American foreign policy.

The president was mindful of the ongoing threat posed by al Qaeda affiliates, especially al Qaeda in the Arabian Peninsula. AQAP hatched the underwear bomber and print cartridge plots in 2009 and 2010, attempting creative means to evade security improvements introduced within transportation systems in the United States and abroad. While lethal, they were focused on less spectacular but more frequent attacks. As the government closely monitored the growing crisis in Syria, there was concern about Westerners who might be drawn to the conflict, develop military on that battlefield, and then return home.

Obama viewed the future of terrorism—rightly—as involving alienated and radicalized homegrown individuals with loose affiliations with or inspired by terrorist networks. Their motivations were more local and less global. They could do damage, but the threat was far different from what the country experienced in 2001. The Tsarnaev brothers who perpetrated the Boston Marathon bombings fit that profile perfectly.

Obama said it was important "to define the nature and scope of this struggle, or else it will define us." He rejected the concept of a "boundless" global war on terror. Obama was clear that he could not promise "the total defeat of terror," but he was increasingly confident it could be managed primarily through targeted U.S. action combined with more effective international partnerships.

The dramatic raid that eliminated bin Laden "cannot be the norm." It was successful, but carried high strategic costs in Pakistan and across the Islamic world. He was mindful that counterterrorism operations, including drone strikes and the civilian casualties that inevitably come with them, risked creating more enemies, but viewed them as more politically sustainable.

With bin Laden dead and al Qaeda on the defensive, Obama publicly suggested Congress revise the authorization for the use of military force (AUMF), the declaration of war that Congress passed in the immediate aftermath of the September 11 attacks.

Even as Obama spoke, the ground was changing. Tom Friedman of the *New York Times* described the Arab uprisings as "a hurricane going through a trailer park." It was no surprise where the storm had the greatest impact—Iraq, Syria, Yemen, Libya, Somalia, and Mali. "The countries that are being hammered first are the artificial ones, those whose borders are straight lines."[35]

The United States wanted to see political, social, and economic reform in the region and the development of new government structures more responsive to the desires of their people and able to generate greater opportunity for populations that were predominantly young, educated, and frustrated. Initially caught by surprise, the autocratic regimes launched counterrevolutions. These fissures provided fertile ground for extremist actors.

Obama enunciated the right goal—at some point, the war does need to end. But the administration narratives regarding al Qaeda's strategic defeat and the receding tide of war were premature, rooted in a misreading of the Arab uprisings and their impact on the threat of violent political extremism to the United States and its allies.

As Derek Chollet noted in *The Long Game*, there were "two eras of Obama's foreign policy: before 2011, and after."[36] The administration was slow to adapt its policies and narratives.

Notwithstanding a desire to pivot to other parts of the world where greater U.S. attention would yield more favorable returns on investment, Obama was wrong to believe that the Middle East would stabilize if the United States simply got out of the way. The White House belatedly recognized that American security remained linked to the intensifying regional conflicts and would require continued political and military involvement.

Obama told soldiers at Fort Bragg on December 14, 2011, as he commemorated the removal of the last U.S. troops from Iraq, that "It's harder to end a war than begin one."[37] Only later would it become clear how true that statement was.

8

THE PIVOT

In mid–October 2011, Secretary of State Hillary Clinton released a detailed review of the administration's regional policy, objectives, and expectations for the next decade. Published in *Foreign Policy* magazine under the title "America's Pacific Century," Clinton suggested that "the United States stands at a pivot point."[1]

Clinton's article both introduced the emerging U.S. strategy regarding Asia and previewed an upcoming presidential trip to the region the following month. The pivot—some within the administration preferred the term "rebalance"—made perfect sense. As Kurt Campbell, one of its key architects, suggested, "the lion's share of the history of the twenty-first century will be written in the Asia-Pacific region." If the Middle East represents an "arc of instability," Campbell sees a region that includes rising powers such as China, India, and Indonesia in addition to American allies such as Australia, Japan, New Zealand, South Korea, Thailand, and the Philippines as an "arc of ascendance."[2]

The region is bound to play a major role in the evolution of most issues of national and global significance—the economy, energy, education, public health, poverty, climate, and security. While political and economic reforms stalled in the Middle East, they continued to progress in a country like Indonesia, no stranger to violent extremism yet able to demonstrate that democracy, a market economy, and a tolerant version of Islam can coexist.

"The Asia-Pacific has become a key driver of global politics," Clinton wrote in *Foreign Policy*. "Just as Asia is critical to America's future, an engaged America is vital to Asia's future."[3]

Obama frequently talked about the need for nation building at home, but a key corollary was the belief that the long-term health of the U.S. economy depended on peace and stability in the Asia-Pacific. The region already produced a quarter of the world's GDP and was expected to generate a significant share of global growth in the immediate future. More and more American jobs were linked to the region—Clinton touted the importance of "commercial diplomacy" as she tried to build a stronger political constituency for the Department of State.

Not only had a new free trade agreement with Korea entered into force in 2012, but the Obama administration hoped to complete a Trans-Pacific Partnership (TPP) agreement among twelve Pacific Rim countries as one of the signature achievements of its second term. Clinton would promote TPP while secretary of state, but later criticize the final product as a candidate for president.

By 2011, many elements of the rebalance were already in place. Given Obama's strong identification with the region, having grown up in Hawaii and spent considerable time in Indonesia, he was America's first Pacific president.[4] The first head of government he welcomed at the White House was the prime minister of Japan. Clinton, breaking with diplomatic tradition, made her first official trip as secretary of state to the region. Her stop in Beijing would underscore both the regional and global importance of the U.S.-China relationship, and its complexity.

While Iran had captured much of the attention regarding Obama's pledge to engage with global adversaries and antagonists, its first success was Burma (also known as Myanmar). There was far less success regarding North Korea, which continued to confound the Obama administration just as it had the Bush administration. But significant regional coordination continued through the so-called Six-Party Process, taking on greater urgency with the leadership succession of Kim Jong-un, who in 2012 became the world's youngest head of state, least experienced, and progressively most unpredictable.

The U.S. military maintained significant capabilities in Japan, South Korea, and Guam that not only represented an important vanguard to deter the likes of North Korea, but also helped allies and friends cope with natural disasters, the most recent involving tsunamis that swamped Indonesia in 2004 and Japan in 2011. Both responses generated enormous regional goodwill.

During Obama's Asian trip in November 2011, in an address to the Australian parliament in Canberra, Obama declared, "The United States is a Pacific power, and we are here to stay."[5] But the pivot quickly ran into a geopolitical problem of perception.

Obama announced plans to station a small Marine contingent in Australia, part of a series of initiatives, but the one that gained disproportionate attention. China viewed it as part of a regional containment plan. And if the Asia-Pacific was now the "in" region, the term suggested some other part of the world must be on its way out.

Europe was concerned that it no longer occupied the importance it once did—the focus of the U.S.-European relationship had shifted significantly toward global economics, not only because of the lingering effects of the global recession but also because there was not an active conflict, although that would soon change with the crisis in Ukraine.

In fact, the White House was consciously moving away from the Middle East, which had been a preoccupation for a quarter century. Given the president's intention to withdraw forces from Iraq by the end of the year, he was interested in reinvesting more diplomatic, economic, and military resources elsewhere in what was anticipated to be a new post-Iraq era. The Asia-Pacific region was where the White House felt it could have the greatest impact and achieve a significant return on investment.

The administration made no secret of its intentions. "It was the President's judgment that we were over-weighted in some areas and regions, including our military actions in the Middle East. At the same time, we were underweighted in other regions, such as the Asia-Pacific. Indeed, we believed this was our key geographic imbalance," National Security Advisor Tom Donilon told The Asia Society candidly.[6] But the Middle East would continue to have its say.

A key goal of the pivot was to establish a better context for the complex relationship between the United States and China. It was not to pursue a "China first" approach to the region, but rather to imbed relations with a rising China within the emerging U.S. Asia-Pacific strategy.[7]

A VITAL RELATIONSHIP, BUT WHAT TO CALL IT?

While seeking to reenergize its engagement with the Asia-Pacific region, the United States and China constitute arguably the most consequential bilateral relationship in the world today. Its character will profoundly influence future regional and global affairs.

"If China develops well, it will benefit the whole world and benefit the United States," Chinese President Xi Jinping said during a visit to the White

House in 2015. "If the U.S. develops well, it will also benefit the world and China."[8]

It is not a G2. Notwithstanding Xi's call for a "new type of major-power relationship," there are too many divergent interests to call this a true partnership.[9] In fact, recent U.S. administrations have struggled to find the right label to describe it. China has its own historical narratives as well.

During the first quarter century following its strategic opening to the world, the emphasis was on gradually integrating China into the international system. As it became a more significant actor, China advanced the concept of a "peaceful rise," later adapted to the phrase "peaceful development" that was viewed as less threatening.[10]

At the same time, with the end of the Cold War, as Michael Mandelbaum suggested in *Mission Failure*, "The main focus of American foreign policy shifted from war to governance," particularly what countries did within their own borders and how they treated their people.[11] China received a major share of attention.

Long before Tahrir Square, there was Tiananmen Square, where an estimated one million people demonstrated in support of students advocating a reform agenda. The protest overlapped with a visit to Beijing by Soviet leader Mikhail Gorbachev, whose economic and political reforms (glasnost and perestroika) were already generating remarkable ripple effects across eastern Europe. Within months, Gorbachev would lose control of his own reform initiative, leading to the end of the Soviet Union.

When the Chinese military moved to disperse the demonstrators in Tiananmen Square in early June 1989, they crushed a large, thirty-foot Styrofoam statue, The Goddess of Liberty, that had served as a centerpiece for the pro-democracy movement. The iconic photo on June 5 of an unidentified man standing in front of a column of tanks—Tank Man as he is colloquially known—dramatically altered global perceptions of China and had a profound impact on U.S. foreign policy and the politics surrounding it.

The realist George H. W. Bush, who had served as U.S. ambassador to China, imposed sanctions immediately after the crackdown, but secretly dispatched his national security advisor, Brent Scowcroft, to maintain a diplomatic channel with Beijing to help them understand the American response. The move was criticized at home, another example where presidents found it difficult to balance the geopolitics and domestic politics of the U.S.-China relationship.[12]

Bill Clinton, during the 1992 campaign, would accuse Bush of "indifference to democracy" and having "coddled the dictators."[13] But as president, he encouraged China's integration in the global system, hoping that its human rights record would improve as a result. While U.S. officials believed that economic growth would promote political reform, the Chinese believed the opposite—that greater prosperity would strengthen their power.[14]

The Clinton administration extended most favored nation status on China and supported its entry into the World Trade Organization (WTO). Both steps dramatically increased the level of trade and investment between the two countries. In the process, China achieved historic levels of economic growth. In his speech accepting the Republican presidential nomination, Donald Trump termed China's entry into the WTO as a mistake, even though for a quarter century integration was a key pillar of U.S. policy supported by both parties.

In 2001, Goldman Sachs first coined the term BRIC to signify the increased importance of emerging economic powers and markets, particularly Brazil, Russia, India, and China; South Africa would be added later.

China presented an unprecedented economic model—a "unique hybrid" with an authoritarian government, yet committed to building a market economy; an emerging economic power and a developing country at the same time, one that lifted billions out of poverty, yet simultaneously became the leading producer of greenhouse gases.[15]

While the Clinton administration described China as a strategic partner, the question arose whether it would take on greater global responsibility. The problem, notes Henry Kissinger in *World Order*, is that "China has no precedent for the role it is asked to play."[16] While China is prepared to cooperate out of its own sense of self-interest, it struggled with the idea of a global good.

The George W. Bush administration, focused initially on big power relations, preferred to view China as a strategic competitor. In fact, there have long been areas where the two countries cooperate and others where they compete. But given China's sheer size and growing international heft, there will always be friction.

In its first weeks, the Bush White House was forced to deal with the aftermath of a collision between a Chinese fighter and a U.S. surveillance aircraft near Hainan Island. The American EP-3 made an emergency landing, with its crew detained until President Bush and Secretary of State Colin Powell resolved the incident with an artfully worded statement that expressed sorrow over the death of the Chinese pilot. It satisfied the Chinese demand for an apology without actually using that word.

With the Bush administration increasingly absorbed by the wars in Afghanistan and Iraq, China worked deliberately to strengthen its posture in the region. It launched a "charm offensive," supporting the region economically in the aftermath of the Asian financial crisis and improving relations with its neighbors. According to Doug Paal of the Carnegie Endowment for International Peace, one clear motivator for China's better behavior was its hopes for a successful Summer Olympics in 2008.[17]

In 2005, Deputy Secretary of State Robert Zoellick encouraged China to become a "responsible stakeholder" in the international system, inferring that a rising China benefits from a stable economic and political order, can play a greater role in setting the rules, but also shares the costs and responsibilities that come with it.

China has its own competing narratives, historically the Middle Kingdom and a global power, but one that was unjustly occupied during what it considered a century of humiliation. In the aftermath of World War II, China evolved into a revolutionary society under Mao that preferred to focus on domestic priorities, yet also felt wrongly isolated by the political imperatives of the Cold War. Even as it began to benefit from the system and exhibit historic levels of economic growth, China still considered the international system as unfair.

With the end of the Cold War, China adapted its ruling narrative to undoing its legacy of humiliation.[18] The "great renewal of the Chinese nation," as President Xi suggested in 2012, has involved restoring Chinese sovereignty over territories that were once ruled by China.

This has included the reunification of China and Hong Kong under the concept of "one country, two systems" and its preoccupation with the status of Taiwan, a recurrent source of friction with the United States, particularly with respect to arms sales, which China considers a relic from the Cold War.

Nationalism has become a crucial political factor upon which the Chinese Communist Party derives its legitimacy.[19] As Chinese and American leaders learned with not only the P-3 incident but also the accidental bombing of the Chinese Embassy in Belgrade during the Kosovo conflict in 1999, Chinese nationalistic sentiment once inflamed is difficult to put back in the bottle, even after the two governments committed to manage the crises. Just as American presidents struggled for decades with the politics surrounding the perceived loss of China, so too Chinese leaders are wary of the domestic implications of any perceived sign of weakness regarding Chinese rights and prerogatives.[20] The flash points that continue to accumulate within the U.S.-China relationship—Taiwan, competing territorial claims in the East and South China Seas, cyber attacks, and North Korea—all have the potential to escalate.

Even as China becomes more comfortable as an influential regional and global player, it still reflects contradictions and ambivalence about its international role—a staunch believer in state sovereignty and noninterference and yet a major source of cyber intrusions and the theft of intellectual property; a defender of freedom of navigation in the face of international piracy and yet an increasingly assertive regional power whose territorial claims compromise international understandings of freedom of navigation; the largest contributor to UN peacekeeping operations and the largest recipient of international financial assistance; skeptical of a global responsibility to address climate change but sensitive to how local environmental concerns impact perceptions of the government's legitimacy; and a beneficiary of stability on the Korean peninsula yet the primary benefactor of the leading regional disruptor, North Korea.

"More than anything, China wants to be prosperous, secure, respected, and left alone in its own geocultural orbit," suggests David Shambaugh of The George Washington University.[21] Over time, not unlike Russia, it sought to establish its own sphere of influence, a concept the United States views as an anachronism even with its own experience with the Monroe Doctrine.[22]

China's leaders and elites increasingly viewed China as a rising power and America, wrongly, as a declining one. But as it became more assertive in restoring its claim to regional predominance, it consistently overplayed its hand. Its territorial ambitions, blunt actions, and unwillingness to consider multilateral solutions to long-standing disputes worked to America's advantage. China's neighbors, fearing Beijing's resurgence, welcomed the American regional reengagement.

MANAGING COMPLEXITY

En route to her first visit to China as secretary of state, Hillary Clinton suggested in impromptu comments to the media that the administration would be realistic in its dealings with the Chinese leadership. She said that formulaic exchanges on issues such as Taiwan and human rights, areas where there is a clear agreement to disagree, did not prevent the United States and China from cooperating on areas of mutual interest, including the global economy or North Korea. Her response was interpreted by some as a deemphasis of human rights, which was not her intent and would not be her practice.★

★The secretary of state always travels with a contingent of journalists who cover the State Department and are steeped in international affairs. During most trips, the secretary will walk to the back of the plane where the media sit and provide broad perspective of U.S. regional interests and the issues expected to dominate upcoming diplomatic discussions. Whatever the secretary says is newsworthy. Media encounters are a vital tool of public

It was an unusual accusation. As First Lady, Hillary Clinton electrified the World Conference on Women in Beijing in 1995 when she said to the consternation of her hosts, "Human rights are women's rights and women's rights are human rights."[23] She would champion the right of global citizens to have access to the Internet and free flow of information without the state's heavy-handed censorship.

Three years later, in one of the most dramatic moments of her tenure, she authorized temporary shelter for human rights activist Chen Guangcheng at the U.S. Embassy in Beijing on the eve of the high-level Strategic and Economic Dialogue. Following blunt discussions with Chinese officials, she resolved a diplomatic standoff. Chen subsequently traveled to the United States, where he became a visiting scholar at New York University.

The incident underscored Clinton's intended point—the relationship between the United States and China will always experience points of friction, but requires focus on economic and regional security, human rights, and other issues simultaneously.

Asian nations place great emphasis on personal diplomacy—showing up is fundamental to success in this part of the world. Given the Bush administration's preoccupation with terrorism, the wars in Afghanistan and Iraq, and the global financial crisis, leaders from the president to his cabinet secretaries were perceived as dedicating less time in the region. Secretary of State Condoleezza Rice, for example, skipped the annual Association of Southeast Asian Nations (ASEAN) Regional Forum in two of her four years in office, which raised questions about U.S. security commitments to its key regional allies.

Clinton advocated "'forward-deployed' diplomacy"—a strong signal to regional partners of greater high-level face-to-face interaction in both multilateral and bilateral settings intended to strengthen existing security alliances; deepen engagement with emerging powers, not just China, but also India and Indonesia; increase involvement within regional organizations, particularly ASEAN and the East Asia Summit; expand trade and investment; and continue the commitment to democracy and human rights.

Obama's regional engagement was mirrored globally. His administration's embrace of the G20 (beyond the G8, which included just Japan) dramatically increased the representation of the Asia-Pacific region, adding Australia, Indonesia, Korea, China, and India to the list of major global political and economic stakeholders. The proposed Trans-Pacific Partnership includes not just Austra-

diplomacy and help to strengthen shared understanding of issues and generate public support for what the United States seeks to accomplish around the world.

lia and Japan, but also Brunei, Malaysia, New Zealand, Singapore, and Vietnam.

When Obama said during the 2008 presidential campaign that he would broaden U.S. engagement with allies and adversaries, Iran was the most dramatic story line. But Burma offered the greatest immediate potential.

Low-key diplomatic talks with Burmese officials had convinced U.S. officials that the Burmese generals who ruled the country were serious about political reform. They released Nobel Laureate Aung San Suu Kyi from house arrest, setting the stage for Clinton to visit Burma two months later and Obama three years after that.

The United States eventually restored full diplomatic relations. Burma held landmark elections in November 2015, with Suu Kyi and her National League for Democracy winning an outright parliamentary majority. In March 2016, Burma named Htin Kyaw as its president, since the existing Burmese constitution included restrictions (no blood relatives who are foreigners, such as Suu Kyi's two sons, who are British citizens) specifically written to deny her the office.

Suu Kyi was named Burma's foreign minister. More than one hundred former prisoners are now parliamentarians. The United States is helping the country consolidate its democratic gains, expand international exchanges, encourage trade, and even develop a military-to-military relationship.[24]

While the Obama administration believed that China had taken advantage of America's preoccupation in the Middle East, it nonetheless viewed Beijing as a "potential partner" in a mutually beneficial relationship that recognized China's legitimate interests but sought to move China to be a more responsible and constructive international player.[25]

The rebalance is still in its early stages, but much has been accomplished. In addition to the administration's historic opening to Burma, relations with India progressed in meaningful ways. The dramatic shift in China's position regarding climate change was significant, since sixteen of the twenty most polluted cities in the world are Chinese.

While the region interpreted the American policy as a classic "balance of power" move in light of China's rising economic and military capability, China viewed the rebalance as an attempt at containment.

BIG COUNTRY

Hillary Clinton once characterized the U.S.-China relationship as "a balance between cooperation and competition."[26] That rightly characterized the friction around unresolved territorial disputes involving China and several of its neighbors. These competing claims to islands and rock piles have important implications regarding freedom of navigation and mineral rights.

At the ASEAN meeting in July 2010, Clinton, while not taking sides on China's territorial disputes with its neighbors, made clear that the United States viewed freedom of navigation as an American core interest. Disputes should be resolved peacefully, without any threat of force, enabling commerce to continue unimpeded.[27] The American position favored international arbitration; China preferred bilateral negotiations.

Stunned that Clinton raised the issue in such a forum, Foreign Minister Yang Jiechi angrily lectured his regional counterparts that China was a "big country," in essence challenging them whether lining up with the United States would serve their long-term interests. Nonetheless, her brief comments "put Beijing on notice that Washington would not accept its unilateral definition of a sphere of influence," summarized James Traub.[28]

"China's policies had actually made the United States more welcome in the region," recalls Jeffrey Bader, who oversaw Asia policy on the White House national security staff.[29]

The United States has repeatedly reinforced its position. When China unilaterally declared an air defense identification zone in the East China Sea in November 2013, likely a response to Japan's nationalization of the disputed Senkaku Islands (the Chinese call them the Diaoyu and contest the present Japanese administration over them), the United States flew a B-52 bomber through the zone without notice to drive home the point that the East China Sea remained international waters.

Likewise, as China constructed a series of man-made islands in the South China Sea and claimed twelve-mile territorial waters around them, the United States sent ships and aircraft through the area. China protested the action, but did not interfere.

Regional fears are that artificial islands on some combination of the Scarborough Shoal (which the Philippines claims) and the Spratly and Paracel chains would enable China to project its growing military power and greatly influence future regional economic development.[30]

While China claimed that America's defense of freedom of navigation is an attempt to militarize the South China Sea—the diplomatic equivalent of the pot calling the kettle black—the next president confronts a difficult policy and political choice whether to up the ante if China continues to expand its reclamation project. "Do we really want to draw a red line here?" asks Bonnie

Glaser of the Center for Strategic and International Studies. "And what would the U.S. do if China simply went ahead anyway?"[31]

President Xi is arguably the most powerful Chinese leader since Deng, but remains alert to threats from within. His anticorruption campaign is a significant response to the gap between the haves and have nots that has emerged in China. Corruption risks undermine the legitimacy of the national government.

The crackdown on most forms of dissent has raised international concerns about China's trajectory and its commitment to the rule of law. "Xi is overextended," suggests one former Obama administration official. The dynamic elevates the potential that Beijing will overreact in response to a future crisis.

"With the collapse of Communist identity, China's legitimacy has been built on the twin foundations of economic growth and nationalist ideology," Campbell wrote in *The Pivot*. Should China's economy slow, "the party is likely to lean more heavily on nationalism."[32]

CHINA'S PLACE IN THE
INTERNATIONAL SYSTEM

Beginning with the Bush administration and continuing with Obama, given that China now has a seat at the leadership table, the question becomes what kind of role does China envision for itself, what is it prepared to contribute, and will it abide by the accepted rules of the international system?[33]

"China does not see itself as rising," suggested Henry Kissinger in 2012, "but a returning power."[34] It has invested heavily in national marketing—promoting brand China through its investment in international broadcasting, the promotion of Chinese language and culture, education exchanges, and hosting major international extravaganzas such as the Olympics and World Expo. But its return on investment has been modest.

China may well also see itself as surpassing the United States, but this does not mean it wants to replace the United States—in truth, it does not see itself as indispensable on the global stage; it does not want that responsibility. It is uncomfortable in the global spotlight, particularly involving issues that are not core interests.

For example, China was dismayed by Russia's annexation of Crimea, given its strong belief in state sovereignty. But it nonetheless refrained from public criticism during the Ukraine crisis. China looks dispassionately at tragedies like Syria for which it has an important but narrow direct interest, access to energy resources in the Middle East.[35]

China uncharacteristically voted in favor of a UN resolution that referred Libya to the International Criminal Court in light of Qaddafi's threatened use of force against his own people. China was greatly influenced by the views of the Arab League and African Union, but did not want the vote to be seen as a precedent. It abstained during the vote on a follow-on resolution regarding the use of force to protect the Libyan people.

"For principled reasons, Beijing does not like internationally sponsored regime change," wrote Thomas Christensen in *The China Challenge*. "For practical reasons, Beijing worries with some justification that the United States and its allies are much better at breaking regimes than they are at replacing them with stable governments."[36]

The United States and China have fundamentally different views regarding global norms such as human rights, the transparent management of markets and currencies, intellectual property rights, and freedom of navigation. These contradictions are unlikely to disappear over time, ensuring high degrees of complexity that will require careful management and strategic patience.

How each country perceives the other matters profoundly: for example, whether China views American power as ascending or in decline; how China defines its core interests; and the extent to which they conflict with America's regional strategy. In turn, while the United States has supported China's rise up until now, will Washington continue to view Beijing as an emerging stakeholder in the international system or a free rider?

Former Deputy Secretary of State James Steinberg and Brookings scholar Michael O'Hanlon stress the importance of "strategic reassurance and strategic resolve" where both countries need to be clear and transparent regarding competing interests, intentions, and red lines.[37]

Notwithstanding its lengthy efforts to integrate China into the global economy, recent actions such as the TPP (which currently excludes China), congressional hesitance to expand China's voting power within the International Monetary Fund, and the curious decision by the Obama administration not to join the Asian Infrastructure Investment Bank (unsuccessfully discouraging others not to join the Chinese-sponsored initiative) seem inconsistent with the longstanding U.S. strategic policy and narrative.[38]

On China's side of the ledger, notwithstanding its assurances that it is not militarizing the South China Sea despite the construction of artificial islands, China has the opportunity to provide strategic reassurance with its response to the clear ruling by an international arbitration panel in The Hague that

Beijing's maritime sovereignty claims are excessive.[39] China claims to have the backing of sixty countries—undoubtedly with the promise of increased aid—who claim to oppose such international arbitration, advancing a narrative that frames the issue as part of the divide between the developed and developing world. How it responds will impact whether the world continues to see China as an ascending or revisionist power.[40]

Its initial response, sharp rhetoric and a public pledge to ignore the ruling, was not encouraging.

International perceptions of China's rise will also be shaped by how it responds to its own inevitable economic challenges such as slowing growth, unprecedented domestic market volatility, and the overdue need to restructure state-owned enterprises. "There is no playbook for rebooting a slowing $10 trillion hybrid economy still in a tug of war between state control and markets," suggests former Treasury Secretary Henry Paulson.[41]

According to Shambaugh, China is already a global *actor*, but only a "partial power." Where the United States enjoys a large global web of formal alliances and strategic partnerships, China only has comparable relationships with North Korea and Pakistan, both of which generate far more complications and costs for Beijing than benefits. Beyond its remarkable economic performance, it has little soft power. It is "a lonely power, lacking close friends and possessing no allies."[42]

Similarly, China currently lacks what Thomas Christensen calls "comprehensive national power," even though it now carries more than enough international heft to frustrate U.S. policies that directly or indirectly threaten Chinese interests or strongly held views of how the international system should and should not function.[43] China's strength at the moment is far more about preventing things from happening that it opposes than making things happen that it favors.

"China has an interest in the stability of the current international system," suggests Christensen, a China policy expert during the Bush administration, "but that does not easily translate into China helping to pay the costs to maintain that system."[44]

For example, Europe hoped China would help the continent deal with its financial crisis, particularly Greece. But it was never likely that China was going to help bail out a country whose economic troubles stemmed significantly from an overly generous social safety net that was far superior to China's. That was never going to be easy for Chinese leaders to explain to their population without significant political risk.

Beijing has been wary of taking actions that jeopardize short-term economic performance and job creation in the service of long-term benefits to the global commons, such as global warming. Only when China recognized both the potential economic benefits of developing green technology and the domestic political imperative to improving the country's air quality and environment did Beijing respond to international demands that China deal with rising emissions generated by its export-led economy.

CHINA POLICY AND POLITICS

Domestic politics regarding China have always been complex. "Liberal Democrats disliked the regime on human rights grounds," wrote John Meacham, while "conservative Republicans remained hostile to what had long been known as 'Red China.' "[45]

The 2016 election was no exception. Early in the campaign, Governor John Kasich of Ohio suggested, "I don't believe we need to make China an enemy. They are a competitor."[46] However, that view was overwhelmed by Trump.

His "Put America First" slogan a mix of protectionism and nativism, Trump built his appeal to conservative and working-class voters around the need to renegotiate commercial relations that he sees as skewed in China's favor. Promising better trade deals, he threatened to impose a 45 percent tariff on Chinese imports in order to address the $505 billion trade deficit, prevent the alleged dumping of goods on American markets, and pressure China to open up its markets to American companies.[47]

At the Republican convention, Trump pledged to pursue a fair trade policy that "protects our jobs and stands up to countries that cheat." He singled out China for its theft of intellectual property and currency manipulation.[48]

Interestingly, notwithstanding Trump's criticism, Beijing seemed to relish the prospect of a pragmatic relationship more focused on commercial interests and less on human rights.[49]

The nominees for both parties expressed doubts about the Trans-Pacific Partnership, despite its being the centerpiece of the Obama administration's pivot to Asia. Hillary Clinton had suggested while in government it would serve as the gold standard in terms of free, fair, and transparent trade with strong protections for workers and the environment. But she argued later that the final version fell short of what she hoped would be achieved, for example, that it did not address currency manipulation.

Trump, suggesting that the TTP would subject America to court rulings from foreign governments, a reality that already exists, vowed to pursue bilateral rather than multilateral trade agreements.[50]

Hoping to gain congressional approval of the TPP before leaving office, Obama addressed campaign criticism that trade worked against American interests, saying that integration is going to continue, "with or without the United States. We can lead that process, or we can sit on the sidelines and watch prosperity pass us by."[51]

In an op-ed in the *Washington Post*, Obama cast the TPP in terms of American leadership, that America should "call the shots" and "write the rules" that other countries not included in the agreement—read China—would have to play by.[52]

North Korea forced itself back onto the global stage and into the 2016 campaign with its claim (probably an exaggeration) that it had successfully tested a hydrogen weapon and a follow-up satellite launch that the United Nations condemned as a prohibited missile test.

While there were calls for more sanctions and placing North Korea back on the U.S. terrorist list (reversing the delisting that occurred during the Bush administration), Trump inferred that China has "tremendous control" over North Korea and would expect Beijing to solve its behavioral problem.[53]

Trump's characterization was exaggerated—Chinese officials are routinely surprised and distressed by the antics of the leaders of their client state and genuinely apprehensive about the impact of their support for North Korea on brand China. In early March 2016, Beijing joined the rest of the United Nations Security Council in voting in favor of tougher sanctions against North Korea.

While China is frustrated with Pyongyang's many provocations, it is unlikely to allow the economic pain to reach a level that jeopardizes the stability of the North Korean government.

The sudden collapse of the North Korean state would result in large numbers of North Koreans seeking to enter China, turbulence that Beijing wants to avoid. At the same time, a soft implosion that results in a prosperous, unified, and democratic Korean peninsula might threaten the legitimacy of the ruling party at home. Beijing also long benefited from the heroic narrative of the Korean war, protecting China and defending its neighbor from the American imperialists.[54]

Former Bush administration negotiator Victor Cha rightly characterized the relationship between China and North Korea as one involving "mutual hostages."[55]

Trump shocked many Asian leaders with his suggestion that Japan and South Korea develop their own nuclear capabilities. In an editorial, a leading South Korean newspaper was "dumbfounded" by the proposal, made largely on economic grounds with little regard for the strategic implications, rightly calling it "penny-wise and pound-foolish."[56]

Strangely, Trump's suggestion that he was willing to speak to North Korean leader Kim Jong-un and would consider withdrawing U.S. forces from the Korean Peninsula received a favorable review in Pyongyang. An editorial in the state outlet *DPRK Today* described Trump as a "wise politician" for taking a position—which it termed "Yankee, Go Home"—that mirrored North Korean policy.[57]

Obama finished his two terms believing that America's future lies far more significantly in the Asia-Pacific region. But he was never able to shift the strategic scales as decisively as he intended. The Middle East remained the most urgent challenge he faced. He was never able to escape its gravitational pull.

9

SOMEONE ELSE'S CIVIL WAR

In remarks to a graduating class of cadets at the U.S. Military Academy in May 2014, President Obama reflected on how much the strategic landscape had changed since he first went to West Point to announce his Afghanistan strategy in 2009.

Obama had withdrawn all American ground combat forces from Iraq, fulfilling his key strategic and political mandate coming into office. He had announced his intention to end the U.S. combat role in Afghanistan by the end of the year and turn responsibility for security of the country over to Afghan forces, supported by a yet-to-be-defined complement of counterterrorism and training forces.

As he would write later in his introduction to the 2015 National Security Strategy, "we have moved beyond the large ground wars in Iraq and Afghanistan that defined so much of American foreign policy over the past decade."[1]

Obama's policies presumed that the United States had achieved what it could in both countries at an acceptable and sustainable cost. What happened next was up to them.

In his West Point speech, he stressed the importance of American leadership. But reflecting on how America leads, Obama differentiated between internationalism—the unique power of the United States to organize and rally the world to solve a major global problem—and interventionism—setting off on military adventures without understanding its costs and risks and building international support and legitimacy.

"Tough talk often draws headlines," Obama said, "but war rarely conforms to slogans."[2]

Yes, but it was Obama who had talked tough about a red line in Syria, only to hesitate at the prospect of military strikes that would draw the United States more deeply into the conflict. His remarks were a reflection of hard lessons learned in Iraq, and relearned in Libya, and the continued struggle of how best to apply them in a still volatile region.

The landscape had indeed changed, but not in ways Obama yet fully understood.

ASSAD'S DAYS ARE NUMBERED

Bashar al-Assad confidently told a reporter from the *Wall Street Journal* in early 2011 that the Arab Spring would not visit Syria.[3] But a protest movement crystallized after images emerged of the brutalized body of a thirteen-year-old boy, Hamza Ali-al-Khateeb, who had written some graffiti about the Arab uprisings on a school building in Saida.

Assad clearly underestimated the changing dynamic within his country and the region: decades of political repression, economic stagnation, and now even climate change. An estimated one million farmers and herders had moved from the countryside to urban areas but lacked meaningful state support. They didn't provide the spark that started the revolution in Syria, but as Tom Friedman of the *New York Times* suggests, "they were ready to join when it did."[4]

American diplomats in Damascus encouraged the Assad regime to respond constructively to the largely peaceful movement, including scheduling new elections that would legitimize Assad's rule in light of the dramatic push for self-determination across the Middle East. The value of such conversations is why the Obama administration returned an ambassador to Syria. Assad would probably have won a free and fair election, but instead he confronted the protests with force.

U.S. Ambassador Robert Ford and his French counterpart visited Hama in a display of solidarity with the Syrian people. Meeting with opposition leaders, Ford was clear that while the United States identified with their cause, it would not send in the military. "After the Iraq war, the last thing we're going to do is send the military to Syria."[5]

Ford was right at the time, although the disintegration of Syria would eventually force a policy change. The Obama administration took a far more cautious approach to events in Syria than in Libya. Unlike Qaddafi, Assad commanded a far more capable military. Unlike Libya's opposition, the

National Transitional Council, Syria's emerging opposition struggled to establish itself as a viable alternative to the Assad government.

Ford's presence in Hama earned the enmity of the Syrian regime, which sent thugs to threaten both the U.S. and French embassies. Secretary of State Hillary Clinton complained publicly about the embassy assault and the failure of the government to protect diplomatic facilities, a fundamental host nation responsibility.

"President Assad is not indispensable," Clinton said, adding, "from our perspective, he has lost legitimacy," a charge Obama would repeat a month later.[6]

As the situation in Syria escalated, the Obama administration demanded that Assad lead a political transition or get out of the way. He did neither. When the president in August 2011 called on Assad to step down, his advisors were confident that Syria was at a tipping point. Assad's days are numbered became an administration talking point.

"Everyone thought nature was going to take care of it," a senior administration official believed.[7]

But having positioned itself on the right side of history, the White House struggled to fashion a coherent strategy behind Obama's declaration.

Looking at Syria, suggests Dennis Ross in retrospect, Obama saw Iraq and feared "entanglement in another ongoing Middle East conflict where our involvement would be costly, lead to nothing, and potentially make things worse."[8]

Ross believed the administration had overlearned the lessons of Iraq. Syria was different, "not an American invasion of a country but an internal uprising against an authoritarian leader."[9] However, Obama saw a potential quagmire.

According to former State Department envoy Fred Hof, who was trying to negotiate a peace agreement between Syria and Israel as the Arab Spring arrived in Damascus, "What the United States would *do* to try to influence Syria's direction never enjoyed the same policy priority as what the United States would *say*" (emphasis in the original).[10]

While there were many inconsistencies in the administration's approach to the Arab Spring, Obama steadily positioned the United States on the side of change, although the U.S. support did not necessarily mean the ability to influence the ultimate destination of these revolutions. Obama's call for a political transition in Syria mirrored his response in other countries that confronted major protests.

The president encouraged an immediate political transition in Egypt. His spokesman, Robert Gibbs, reinforced his words, saying "now means yesterday."[11]

In June 2011, the White House backed a political transition in Yemen after its longtime leader, Ali Abdullah Saleh, suffered serious injuries following violent protests and an assassination attempt. The president would identify Yemen's transition as a model even though his successor, Abd Rabbuh Mansur Hadi, was a political insider elevated through a single-candidate election. Hadi's government eventually collapsed when challenged by a rival Houthi faction backed by Saleh and supported by Iran.

The United States was far more muted regarding Bahrain, where the Shia majority population organized dramatic protests that were put down with the help of other Gulf states, especially Saudi Arabia. The government blew up Pearl Square, Bahrain's equivalent to Tahrir Square, to discourage further public protests. Washington did promote an independent commission of inquiry that it hoped would open the door for political reforms, but liberalization was stifled by the Sunni monarchy that feared Iran would take advantage.

The Obama administration declared that Qaddafi had lost his legitimacy by turning his security forces against his people. But if the Libyan people merited protection, then what about the Syrian people? By the time the president called for Assad's departure, more people had been killed in violence in Syria than in Libya.*

For an administration that placed great importance on international legitimacy, the lack of an authorizing resolution by the United Nations was crucial. Even with Obama's strong belief in the importance of American leadership, he viewed the responsibility to protect civilian populations from their governments as an international one.[12] The NATO intervention in Libya enforced a United Nations Security Council resolution.

But as Syria reached a crisis stage, Vladimir Putin had replaced Dmitri Medvedev as Russian president and Moscow's regional policy hardened. Where America saw potential democrats in the protest movements, Putin saw troublemakers or terrorists. He was uninterested in another color revolution that threatened Russian interests. Unlike Libya, there would be no international mandate for Syria.

---

*After leaving the State Department, I tweeted that Obama had established a "Qaddafi standard." If the Libyan leader had lost his legitimacy, so too had Assad. Critics later called Obama's public call for Assad's departure a mistake, given the absence of a follow-on implementing policy, but it was consistent with how most Americans view the U.S. role in the world. In hindsight, given the president's public declaration, the administration should have provided greater direct or indirect support to the Syrian opposition.

The Obama administration acknowledged the potential for Syria to become a regional "magnet for terrorism."[13] On January 24, 2012, a year after the start of the Arab Spring, al Qaeda declared its first franchise in Syria, Jabhat al-Nusra. A number of regional players quietly backed the jihadists as the conflict's most effective fighters.

At the same time, the Assad regime blatantly manipulated the conflict, turning a blind eye to the rise of the Islamic State as part of a deliberate strategy to divide the opposition, claim it was fighting terrorism, and justify its brutal suppression of the revolt. Russia along with Iran would become Assad's key international defenders.

While the Obama administration supported the moderate Syrian opposition, it hesitated to provide significant lethal assistance. The president would reject a CIA proposal, endorsed by Clinton and Secretary of Defense Leon Panetta, for an expanded train-and-equip program.[14]

"For Clinton, the goal was not to topple Assad but to force him to negotiate his departure," suggested James Traub. "Force was a tool of diplomacy."[15]

As Deputy National Security Advisor Ben Rhodes explained, "the president did not see where a more interventionist option led other than deeper involvement in an extraordinarily complex conflict that showed no signs of having a military solution."[16]

As its policy limped forward, Obama drew a red line around the use of chemical weapons. And then the Syrians crossed it.

PROCESS FAILURE

As the administration mulled its options in response to the chemical weapons attack that killed more than one thousand, most of them children, Secretary of State John Kerry believed the credibility of the United States was at stake.

"Will they remember that the Assad regime was stopped from those weapons' current or future use," Kerry asked, "or will they remember that the world stood aside and created impunity?"[17]

Kerry conveyed a sense of urgency. He did not believe the United States could afford to wait for the United Nations investigation that was unlikely to reveal more than was already known.[18] But the push seemed to resemble the Bush administration's rush to invade Iraq even as the UN searched for weapons of mass destruction.

Kerry acknowledged that the administration's response would be threading multiple policy needles, holding the Assad regime responsible for its transgression of international norms without assuming responsibility of Syria's civil war; and mounting a credible military response in the face of domestic opposition to direct involvement in another Middle Eastern conflict.

Obama, Kerry said, is "a President who does what he says that he will do."[19]

But behind the scenes, there was an ongoing internal debate regarding the legal authority to take action. Given the lack of a UN resolution, or even a NATO commitment as occurred with Kosovo, there was no clear international authority for what the White House contemplated—military action in response to an alleged war crime that had already occurred and thus did not represent the kind of imminent threat to civilian life as was the case in Libya.[20]

After the unexpected rejection by the British House of Commons, the last available option to enhance the legitimacy of military action was through Congress. As a candidate for president, Obama made clear that absent an imminent threat, he did not believe a president had the authority to order a military attack without congressional approval.[21] Now he confronted just such a scenario.

Obama's national security team was skeptical that Congress, sharply divided along partisan lines, was capable of acting decisively and favored a military strike based on the president's inherent authority as commander-in-chief.[22] A key holdout was Chief of Staff Denis McDonough, who did not believe the military action envisioned would make a significant difference on the ground.[23]

Obama and McDonough went for a walk on the White House grounds, arguably twenty-four hours too late. If the president doubted the emerging plan, he should not have authorized his secretary of state to make a compelling public call for action. If the president needed the support of Congress, he should have developed a realistic legislative strategy before announcing his decision.

Instead, when the commander-in-chief reached the podium in the Rose Garden, Obama put his finger on the trigger but asked an antagonistic Congress for permission to pull it. Despite being a leader that prized careful deliberation, the prospect of a vote was never discussed in detail with his leadership team.[24]

Obama allowed his foreign policy rhetoric to get too far ahead of domestic politics. For one of the only times in his presidency, he leaped beyond the policy and political boundaries constructed during the 2008 campaign. While Obama thought he had the votes, the last-minute shift in strategy and failure to gain a vote severely undermined the credibility of not just his Syria policy, but U.S. leadership in the region and beyond.

Obama eventually achieved an important result, with help from an unexpected source, but the policy and political process failure surrounding it would dog the Obama administration for the remainder of its term.

PUTIN TO THE RESCUE

Calling the chemical attack "an assault on human dignity" and "a serious danger to our national security," Obama announced that he had decided to take military action against Syria. The action would be "limited in duration and scope" but would "hold the Assad regime accountable for their use of chemical weapons, deter this kind of behavior, and degrade their capacity to carry it out."[25]

But while believing he already had the authority as commander-in-chief to act, Obama formally asked Congress to authorize a military response. Despite the urgency that Kerry had conveyed in his powerful indictment of the Assad regime, Obama awkwardly termed the situation "not time-sensitive." The matter was "too big for business as usual," but Obama chose to hold fire until Congress returned from its August recess.

Obama found himself back in the gray area that presidents have experienced since the end of the Cold War—where was the line where the exceptional nation, charged with enforcing international norms, became the world's policeman, the hyperpower acting beyond perceived international legitimacy and support?

Given the still fresh scars from Iraq, there was little appetite among members in both parties for intervention in Syria. Despite the construction of more gerrymandered congressional districts that left one party or the other with significant electoral advantages, incumbents have become increasingly leery of tough votes that might spark a public backlash or a primary challenge.

The White House believed there was sufficient support in Congress. But while the administration worked Capitol Hill, most members were still in their home districts and hearing from skeptical constituents. They began to retreat.

Obama invoked Rwanda, where the international community failed to act, and Kosovo, where it did despite paralysis within the UN Security Council. The analogies were problematic. Obama was not intervening to stop the slaughter in Syria, nor did he envision a sustained campaign to force Assad to retreat.

Kerry urged Congress to vote in favor of military action, saying "This is not the time to be spectators to slaughter."[26] He placed Assad in the company of Adolf Hitler and Saddam Hussein, two leaders who posed a sufficient threat to global security that the United States felt compelled to militarily remove them from power.

Despite these comparisons, Kerry admitted, "We're not going to war."[27] Instead, he described the challenge as holding Assad accountable through targeted strikes "without assuming responsibility for Syria's civil war."[28]

During a stop in Sweden en route to the G20 Summit, Obama attempted to redefine the red line as drawn when the international community outlawed the use of chemical weapons and Congress ratified the Chemical Weapons Convention. "I didn't set a red line; the world set a red line," the president suggested. "Congress set a red line when it ratified that treaty."[29]

During a thoughtful give-and-take with reporters at the conclusion of the G20 conference in St. Petersburg, the president emphasized that he sought the congressional debate expressly because Syria did not represent a direct threat to the United States. He acknowledged that "experience with the war in Iraq colors how people view this situation not just back home in America, but also here in Europe and around the world."[30]

For his part, Putin refused to acknowledge the Assad regime's responsibility for the atrocity. A majority of G20 leaders disagreed with him regarding the basic facts of the incident, but shared his concern about the danger of taking military action without an authorizing UN resolution. Putin reinforced this point publicly in a subsequent opinion piece in the *New York Times*.

Suggesting there are no "champions of democracy in Syria," Putin pointed directly to the chaos that followed interventions in Iraq and Libya and encouraged Americans to "ask why their government would want to repeat recent mistakes."[31]

An offhanded comment by Kerry following a meeting in London led to a Russian initiative and an international agreement that Syria would join the Chemical Weapons Convention and destroy its chemical weapons stocks as an alternative to a military strike.

As part of the Nunn–Lugar nonproliferation dialogue between U.S. and Russian officials through the years, representatives from both countries had done some joint planning on just such a scenario. After Obama hesitated in the Rose Garden, Israel encouraged Moscow to force Syria to give up its weapons as the best achievable outcome. While effectively neutralizing a critical Israeli security vulnerability, senior Israeli officials nonetheless considered the episode a "disaster." As one suggested after the fact, "America cannot draw a line and then pull back."[32]

The problem wasn't that the president drew the red line, but that the administration did insufficient planning regarding what would happen if or when it was crossed.

"They were making it up as they went along," said one former Obama administration official. "Instead of an opportunity for coercive diplomacy, they backed into a resolution and got no credit."[33]

In the months leading up to the crisis, the administration spent considerable time reviewing military options for attacking Syria's chemical sites, but it wasn't until Kerry's ad-libbed comment that diplomacy took center stage. At the time of the Syria crisis, secret talks with Iran suggested the potential for a breakthrough that would enable long-sought international negotiations regarding Iran's nuclear program. The Iranians suggested that a strike against Assad, their most important regional ally, would be considered an act of war that would kill the prospect of nuclear talks, Obama's top regional priority.[34]

Even with these conflicting priorities, had the Obama administration from the outset linked the demand that Syria give up its chemical weapons or face military action, it could have achieved an impressive triple play: eliminated a compelling threat to Israel's security, preserved the prospect of negotiations with Iran, and enhanced the credibility of American power.

"President Obama vacillated, first indicating that he was prepared to order some strikes, then retreating and agreeing to submit the matter to Congress. The latter was, as he well knew, an almost certain way to scotch any action," reflected Leon Panetta later. "The result was a blow to American credibility."[35]

Saudi Arabia's foreign minister, Prince Saud al-Faisal, pointedly criticized the Security Council for "reducing the Syrian crisis to merely destroying chemical weapons" while failing to solve "one of the greatest humanitarian disasters of our time."[36] Protesting the lack of major-power action, the Kingdom took the unprecedented step of declining to accept the region's rotating seat on the Security Council.

Allies in Europe and Asia, protected by U.S. treaty commitments, also took note.

"I don't think we should remove another dictator with force—we learned from Iraq that doing so makes us responsible for all that comes next," Obama said on September 10 as he asked Congress to postpone a vote he was almost certain to lose while the Security Council finished the details of the agreement to eliminate Syria's chemical weapons.[37]

It was a lesson that Obama learned in Libya and applied in Syria. Obama feared that initiating military action would create pressure to assume a greater role and eventually remove Assad by force. Drawing upon his inner Powell, Obama was concerned about taking small steps that would not be successful and create a dynamic that would make it hard to leave. He also considered partial measures such as providing lethal assistance or establishing a safe zone as "half-baked ideas" without a clear understanding of how they would be sustained.[38]

As Stephen Sestanovich wrote in *Maximalist*, "Yet whatever the prestige costs—and they were high—Syria was not a problem that Obama ever believed he had to solve."[39] On the other hand, without greater military pressure on the Assad regime, the prospects of a political settlement became increasingly remote.[40]

Even with the agreement to destroy Syria's chemical weapons, Assad was free to exploit clear conventional-weapon advantages. Over time, even that line blurred as he employed air-delivered barrel bombs filled with chlorine to devastating effect on combatants and civilians alike.

The net effect was "a de facto end to US efforts to push [the Assad] regime out of power," believed Walter Russell Mead.[41] Cynically, many in the region viewed the United States as complicit in Assad's survival for its failure to launch military strikes or provide greater support to the Syrian opposition.

But soon another player would emerge in Syria and Iraq that would dramatically alter both U.S. policy and politics.

THE JV TEAM

In early 2014, in an interview with *New Yorker* Editor David Remnick, as the Islamic State began its advance across the Sunni provinces of Iraq, taking over Fallujah, a heavily contested city during the American occupation and ensuring insurgency, Obama attempted to distinguish between core al Qaeda, still focused on attacking the American homeland, and other jihadists engaged in local sectarian power struggles.

Clearly underestimating its capability, Obama termed the Islamic State "a JV team." But by the time he said that, the Islamic State was already larger than al Qaeda ever was and acting as much like a conventional army as an insurgent force.[42]

Within months, the Islamic State would gain more territory, adding the cities of Mosul and Ramadi. The president was critical of the dismal performance of Iraqi security forces that, despite a multibillion-dollar American invest-ment, were "not willing to stand and fight."[43] Obama rightly highlighted sectarian political differences that contributed to significant Sunni support for the Islamic State and pushed for a political change at the top—Haider al-Abadi would succeed Nouri al-Maliki as prime minister.

Obama would take some criticism for failing to reach agreement with Iraq on a follow-on military mission, but it was hard to see how 10,000 troops could succeed where 100,000 troops had previously failed to turn Iraq into a functioning democracy.

The break in the U.S. presence between 2011 and 2014 enabled a national and regional reset of perceptions of the U.S.-Iraqi relationship and the legitimacy of the U.S. role in the region. Now it was acting at the invitation of the Iraqi government as part of a multinational campaign to retake territory from the Islamic State. Obama put the mission in the context of saving lives, not defending U.S. security. Initially, he did not believe U.S. forces would be in Iraq for long.

"When you have a unique circumstance in which genocide is threatened, and a country is willing to have us in there, you have a strong international consensus that these people need to be protected and where we have the capacity to do so, then we have an obligation to do so."[44]

The U.S. response reestablished a familiar domestic political fault line, with Republicans accusing the president of not doing enough and Democrats expressing concern that the slope to a deeper commitment in the struggle was becoming slippery. John McCain suggested Obama was guilty of "grudging incrementalism," which harkened back to a conservative critique of the flawed strategy in Vietnam.[45]

But even as U.S. forces reengaged in Iraq and became a combatant in Syria's civil war, a step he had avoided a year earlier, Obama made clear there were limits. "We cannot do for them what they are unwilling to do for them-selves."[46]

The White House characterized the new effort as a counterterrorism strategy, but the Islamic State actually controlled an area equivalent to neigh-boring Jordan. As it showed unexpected ability to hold and govern territory, it had the look and feel of a conventional army, not a terrorist network.

#MESSAGE TO AMERICA

On August 19, 2014, the Islamic State released a gruesome video entitled "A Message to #America (from the #IslamicState)." The use of hashtags underscored the media sophistication of this latest extremist player. It certainly represented a sharp contrast with the use of audio and videotapes by Osama bin Laden and Ayman al-Zawahiri, which frequently referred to events that occurred weeks earlier. The Islamic State was not reacting to events; it was driving them.

In the video, a hooded man initially nicknamed Jihadi John in the West and later identified as Mohammed Emwazi, a British citizen, accused Obama of aggression toward the Islamic State. Picking up a theme from al Qaeda, Emzawi, later killed in a drone strike in November 2015 in Raqqa, accused the United States of being at war against Islam, the frame the Obama administration had spent six years trying to counteract.

Journalist James Foley was then beheaded in retribution.

Declaring that the Islamic State had no place in the twenty-first century, Obama quickly adjusted his rhetoric. Consistent with his view of America as the exceptional nation, he talked about the need for a regional coalition to oppose the Islamic State, recognized it represented a long-term challenge, and acknowledged it would take time to develop an appropriate response.

"We don't have a strategy yet," he admitted in late August.[47]

Less than a week later, a second video was released revealing the beheading of journalist Steven Sotloff. In the video, the Islamic State warned countries about an evil alliance with America. The message this time, primarily to Great Britain: back off and leave us alone. To reinforce its point, two aid workers would be subsequently murdered.

As with Zarqawi's video years earlier documenting the killing of Nicholas Berg, both Sotloff and Foley were dressed in orange jumpsuits, a reminder of the continued propaganda value of the Guantanamo prison.

The significant use of social media and brutality of message was targeted at young Muslims, particularly in the West, a sophisticated and successful strategy that lent cache to the caliphate. The Islamic State's online magazine, *Dabiq*, named after a Syrian village associated with an anticipated apocalyptic battle with Christian forces, consistently touted its successes.[48]

Thousands of Westerners were enticed to join their ranks and travel to Syria. At the same time, the Islamic State sought to encourage supporters to attack in place—former State Department official Alberto Fernandez terms it "D.I.Y. jihad"—that represented an outsourcing of the threat without an attacker ever being in physical contact with a recruiter.[49]

The radicalized couple that committed the San Bernardino shooting in November 2015 fit this profile. They were described by the Islamic State as "soldiers of the caliphate," but did not receive any advance training or direction.[50] Neither did the attacker at an Orlando nightclub in June 2016 who called 911 and pledged allegiance to the Islamic State moments before committing the worst mass shooting in U.S. history.

The Islamic State demonstrated unprecedented savvy in its employment of information technology to radicalize and recruit a new generation of jihadists. The Internet represented "a virtual sea of jihadist recruiters, cheerleaders, and fellow travelers," suggests journalist and reseacher Peter Bergen.[51] Unlike al Qaeda, which practiced some selectivity in its recruiting, the Islamic State appeal was more broad-based. All were welcome, although it seemed to attract individuals whose prospects were limited, who had suffered a major setback in life, and who were drawn to the opportunity to move from "zero to hero" with one dramatic violent act.[52] By crowdsourcing extremism, the movement propagated its appeal, ideology, and tactics without requiring anyone to travel, long one of the vulnerabilities of such networks. An estimated forty-three thousand Twitter accounts were associated with the Islamic State, challenging the ability of governments, working with social media companies, to effectively deny the Islamic State use of the Internet. By applying network restrictions on violent hate speech, collective efforts made it somewhat harder for the Islamic State to communicate online, although there were practical limits to what could be achieved.

Some perspective is warranted. According to Bergen, since 9/11, each case of a successful attack involving one or more fatalities carried out within the United States was carried out by a lone wolf.[53] Such attacks are on par with other forms of political extremism, whether white supremacists or antiabortion zealots. In fact, an American is five thousand times more likely to be killed in a gun incident than by terrorists inspired by Binladenism.[54]

The media campaign complemented the Islamic State's dramatic military advance. Gradually controlling and governing substantial territory, it surpassed al Qaeda as the wealthiest and most attractive global extremist brand.[55] This early success was fundamental to the appeal of the Islamic State.

Conversely, as the international coalition gradually loosed the Islamic State's grip on territory and squeezed its financing, it adapted its approach. Its emphasis on radicalization-in-place reflected its diminished ability to support and pay out-of-area fighters. Over time it became clearer that life in the Islamic State's realm was hardly the idyllic utopia portrayed in its media messaging.

Whether or not the Islamic State intended to draw the United States deeper into the conflicts in Syria and Iraq, the brutal actions perpetrated in the name of Islam generated a negative and strategically significant response. More than sixty nations, including most in the region, joined an opposing coalition.

The response involved military and political action. A significant part of the effort involved the amplification of Muslim voices attempting to discredit and delegitimize the Islamic State.

Inside extremist circles, the Islamic State also had opposition. It disagreed with Jabhat al-Nusra over strategy and tactics and formally split from al Qaeda in February 2014.[56] The emergence of al-Nusra, arguably the most effective opposition force in the war, undermined the Obama administration narrative that al Qaeda was on a path to a strategic defeat, although it too dropped its affiliation with al Qaeda in July 2016 as it attempted to reposition itself within the Syrian opposition hierarchy.

DEGRADE AND DESTROY

On September 10, 2014, in a prime-time address a week after the Sotloff tape, President Obama stepped to a podium on the State Floor of the White House and delivered perhaps the most consequential speech of his presidency. Only fourteen minutes in length, it was a speech he never expected to give.

Over the previous month, U.S. forces had conducted military strikes in Iraq aimed at halting an Islamic State advance toward Erbil that threatened American diplomats assigned there and protecting civilians from potential acts of genocide on Mount Sinjar. In both instances, Obama characterized the operations as limited life-saving actions utilizing unique American military capabilities.

Just two weeks earlier, he suggested the Islamic State's claim of being at war with the United States and the West was a matter of "expediency."[57] But the beheadings of two Americans, an Iraqi political crisis, and fears that the Islamic State could threaten Baghdad convinced the Obama administration and key regional allies that a broader regional campaign was necessary.

The United States would not just form a regional coalition; it would lead it. The stated imperative was no longer to just contain the Islamic State, but to "degrade, and ultimately destroy" it. The United States was already bombing the Islamic State and al Qaeda from the air, but now Obama was also introducing 475 special operations forces to improve intelligence collection and training of Iraqi forces. While the president emphasized that the United States would not "get dragged into another ground war in Iraq," it was now at war with the caliphate.[58]

Initially, the Obama administration distinguished its efforts in Iraq and Syria, but eventually understood it could not succeed without effective action on both sides of the border. Two weeks later, the president announced on the South Lawn that the air campaign now extended into Syria, where it targeted a mysterious element, the Khorasan Group, formed at the direction of Zawahiri, the al Qaeda leader, and actively plotting against the United States.[59]

The complexity of the Syrian conflict quickly created major policy complications. In Syria, the United States made a conscious decision to fight the Islamic State, but not the Assad regime. It conditioned its support to the Syrian opposition on that basis, even though most combatants, including the moderate opposition, considered Assad the primary adversary.

Given the fluidity of the Syrian conflict, it became increasingly hard on the ground to isolate the good guys from the bad guys—those elements of the opposition that were interested in building a pluralistic country and those with competing visions of a far more religious and conservative society at odds with the modern world. The Obama administration created an arduous vetting process around those who qualified for American support, which in turn reduced its impact.

It attempted to step up support for the Pentagon train-and-equip program for the moderate Syrian opposition. Ultimately, it failed. There were simply too few fighters. Months into the program, only a handful were still fighting, and at one point they were forced to surrender some of their equipment to al-Nusra.[60]

The Obama administration responded to that setback by developing a more effective partnership among the Kurds and various Syrian rebel groups, although this step threatened the unity of the international coalition. Turkey, for example, was wary of how support for the Syrian People's Protection Units or YPG would affect its long-standing struggle with the Kurdistan Workers' Party or PKK.

In fact, given the competing visions of how a future Syrian state should be governed, with the United States the sole major combatant seeking to establish an ethnically and religiously inclusive modern state, it led one regional expert to conclude, "America has no real allies in the Middle East."[61]

A year after the intervention in Iraq and Syria, Obama acknowledged in an interview with *60 Minutes* that so far it had failed to "change the dynamic inside of Syria" even if it had stalled the Islamic State's momentum. Saying "there aren't any silver bullets," he reiterated that he did not see a military solution, whether that involved the United States or Russia for that matter. He said defeating the Islamic State would only happen when Sunnis in the region were "working in a concerted way to get rid of them."[62]

Obama refused to send several hundred thousand troops back to the Middle East as the sole measure of American strength. "There are people who would like to see us do that. And unless we do that, they'll suggest we're in retreat." Obama criticized the idea of sending large numbers of forces back "to be, not just the police, but the governors of this region." That, he said, would be "a bad strategy."[63]

The Obama administration, acknowledged Secretary of Defense Ash Carter, was ultimately not prepared to "Americanize the conflict."[64]

The United States relaunched international talks in October 2015 in hopes of achieving a political solution over time. While continuing to insist that Assad had to go, absent significant shift in strategic calculations by Russia or Iran, Assad's primary protectors, there was no viable path to achieve it.

The stalemate guaranteed that Obama would hand to his successor an active, complex, and open-ended war in the Middle East. The tide of war wasn't receding; the Islamic State would outlast the Obama administration.

10

RESET

In a speech to a young audience in Brussels in March 2014, against the backdrop of a rising crisis over Ukraine, President Obama disputed the idea that Russia and the West were reengaged in a new Cold War. Russia was not threatening nuclear annihilation nor advancing a competing global ideology, although Vladimir Putin claimed to be defending conservative principles against Western decadence.

Russia was challenging America's predominant influence within the global system. Since the end of the Cold War, four successive U.S. administrations sought to integrate Russia into the liberal international order. But Putin, who considered the demise of the Soviet Union a historic catastrophe, believed that Washington did not take Russian interests adequately into account. He came to see Western conspiracies both near and far, defined his increasingly repressive rule in terms of Russian nationalism, and repositioned Moscow once again as an American antagonist.[1]

Obama did acknowledge a "contest of ideas" involving two vastly different interpretations of how the world is supposed to work.

Four months earlier, Russia pressured the government of Viktor Yanukovych to back out of an association agreement with the European Union. Instead, Russia offered Ukraine billions in economic assistance to join Russia's facsimile, the Eurasian Economic Union. The controversy sparked contentious protests centered in Kiev's Maidan Square and sporadic violent confrontations with government security forces.

In late February, there appeared to be a diplomatic breakthrough to form a coalition government and hold early elections. But before the ink on the political settlement was dry, Yanukovych and his inner circle fled Kiev. The

Ukrainian parliament rapidly voted him out of office and installed a government of technocrats sympathetic with Ukraine's western tilt.

Putin saw yet another color revolution developing in his own backyard and the prospect of the European Union or even the North Atlantic Treaty Organization right at his doorstep. NATO expansion was a long-standing Russian grievance, but Putin's real concern was direct political and economic competition.[2] Putin did everything he could to prevent Ukraine from moving beyond Moscow's gravitational pull.

The Ukraine crisis unfolded just months after the United States and Russia collaborated on the elimination of Syria's chemical weapons stocks in response to the Assad regime's violation of the U.S. red line. Obama considered the agreement in lieu of military action as liberation from the "Washington playbook" that tends to militarize international confrontations.[3] Many American allies viewed it as a disaster to threaten force and not follow through. The stakes only seemed to escalate further when Putin saw his own need for military action in Syria and never hesitated.

In Ukraine, Moscow's tactics did seem to reflect a prior age, infiltrating irregular forces—green men without military insignia and other "volunteers"—to augment Russian forces already stationed there by mutual agreement. Under the guise of protecting Russian-speaking citizens (a large number of Soviet soldiers chose to retire in Crimea, given its temperate climate), a rushed and rigged popular referendum regifted Crimea to Russia, reversing an action by Nikita Khrushchev sixty years earlier. And Russian separatists supported by Russian weaponry took control of Ukraine's eastern provinces, embarrassing Ukrainian forces that were poorly equipped and badly led.

Geopolitics were back, the use of overt and covert action to pressure, destabilize, and change the borders of Ukraine. So was propaganda, the manipulation of information and outright deceit that unified domestic public opinion and divided key publics abroad.

Obama called Russia's actions "unacceptable in the 21st Century," ironically the same mantra George W. Bush used in 2008 to describe Russia's intervention in Georgia. Both Obama and Bush attempted to form a pragmatic relationship with Putin only to become deeply disillusioned.

Obama labeled Russia a regional power acting from a position of weakness. While there was little doubt Putin was playing the weaker hand—Russia's long-term economic, political, and demographic challenges are significant—he did so with the instinct of a gambler. Putin also had clear advantages. The histories and cultures of the two countries were closely intertwined; Ukraine was far more important to Russia than the United States.

While Obama rejected the analogy that these events marked moves on a new Cold War "chessboard," as time went on, it was hard to deny the renewed rivalry. Obama did not look at the world in zero-sum terms, but Putin certainly did. The perception resonated in every Western capital.

Suddenly, the president of the United States was speaking publicly about Article 5 of the NATO Charter—an attack on one is considered an attack on all. For all of the talk over two decades about a new NATO, prepared to address global threats, everyone was focused on the old NATO and its classic mission of deterring Russia.

Even as the Obama administration sought to find common ground in Syria after its intervention to prop up the Assad government, Russia appeared to attempt to interfere in the 2016 U.S. election. Russian hackers were believed to have burrowed into the Democratic National Committee computer network and passed emails to WikiLeaks to embarrass the candidate Russia knows only too well. They also probed state election databases, perhaps to undermine the voting public's confidence in the democratic process.

It remains to be seen whether Putin is driving Russia's prevailing revisionist and anti-Western posture or is a product of it. If the former, the challenge for the United States is to manage the coming decade while hoping for change over time. If the latter, it requires a fundamental rethinking of the strategy that has guided the United States and the West since the end of the Cold War. Either way, he is likely to be a significant thorn in the side for most of the next president's time in office. Another reset is highly unlikely.

EVIL EMPIRE

George F. Kennan, reprising his legendary Long Telegram as "X" in an essay in *Foreign Affairs* in 1947, saw the Soviets as greatly influenced by Russian history and tradition, which viewed the outside world as "hostile," necessitating "the cultivation of a semi-myth" of implacable antagonism. Kennan recognized that "we are going to continue for a long time to find the Russians difficult to deal with."[4]

Kennan advocated "a long-term, patient but firm and vigilant containment of Russian expansive tendencies" without "superfluous gestures of outward 'toughness.'"[5] He was confident the Russian system contained the "seeds of its own decay" and believed that an effective policy response should include an information campaign that placed communism and capitalism in stark relief.

The United States, Kennan suggested, "need only measure up to its own best traditions" while "accepting the responsibilities of moral and political leadership that history plainly intended them to bear."[6] Kennan viewed the Soviet threat as political, not military, and was dismayed at the militarization of his containment strategy.[7]

The guiding strategic narrative during the Cold War really *was* about countries that were with us or against us. There was a conceptual Iron Curtain and an actual Berlin Wall that separated East and West. Right or wrong, virtually every square inch of territory was contested; so were the hearts and minds of a global population.

Even though the United States became more confident over time that it would ultimately win the Cold War, its successful end was far from preordained. As Yale historian John Lewis Gaddis wrote, "It was at least as easy to believe, in 1945, that authoritarian communism was the wave of the future as that democratic capitalism was."[8]

"The Cold War," added Gaddis, "was not just a geopolitical rivalry or a nuclear arms race; it was a competition."[9] No president publicly embraced that competition more than Ronald Reagan.

Coming into office with the wounds from Vietnam still sensitive and the hostage crisis with Iran still fresh, Reagan rejected Nixon's realpolitik and embraced American exceptionalism. Reagan was determined to restore faith in American leadership. The Soviet Union was his foil.

Reagan steadily confronted Moscow on the global stage, drawing contrasts at every turn between the dynamism of the United States and the West and the bleak prospects behind the Iron Curtain. Reagan significantly increased defense spending and launched an ambitious if improbable missile defense program dubbed Star Wars after the popular movie. Even though the missile shield never worked as it was imagined and became a contentious domestic political issue, its very audaciousness played into Moscow's calculation that the status quo was unsustainable.

He supported anticommunist governments in the Western Hemisphere and authorized various covert actions in Nicaragua and El Salvador that blurred the line between war and peace. The ensuing Iran-Contra political crisis threatened his presidency.

Through Reagan's CIA and with the remarkable support of Congressman Charlie Wilson, the United States surreptitiously funneled significant arms, including Stinger missiles, to the mujahideen in Afghanistan. For every dollar the United States fed to the insurrection, the Soviets were forced to spend ten to counter.[10] The Soviet defeat was a significant factor in the Cold War's denouement, albeit with unintended consequences, indirectly giving rise to al Qaeda.

Despite opposition from his advisors, Reagan branded the Soviet Union the "evil empire."[11] He viewed the Cold War in moral, not just geopolitical terms—a "struggle of ideas and economic systems."[12] Reagan was willing to do business with Gorbachev—he achieved meaningful arms reductions, including intermediate-range nuclear missiles—but he refused to accept the notion of parity. Instead Reagan sought to strip the Soviets of their political legitimacy.

To most, the Berlin Wall became a vivid manifestation of the inferiority of the communist system. While confident the Soviet Union would end up "on the ash heap of history," Reagan also viewed it as an impediment to its ability to transform.

On June 12, 1987, standing in front of the Brandenburg Gate in Berlin, ever the Great Communicator, Reagan called on Soviet leader Mikhail Gorbachev to "tear down this wall." According to journalist and author James Mann, the exhortation was neither a moment of triumphalism nor a publicity stunt. It was rather a sophisticated argument intended to encourage and enable the Soviet Union to eventually integrate into the international system.[13]

Reagan encouraged the nascent changes introduced by Gorbachev, saying, "We welcome change and openness; for we believe that freedom and security go together, that the advance of human liberty can only strengthen the cause of world peace."[14]

With oil prices falling dramatically, if Gorbachev wanted to improve his economy, he had little choice but to reform. Gorbachev thought he could have the best of both worlds—undertake needed political and economic reforms and still maintain control of the communist system. He was wrong.

"Gorbachev unintentionally destroyed the Soviet system," Mann wrote. "Reagan gave him the help he needed to do it."[15]

THE HEDGE

President George H. W. Bush deftly managed the final demise of the Soviet Union. Bush did not fully agree with Reagan's strident public posture. Displaying far-sighted vision, Bush declined to "dance" on the Berlin Wall and gave Gorbachev sufficient diplomatic room that ensured his acquiescence regarding major structural changes in Europe, including the unification of Germany and its continued membership in NATO.

Within two years, the Soviet Union ceased to exist as the leaders of Russia, Belarus, and Ukraine in December 1991 formed the Commonwealth of Independent States. Of note, Ukraine's leader at the time, Leonid Kravchuk, rejected Russian proposals for the CIS to confer citizenship, form a security alliance, or elect a joint parliament.[16]

As the Clinton administration took over, a major concern was the challenge of "loose nukes." The demise of the Soviet Union left three countries in possession of inherited Soviet nuclear capabilities—Ukraine, Belarus, and Kazakhstan. Had it decided to keep its nuclear weapons, Ukraine would have been the third-largest nuclear power in the world. Instead, the United States, Russia, and Ukraine negotiated a trilateral statement that pledged respect for Ukraine's existing boundaries. It was codified in December 1994 in the Budapest Memorandum, eventually endorsed by the permanent five of the UN Security Council, that committed the parties to refrain from "the use of force against the territorial integrity and political independence of Ukraine."[17]

During the 2014 crisis over the annexation of Crimea, Russia justified its action with the dubious claim that the West abrogated the agreement by conspiring to overthrow the Yanukovych government.[18]

In his first trip to Moscow as president, Bill Clinton described America's post–Cold War hopes for Russia in a televised town hall meeting with local students. Russia's future would depend on how it answered three questions: Would Russia create a market economy or turn back? Would Russia remain committed to democracy or restrict it? Would Russia define its power and role in the world "in yesterday's terms or tomorrow's?"[19]

After decades of containment that assumed Soviet strength, Clinton viewed his challenge as trying to manage Russia's weakness, keeping it focused on building a new, modern system of governance rather than recovering what it had lost. There was a clear understanding that, if the revolution that Russia launched with the end of the Soviet Union failed to deliver clear benefits, hard-line forces could reemerge.

Notwithstanding Francis Fukuyama's famous prediction of an end to history and the presumed triumph of Western liberal democracy, the emerging U.S. policy included hedges against Russian revisionism.

One was NATO expansion, although as Henry Kissinger noted in *World Order*, it was justified less on security grounds than "as a sensible method of 'locking in' democratic gains."[20] Russia and the United States would agree to disagree over what was permitted beyond the acceptance of a unified Germany within NATO, but the Clinton administration felt that the prospect of NATO membership would provide an impetus for the nations of central and eastern

Europe to remain committed to democratic values and institutions. Among its chief critics was none other than George Kennan, who considered the policy a "strategic blunder of potentially epic proportions."[21]

While there was grudging cooperation regarding Bosnia, the 1999 NATO air war in Kosovo and the province's eventual declaration of independence would have a deep impact on the relationship. Putin, who was chief of the Federal Security Service (FSB) at the time of the conflict, became prime minister two months after it ended and succeeded Boris Yeltsin as president at the end of the year.

The NATO intervention over Kosovo "infuriated Russia in ways American and European leaders failed to appreciate," suggested Steven Lee Myers in *The New Tsar*.[22] Putin had a vastly different interpretation of how the Cold War ended, what that meant in terms of a revised world order, and the international prerogatives that went with it.[23]

Putin believed the United States was taking advantage of Russia's weakness. The Russian economy had almost collapsed, with the ruble losing 40 percent of its value. And now Washington was leading a military campaign against its Serb allies without an authorizing resolution from the United Nations. The NATO rationale, intervening against a sovereign government engaged in a conflict with a restive province, cut close to home, since Moscow was waging its own brutal struggle at the same time in Chechnya.[24]

As the George W. Bush administration came to office, it was focused on the importance of big power relationships, including Russia. Bush's foreign policy advisors believed the Clinton policy toward Russia relied too heavily on Boris Yeltsin.[25] Ironically, after his first meeting with Putin, the president went out of his way to express his trust in Putin, saying "I was able to get a sense of his soul."[26]

In that first meeting in Slovenia, Bush declared his intention to abrogate the ABM Treaty. The issue of missile defense would remain a bone of contention during both the Bush and Obama administrations. Russian officials were never convinced the system was targeted against the growing missile threat from Iran.

For his part, Putin expressed deep concern about Pakistan, the links between its intelligence services and al Qaeda, and an array of extremists funded by Saudi Arabia.[27] Three months later, on September 11, Putin was the first world leader to call the White House after the attacks of September 11, pledging to work with the United States in a common struggle against terrorism, which he termed "the plague of the 21st Century."[28]

The post–September 11 period represented the high-water mark in relations between Washington and Putin's Russia. He went so far as to suggest a "strategic partnership," drawing parallels between the wars in Afghanistan and Chechnya.[29]

As Bush turned his focus toward Iraq, Putin sent an emissary to Baghdad ahead of the threatened U.S. invasion in an effort to convince Saddam Hussein to resign. While Russia also joined France and Germany in opposing a UN resolution authorizing military action, Putin made what Bush considered a "friendship call" hours after the first bombs dropped in Baghdad, warning that the war was going to be far more difficult than the Americans anticipated.[30]

As he tried to construct a relationship with Bush, Putin's bargain with the Russian people was order in lieu of genuine politics. He equated Western democracy with the chaos that accompanied the end of the Soviet Union. Putin's view of governance was managed democracy, meaning public affirmation of political and policy choices made by a small circle of figures entrusted with the function and preservation of the state. Putin likened his model to Japan and its dominant Liberal Democratic Party.[31] It was a selective comparison, since Japan has tumultuous politics, a vigorous civil society, and a large and free independent media. All are under attack in Russia.

But in truth, suggested Peter Baker and Susan Glasser in *Kremlin Rising*, "the counterrevolution launched by Putin and his circle was not about completing the transition to democracy; it was about rolling it back," what one Russian politician called a "constitutional coup d'etat."[32]

Many of the modern tools of political communication Putin viewed as threats to public order. "He considered the state networks a 'national resource' as precious as oil or gas."[33] Putin would closely associate independent media and social media with the protests that erupted in Moscow in 2011. By 2016, recognizing the threat posed by communication technologies (nothing new to Russian authorities), truly independent media had either been bought out or driven out of business. And Kremlin censors had blocked more than one million websites.[34]

Putin in 2008 was term limited and yielded the presidency to a longtime associate and hand-picked successor, Dmitri Medvedev, while assuming the role of prime minister. Just before the transition, Kosovo declared independence and NATO leaders meeting in Bucharest considered a membership action plan for Ukraine and Georgia. While a divided alliance tabled the move, NATO appeared willing to move ahead sometime in the future.

Georgian President Mikheil Saakashvili, perhaps emboldened by the NATO consideration, took military action to regain control of South Ossetia and Abkhazia, two contested pro-Russian provinces that had been occupied by Russian peacekeepers since the end of the Cold War. In response, Russian forces drove deep into Georgian territory, intent to embarrass Saakashvili, weaken Georgian forces, and send a clear message to Ukraine regarding the risks of a closer relationship with Europe.

"The Russians had baited a trap, and the impetuous Saakashvili walked right into it," Robert Gates wrote in *Duty*.[35] Medvedev suggested the Russian action was intended to protect the lives of Russian citizens within the threatened provinces, a logic Putin would reuse in Crimea.[36]

RESET

Vice President Joe Biden is credited with originating the frame that became an all-purpose description of U.S. objectives in its relations with Russia. "It is time to hit the reset button," Biden said early in the administration.[37]

As a policy, the reset involved cooperating with Russia where possible, being firm where interests clearly diverged, and engaging with the Russian people regarding the importance of respect for human rights, an independent judiciary, and free media, hallmarks of a society that is reasonably democratic and prosperous.[38]

Secretary of State Hillary Clinton actually presented a reset button to her counterpart, Foreign Minister Sergei Lavrov, an icebreaking gesture that also captured the complexity of the relationship when Lavrov suggested there had been a mistranslation of the reset term. The Americans labeled the button *peregruzka*, which actually meant overcharged or overloaded, which it turns out is exactly what happened, as the circuits in the relationship eventually tripped.

According to Stanford professors Kathryn Stoner and Michael McFaul, the latter overseeing Russia policy on the National Security Council staff and then serving as U.S. ambassador in Moscow during the Obama administration, the reset actually did produce results. This included the New Start Treaty, the Northern Distribution Network (which enabled resupply of U.S. forces in Afghanistan), Kremlin support for Iran sanctions (UN Resolution 1929) and its abstention regarding Libya (UN Resolutions 1970 and 1973), and Moscow's membership in the World Trade Organization.[39] By the same token, Putin believed Medvedev had been misled about Libya, as the campaign increasingly supported Qaddafi's overthrow.[40]

The Obama administration restructured the missile defense program it inherited from the Bush administration, introducing a more dynamic arrangement that would establish a capability in Europe more quickly but one also intended to assuage Russian concerns. While Obama sought "flexibility" with Russia regarding its missile defense concerns, Moscow never relented.[41]

Stoner and McFaul believe the reset ended in 2012 when significant demonstrations began in the aftermath of less than free and fair parliamentary elections followed by news that Putin planned to return to the presidency. While much would be made of the contrasting styles of the U.S. and Russian leaders, Putin needed the conflict with the liberal West and the hegemonic United States—renewed threats against the Motherland—to reinforce his sagging political legitimacy and popularity.[42]

The reset became an issue during the 2012 campaign when Republican candidate Mitt Romney highlighted Russia as a key geopolitical foe and accused Obama (unfairly) as looking at Putin with "rose-colored glasses." Obama derided Romney's focus on Russia as a priority from the 1980s, reminding him that "the Cold War's been over for 20 years."[43]

Whether Romney's analysis was prescience or coincidence, Obama clearly underestimated the degree to which Putin's Russia would become a preoccupation during his second term. With Putin back at the helm in Russia, the "reset had no sequel."[44]

OFF-RAMPS

The demise of the Soviet Union left twenty-five million citizens of Russian descent beyond its borders, a major reason why Putin lamented "the demise of the historical Russian idea" and was determined to restore it.[45] He advanced a kind of Putin Doctrine, a corollary to America's Monroe Doctrine that presumed regional prerogatives to protect Russia's interests.

The Ukraine crisis fit Putin's narrative of a new Russia—Novorossiya—that projected renewed Russian strength and influence. It came on the heels of the Winter Olympics in Sochi, the first time Russia had hosted an Olympics since 1980. Ironically, those Summer Games were widely boycotted due to Soviet actions in Afghanistan. Before the 2016 Olympic Games in Rio de Janeiro, a number of Russian athletes would be banned for systematic doping violations, adding another grievance to the ledger.

The Sochi Games cost a staggering $51 billion.[46] But regardless of the price, Putin positioned Russia right where he thought it belonged, "at the global center of gravity, a rich, indispensable nation playing host to the world."[47] As an investment in international public diplomacy, the goodwill generated by the Sochi Games would be squandered. As an investment in domestic politics, Putin would be richly rewarded.

The United States established four policy objectives: support for Ukraine; reassurance of NATO allies, particularly those closest to the conflict; identifying ways to impose costs on Russia; and leaving open a path to deescalation. The White House framed its response in terms of universal rights and the aspirations of the Ukrainian people.

There was some criticism the Obama administration improperly encouraged the Maidan protesters. Others suggested the White House needlessly pushed Russian buttons given its historical interests and influence in Ukraine. A subset argued that this was just another manifestation of the folly of expanding NATO.

Some of Obama's critics admired Putin's decisiveness, although there were legitimate questions whether he was guided by strategy or impulse. Kissinger believed the re-acquisition of Crimea was to protect Russia from potential NATO expansion. It certainly played well among the Russian population.[48]

The crisis in Ukraine caught the U.S. and European strategy for Russia coming and going. The long-term goal was to fully integrate Russia into the international system and provide both a stake and the incentive to play by the rules. The policy had been sufficiently successful given the rise of global interdependence that isolation was impossible to achieve, either economically or politically.

For example, Europe did business with Russia and was reliant on Russian energy to a significant degree. As Europe worked to diversify its energy supply, Russia found an eager buyer in China. Following the emergence of the Islamic State, the Obama administration reluctantly concluded there was no solution to Syria without Russia's cooperation.

Ukraine tested the Obama definition of American exceptionalism, meaning the ability to rally the international community to the defense of international norms. There was some reluctance among European allies that still believed integration was the best approach, although that receded when Ukrainian separatists using a Russian antiaircraft battery downed Malaysian Air Flight 17, killing all 298 civilians and crew onboard. The incident validated Obama's caution against providing lethal weapons to Ukraine—great uncertainty regarding how they ultimately will be employed.[49]

Working with European leaders, Obama initiated multiple rounds of sanctions, focused on Putin's favored financial oligarchs. There were clear impacts—international capital flight, stock market declines, depreciation of the ruble, and rising interest rates, especially when coupled with the sharp drop in the prices of oil and gas. Russia was expelled from the G7. Russia paid a steep price, but within a range Putin was willing to bear.

While Obama considered Putin's actions as "a wrong-headed desire to re-create the glories of the Soviet empire," there was a limit to what he could do.[50] He acknowledged that Russia would not be dislodged by force. While Obama talked about available off-ramps to encourage Russia to resolve the crisis, Putin drove past all of them. In fact, few national leaders would feel the need to change course with an 85 percent approval rating.

The key over the long term remains the Western commitment to provide sufficient resources to help reform the Ukrainian economy and redeem the choice of a majority of its citizens to develop closer ties with the West. That becomes a more difficult proposition with the Brexit vote.

As if adding insult to injury, in the middle of the Ukraine crisis, Edward Snowden leaked highly classified documents to select news sources and then fled to Moscow. Putin was undoubtedly surprised by the development, but granted Snowden asylum. He was able to portray himself internationally—at least for one moment—as a defender of human rights, even as he expelled various American civil society organizations and used Russia's surveillance technologies to increase control of its networks and stifle dissent.

Obama considered Putin "on the wrong side of history" in Ukraine. But Putin was focused on his own historical lessons.

PUTIN'S LEAP INTO SYRIA

In Syria in September 2015, Putin saw another Russian ally in danger and jumped decisively into the middle of a civil war that Obama had studiously sought to avoid.

Whereas Obama believed he was applying the lessons of Iraq in his limited air campaign against the Islamic State, Putin invoked Hitler and the cooperation that the allied nations showed in recognizing a larger common adversary. Ironically, Yalta, where Roosevelt, Churchill, and Stalin met during World War II, was part of Russia at the time, given to Ukraine and then taken back in 2014.[51]

"We support the legitimate government of Syria," Putin told Charlie Rose in a *60 Minutes* interview just before his UN General Assembly appearance in September 2015. He also drew parallels to the chaos that followed

Western military incursions in Iraq and Libya, chiding the American leadership and audience about its belief in American exceptionalism, saying disingenuously that Russia does not have "an obsession with being a superpower in the international arena."[52]

While Putin claimed to be fighting the Islamic State, within days it became clear his real target was all opposition to the Assad regime, including the moderate Syrian opposition supported by the United States. Moscow established a de facto alliance with Iran that gave renewed life to the Assad regime. If the Obama administration continued to believe that Assad's days are numbered, Russia's intervention added months and perhaps years to that total. As of early 2016, American intelligence officials acknowledged that Assad was now likely to remain "a player on the stage longer term."[53]

If the United States wanted to defeat the Islamic State, Putin believed it would have to accept Assad as an ally. This put the United States in a policy no-man's-land. Lacking any guarantee that Assad would depart, whether sooner or later, the United States had no apparent means of ending the Syrian conflict.★

According to former Secretary of State Condoleezza Rice and former Secretary of Defense Robert Gates, Putin employed "old-fashioned great-power politics" that strengthened his position at home and abroad. Given that "diplomacy follows the facts on the ground," Putin created a favorable "military balance of power" in Syria that gave him clear advantages in determining an acceptable political solution.[54]

Putin's Syria gamble was a shrewd play that preserved Russia's last bastion of influence in the Middle East and access to a key base in the Mediterranean and, given the struggles in Europe to cope with the dramatic migration crisis, created the prospect of an end to Russia's political isolation over Ukraine.

However, even as he scaled back the Russian intervention after five months, there are long-term risks as well. With an estimated two thousand Russians within the ranks of the Islamic State, Putin placed Russia at the center of a perceived holy war in the heart of the Middle East, the very place the United States occupied beginning in 2003.

Almost immediately, there was a new narrative advanced by conservative Saudi clerics warning of an "Orthodox crusader Russia," drawing comparisons between Syria and the Soviet experience in Afghanistan a generation earlier.[55]

★It is best to think of Syria as multiple conflicts: Assad against the Syrian opposition; the Islamic State against the United States and the regional coalition; the Islamic State against other extremist groups, including Jabhat al-Nusra; Iran and the Gulf states; the Turks and the Kurds; in the background Israel and Hezbollah; and a renewed competition between the United States and Russia.

In response, the Islamic State brought down a Russian civilian airliner over Egypt in late 2015, although it also reinforced the Putin narrative that it intervened in Syria to fight terrorists.

Obama, frustrated at suggestions that he was being outmaneuvered by Putin, considered Putin's intervention a "blind alley" that reached back to "the days of the tsars."[56] Lurching from crisis to crisis may well boost Putin's political poll numbers, Obama pointed out, but Russia's economy was expected to contract by 4 percent in 2015. The Obama administration believed that the best Putin could hope to achieve was "to prevent Assad from losing."[57]

But that was the point. His employment of military force created "geopolitical space" that improved the chances of an outcome consistent with Russia's interests.[58] How wedded Russia was to Assad is unclear, but it was inclined to protect him at least until an acceptable alternative is visible. The problem for Washington was that there wasn't one, leaving no clear path forward.

As the United States and United Nations pushed in early 2016 for a renewal of international talks aimed at achieving a ceasefire and launching a political transition, it was the opposition that balked at direct negotiations. The Syrian regime, now with the upper hand on the ground, sent a delegation prepared to negotiate without preconditions. Not surprisingly, the talks were suspended within days without progress.

"Russia and Iran have wanted Bashar al-Assad politically alive far more than Washington has wanted him dead," thought former State Department official Fred Hof.[59]

Notwithstanding Russia's evident weaknesses—an economy too heavily dependent on extractive resources, declining demographics, endemic corruption, and political isolation—Russia is a revisionist power that demonstrated the ability to undermine the credibility of American power.

RUSSIA PROBLEM OR PUTIN PROBLEM?

After a somewhat promising yet unpredictable relationship with the government of Boris Yeltsin during the Clinton administration, both the Bush and Obama administrations saw hopes of a productive relationship with Russia turn to disillusionment. So what's next?

While sanctions have imposed costs on Russia over time, they have gone as far as they can go. While the United States has relatively little invested in Russia, Russia has natural resources that the world needs. Putin is paying a price, but there are no major cleavages among Russia's elites that would suggest imminent political change. However, Putin's survival is not guaranteed, particularly if low energy prices and sustained political pressure continue to cause problems for Russia's oligarchy.

As problematic as the relationship is at the end of 2016, the next president should not anticipate it will get better. Putin developed into Obama's antagonist in chief, a dynamic Secretary of State Hillary Clinton saw first-hand. Her critical comments about Putin's reelection in 2012 clearly stuck with him. Russian hackers, with the help of WikiLeaks founder Julian Assange, who made no attempt to hide his animosity, were eager to return the favor as she campaigned to succeed Obama. Nonetheless, even with Russia's troubling behavior, there is a clear need to work to prevent the relationship from declining further. The watchword is not engagement, but rather crisis management.

The next president has to determine if the United States has a Putin problem or a Russia problem. Putin has been portrayed by some as a grand strategist, but in reality he is a gambler, a far better tactician than strategist. In Ukraine, Putin "was making decisions alone and off the cuff."[60] Perhaps this explains the admiration expressed by Donald Trump, who went so far as to describe him as "a very bright and talented man."[61]

Is Putin a rational actor? There are reasons to believe he is, given his dogged pursuit of what he sees as Russia's interests—protecting its interests in its immediate neighborhood in Ukraine; preserving its last bastion of significant influence in the Middle East in Syria; and viewing Bashar al-Assad as the lesser of evils compared with the Islamic State. But he appears increasingly reckless as well.

At present, the dynamic that surrounds Russia and Putin appears to be self-reinforcing. Washington cannot assume that what comes after Putin will be better as Moscow becomes more isolated. Since 2012, scores of organizations have been banned as "undesirable," including the National Endowment for Democracy and MacArthur Foundation. More than one hundred groups have been labeled as "foreign agents" for receiving outside funding in support of, for example, work on human rights.[62]

There is not necessarily a clear alternative on the horizon. Dmitri Medvedev in his one term as president demonstrated different instincts at times and seemed to recognize many of Russia's strategic deficits. According to former Secretary of Defense Gates, Medvedev "had realistic ideas about how to deal with them, including the need to more closely align with the West and to attract foreign investment."[63]

It is unclear whether Medvedev represents a new kind of leader who could emerge if Russia's political system evolves, or was simply an attractive hologram controlled by Putin and the system that created him. A State Department cable released by WikiLeaks would characterize Medvedev as Robin to Putin's Batman.

Russia under Gorbachev achieved a certain level of soft power because Gorbachev was willing to envision a different relationship with the rest of the world. Russia under Putin has largely abandoned this arena. Under Putin, politics became a form of "performance art."[64] There were staged events and carefully choreographed media performances that gave the aura of participatory politics when in fact key decisions were made out of the public view by an increasingly narrowing circle of hard-line advisors.

Andrew Weiss, vice president of studies at the Carnegie Endowment for International Peace, suggests Putin is an impulsive leader focused not on grand strategy but short-term opportunism rooted in Russian nationalism and hostility toward the West.

"We're going to have an outlier Russia for the foreseeable future," he predicts.[65]

Weiss sees both a limited appetite for cooperation and a narrowing field of common interests. While the United States and Russia have worked effectively together in the area of nuclear nonproliferation—the Iran deal is the latest example—a more realistic goal is simply avoiding a direct confrontation, whether related to Ukraine, Syria, or some future crisis.

Stoner and McFaul advocate a strategy of selective engagement and selective containment of Russia until economic and political pressure on Russia creates conditions for a shift in policy in Moscow. The United States and Europe should resist the temptation to return to business as usual while countering Putin's propaganda and engaging more broadly with Russian citizens. This will take time and determination.[66]

Obama went out of his way—rightly—to avoid making the relationship personal, although the closer he came to the end of his second term, the more candid he became regarding what he viewed as Putin's policy failures. This is actually where the next president should begin—prepared to cooperate where American and Russian interests align, but clear about the areas of disagreement that are likely to dominate the relationship for the foreseeable future.

With China, there is an understanding that Beijing usually responds more constructively to criticism in private. With Russia, there is a clear battle of ideas under way. The next administration should embrace that contest vigorously and publicly. Putin has brought back propaganda with a vengeance. The United States should not shy away from this arena.

The contest is not about trying to change Putin's mind or those around him. It is about reinforcing the perceived common cause among those who are most likely to be affected by Putin's policies and actions.

In the 2016 campaign, there was a fair amount of discussion regarding how to engage Putin. In contrast to Romney's caution in 2012, Trump expressed admiration for Putin's leadership style and envisioned the ability to work constructively with him. Uniquely, he saw virtue in Russia's deeper intervention in Syria, saying "if Putin wants to go and knock the hell out of ISIS, I am all for it."[67] He even seemed to invite Putin to release more of Hillary Clinton's emails, which he walked back after a public backlash.[68]

Clinton, while defending the Obama administration's reset policy with Russia, was rightly critical of Moscow's destabilizing actions in Ukraine and direct military intervention in Syria. While citing constructive results with Medvedev, including sanctions against Iran and cooperation with Afghanistan, she acknowledged that the relationship changed when Putin returned to office.

When asked whether there should be another reset with Russia, Clinton said, "It would depend on what I got for it." One way or another, the former secretary of state said, "we have to figure out how to deal with him."[69]

Support for Ukraine's political, economic, and military development is crucial. NATO has and must continue to bolster its presence in central and eastern Europe, reassuring the Baltic States and the Black Sea region regarding its Article 5 commitments.

However, it is unlikely Crimea will be returned anytime soon. Together with Russia's disturbing interference in the 2016 campaign, there is no immediate prospect of a normal relationship with Russia.

That said, there are still important areas of potential cooperation with Russia—arms control, the Islamic State, the Arctic, and even climate change. As former Senator Sam Nunn suggests, given that the two countries together hold the preponderance of nuclear weapons and related material, "the United States and Russia cannot afford to treat dialogue as a bargaining chip."[70]

Even with Moscow's interventions in Ukraine and Syria, the American people view Russia primarily as a problem, but not an adversary, which provides some constructive policy options for the new president.[71] The goal, suggests Robert Legvold, is to keep the new Cold War "as short and shallow as possible."[72] But the current dynamic will last for years.

Even as U.S.-Russian relations deteriorated, there was one area where cooperation remained undisturbed, that being nuclear negotiations with Iran. But there were limits.

11

A GOOD DEAL

Just prior to the Iranian election in 2009, Ray Takeyh, then a State Department deputy to Dennis Ross, told the *New York Times* that the Obama administration's goal in its approach to Iran was "to inject a degree of rationality into this relationship, reduce it to two nations with some differences and some common interests—get beyond the incendiary rhetoric."[1]

Given the deep mistrust and antagonism that had developed between the two countries, and a mutual ignorance of their internal politics given the lack of diplomatic relations for more than three decades, the task would not be easy. Nothing about Iran over the three decades since its revolution and the subsequent hostage crisis had been easy.

The Obama administration had launched a "new era of engagement," and the centerpiece was the P5 + 1 negotiations regarding Iran's nuclear program (the Europeans referred to the talks as the E3 + 3).

After the false start in 2009, the negotiations were surprisingly constructive, predictably challenging and complex, and ultimately historic. After years of missed opportunities, both countries were prepared to engage at the same time. Over time, the diplomatic leading actors directly involved, especially Secretary of State John Kerry and Foreign Minister Mohammad Javad Zarif, developed a professional and personal rapport. Despite difficult moments, they led their respective teams across the finish line.

A crucial addition to the American negotiating team was Secretary of Energy Ernest Moniz. Backed by experts across the American nuclear complex, he would be pivotal in identifying the technical steps required to add real time to the Iranian nuclear clock and defending the administration narrative

179

that it had successfully blocked Tehran's path to a weapon for at least fifteen years.

THE ELECTION

The process proceeded as well as the Obama administration hoped, but it just took four years longer than anticipated. There was a significant opening after the Iranian election—not the 2009 election when President Mahmoud Ahmadinejad was returned to office through a disputed result, but the 2013 election when the Iranian people returned the pragmatists to power. President Hassan Rouhani, himself a former nuclear negotiator, was prepared to try again, with the evident blessing of Ayatollah Ali Khamenei.

The United States and Iran developed competing narratives around the nuclear negotiations that were contradictory, but not necessarily incompatible.

The American narrative was that the failure of Iran to engage constructively and accept the Tehran Research Reactor proposal in 2009—shipping out its stock of enriched fuel in return for a guaranteed fuel source to meet a legitimate need—led to the pressure track where the United States orchestrated increased national and international sanctions that further isolated Iran politically and crippled it economically.

The sanctions, including additional measures passed by Congress despite administration objections, effectively curtailed Iran's access to the global financial system.[2] The Iranian people, with high aspirations but low opportunities given the government's pariah status, elected a leader who seemed capable of constructing a better relationship with the international community and the United States.

The view from Tehran, notwithstanding the economic pressure, was that after years of defending Iran's rights under the Non-Proliferation Treaty, the United States and other major international players finally accepted Iran's position that its peaceful civilian nuclear program must include a guaranteed indigenous source of nuclear fuel. Iran considered that it had a "right" to enrich (a view not shared by the international community) within the terms of the NPT and Additional Protocol. Iran wasn't forced to make a deal; the international community finally was willing to make a deal based on terms that Tehran had consistently advocated.

As with most narratives, there is truth in each, although flaws as well. No doubt Iran was suffering economically, both due to sanctions and long-standing economic mismanagement. For Rouhani to have a successful presidency, he needed to improve Iran's economic performance, and sanctions relief certainly enhances those prospects. But it is also true that the United States softened its positions regarding enrichment and accountability for past activity in order to reach an agreement.

In other words, it was a real negotiation. Neither side got everything it wanted.

The politics of the Iran deal were fraught on both sides. The two presidential staffs contemplated a brief meeting between Obama and Rouhani on the margins of the United Nations General Assembly but settled on a phone call instead. Even a polite handshake between Obama and Zarif created political blowback in Tehran. As negotiations entered the final phase, Republican senators released a letter threatening to reverse any agreement that was reached.

The U.S. mantra of all options on the table suggested to Iran that it was not interested in a relationship based on mutual respect, but one based on intimidation. While Obama pledged never to allow Iran to gain an actual weapon, "the harder question, never discussed on the campaign trail, would be how close to that goal Obama would allow the Iranians to get."[3]

While the Obama administration acknowledged Iran's interest in civilian nuclear energy without considering it an explicit right, the president took note of the Supreme Leader's fatwa against nuclear weapons, reaffirmed by President Rouhani, and decided to test these public commitments.

"So these statements made by our respective governments should offer the basis for a meaningful agreement," Obama said at the United Nations General Assembly in 2013. "But to succeed, conciliatory words will have to be matched by actions that are transparent and verifiable. After all, it's the Iranian government's choices that have led to the comprehensive sanctions that are currently in place."[4]

For Trita Parsi, the key to this exchange was the West's acceptance of the reality that Iran was never going to accept a zero option regarding enrichment. Once that bridge was crossed, the negotiation became possible.[5] But that concession keyed the opposition to the negotiation, particularly from a key U.S. ally.

BAD DEAL

The Israelis had been cool to negotiations from the beginning of the Obama administration. In his first visit in May 2009, Prime Minister Benjamin Netanyahu recognized the potential value of testing Iran's willingness to negotiate but was concerned that it not be allowed to string them out as it inched closer to a weapons capability.

Netanyahu's Minister of Defense, Ehud Barak, talked repeatedly about an approaching "zone of immunity" after which Iran's nuclear program could not be effectively stopped or attacked. Israel sought to limit the time period for negotiations, keep the military option on the table, and define any deal as requiring zero enrichment, a very different bottom line than the Americans ultimately drew.

In truth, the only way to guarantee zero enrichment was to invade the country and replace the government with one committed to denuclearization. The existing Iranian regime was not about to surrender to the West, particularly since the nuclear program enjoyed considerable popular support.

"Without a deal, we risk even more war in the Middle East," said Obama.[6]

That left only one viable alternative, negotiating on the basis of a limited nuclear capability while restricting the potential for a breakout. According to the U.S. negotiating team, achieving that outcome resembled solving a Rubik's cube.

However, Netanyahu, an aggressive and surprisingly public critic of the agreement, felt that as the negotiations progressed, the Obama administration yielded too much on sanctions, giving up important leverage. Netanyahu believed that Obama felt obligated to make a deal because American politics ruled out the use of force.[7]

As the Obama administration closed in on a deal between Iran and the international community, Netanyahu took the unprecedented step of addressing the U.S. Congress, wading directly into the middle of the American domestic political divide.

Beginning his remarks, Netanyahu mentioned that "some perceive my being here as political. That was never my intention." In fact, his speech was all about politics. He effectively challenged the Republican-led Congress to block implementation of what he considered "a very bad deal. We're better off without it."[8]

The Israeli prime minister both anticipated and rebutted the Obama administration's strongest arguments for the deal. The alternative was not war, but a better deal.

From Israel's vantage point, the agreement allowed Iran to retain a large nuclear infrastructure that either encouraged "hide and cheat" while it remained in force or enabled a short breakout period once it expired. "This doesn't block Iran's path to a bomb," Netanyahu said, "it paves Iran's path to the bomb."[9]

Before receiving any sanctions relief, Netanyahu believed Iran should first stop its aggression within the Middle East, its support for terrorism, and its threats against Israel. "If Iran wants to be treated as a normal country," he said, "let it act like a normal country."

Reminding U.S. lawmakers that few countries had more American blood on their hands and continued to embrace the Death to America narrative, Netanyahu cautioned that there were no overlapping interests with Iran. Even when it comes to fighting the Islamic State, "the enemy of your enemy is your enemy."[10]

While he portrayed Iran as vulnerable given continued international pressure and declining oil prices, at the same time Netanyahu suggested it now dominated four Arab capitals—Baghdad, Damascus, Beirut, and Sana'a—dramatically extending its influence as the existing regional order collapsed.

Less than a week after Netanyahu's speech, Senator Tom Cotton, a first-term Republican from Arkansas, released an open letter signed by forty-six Senate colleagues addressed to the Leaders of the Islamic Republic of Iran. The letter was ostensibly to acquaint Iran's leadership of the U.S. constitutional process regarding the ratification of international agreements.[11]

Since the signatories were all Republicans, it represented a de facto presidential campaign plank. A future president, presumably a Republican, could revoke the agreement "with the stroke of a pen" and a future Congress "could modify the terms of the agreement at any time."[12]

There was considerable concern about the implications of the more than $100 billion in frozen assets that would be available to Iran with the lifting of sanctions tied to its nuclear programs. (Iran would not gain relief from sanctions related to its human rights record and support for terrorism.)

Critics of the deal frequently suggest that a better deal was readily available, without recognizing how recent American actions have impacted the strategic calculations of rogue regimes like Iran and North Korea and the consequent value they see in nuclear deterrence.

Saddam Hussein started a nuclear program, but never built an actual weapon. He was eventually overthrown. Muammar Qaddafi started a nuclear program and voluntarily gave it up. He was eventually overthrown. Kim Jong-il claimed to be willing to denuclearize but never actually did. His son, Kim Jong-un, has given up all pretenses and now appears to be perfecting North Korea's capability as a regime survival strategy.

Ayatollah Ali Khamenei termed an actual nuclear weapon as haram or forbidden while positioning Tehran as a potential nuclear power, a strategic hedge in the event the revolutionary government felt threatened in the future. There is no reason to believe that a better deal was possible.[13]

As Obama rebutted, it was unrealistic that sanctions would force an Iranian capitulation regarding what it views as a "right" to have a nuclear program, or that sanctions could continue indefinitely. "We put sanctions in place to get a diplomatic resolution, and that is what we have done."[14]

NO ALTERNATIVE

The nuclear agreement with Iran involved not just the United States, but also Russia, China, Great Britain, France, Germany, and the European Union. In fact, diplomats representing America's closest allies made clear to members of Congress that their governments would not support renegotiation.

In a follow-on speech at American University, Obama suggested "our closest allies in Europe, or in Asia—much less China or Russia—certainly are not going to agree to enforce existing sanctions for another 5, 10, 15 years according to the dictates of the U.S. Congress."[15]

The United States paid a relatively low price for sanctions, since it did no business with Iran. Other countries that imported oil from Iran had far more developed economic relationships. Obama argued that sanctions by themselves were never going to result in Iranian capitulation as critics suggested. Without a deal, there would be no lasting constraints on Iran's civilian nuclear program.

As Secretary of State John Kerry said in a speech in Philadelphia, sanctions did not stop Iran's march toward a nuclear weapon capability; a negotiated agreement did.

Iran complied with its obligations under the Joint Plan of Action. The breakout time under the agreement is according to the administration now at least a year, with all pathways to an actual weapon closed off.

In choosing American University as the speech site, the White House consciously drew parallels to John F. Kennedy's commencement speech in June 1963 where he not only announced plans to negotiate a partial test ban treaty with the Soviet Union (and Britain) but signaled in the aftermath of the Cuban Missile Crisis that the United States would not start a war with the Soviet Union.

Obama also drew parallels to Ronald Reagan's willingness to negotiate with the Soviet Union—"a far greater existential threat to us than Iran will ever be"—even as he labeled them the "evil empire." Reagan also allowed members of the National Security staff to negotiate with Iran regarding the return of American hostages in Lebanon (although it would lead to a cover-up and scandal that threatened the Reagan presidency).

Ironically, one of the key figures in Iran-Contra, Richard Secord, a retired Air Force major general, was among 190 retired flag officers who wrote an open letter to Congress opposing the agreement as "unverifiable."[16]

David Ignatius of the *Washington Post* termed the Iran agreement, both the negotiation itself and the successful defense before a skeptical Congress, as "the strategic success" of the Obama presidency.[17]

No deal is perfect, but the nuclear agreement required Iran to take unprecedented steps to dismantle a significant portion of an active nuclear program in which it had invested billions of dollars: shipping nuclear fuel out of the country, removing thousands of centrifuges, and repurposing major nuclear facilities.

The deal provided for around-the-clock access to declared nuclear facilities and managed access to undeclared sites where there may be suspicions of illicit activity. The conventional arms embargo against Iran would be lifted in five years and the ban on the purchase of missile technology would end in eight years.

Obama in an interview with Tom Friedman of the *New York Times*, expressed hope that the Iran deal would lead "to a more constructive relationship with the world community." But the administration stressed that the deal dealt with one specific area of concern. "We are not measuring this deal by whether it is changing the regime inside of Iran," Obama said later. "We're not measuring this deal by whether we are solving every problem that can be traced back to Iran, whether we are eliminating all their nefarious activities around the globe."[18]

In fact, the Obama admisistration had hopes Iran would be more cooperative in battling the Islamic State or resolving the Syrian civil war. Those hopes went unfulfilled as Iran and Russia intervened directly to protect the Assad regime.

Some were critical that the United States would negotiate with Iran at all. But Obama was quick to point out that "you don't make deals like this with your friends."[19] He put the choice starkly as "between diplomacy or some form of war—maybe not tomorrow, maybe not three months from now, but soon."[20]

In the criticism of the deal with Iran, the president saw the same dynamic that propelled the United States into Iraq. The same people criticizing the deal with Iran are the same who advocated for the invasion of Iraq. Ironically, the president pointed out, the prime beneficiary of that action was Iran, which saw its strategic position in the region enhanced by the elimination of its primary nemesis, Saddam Hussein.

Obama reiterated a valid concern that, in the absence of an agreement, there was a risk of a regional arms race. The deal was described as a "leap of faith" or "roll of the dice," a belief that kicking the nuclear can down the road ten to fifteen years represents sufficient "time and space to restructure one of the United States' deepest adversarial relationships."[21]

October 18, 2015, became "adoption day" when, following approval of the nuclear deal by the Guardian Council and parliament, Iran began to mothball thousands of centrifuges, convert enrichment plants to more benign uses, and ship most of its existing nuclear fuel stockpile out of the country. Just as the United States and international community closely monitored Iran's compliance, Tehran set up its own watchdog to ensure that the promised sanctions relief was forthcoming. The government felt it needed to demonstrate an end to Iran's economic isolation before March elections in order to hold off hard-liners opposed to the deal.[22]

The International Atomic Energy Agency formally closed its investigation into Iran's past nuclear weapons activities on December 15 as part of the implementation of the nuclear deal.

Despite majorities in both houses of Congress, Republicans did not have a sufficient majority to block implementation of the Iran nuclear deal; instead, they decided to run against it in the 2016 campaign.

MUNICH NARRATIVE REAPPEARS ON CUE

The Iran deal brought back the decades-old debate regarding engagement and appeasement. Almost on cue, Senator Lindsey Graham of South Carolina called Obama "the Neville Chamberlain of our time."[23] Critics decried the negotiation, believing that the joint plan of action legitimated Iran's nuclear program and left Tehran with a plausible path to an actual weapon if it ever chose to do so.

Obama rejected the idea that negotiating with a "malevolent adversary" represented appeasement. Obama rightly suggested that "total surrender" was never a realistic option.[24]

Never one to avoid hyperbole, Donald Trump called it "the worst deal I've ever seen negotiated."[25] Senator Ted Cruz called it "catastrophic" and was one of several candidates who pledged "on the very first day in office, to rip to shreds this Iranian nuclear deal."[26]

The strident opposition seemed to have an impact on public opinion, which steadily declined between the successful conclusion of negotiations and its implementation. By the fall of 2015, Americans were evenly split if not narrowly opposed to the deal.[27]

Senator Marco Rubio, critical of Obama's "open hand to Iran," called the deal an elevation of politics over policy, "legacy over leadership, and adversaries over allies." Recognizing that the deal's signatories were unlikely to agree to renegotiate its terms, Rubio pledged to employ sanctions against any entity that pursued commercial opportunities with Iran. Nations of the world would be confronted with a choice. "They can do business with Iran, or they can do business with America, and I am very confident they're going to choose America before they choose the Iranian economy."[28]

An ardent believer in American strength and leadership, Rubio overlooked the devastating impact such a policy would have on relations with the major global players directly involved in or supportive of the nuclear deal.

There was concern expressed about the implications from Democrats as well. Explaining his opposition to the deal, Maryland senator Benjamin Cardin, ranking member of the Senate Foreign Relations Committee, suggested that the P5 + 1 agreement "legitimizes Iran's nuclear program," overlooking the fact that the Non-Proliferation Treaty entitled states in good standing to pursue peaceful civilian nuclear capability.[29]

Jeb Bush was one of the few to call out the rejectionists, quipping that "it is not a strategy to tear up an agreement."[30] Although Bush would not survive what became a remarkable antiestablishment campaign, some members of the Republican national security establishment spoke out in favor of the deal.

Former National Security Advisor Brent Scowcroft suggested in an op-ed in the *Washington Post* that the nuclear deal represents a potential "epochal moment" on a par with Richard Nixon's opening with China or Ronald Reagan and George H. W. Bush's management of the decline and end of the Soviet Union.[31]

Scowcroft viewed the deal as a test of the U.S. leadership in the Middle East and whether it has the will to continue to play a constructive role in the region. He did not see a credible alternative to the negotiated agreement.

"If we walk away, we walk away alone," Scowcroft cautioned. "The world's leading powers worked together effectively because of U.S. leadership. To turn our back on this accomplishment would be an abdication of the United States' unique role and responsibility."[32]

The Obama administration downplayed the damage to American credibility with its circuitous approach to the Syrian red line, but nonetheless viewed the Iran deal as a key test. Obama said rejection of the deal would undermine "America's credibility as the anchor of the international system."[33] Added John Kerry, it would be "a self-destructive blow to our nation's credibility and leadership."[34]

Obama acknowledged the "partisan prism" through which the deal was being evaluated. Ironically, joining him in that concern was the man he defeated in the 2008 presidential campaign, John McCain, who viewed with regret the fact that the agreement would be the first major treaty that did not have bipartisan support (which he defined as at least one member of the Senate voting for an agreement negotiated by a president of the other party). Of course, that was not a sufficient reason for McCain himself to vote for the agreement.

Senate Democrats assembled forty-two votes to block any effort to formally reject the Iran nuclear deal, relieving Obama from having to veto a resolution of disapproval.[35]

NOW WHAT?

On the Democratic side, former Secretary of State Hillary Clinton believed the nuclear deal "accomplishes the major goals we set out to achieve," establishing a verification regime and extending the time available to detect any cheating. She viewed Iran as the "subject" of the agreement, not as a "partner" in its implementation.[36] She called the deal a "balancing of risk," not a "perfect solution." She was critical of Republican pledges to tear it up, saying that is "not leadership. That's recklessness."[37] She pledged to be vigilant if Iran violated its terms.

Clinton was far more skeptical regarding the prospects of improved relations with Iran in the foreseeable future. To some extent reprising her position from the 2008 campaign, where she supported a diplomatic initiative under the right conditions—the very path that she and Obama took with Iran and the nuclear negotiation—she viewed the prospect of normalization as leverage to change Iranian behavior. She preferred a step-by-step approach where "you have to get action for action."[38]

She listed several preconditions—getting out of Syria, ceasing support for Hezbollah and Hamas and its hostility toward Israel, in other words dramatically reshaping its regional policies—before she could envision normal relations.[39]

Clinton did not expect the agreement to yield a diplomatic opening with Iran or a meaningful change in Iran's behavior. "We've had one good day over 36 years," she told a debate audience in South Carolina in early 2016. "I think we need more good days before we move more rapidly toward any kind of normalization."

Clinton's caution was actually shared in Tehran. In an interview with CBS's *60 Minutes*, President Rouhani signaled that the process of rebuilding trust will take time from Tehran's vantage point as well.

"The enmity that existed between the United States and Iran over the decades, the distance, the disagreements, the lack of trust, will not go away soon. What's important is which direction are we heading?" Rouhani said through a translator. "I believe we have taken the first steps towards decreasing this enmity."[40]

While the Iranian people welcome the opening with the West, Iran's leadership remains wary. The relationship still carries significant political baggage that accumulated over decades. The strategic narratives of the two countries—the Great Satan interfering in the sovereign affairs of Middle Eastern states and a great civilization hijacked by a malign religious ideology—still have currency.

When asked about Iran's narrative, Rouhani explained that "Satan in our religious parlance is used to refer to that power that tricks others and whose words are not clear words [and] do not match reality."[41]

It's not clear that the American narrative will evolve significantly either. Notwithstanding progress on the nuclear issue, the Iranian regime has a poor human rights record and represses political dissent. Prospects for economic development are problematic, since the Iranian Revolutionary Guard Corps, a designated terrorist entity, remains deeply imbedded in the Iranian economy.

The White House was rightly understated regarding the prospects of normalized relations. Perhaps as a reflection of the need to balance politics in Iran, Tehran followed the nuclear deal with a series of controversial missile tests by the Iranian Revolutionary Guard Corps. The Obama administration indicated potential support for additional sanctions in response.

There are hard-line forces within the Islamic Republic that are invested in the status quo politically, militarily, and economically. How much the regime feels it needs to respond to popular sentiment remains to be seen. Conservatives on both sides have the interest in seeing the nuclear agreement fail and ability to impose political costs on any future cooperation.

But like the resumption of diplomatic ties with Cuba, the deal inevitably raises the expectations of the Iranian people for an end to the country's isolation, expectations that Iran's sclerotic religious leadership will find both unnerving and difficult to manage.

Unlike Cuba, there will not be embassies being opened anytime soon. The next president should consider establishing mutual interest sections to facilitate increased travel and exchanges while also expanding routine diplomatic contact that will enable communications between the two countries to mature.

Unlike China, where the opening to the United States and the West occurred as a result of Mao's strategic shift, the nuclear deal may create a comparable opening, but it will take some time to know.

"Iran will be and should be a regional power," Obama said. "They have the ability now to take some decisive steps to move toward a more constructive relationship with the world community."[42]

As Obama discovered, even though political leaders of all stripes acknowledge the independence and interconnections of the twenty-first-century world, powerful historical narratives from the twentieth century have not gone away. Notwithstanding successful bipartisan engagement with the Soviet Union throughout the Cold War, presidents who engage adversaries are accused of appeasement—negotiations are viewed as a reward rather than a realistic means of resolving problems at the lowest possible cost.

The lesson of Munich was misapplied with Vietnam, resulting in a gradual drift toward a war that was strategically unnecessary. By engaging without precondition in nuclear negotiations with Iran, Obama rightly ignored the rhetoric of appeasement and reached an agreement that is arguably his most significant foreign accomplishment.

Whether or not it yields greater moderation in Tehran, it substantially lowered the risk of an unwanted military confrontation that was far more likely than not to result in the very outcome the United States wished to avoid—a nuclear-capable Iran. Beyond the nuclear agreement, it is unclear what either country wants out of the relationship. Regular high-level dialogue is necessary to find common ground for cooperation where possible, take steps that reduce sources of friction (such as an exchange of prisoners, including jailed journalists), and work toward the eventual resumption of normalized diplomatic relations, not as a reward but recognition of reality in the Middle East.

Aside from the nuclear agreement itself, the negotiation produced a direct, high-level, and effective channel of communication between the U.S. and Iranian governments, the first time that has existed in more than thirty-five years. The presidents of the two countries had a brief conversation by phone. The foreign ministers of the two countries worked on a first-name basis. Their respective staffs have achieved a high level of familiarity, if not yet trust.

Iran's fulfillment of its obligations under the nuclear deal coincided with an incident in the Persian Gulf where U.S. sailors, due to a navigation error, drifted into Iranian waters and were briefly detained by Iranian authorities. Following a flurry of diplomatic activity, the sailors were quickly repatriated, although not before Iran released a video that showed the sailors with their hands up.

The fact that the incident was quickly resolved demonstrates the fruits of constructive engagement and the increasing ability of the two countries to work together. Yet Senator Ted Cruz called the incident "heartbreaking" and threatened "the full force and fury of the United States of America" in response to any seizure of American service members if he were president.[43]

The first round of Iranian elections following the nuclear deal appeared to favor the engagers among the regime's leadership. All but one of the candidates supported by the Rouhani camp earned seats within the Assembly of Experts, the body that will appoint a new supreme leader.

After the Gulf War, the Bush administration excluded Iran from the Madrid Conference, suggesting that it did not have a role to play in the "new world order" that was being established. A quarter century later, the United States has begrudgingly recognized that Iran is a regional power and will have an impact one way or another.

The Obama administration seemed to acknowledge in 2015 that there could be no solution to the challenge in Syria without including Iran directly in a political solution. As foreign ministers gathered in Vienna in late October to try to reenergize the stalled political process, the first such gathering since the successful conclusion of nuclear talks, Iran sent its foreign minister, although no convergence of interests is yet visible.

Iran adopted a posture similar to Russia's regarding the future of Bashar al-Assad. Fight terrorism, secure the country again, and then talk about how the country should be governed. At the same time, Saudi Arabia looked to increase the costs to Iran for its support of Assad and the Houthis in Yemen.

In an unprecedented step, Prince Turki bin Faisal Al Saud, a member of the Saudi royal family, attended a conference in Paris in July 2016 sponsored by the exiled National Council of Resistance in Iran and all but endorsed regime change, a gesture Tehran will undoubtedly view as a grave threat. The

Saudi action will certainly intensify the rivalry that underlies the conflicts in both Syria and Yemen.

While it will be up to the next president to chart where the U.S. relationship with Iran proceeds beyond the nuclear deal, as Obama approached the end of his time in office, he became more assertive about what it accomplished.

"Iran is now being subjected to the most comprehensive inspection regimen ever negotiated to monitor a nuclear program," he wrote in the *Washington Post* on the eve of his last Nuclear Security Summit. "In other words, under this deal, the world has prevented yet another nation from getting a nuclear weapon."[44]

The next president may have concerns whether the deal will ultimately accomplish that objective, but is unlikely to change it.

12

GOOD ENOUGH

President Obama pledged while campaigning for the presidency to commit greater resources to Afghanistan, as part of a strategy he reframed as the war against al Qaeda. "There must be no safe haven for those who plot to kill Americans," he suggested in a 2007 *Foreign Affairs* article, drawing a parallel between the war against al Qaeda and the Cold War.[1]

Once in office, after a detailed policy review, he announced in late 2009 that a military and civilian surge would stabilize Afghanistan, reverse the Taliban's momentum, strengthen Afghan security forces, and transition to a long-term multilateral partnership. By August 2010, there were close to 140,000 American and NATO troops in the country.

The administration hoped to reduce the capability of the Taliban and convince them to give up the fight; improve the performance and legitimacy of the Afghan government; and jump-start the economy by expanding regional trade. If successful, this would over time make the country more stable and international support more sustainable. There was no doubt the country would need considerable outside support for an indefinite period.

But Obama made clear he was not making an open-ended commitment, which he said "was not necessary in order for us to meet our national interests as properly defined."[2] The United States would help create an Afghanistan that was "good enough" to hold its own and avoid being a future safe haven for global terrorists. It would not be a perfect place.

Obama was wary of military solutions to complex political situations that tended to yield unwelcome consequences. He was, says Boston University Professor Andrew Bacevich, much more reluctant than his predecessors to "sound crusading notes" in the employment of military force.[3] He tried to reorient the war in Afghanistan back to its original purpose, the one the American people actually signed up for—defeating al Qaeda.[4]

But by agreeing to the military's counterinsurgency strategy—even for a limited period—Obama inadvertently intensified the fight against the Taliban, an extremist group that was a threat to Afghanistan but not the United States, a war that was not necessarily vital to American security.

However, even the limited war that Obama was prepared to wage was problematic. According to former American diplomat Peter Tomsen, "there has never been a possibility that the United States and its allies could win the war against the Taliban. Only Afghans themselves can do that."[5]

While the Afghans did steadily improve their military capability, it was not fast enough to match the political timetable Obama believed he confronted. Other critical elements of the strategy lagged further behind, including the pervasive challenge of Afghan government corruption, fed by levels of international assistance that Afghanistan could not absorb and bumper poppy crops that funded the insurgency and undermined the development of a legal economy.

There were too many disconnects between what was possible and necessary, and not enough pressure on adversaries and allies to change course. The Obama administration had a plan, but none of the pieces fit together easily.

Despite his best efforts, Afghanistan turned out to be a war that Obama technically ended but in reality could not turn off, without risking the collapse of the Kabul government and the American regional strategy. In July 2016, the president announced that 8,400 U.S. personnel would remain when he left office to continue supporting Afghan forces and guard against the renewed threat posed by the Taliban, al Qaeda, and the Islamic State.

IN SEARCH OF A POLITICAL SOLUTION

The White House acknowledged that the timetable the president outlined in December 2009 at West Point was driven by the limits of the available support for a war that was already more than eight years old. To "purchase more time and resources for the policy," explained Ben Rhodes, a deputy national security advisor and Obama's foreign policy speechwriter, the president was forced to specify "the limits of what we would do."[6]

The emerging strategy in Afghanistan confronted local realities that could either help or hinder American designs for the country. The warlords, as they were termed, were an integral part of Afghan society; no plan was likely to succeed without them. The Taliban was the most powerful indigenous political force in the country. No revised system of government was likely to mature if they continued to attack it. The United States had taken far too long before recognizing the need for a viable peace process, giving the Taliban valuable time to recover after being driven from power in 2011.

The Bush administration refused to negotiate with the Taliban despite having significant leverage in the very early stages of the conflict. In December 2001, a group of high-ranking Taliban representatives signaled to the incoming interim Afghan president, Hamid Karzai, that they were willing to negotiate a settlement in return for immunity. The White House was not interested.[7] Subsequent Taliban peace feelers were scotched by Karzai and Pakistan, who feared being cut out of the negotiating process since the Taliban preferred talking to Washington if anyone.[8]

After Obama announced the surge in 2009, the military preferred to wait for the tide to turn on the battlefield before launching negotiations.[9] Another factor was domestic political risk. As former State Department official Vali Nasr acknowledged, "talking to terrorists is not good politics."[10]

As Washington developed a negotiating strategy, there were valid concerns that a political settlement would jeopardize significant social advances, particularly regarding opportunity for women and education for girls. Hillary Clinton told Afghan officials repeatedly that peace could not be achieved at the expense of half of Afghan society. She articulated a balanced path forward in a February 2011 speech to the Asia Society.[11]

The U.S. core conditions for a political settlement were the Taliban must break with al Qaeda, abandon violence, and abide by the Afghan constitution, meaning that they must accept a meaningful role for women in Afghan society.[12] The Taliban themselves were divided on their continued association with al Qaeda, although there was never evidence of a break.[13]

When negotiations finally started in 2010, the early meetings were dominated by a prisoner swap that the Obama administration would ultimately engineer involving five Taliban detainees at Guantanamo and an Army soldier who was subsequently charged with deserting his post. The White House endured withering criticism for the trade, even though it reflected a sacrosanct military commitment not to leave soldiers behind.★

★While there was a legitimate question whether the Taliban fighters could return to the fight, the administration neutralized those concerns, working with Qatar to host and monitor them. Despite the fact that Sergeant Bowe Bergdahl had apparently abandoned his post, in the process putting fellow soldiers at risk, the administration orchestrated a Rose Garden ceremony with the president and Bergdahl's parents, failing to recognize the severity of the

Special representative Richard Holbrooke sought to increase trade and transit between Afghanistan and Pakistan to improve the prospects of regional cooperation and integration. The two countries signed a trade agreement in 2010, part of the New Silk Road initiative designed to restore Afghanistan's historical role as a regional trading hub. But Pakistan remained wary that Afghanistan was an insecure back door and security vulnerability vis-à-vis India.

At roughly the same time, the White House was charting an exit strategy. In July 2010, at the NATO Summit in Lisbon, Karzai publicly committed to assume full responsibility for Afghan security, a bold pledge that exceeded its actual capabilities. Whether realistic, it dovetailed with political imperatives both in Kabul and Washington.

General David Petraeus, who was regional commander as the review unfolded and commander in Afghanistan at the height of the surge, did not believe that the politics of the moment required a troop reduction. Political capital, he believed, was renewable, provided there was progress.[14] He would misjudge both the politics and the president. The Afghan war cost $119 billion in 2011, a level the White House believed could not be sustained.

Obama, suggested Fred Kaplan in *The Insurgents*, viewed his Afghanistan strategy as a gamble that didn't pay off. Taking advantage of the death of bin Laden, he was "pulling the plug on COIN" and scaling back the U.S. commitment to Afghanistan.[15]

When Obama announced in June 2011 that he was sticking to the timeline established at West Point to reverse the surge, he was effectively shifting from counterinsurgency to a counterterrorism approach.

At the NATO Summit in Chicago, Afghanistan affirmed that the transition process would begin in mid-2013, with Afghan forces taking the lead in security operations in all Afghan provinces by the end of 2014, supported by U.S. and NATO forces.[16]

While Obama felt the need to publicly limit his commitment to Afghanistan in order to sustain public support for his strategy, it undermined the prospects for a successful political negotiation. The Obama administration attempted a talk while leaving approach, although it was never clear how committed the Taliban was to the process.[17]

As Henry Kissinger suggested in a meeting with Obama's Afghanistan negotiating team in 2011, "You should never be negotiating a peace when the

_____

pending military investigation. The president should have called the Bergdahls after his release and then released a written statement reiterating America's commitment to always bring soldiers home from any battlefield.

opposing force knows you are leaving."[18] But that horse had already left the barn two years earlier, a fact Kissinger undoubtedly knew.

The failure of the political track didn't surprise insiders who knew Afghanistan best. The Taliban was "a religious *movement*, never a political *party*" (emphasis in the original), wrote CIA station chief Robert Grenier in his book *88 Days to Kandahar*.[19]

"It was an impossible task to convince the Taliban that it should operate inside the Afghan political system rather than outside of it," suggested former Acting CIA Director Michael Morell.[20]

The United States never arrived at a political end state in Afghanistan that the region, particularly Pakistan, would support. Pakistani policy was built on the premise that the United States would leave Afghanistan. So was U.S. policy. This was always a fundamental hole in the American strategy.

THE ALLY FROM HELL

Talking at a breakfast with foreign policy reporters in Washington in early 2013, Pakistani ambassador to the United States Sherry Rehman condemned the use of U.S. drones against terrorist targets within Pakistan as counterproductive and illegal.

"We see them as a direct violation of our sovereignty." She denied that the government in Islamabad secretly collaborated with the United States regarding drone operations, insisting, "There is no policy of quiet complacency, no wink and nod."[21]

But there is strong evidence that some elements of the Pakistani government, in particular its military and intelligence leaders, were quite aware of what the United States was doing.[22] In fact, there was an "unspoken deal" between the governments that operations would be under the control of the Central Intelligence Agency, allowing plausible deniability on both sides regarding the targeting of extremists out of concern over Pakistani public opinion.[23]

The United States treated drone operations as secret, even though their use is well cataloged by the Pakistani media and international nongovernmental organizations. Pakistan would cooperate privately while denying it publicly. Pakistan participated in targeting decisions for its own security purposes, but would manipulate local public sentiment when the United States targeted its extremist allies.[24]

In November 2008, Pakistan's president, Asif Ali Zadari, assured CIA Director Michael Hayden he could manage the politics of continued drone strikes against al Qaeda's senior leadership.[25] But as a general rule, Pakistan's ISI preferred not to involve civilian leaders in decisions surrounding U.S. operations in Pakistan.[26] For its own reasons, the Pakistani military did not feel it could acknowledge the degree to which its security relied on the United States, hardly the makings of a strategic partnership.

In 2001, in the aftermath of the attacks of September 11, the Bush administration demanded that the Musharraf government condemn the al Qaeda attacks, deny al Qaeda a safe haven in Pakistan, cooperate with the United States in its Afghan mission, and break diplomatic relations with the Taliban. According to Husain Haqqani, former Pakistani ambassador to the United States, Musharraf made a tactical, but not a strategic choice. Pakistan would cooperate in some ways, but not others.[27]

Pakistani forces were instrumental in the capture of Khalid Sheikh Mohammed, the mastermind of the 9/11 attacks. The picture of a disheveled terrorist wearing a ratty T-shirt had a significant impact on global perceptions of the supposed glamour of al Qaeda's war with the United States.[28]

But Pakistan did far less regarding the Taliban. The greatest concern for Pakistan was that the United States would again turn its back on the region, leaving Pakistan to pick up the pieces. Its support for various groups on both sides of its border with Afghanistan was a hedging strategy against India. Pakistan's ill-advised agreement in 2006 to end Pakistani military operations in the FATA, the Waziristan Accord, was a crucial factor in the Taliban's comeback.[29]

Pakistan "mastered the art of pretending to help the United States while actually supporting its most deadly foes," says Fareed Zakaria.[30] Given that it is a nuclear power with the fastest-growing arsenal in the world, Washington seldom called Islamabad on its double-dealing.

Grenier described relations between the United States and Pakistan as "layered, institutionalized duplicity."[31] Inside the U.S. government, Pakistan was considered the "ally from hell."[32]

A key insight from the 2009 strategic review was that Pakistan was of far greater importance in combating terrorism than Afghanistan. Yet when Obama offered Islamabad a fundamentally different relationship, the Pakistani government demurred. It was unwilling to give up its preoccupation with India and envision a different future.

The total lack of trust between the countries was apparent during the Raymond Davis incident in early 2011. Davis, a U.S. intelligence operative, was arrested after shooting two Pakistani citizens who threatened him. A third

Pakistani citizen was run over by an American Consulate vehicle as it responded in haste to the scene. The United States invoked the Vienna Convention and demanded his release. Pakistan denied that he had diplomatic immunity, but eventually released him after payment of damages to the families of the deceased.*

In the aftermath of the Abbottabad raid, Pakistan initially attempted to convey that the death of bin Laden was a shared victory against international terrorism. But the Pakistani public felt humiliated by the fact that American forces were inside Pakistani territory for a lengthy period of time without being detected.[33] According to a poll taken weeks later, two-thirds of Pakistanis condemned the action.[34] The Pakistani government fell back on familiar ground, criticizing the United States for violating its sovereignty. The fear, rational or not, was that if the United States entered Pakistan to get bin Laden, it could do so to take possession of the country's nuclear arsenal.

Following a November 2011 incident along the border with Afghanistan that resulted in the deaths of twenty-four Pakistanis, Pakistan suspended support to NATO for military operations in Afghanistan, blocking the movement of supplies from Pakistani ports across the border. For months, Washington pointedly declined to apologize for the miscommunication that led to the friendly fire incident.

Pakistan's parliament demanded a suspension of drone operations. The administration ignored the request.[35] Not for the first time, Washington sacrificed its long-term solution to political extremism—a more effective allied government in Islamabad genuinely responsive to its population—for short-term tactical gains.

This failure to communicate regarding drone operations was strategically short-sighted. Given Pakistan's nexus to violent political extremism, the "don't ask don't tell" policy prevented the use of public diplomacy to build greater

---

*Various news media outlets learned that Davis was a contractor with the CIA. Believing his life was in danger, U.S. officials including the author made requests to senior editors that reporters withhold that detail from news stories while the sensitive negotiations regarding his release continued. The U.S. media agreed unless or until it was reported elsewhere. While committed to independent reporting of government activity as a fundamental first amendment right and responsibility, most journalists and editors are willing to listen to government concerns and adjust their coverage when lives are at stake. In this case, within days, Pakistani media reported that Davis worked for the CIA and the American media followed suit. During WikiLeaks, the media withheld the identities of civilians who were mentioned in diplomatic cables because of legitimate concerns that, particularly in authoritarian countries, their lives would be in jeopardy. Such requests are rare and must be compelling, but such cooperation represents an appropriate balancing of national interests.

public understanding regarding the importance of drone operations to both U.S. and Pakistani security.[36]

A year after the bin Laden raid, according to a Pew Research Center poll, three out of four Pakistanis considered the United States an "enemy." Only 8 percent viewed the United States as a "partner."[37] Drones were a key factor.

In a speech at the National Defense University, Obama acknowledged the severe impact the bin Laden raid had on Pakistani public opinion and U.S.-Pakistani relations, but not drones, at least not explicitly.

Given the secrecy surrounding drone operations, most Pakistanis considered the conflict as America's war, even though their country was threatened by extremism as well. The American silence enabled the Pakistani government to control the narrative around drone strikes, which it did to the detriment of the overall U.S. strategy.

More recently, there are promising signs that anti–American sentiment is moderating in Pakistan. A Pew Poll in 2014 revealed a declining majority still hold negative views of the United States. One reason is the perception of threat by Pakistanis that extremists now pose to Pakistan itself.[38] Another is a shift in strategy where drone strikes in Pakistan have become less frequent. The "blowback effect" from the drone campaign may not be radicalizing the Pakistani population, although it is not "winning hearts and minds" either.[39]

According to Tomsen, the former U.S. envoy to Afghanistan, "neither the Bush administration nor the Obama administration fully grasped the true depth of Pakistan's duplicity; the U.S. war in Afghanistan has been, in no small part, a war against Washington's putative partners in Islamabad."[40]

For years, Pakistan provided safe haven to extremists, including the Haqqani network, which launched repeated attacks against U.S. personnel in Afghanistan and gradually became more integrated with the Taliban leadership. Pakistan believed that chaos in Afghanistan was good for them, providing strategic depth to offset Indian influence.

Over time, encouraged by U.S. interlocutors, Pakistani officials began to recognize that at least some of the groups they continued to harbor represented a real threat to Pakistan as well. The Pakistani military has devoted greater resources to fighting terrorism. In turn, China has encouraged greater Pakistani support for talks between the Taliban and Afghanistan.

In late 2014, militants in Pakistan attacked a government-run school in Peshawar, killing 157 students and teachers. In early 2016, the Pakistani Taliban claimed credit for an attack against Christians in Lahore that killed at least seventy people, including thirty children. Both events sparked public protests that the government is not doing enough to combat political extremism.

Only 9 percent of Pakistanis have a favorable view of the Islamic State, although 62 percent according to a Pew poll had no opinion.[41] But it is unclear that public discontent has yet translated into a different strategic choice by Pakistani authorities.

But ultimately Obama's surge was not successful "because he could not convince, cajole, or pressure Pakistan to play a more positive role there," suggests the *Atlantic*'s Jeffrey Goldberg.[42] As he prepared to leave office, Obama pointedly questioned whether Pakistan was an ally at all.

THE ZERO OPTION

On May 1, 2012, in a televised address to the American people from Bagram Air Base in Afghanistan, President Obama announced that the U.S. and NATO combat mission would end by December 2014. During a transition period, American and NATO forces would continue to train and advise the 352,000-strong Afghan security forces and conduct counterterrorism operations against the regional remnants of al Qaeda.

While acknowledging that the Afghan war had taken longer than anticipated, Obama believed the tide had turned. The increased emphasis on Afghanistan and Pakistan had broken the Taliban's momentum and brought the defeat of al Qaeda within reach.

Two years later, in a Rose Garden statement, Obama reaffirmed that the United States would end its combat mission in Afghanistan by the end of the year, leaving fewer than ten thousand American troops in Afghanistan in a support role. Force levels would be cut in half by the end of 2015 and the drawdown would be completed by the end of 2016, leaving a security assistance detachment within the American Embassy to continue to coordinate long-term military assistance to the Afghan government.[43]

Describing its relationship with Afghanistan as a strategic partnership, the administration remained skeptical of a long-term presence. "The path," said an unnamed senior official, "is not toward the Korea model."[44] Obama touted the fact that, having inherited active land wars with 180,000 ground troops in harm's way, he anticipated that none would remain engaged in combat when he left office.

While expressing an ongoing commitment to a "sovereign, secure, stable, and unified Afghanistan," Obama acknowledged that despite a decade and a half of effort, "Afghanistan will not be a perfect place, and it is not America's responsibility to make it one."[45]

At the time, Obama was confronting yet another disputed election in Afghanistan as Ashraf Ghani and Abdullah Abdullah jockeyed for the top spot with yet again claims of widespread fraud. Eventually the two worked out an arrangement to share power, with Ghani as president and Abdullah as a newly created chief executive officer.

When Ghani made his first visit to Washington as president, he convinced a skeptical Obama to be more flexible with his exit strategy, keeping a larger number of U.S. forces in Afghanistan through the end of 2015.

The president and his staff were reluctant to keep as many as ten thousand American soldiers in Afghanistan at a prospective cost of $10 to 15 billion per year. But in early August 2015 when General Martin Dempsey, the outgoing chairman of the Joint Chiefs, proposed five thousand troops to stem the growing Islamic State presence in the country and continue to battle al Qaeda, Obama responded, "I think that's an argument that can be made to the American people."[46]

The announcement came on the heels of a major Taliban incursion into Kunduz, the first time the Taliban had controlled a major Afghan city since 2001. While Afghan forces were able to retake control of the city two weeks later, the counteroffensive required significant U.S. support that included air strikes and special forces.

There is strong evidence that Pakistan facilitated the Taliban resurgence, continued to shelter violent jihadis, and have even had a hand in the rise of the Islamic State in the region.[47] A May 2016 U.S. drone strike killed Taliban leader Akhtar Mohammad Mansour in Baluchistan, the first such attack in that part of the country. The action crossed a Pakistani red line that limited drone operations to its tribal areas, but American officials viewed Mansour as an obstacle to a negotiated settlement with the Afghan government and saw an opportunity to confront its recalcitrant ally over its relationship with the Taliban.[48]

In fact, the U.S. safe haven strategy was at risk of failing. The idea that Afghanistan could assume full responsibility for its security on an accelerated timetable absent a peace agreement was too good to be true. A new regional al Qaeda affiliate was able to establish a large training camp near Kandahar, necessitating military action by U.S. special operations and air forces.[49] The developments undermined the administration's metanarrative regarding Afghanistan—that the Taliban's momentum had been reversed, that Afghanistan was able to defend itself, that core al Qaeda and its closest allies were on a path to defeat, and that Afghanistan could not again become a terrorist safe haven.

Obama was undoubtedly chastened by the experience in Iraq, where he fulfilled his commitment to the American people to withdraw all U.S. forces from the country, only to see Iraqi security forces collapse in the face of a challenge from the Islamic State.

Obama bit the bullet.

"The security situation remains precarious," Obama acknowledged when announcing the extension of the U.S. training and counterterrorism missions.[50] Obama suggested a U.S. troop presence would likely be required until the Afghan government and Taliban reconcile.

While welcoming Mr. Obama's decision to retain U.S. forces past 2016 to continue to train Afghan forces and conduct counterterrorism operations, experts with deep experience with the country believe that the United States needs to maintain not just an active advisory capability but sufficient air power in the country to support Afghan forces, a military capability Afghanistan does not yet have.

The White House broadened the existing rules of engagement to allow more direct support to Afghan forces, hoping again to increase pressure on the Taliban to negotiate.[51] But the action further blurred the line between combat, which the president ostensibly ended in 2014, and support, which still places U.S. forces at risk.[52]

The administration resisted comparisons to the Korea model, but ultimately understood that a realistic stabilization process takes a long time, just as Korea did. Notwithstanding Obama's concern about the long-term affordability of the mission, Afghanistan is projected to require as much as $15 billion per year in support.[53]

What happens next falls to another president, the seventh required to struggle with the implications of conflict in Afghanistan—the first three in the context of the Cold War and the next four in the context of combating terrorism. But with the peace talks stalled and threats to the country still significant—both conditions that remain in Korea decades after an armistice—the military is now preparing for an extended presence. The term exit strategy "has largely disappeared from the military's lexicon."[54]

Obama reconceptualized the war on terror that he inherited. He established clear boundaries regarding how it would be waged. But he could not end it. In fact, the three wars he inherited merged into one. It needs to be reconceptualized yet again.

13

WAR WITHIN ISLAM

The Bush administration declared a war on terror that in retrospect was too broad and could not be realistically waged and won. The Obama administration reconstituted the struggle as the war against al Qaeda, exchanging what amounted to perpetual war for a tighter focus on those responsible for September 11, a challenge that could reach a logical end. But given the evolution of the threat, the 2011 Arab uprisings, and the rise of the Islamic State, this formulation proved to be too narrow.

The Middle East is involved now in a multidimensional transition that is likely to take decades to resolve. At one level, it is about what constitutes and who represents Islam. This sectarian struggle underlies the geopolitical rivalry between Iran and the major Gulf states. It is also about the nature of Islamic society and its relationship to the modern and secular world.

At another, it is a crisis of governance and the viability of states formed one hundred years ago. Many of the region's failing republics—Syria, Iraq, Yemen, and Libya—are countries with straight-lined borders with competing ethnic, religious, and tribal constituencies. Given the zero–sum identity politics of the time, there is little trust in central governing structures and no existing conception of inclusive governance. No Washingtons, Jeffersons, Lincolns, or Roosevelts have emerged to guide them out of the existing storm. Their survival in their current form is far from assured.

This ongoing challenge requires reconceptualization yet again. Just saying radical Islamic terrorism misses the mark. That label is far more about tactics than the broader conflict itself. But what we call it—up to now a war on terror and a war against al Qaeda—is actually quite important. Understanding its true nature is fundamental to developing a coherent and effective strategy that employs the right tools, avoids unintended consequences, sets appropriate expectations, and actually makes us safer.

To get there, it is important to recognize how the threat has evolved over the past fifteen years.

The first generation revolved around a series of incidents beginning during the 1990s that culminated with the attacks of September 11. Osama bin Laden and his core al Qaeda movement represented jihad's first generation.

America was at the center of al Qaeda's declared war—the "far enemy." Bin Laden was motivated by the perceived impact of U.S. policies on the Middle East—the occupation of sacred Muslim lands and support for Israel at the perceived expense of the Palestinians.

Bin Laden preferred carefully planned and dramatic attacks to gain notoriety and build popular support for the al Qaeda movement. He became the face of international terrorism. After he was driven from his sanctuary in Afghanistan, he receded from view but relied on audio and videotapes to stay relevant. A bin Laden message, released on the eve of the 2004 U.S. presidential election, may have had a decisive impact on the result.

The ill-advised American invasion of Iraq enabled al Qaeda to launch a comeback and establish an operational capability in the heart of the Middle East. The movement evolved to include franchises in the Arabian Peninsula, Levant, and Sahil and sympathizers in many parts of the world.

Support within the Muslim world for al Qaeda dropped significantly in light of the brutality of al Qaeda's affiliate in Iraq and a recognition that most of its victims were Muslims, not Westerners. By the end of the first decade of the twenty-first century, while it was clear that terrorism remained a potent weapon, it was reasonable to conclude that the threat posed by al Qaeda was diminishing.

At the same time, new leaders emerged committed to establishing a caliphate sooner rather than later. One was Abu Musab al-Zarqawi, the leader of al Qaeda in Iraq. Another was Anwar al-Awlaki, who became the movement's most captivating public figure even before bin Laden's death. Despite his American citizenship and Western upbringing, Awlaki viewed the world as bipolar, between believers and nonbelievers, the flip side of the Bush conception of a world that was with or against the West.

With the help of Awlaki and others who appreciated the potential of information and communication technology, al Qaeda evolved into its second generation and attained global reach. Al Qaeda in the Arabian Peninsula became the movement's most potent franchise. It launched an online magazine, *Inspire*. Awlaki made regular use of blogs and YouTube, products that continue to have potency well beyond his death. The Charlie Hebdo, San Bernardino, and Orlando attackers appear to have been inspired by Awlaki's online videos.

The San Bernardino perpetrators "marinated in extremist ideology and planning for a long time before they finally made a decision to act," suggested Bruce Riedel of Brookings.[1]

The Arab uprisings initially appeared to be a strong refutation of al Qaeda. Political change could be accomplished through peaceful protest rather than violence. Sadly the political and security vacuums that developed in Syria, Libya, and Yemen created new opportunities for a wide array of Islamic actors, including al Qaeda and eventually a rival offshoot.

As the Islamic State has achieved de facto rule over portions of Iraq and Syria and demonstrated a surprising ability to defend that territory, we entered the caliphate phase of the struggle. An estimated thirty thousand foreign fighters from one hundred countries around the world have fought on behalf of the Islamic State, a worrying if relatively small number from the United States. A wide range of Islamist actors worldwide have pledged allegiance to the Islamic State, a mix of local insurgencies under a single authority representing a new form of "distributed warfare."[2]

The Islamic State has also encouraged do-it-yourself terrorism for those unable to reach its battleground principalities. This is jihad 3.0.[3] The conflict has evolved in fundamental ways since 2001. Even with the San Bernardino and Orlando shootings, or seemingly random events perpetrated by disturbed individuals driving a truck into a large crowd or wielding an axe at train passengers, this latest phase is far less about what the United States does in the Middle East and far more about how the Arab world will be structured and governed going forward.

NO LONGER ABOUT US

After 9/11, the U.S. government initially asked itself, "Why do they hate us?" It was the wrong question.

Over time, a deeper, more nuanced understanding of the challenge in the Middle East developed. It was less about what America represents and far more about what America does, actions perceived as unfair, hypocritical, and inhibiting the region's advancement.[4] As the Defense Science Board said in its 2004 report, "Muslims do not 'hate our freedom,' but rather, they hate our policies."[5]

After 9/11, politicians from both parties committed themselves to do "whatever it takes" to defeat terrorism. In the process, the United States overreacted. The frame of a war on terror was too ambitious.

In Afghanistan, the United States quickly eliminated the al Qaeda safe haven and dispatched the Taliban government that had provided it shelter, but squandered its early strategic advantage and ended up at war with a group with local rather than global ambitions. The understandable concern about terrorists in possession of weapons of mass destruction led the Bush administration to make an erroneous supposition that a secular leader like Saddam Hussein would share dangerous capabilities with the adversary of an adversary that nonetheless viewed him as an apostate leader.

In his 1996 and 1998 fatwas declaring war on America, bin Laden's justification included the presence of U.S. troops on sacred Muslim lands in the aftermath of the Gulf War; the suffering of the Iraqi people due to international sanctions; and American support for Israel as well as secular and corrupt leaders across the region.[6] While rooting out al Qaeda from its sanctuary in Afghanistan was certainly necessary, the Iraq invasion validated bin Laden's narrative that the United States was at war with Islam.

Zarqawi mounted a formidable insurgency against the American mission, but his purpose was not just to drive the United States out of Iraq but also drive the Shiite government America helped install out of power. He deliberately sparked a sectarian "internal war within Islam" to achieve both objectives.[7]

When he arrived in office, Obama crafted a deliberate strategy to reverse the perception of a war with Islam, reducing the U.S. military footprint in the region while driving home the reality that Muslims were the primary victims of bin Laden's war.[8] The al Qaeda brand steadily lost its luster within the Islamic world and much of its capability as well. By 2011, core al Qaeda's primary function was as "a communications company."[9] Bin Laden, its chief spokesperson, at the time of his demise, understood this was a battle that al Qaeda was losing.

At the same time, Zarqawi and his successors, aided by the Arab uprisings and the collapse of effective governance in several countries, changed the nature of the conflict. The "far enemy," the United States, became a less immediate concern. The conflict was far more about an array of "near enemies," from the existing power structures and extremist competitors to the Shia and other religious and ethnic minorities.[10] The Islamic State's battles with the governments in Iraq and Syria, along with key defenders like Hezbollah and the Iran Revolutionary Guard Corps, and insurgent rivals like the Jabhat al-Nusra, are a reflection of this shift.

As the Islamic State's grip loosened on its territory, it expanded its ability to strike beyond its borders with the Paris and Brussels attacks, the downing of the Russian airliner in Egypt, the shootings in San Bernardino and Orlando, and the sequenced incidents in Turkey, Saudi Arabia, and Bangladesh.

"Hit everyone and everything," suggested one operative in an interview in the group's online French language magazine, *Dar al-Islam*.[11] Some attacks were directed by its core leadership, but many were inspired instead. In some cases, religious ideology was not a motivation, but used by true dead-enders to validate a decision to commit murder. The Islamic State was happy to designate them after the fact as soldiers for the cause. Its supporters demonstrated a sensitivity to past mistakes—in Bangladesh, foreigners were singled out and Muslims spared.[12] But the intention was clear, striking at social functions that connect people to a larger community, attempting to drive a wedge between the Islamic and secular worlds.

For a long time, "the perception that ISIS is doing well" created more followers.[13] Even as the Islamic State's hold on territory in Iraq and Syria became more tenuous, it has continued to acquire affiliate groups around the world. With fifty affiliates in twenty-one countries, and thirty-three "provinces" in eleven of those countries, there is a growing recognition that the Islamic State represents a "threat to global security" according to SITE's Rita Katz.[14] This structure will allow the movement to survive if (or when) the caliphate fails.

James Clapper, Obama's director of national intelligence, assessed in early 2016 that "there are now more Sunni violent extremist groups, members and safe havens than at any point in history."[15] That said, even with the Islamic State's ability to inspire supporters to launch attacks like those in San Bernardino and Orlando, more people were killed by right-wing extremists than jihadists.[16]

But the conflict's dynamic has changed. America is no longer at its center.

This is no longer bin Laden's war, but, says former CIA operative Robert Grenier, "an internal struggle for the future of the Muslim world."[17] Adds Anthony Cordesman of the Center for Strategic and International Studies, this regional struggle "is a 'clash within a civilization,' not a clash between them."[18]

But as of this writing in 2016, conflicts across the Middle East that gave life to the Islamic State and a rebirth to al Qaeda show no sign of diminishing. It is unclear if the Islamic world but particularly the Arab states can resolve these conflicts, but particularly Syria, without greater involvement by the United States.

DO NO HARM

In October 2003, Secretary of Defense Donald Rumsfeld drafted a "snow-flake," one of many memos he sent posing critical questions to his top civilian and military leaders. Entitled "Global War on Terrorism," Rumsfeld questioned whether they were focused on the right metrics to know whether the war was being won or lost.

Asked Rumsfeld, "Are we capturing, killing or deterring and dissuading more extremists every day than the madrassas and the radical clerics are recruiting, training and deploying against us?"[19]

Obama echoed Rumsfeld in his 2014 commencement speech at West Point, saying that "our actions should meet a simple test: We must not create more enemies than we take off the battlefield."[20]

The war on terror was initially understood to be primarily a political struggle—frequently identified as winning a battle for hearts and minds, ideas, or narratives. Notwithstanding the analogy of the Cold War, which involved steadily delegitimizing the Soviet Union and its communist ideology, Islamist extremism never posed an existential threat to the United States, even with dire scenarios involving chemical, biological, or nuclear weapons.

Leaders have consistently said that the United States cannot kill its way to victory, but for a variety of reasons, the war thus far has relied disproportionately on military force as the leading element of the American strategy.

To a significant degree, Obama crafted a realist strategy against al Qaeda and later the Islamic State around this core idea: first and foremost, do no harm. Avoid placing U.S. forces on the ground in the middle of conflicts that they cannot end and involving a postconflict commitment that is unlikely to work and is not affordable. In other words, Obama sought to fight the war in ways that play to America's technological strengths, particularly the employment of better intelligence and drones, while reducing the actions that trigger extremist narratives regarding the occupation of sacred lands that actually produce more terrorists.

Notwithstanding conservative criticism like that of Charles Krauthammer regarding the president's "ambivalence about the very idea of the war on terror," the Obama administration has been right to avoid getting drawn into the middle of civil wars for which multiple regional players have far more vital interests.[21] The United States should not pretend to understand the historical, religious, and cultural factors underneath these conflicts.[22]

America has not disengaged from the Middle East. It has applied military force more judiciously, generally avoiding actions that exacerbate the threat to the United States. At the same time, given the strategic objective of preventing the emergence of new extremist safe havens, the United States was slow to recognize how the Arab uprisings in 2011 fundamentally changed the conflict.

At first, the Arab Spring seemed to represent an affirmation of this cautious approach. Suddenly, the autocratic republics were teetering and people were empowered. Even the monarchies that could quell discontent through oil wealth understood that they needed to improve the basic social contract with their educated, ambitious, and underemployed populations.

But over the past couple of years, governing institutions have weakened. Regional security forces have underperformed. States have literally fractured. Viable political solutions have been handicapped by a lack of unity among key regional states and external stakeholders, including the United States and Russia. Except in Tunisia, opposition movements have not been able to present themselves as viable political alternatives or to sustain broad-based popular support.

Now there is a question whether time works in favor of the United States or the Islamic State. The longer the Islamic State caliphate governs real territory in Iraq and Syria, the greater its ideology takes hold in the Middle East and beyond. The U.S. strategy assumes that the major players within the Islamic world will band together eventually to defeat it. This is an open question given significant differences among key regional states—Saudi Arabia, Qatar, Turkey, and Iran—over what the conflict is about and what the end result should be.

What the United States considers a shared struggle against the Islamic State, most of its partners view as a zero-sum proxy battle for regional influence.

Obama framed the challenge in 2014 when he resumed combat operations in Iraq and launched air strikes in Syria: degrade and ultimately destroy the Islamic State. Perhaps a better formulation of the challenge is to degrade, discredit, and defeat the Islamic State and then stabilize the region, rebuild governing structures, and develop and integrate the region more significantly into the international system.

DEGRADE, DEFEAT, AND DISCREDIT

Degrading the Islamic State is a military challenge. Discrediting the Islamic State is a religious and ideological challenge. Defeating the Islamic State is a political challenge. According to Peter Bergen, "politics and theology merge with the caliphate."[23] As it stands now, defeating the ideology behind the Islamic State begins with eliminating the caliphate, but it doesn't end there. To prevent its return, better governance must be implemented in its place.

Since relaunching military strikes in Iraq and extending them to Syria, the U.S. military has taken the lead to degrade the Islamic State. It increased the presence of advisors and special operations forces to improve intelligence collection and attack the Islamic State leadership structure. Over time, the campaign began to demonstrate results. By mid-2016, air strikes on supply lines have cut its oil output by 30 percent.[24] The amount of territory held by the Islamic State steadily declined in both Iraq and Syria as local forces improved with American help. The dramatic drop in oil prices helped as well. All of this has made it more difficult to provide pay and benefits for its fighters, many of whom are "for-profit militants," creating recruitment and retention challenges within the ranks.[25]

There was some indication that the Islamic State's increased emphasis on attacks in the West reflected the pressure it was experiencing in Syria and Iraq. By mid-2016, it had lost its hold on several major cities, including Ramadi and Fallujah, as well as its battlefield commanders. "We are systematically eliminating ISIL's cabinet," said Secretary of Defense Ash Carter.[26]

The Islamic State's inability to defend its territory erodes its legitimacy. According to William McCants of Brookings, "the ideological fight is the actual fight."[27] For example, some Sunni sheiks in Iraq joined the effort against the Islamic State not because they backed the new government in Baghdad, but because they became convinced that the American side was now winning.[28]

Pentagon officials admit that the existing "outside-in" strategy that relies primarily on air power has its limits. The defeat of the Islamic State requires a ground force. The Iraqi military has steadily improved. The Syrian order of battle is more complex, relying on proxy forces to do the job.

Ideally, if military forces representing moderate Arab states rooted in the modern world can defeat radical forces rooted in the seventh century, supported by the United States and the West, it creates the right dynamic for the desired long-term political, social, and religious outcome. But who does this and how matters, and will affect the prospects of a political settlement. Competing (and perhaps incompatible) interests were apparent in mid-2016 in the struggle to reach agreement with Russia over which groups to target and the clash between NATO ally Turkey and Kurdish forces supported by U.S. special operations even as the military campaign was gaining momentum against the Islamic State.

Beyond success on the battlefield, there is also what Iraqi Prime Minister Haider al-Abadi has termed a "psychological war" against its "false narrative."[29] This requires discrediting perceptions of the Islamic State as an idyllic Muslim society, what former U.S. Special Presidential Envoy John Allen described as "defeating Daesh as an idea."[30]

The United States can play a significant role, particularly detecting active plots and deterring its own citizens from supporting the Islamic State cause. But it's unclear that the United States can be the decisive actor in such a sectarian struggle.

The Islamic State has changed al Qaeda's recruitment model, which relied heavily on face-to-face contact. Its ability to attract followers does not require travel, which makes radicalization and activation harder to detect. Much of its radicalization effort is online.

Those who have attempted to travel to Syria, including a meaningful number of Americans, were heavily influenced by online propaganda or interactions on social media with foreign individuals they never met.[31]

The Islamic State generates upwards of two hundred thousand tweets per day according to the House Homeland Security Committee Chairman Michael McCaul. "Terrorism has gone viral," he said.[32] In contrast to al Qaeda's use of couriers and videotapes that would emerge in public weeks or months behind events, the Islamic State operated in real-time. The caliphate was not "a far-off dream," but instead "here and now."[33]

While there should be efforts to disrupt the ability of the Islamic State to carry out its online activity, it is going to continue to communicate. The modern media environment is simply too dense and integrated. "Blaming the Internet for radicalization is really blaming any form of communication for radicalization," suggests former CIA analyst Marc Sageman.[34]

Attempting to shut down Islamic State communications may be counterproductive. All communications leave digital exhaust that can be valuable for intelligence agencies and law enforcement. But any systematic governmental attempt to deny the Islamic State the ability to communicate can be used by autocratic regimes, some American allies, to justify repression of protected speech. A better approach is to continue to work with the private sector to apply routine terms of service, which preclude speech that advocates violence and hatred.

In early 2016, the U.S. government revamped its effort to counter violent extremism. At the State Department, the Center for Strategic Counterterrorism Communications was rebranded the Global Engagement Center. Domestic counterradicalization efforts were also beefed up within the Department of Homeland Security.

Despite claims the United States was lagging behind the Islamic State in the digital dimension of the struggle, more effort should be focused on supporting countermessaging centers within the Islamic world.[35] America will not be the most credible messenger as various movements seek to discredit the extremist interpretations of the Koran. This is ultimately not a debate the United States can lead. Said one unnamed official, "it's not the U.S. government that is going to break the brand" of the Islamic State.[36]

In an interview with CNN's Fareed Zakaria, Obama resisted the notion that the United States was involved in a "religious war."[37] But the Islamic State is.

There are sound strategic reasons to avoid the kind of divisive rhetoric presented during the 2016 presidential campaign. For one, self-proclaimed caliphs such as bin Laden and Abu Bakir al-Baghdadi, the leader of the Islamic State, feed off the perception of an intractable divide with the Islamic world.

But even Muslims who reject the Islamic State understand the religious context behind its declaration of a caliphate. It comes straight from Islam.[38]

"Islamist terrorism does have some kind of a relationship to the religion of Islam, something that cannot be wished away by claims that Islam is simply a religion of peace, or by a desire not to offend," says Peter Bergen in *United States of Jihad*, explaining the evolution of the threat in America.[39]

That said, Omar Mateen, the angry and conflicted bully who perpetrated the attack on the Pulse nightclub in Orlando, declared allegiance to the Islamic State but may well have used religion as a veneer to justify what Obama rightly termed both an act of terror and a hate crime.

The United States should find ways to bolster voices that view Islam as compatible with the modern world while helping the Islamic world confront and contain those who preach intolerance and manipulate religious teachings to justify extreme violence.[40]

What is needed is a broader debate within the Islamic world regarding the Islamic State's brutal practices and whether they can be justified by the

Koran. The Islamic world needs to confront the Gulf states that continue to promote a less tolerant version of Islam that can make the leap to jihadism shorter. "Saudi Arabia is destroying Islam," said a cleric from Kosovo, a moderate Islamic state that has seen a disturbing number of citizens drawn to fight for the Islamic State.[41]

Even though a core element of its appeal, the Islamic State will be undone by its own brutality, in the very same way its predecessor, al Qaeda in Iraq, lost support. Few want to live in the society they attempted to form.[42] Discrediting the Islamic State will also require justice, prosecuting those responsible for crimes against humanity, as well as a process of truth and reconciliation that accounts for what took place and reestablishes the boundaries of acceptable behavior in a modern civil society. This process will take decades.[43]

If degrading and defeating the caliphate is crucial to destroying and discrediting the Islamic State, this requires a far more unified regional response than has been the case thus far. It is one thing to say that the Islamic State represents a perversion of the teachings of Islam. It is another to unify a deeply divided region against a common adversary and in the process uphold the sovereignty of states that are increasingly divided along sectarian or tribal lines. "When political dynamics fail, people turn back to religion," explained Rami Khouri of the American University in Beirut.[44]

But a comprehensive political solution is still a distant prospect. For all of its concern about the implications of the day after, the Obama administration never developed a coherent or realistic answer to the question.

STABILIZE, REBUILD, AND DEVELOP

But taking back territory is the first step in a lengthy process. To truly defeat the Islamic State, it is also necessary to put something better in its place. This, Gideon Rose wrote in *How Wars End,* "is all about politics."[45] As the United States has learned at great cost, this is not easy.

Contrary to American hopes, Iraq was not self-ordering. There was not enough planning regarding who or what would succeed Saddam Hussein. Despite that experience, the Obama administration repeated the same mistake in Libya, albeit without the enormous costs.

"U.S. officials have assumed that all the United States has to do is get rid of the bad guys and the post war peace will take care of itself," suggests Max

Boot. "But it simply isn't so. Generating order out of chaos is one of the hardest tasks any country can attempt."[46]

The challenge of ungoverned space across the Middle East and North Africa cannot be solved through a temporary surge. It is an "ultramarathon" that involves a generational challenge to stabilize conflict areas, address humanitarian needs, rebuild governing institutions, and establish traditions of self-determination and the peaceful transfer of power.

This is the heart of the prevailing U.S. counterterrorism strategy, which the Obama administration viewed with considerable ambivalence. While countries such as Libya and Syria do not represent vital interests in their own right, they are when significant swaths of territory become terrorist safe havens. Somalia was a strategic backwater in 1992 when U.S. forces were dispatched to address a humanitarian crisis. A decade later, Somalia was far more consequential with al Shabaab, an al Qaeda affiliate, in control of Mogadishu and launching attacks against neighboring Kenya.

Other than military action, the United States has yet to develop a long-term political strategy for the growing list of conflict countries that confront extremist insurgencies.

In Libya, the United States remains far more focused on attacking the Islamic State stronghold in and around Sirte than increasing the effectiveness of the new government of national unity in Tripoli.

In Egypt, regardless of the strength of the Egyptian military, rising youth unemployment, falling tourism, and increased political repression create economic weaknesses that will leave the country vulnerable to radicalization. Farea al-Muslimi, a visiting scholar with the Carnegie Middle East Center in Beirut, described Yemen at present as a country with "no national agenda, and a lot of guns."[47]

In March 2016, the Kurdish Democratic Union Party (PYD) unilaterally declared a federal region in northern Syria that includes three self-governing cantons. A tribal leader suggested the move was "just blowing bubbles." The Kurds, on the other hand, insisted that some kind of federal structure is the only hope of ending the conflict, that going back to the "old Syria" is impossible, a point that even Obama has made.[48] Turkey sees a Syrian state run by a PKK affiliate as a national security threat.

Across the border in Iraq, the already autonomous Kurdish region again ponders independence.[49] At least one Kurdish leader has termed Iraq not just a failed state but a "conceptual failure."[50]

"The puzzle is, how do you glue these states back together again," asks Fawaz Gerges of the London School of Economics and Political Science. "They're gone into a million pieces."[51]

The Islamic State has for the moment erased the border between Iraq and Syria. Iraq could be one country or three. Syria could be one country or four. Not so long ago, Yemen was two countries, North and South. That divide has returned in the existing conflict between the Yemeni government, Houthis, and other factions. Libya is riven with large numbers of armed tribes and for a long time had not one government but two.

Whether existing boundaries drawn a century ago under Sykes–Picot survive depends on the quality and character of governments put in place if and when there are ceasefires and peace agreements.

At that point, as countries enter the postconflict phase, a core question lingers. Who will be the enforcer? Egypt used to look after Libya; now it has more than enough to worry about within its own borders. Saudi Arabia intervened in Yemen, but will struggle to find common cause with Iran. While Iraq regained control of Ramadi and Fallujah in 2016, whether a Shia-led government is prepared to rebuild these Sunni-dominated cities will say a great deal about the future of the country.

The United States has an interest in each of these places—perhaps vital, perhaps not—but as Stephen Biddle of The George Washington University acknowledges, "Our interests align with none of our allies in this conflict."[52]

Lebanese Prime Minister Tammam Salam told President Obama shortly after launching air strikes in Iraq and Syria that he recognized the importance of the U.S. no-boots-on-the-ground policy, but that ultimately there would need to be a ground campaign to defeat the Islamic State. Salam believed the United States could use the international and regional coalition formed against the Islamic State as a foundation.[53]

There is a danger, suggests Columbia's Richard Betts, that "American leaders have drawn too firm a lesson from the wars in Afghanistan and Iraq: never put boots on the ground."[54]

The next president should be prepared to place some additional boots on the ground together with other key stakeholders, not to impose a solution on the warring parties in any of these conflicts but to stabilize the situation once a peace agreement becomes feasible. In Syria, America would need to include all key stakeholders in the process, set realistic objectives, and construct a strategy that can sustain public support for years.[55] This would require the inclusion of key regional countries, including Turkey, Jordan, Saudi Arabia, and Iran, as well as external powers including Russia.

Yes, this would be a return to nation-building, but on a different model that is less reliant on hundreds of thousands of troops. The emphasis should be rebuilding from the bottom up, not the top down. Effective state building requires developing local structures where everyone is invested from the outset. Then the parties can determine what kind of federalized structure makes sense.

Democracy may well be a significant part of the solution to violent political extremism, but two critical lines are moving in the wrong direction. Given the rise of the Islamic State and recovery of al Qaeda, violent political extremism is on the rise, but so is authoritarianism. Global freedom has declined for ten consecutive years.[56]

Sobered by the experience of the past fifteen years, the next president needs to be mindful how difficult and lengthy the process is. "Revolutions can get hijacked," reminds David Kramer, former head of Freedom House. "In these transitions, we need to avoid premature labels."[57]

The fact is the United States needs to devote greater resources to democracy and development over time. It must also be firmer with countries in transition regarding the need for even-handed policing, an independent judiciary, a free press, the fair treatment of political opponents, the need for genuinely competitive elections, and the peaceful transfer of power.

American policies geared toward "freedom" or "democratic enlargement" are appropriate, but need to be realistic. Concepts of tolerance and inclusion cannot be instilled in one election cycle. They must be carefully nurtured over extended periods.

Success does not come with the first election. In fact, recent experience suggests that if elections occur and governments form too quickly, without an adequate institutional foundation to support political pluralism, countries can easily slide backward and conflicts intensify again. That danger certainly exists in Syria.

"Democracy involves first majority rule and second minority rights," reminds Chris Hill, former U.S. ambassador to Iraq and now dean of the University of Denver's Korbel School of International Studies. "No one in the region yet gets to step two."[58]

To the extent the conflicts in Syria and Iraq are fueled by rising sectarianism in the Middle East, this represents, as the president told *Vox*, a "generational challenge in the Muslim world" that cannot be solved by "simply invading every country where disorder breaks out." The United States must help solve these conflicts, "but we can't do it for them."[59]

A PRESIDENCY AT WAR

The new president faces twin strategic dilemmas. First, will the strategy that Obama outlined and the major candidates for president in 2016 supported (whether they admitted it or not) succeed? In other words, can the United States defeat the Islamic State without taking responsibility for the broader Syrian civil war? And second, given the bipartisan political consensus against deploying U.S. combat troops to Syria, if and when a peace agreement and ceasefire is achieved, can the region on its own stabilize and rebuild Syria without sowing the seeds of a future sectarian conflict? In other words, can the United States ensure that Syria does not become a future extremist safe haven without putting more American boots on the ground?

The answer to those questions is, probably not.

Eight years ago, the Israeli–Palestinian conflict was at the center of politics in the Middle East. That is no longer the case. It is now Syria. And, according to former Director of Central Intelligence (and U.S. commander in Iraq) David Petraeus, the Syrian conflict is a "geopolitical Chernobyl" that is spreading instability and extremism across the region that will take time to cap and then years to reverse.[60]

Suggestions that Syria would have turned out differently if Obama had been more assertive early in the conflict fail to adequately account for the complexity of the conflict and the role played by a wide range of players—the Assad regime, Iran, Russia, the Islamic State, Turkey, and the Gulf states.

The fact is, Syria is not one conflict. The Islamic State is fighting for a caliphate. The United States is committed to the caliphate's destruction. The so-called moderate opposition, supported by Turkey and others, is fighting the Assad regime. Turkey wants Assad to go, but is worried that the Kurds will gain in the process. Russia, which claims it is fighting the Islamic State, is determined to prevent the regime's collapse and any political transition that changes the nature of the Syrian government. Iran is trying to preserve its links through Syria to project influence across the Middle East. A range of Sunni states, in particular Saudi Arabia and the Gulf states, are opposed.

At a minimum, this means that the next president will be a president at war, either engaged directly against the likes of al Qaeda, the Islamic State, or its successors, or dealing with an extended postconflict period in Yemen, Libya, or Somalia, but especially in Iraq and Syria.

The Obama administration mismanaged several aspects of its Syria strategy—its expectation that Assad's days were numbered, its impulsive execution around the red line, and its half-hearted support for the Syrian opposition—but its caution was appropriate.

Thus far, the United States has focused on the dimension of the Syrian conflict that does impact American security—the Islamic State. The United States has avoided a critical mistake made in the Iraq conflict, launching an invasion that validated al Qaeda's narrative of the occupation of sacred Muslim lands and fed the perception of a war between the Islamic world and the West.

When the Islamic State beheaded hostage Peter Kassig in Dabiq, a small town in northern Syria where an eighth-century caliph attempted unsuccessfully to defeat the Romans, Kassig's executioner said they were "burying the first American crusader in Dabiq, eagerly waiting for the remainder of your armies to arrive."[61] Notwithstanding sporadic attacks by disaffected Westerners inspired by the Islamic State, the United States has wisely avoided creating a strategic framework that plays into its apocalyptic vision of a clash of civilizations.

Obama was right when he said that Syria is fractured to the point that the "return to a pre-war status quo is a fantasy."[62] But the administration struggled to develop a political process that could achieve an international consensus regarding how to administer Syria during a political transition, ensure the delivery of humanitarian assistance, stabilize the country, resettle refugees and those displaced by the conflict, and begin a lengthy and costly rebuilding and recovery process. That responsibility falls to the new administration.

Political change, suggests Nancy Youssef of the *Daily Beast*, must be organic, with an emphasis on "structural problems within the region that allow ISIS to grow."[63] In both Afghanistan and Iraq, the United States spent too much time focused on national institutions that were disconnected from local needs rather than developing more effective institutions from the ground up. Of course, in Libya, there was an indigenous solution, but the Libyans were unable to transcend regional and tribal rivalries.

In the short term, the emphasis should be on deescalating the Syrian civil war and sustaining a durable ceasefire. Such a step should begin to stem the rate of internal displacement, external refugees, and radicalization. The emphasis in the midterm should be local governance, including existence of a largely autonomous Kurdish region. Long-term questions, including how to govern a unified Syria, putting in place a new constitution, reforming government institutions, rebuilding the economy, and developing an inclusive civil society will involve a major commitment over a decade or more.[64]

Both the Bush and Obama administrations erred in believing in Iraq and Libya that a new order would be self-establishing. The depth of the tragedy in Syria—as of mid-2016, more than four hundred thousand people killed and a majority of its population displaced—exceeds anything the international community confronted in Iraq or Libya.[65]   Some additional U.S. forces may be required—the American public appears to be open to a larger effort if carefully tailored to U.S. strengths and interests—but certainly nothing resembling the American invasion forces of 1991 or 2003.

The United States remains rightfully chastened by the cost of full-on nation building given the disastrous experience in Iraq. But there is a compelling strategic need to improve governance and build market-based economies that can generate jobs for the region's highly educated, connected, and frustrated youth. As of 2015, youth unemployment remains at 25 percent in Algeria, 26 percent in Egypt, and even 40 percent in Tunisia, the lone remaining fragile bright spot from the Arab Spring.[66]

Even though it was a young Tunisian, Mohammed Bouazizi, whose protest over government corruption and indifference sparked the Arab uprisings, on a per capita basis more Tunisians have been drawn to the ranks of the Islamic State than any other regional country.[67] Reducing violent political extremism requires greater economic development where hundreds of thousands of unemployed university graduates represent an inviting target for the Islamic State and like-minded groups.[68]

The United States will need to assume a significant role in the stabilization and recovery effort. This should not be viewed as a diversion, but rather as a vital component of the existing counterterrorism strategy, precluding the emergence of extremist safe havens. The long-term goal is not just military success, but long-term political stability. As Jessica Stern and J. M. Berger argue in *ISIS: The State of Terror*, "a failed state is the worst of all popular outcomes."[69]

New York Times columnist Tom Friedman underscored the depth of the regional economic deficit and what it will take to reverse existing trends. "Sixty years ago, Egypt and South Korea had the same per capita income," Friedman said in remarks at the Center for Strategic and International Studies. "Today, South Korea's GDP is three times the entire Arab world."[70]

Killing the bad guys alone will not end the threat of terrorism to the United States and its allies. Economics and governance are fundamental aspects of defeating the Islamic State. Growing diverse, market-based economies across the region that generate jobs and fair wages for a young but educated population is crucial to blunting the pull of the Islamic State, whose appeal is as much about money as it is ideology.

Obama judged that the United States for all its power does not have the ability to impose a political order on another country in a time frame and at a cost that the American people are willing to bear. The new president must enlarge the political space that will enable a new approach focused not on the mistakes of the past but on the security needs of the future. That will require changing the dominant national security narrative that emerged from the 2016 campaign.

14

NO BOOTS ON THE GROUND

A n August 2015 Gallup poll in the early stages of the presidential campaign suggested that only 19 percent of the American electorate considered foreign policy the leading challenge facing America. Only 3 percent listed the Islamic State.[1]

Within months, attacks in the United States, France, Egypt, and elsewhere either directed, inspired, or validated by the Islamic State—a radicalized couple in San Bernardino that used military-style weapons to kill fourteen; a cell that employed automatic weapons and suicide vests to kill 130 civilians in Paris and then struck the Brussels airport as well; an affiliate that smuggled a bomb on board a Russian airliner in Egypt, killing all 224 passengers on board; and suicide bombings in Turkey, Lebanon, Libya, and other locations—generated a sea change in the salience of the ongoing threat of terrorism to the United States and its allies.

Its importance intensified yet again with the attack on an Orlando nightclub that killed forty-nine people and wounded fifty-three, many of them members of the LGBT community, by another radicalized lone wolf who called 911 to swear allegiance to the Islamic State in the midst of the incident.

The 2016 presidential campaign suddenly revolved significantly and unexpectedly around national security, and became a referendum on the Obama administration strategy regarding how to protect Americans at home and defeat the caliphate abroad. Attempted terrorist attacks in New York, New Jersey, and Minnesota in September, just as the campaign reached the stretch drive, further reinforced the prevailing partisan divide, with Democrats claiming the mantle of experience and temperament to deal with this complex long-term challenge and Republicans sounding tougher and promising to be stronger.

By May 2016, a clear majority of Americans across the political spectrum viewed the Islamic State as the leading threat to the United States. The public supported existing military efforts to defeat the Islamic State, although there are significant divisions whether military force is the best course to defeat terrorism, whether current efforts will go far enough or potentially too far, and whether to send ground troops to Iraq or Syria.[2]

While the political rhetoric sharpened, especially Donald Trump's proposals regarding walls and travel bans, the dominant national security narrative during the 2016 campaign was actually consistent across both political parties.

After San Bernardino, Senator Ted Cruz said, "We need to focus on killing the bad guys, not getting stuck in Middle Eastern civil wars that don't keep America safe."[3] Barack Obama could not have described his policy regarding Syria more succinctly.

Cruz's comments reflected the political boundaries that were drawn during the 2008 presidential campaign—the prevailing skepticism regarding major ground wars and nation building—and largely remained intact eight years later.

Candidates from both parties pledged more aggressive action, advocating a myriad of tactical options to reduce Syria's impact on the broader security environment, utilizing U.S. airpower; improved intelligence and situational awareness; special operations; and regional force training, planning, and coordination to degrade the Islamic State. None of the frontrunners advocated employing American ground troops in significant numbers. While there was some support for U.S. forces as part of a regional coalition, no one believed the United States should assume primary responsibility for the Syrian crisis.

Much less attention was paid to the underlying political and economic factors across the Middle East and North Africa that enabled the rapid Islamic State advance in Syria and Iraq and have contributed to its expansion into Afghanistan, Libya, and other states. Like the Obama administration, all of the major candidates for president struggled to delineate how to defeat the Islamic State, considered a vital American interest, without being drawn more deeply into the wider Syrian civil war.

Obama believed that defeating the Islamic State was linked to removing Assad from power to end Syria's civil war, but pursued them on separate tracks. A few candidates believed it was a mistake to push Assad aside.

As the new administration takes office, the Islamic State has lost significant ground and an increasing number of its leaders, yet appears to be expanding from a regional challenge to a global movement. This is everything al Qaeda was, and more.

What became clear through the 2016 campaign was that the process of degrading and defeating the Islamic State—taking back territory in Iraq and Syria; stabilizing conflict countries to prevent safe havens and reversing the humanitarian crisis that has displaced millions both within and beyond the region; disrupting the process of radicalization and reducing the threat posed by radicalized lone wolves inspired but not directed by terrorist networks; constructing viable governing institutions; and rebuilding reasonably inclusive civil societies—will extend well beyond one or two presidential terms.

POWER POLITICS

Both parties believe in U.S. global leadership. The better question is not whether to lead, but how, where, for what purpose, and at what cost.

Pledging not to surrender to the "false song of globalism," Donald Trump advanced a far more nationalistic and populist theme of "America First." In a major foreign policy speech after becoming the presumptive favorite for the Republican nomination, Trump pledged to stop China's "theft" of American jobs, be more prepared to walk away from negotiations with adversaries, require allies to pay more for mutual defense, build a stronger military, yet be more restrained regarding the use of force.[4]

"We will not be ripped off anymore," he reiterated to the *New York Times*.[5]

Trump strongly signaled that interests should guide American foreign policy, expressing skepticism for the kind of humanitarian intervention advocated by Hillary Clinton and launched by Barack Obama in Libya. He criticized Obama for supporting "radical change" in countries like Egypt, even suggesting that it's a "dangerous idea" to promote Western-style democracy to countries with no experience with it.[6]

While all of the major Republican presidential candidates suggested that the government should spend more time addressing challenges at home rather than trying—and failing—to fix intractable problems abroad, Trump was by far the most isolationist. But while trying to "shake the rust off of America's foreign policy," Trump attacked the very basis of international alliances and trade that are key elements of its foundation.

Trump criticized Obama for undermining perceptions of American leadership. But his suggestions that the United States was overextended, that allies need to shoulder more responsibility for their own security, and that Washington should seek better deals in negotiations with friends and foes left much of the world questioning the future of American foreign policy. The fact that Trump values "unpredictability" only exacerbated existing concerns regarding the perceived credibility and legitimacy of American power.

Others sought greater balance. "We don't have to be the world's policeman," Senator Marco Rubio said. "But we certainly have to be the world's leader."[7] There is not a clear line between the two. A stable and prosperous world does need a leader, but when necessary it can also require a defender or enforcer. Delineating among those roles was a challenge for the major candidates just as it was for Obama.

At one level, it is the difference between internationalism and interventionism. In describing America as the exceptional nation, President Obama consistently alluded to the unique ability of the United States to catalyze the world to unite and act together to solve an important global or regional issue. When there's a problem, Obama remarked on multiple occasions, the world calls Washington, not Moscow or Beijing.

John Ikenberry wrote in *Liberal Leviathan*, the United States after the Cold War became the "owner and operator" of the liberal capitalist political system that it largely designed.[8] In turn, Michael Mandelbaum in *The Case for Goliath* calls the United States the world's "order-maker," providing public goods, particularly security, to this global system.[9]

Obama was right to suggest in 2014 that "by most measures, America has never been stronger relative to the rest of the world. Those who argue otherwise—who suggest that America is in decline, or has seen its global leadership slip away—are either misreading history or engaged in partisan politics."[10]

But there are outlier states and nonstate actors that seek to undermine America's preeminent posture within the international system, but who choose not to play by agreed-upon rules. Since the end of the Cold War, the United States has most often served as the primary enforcer against transgressors who threaten the system or act outside acceptable boundaries. During his two terms, Obama sought to renegotiate the circumstances under which America would play this role and shoulder the attendant costs.

The United States retained the right to act alone when its vital interests were threatened, as with the Osama bin Laden raid. But during his time in office, Obama narrowed the definition of what was vital. He never considered the fate of Bashar al-Assad a vital interest, nor the Islamic State an existential threat even with the horrific levels of death, destruction, and displacement.

In turn, Obama made clear that where interests were important but not vital, the United States would act with international partners and clear authority. But other rising powers, most notably Russia, had their own interests, could frustrate the United States' ability to achieve international consensus, and demonstrated a willingness to act where the United States hesitated.

While the Democratic candidates defended the choices that Obama made on the international stage—Hillary Clinton in particular since she served as his secretary of state—Republicans criticized Obama's foreign policy within an increasingly complex international environment and the alleged weakness it projected.

As one example, Senator Lindsey Graham suggested that Russian President Vladimir Putin would not have infiltrated troops into Ukraine if Ronald Reagan were president. Graham ignored the fact that Putin deployed military forces against Georgia in 2008 while George W. Bush, no shrinking violet, was still in office.[11] Robert Kagan viewed such rhetoric—the belief that the world should jump when Washington snaps its fingers—as "a nostalgia fantasy."[12] The United States does not always get what it wants, and never could.

Trump actually commended Putin as "a very strong leader for Russia." Oddly, given the crisis in Ukraine, Trump parlayed that position with a belief that the United States does not get as much from NATO as it once did. "NATO was set up at a different time," he told the *Washington Post* editorial board, "when we were a richer country."[13]

Even though several Republican candidates accused Obama of strategic disengagement, Trump believed that European nations should assume greater security responsibility, a view that Obama tried to put into practice in Libya with disappointing results. While Trump believed that European allies should spend more on their own defense, the reality is just the opposite. Particularly given the Brexit vote, Europe will be hard-pressed to sustain defense spending at current levels. He also suggested that allies like Saudi Arabia, Japan, and South Korea should pay more for the protection America provides.

Taking a stab at a personalized doctrine, Trump wanted America to be strong enough that "Nobody is going to mess with us."[14] If only the world were that simple. While the solution involves more than just talking tougher, a critical backdrop to the 2016 campaign was the return of geopolitics, given the Russian interventions in Ukraine and Syria as well as the Chinese buildup in the South and East China Seas.

Notwithstanding George W. Bush's freedom agenda, the Republican field seemed to strike a far more realist chord, recognizing the perceived value of strong leaders who could nonetheless maintain security. Senator Ted Cruz on multiple occasions commended President Abdel Fattah el-Sisi of Egypt despite his crackdown on Egyptian civil society.[15] Multiple candidates criticized the overthrow of Saddam Hussein and Muammar Qaddafi and the political vacuums that resulted.

"For a full generation we have not had to think too much about whether something done or undone in foreign policy promotes or endangers our vital interests," suggested Walter Russell Mead. He believed the next administration needs to improve America's understanding of "what matters and why" and develop a more coherent Eurasian strategy that better integrates European, Middle Eastern, South Asian, and East Asian policy. The focus should be less on individual issues and more about geopolitical context.[16]

Democrats and Republicans have sparred continually in recent decades over national security, offering competing narratives over what it means to be "strong," to demonstrate "leadership," to do whatever it takes to keep America safe. An assertive tone is usually paired with a focus on military capability and alleged "gaps" in our arsenal. 2016 was no different.

Several Republican candidates decried the state of military readiness and highlighted the declining numbers of aircraft and ships in the inventory, ignoring the fact that individual weapon systems are far more capable and can deliver greater firepower in any corner of the world.

But as the general election approached, the Democrats sought to turn the tables on what was traditionally solid Republican ground. During her acceptance speech at the Democratic National Convention, Hillary Clinton criticized Trump for calling the military a "disaster," instead terming the armed forces a "national treasure."[17]

The debate underscored that for all the theoretical discussion of smart power—the need to employ all dimensions of American power, particularly against an insurgent network like al Qaeda or a proto-state like the Islamic State—when it comes to American politics, being viewed as strong on national security remains one-dimensional.

The 2016 campaign reinforced how little support exists for the political and development tools that will be more effective over the long run in reducing violent political extremism. As David Ignatius of the *Washington Post* wrote, presidential candidates who employ "back to the future" rhetoric regarding the use of force ignore how "the world has changed, which render old models of U.S. power much less relevant."[18]

Clinton was more forthcoming than Trump regarding what will be required in Syria and other countries not just to defeat the Islamic State but to prevent Syria and other conflict states from becoming extremist safe havens.

Key steps include delivering humanitarian assistance, stabilizing war-torn societies, rebuilding infrastructure, establishing more effective governance, disarming factions and tribes that threaten the sovereignty of the state, developing market economies that create jobs, particularly for the young, and instilling a mind-set of more inclusivity and tolerance.

This is an imposing list that will severely test international capabilities. While the burden is shared and should not fall primarily on the United States, American leadership and sustained engagement will be important.

The debate underscored the same political dichotomy that Obama struggled to resolve during his two terms—an expansive narrative regarding America's vital role in the world but a narrowing political space regarding what the American people are willing to support.

Notwithstanding Trump's confidence that no one will challenge an America that he leads—as if just saying that's the case will make it so—he also seemed to be comfortable with letting others take the lead in solving problems that he does not see as being of vital importance, expressing for example a lack of concern regarding Putin's intervention in Syria.

"At some point," Trump said in a radio interview in 2015, "we can't be the policemen of the world. We have to rebuild our own country."[19] Obama stressed the same thing throughout his presidency. But the next president faces a different strategic landscape.

LIMITED INTERVENTIONISM

Criticism of the Obama administration during the 2016 campaign centered on perceived uncertainty and an unwillingness to employ military force in a decisive way. Much of it revolved around tactical judgments—failing to adequately support the moderate Syrian opposition or establish a no-fly zone early in the civil war.

But every candidate for president in 2016 accepted the Obama administration's conception of the challenge in Syria. Most candidates advocated an approach to the Islamic State that was activist, but only modestly interventionist. Although each candidate pledged a more intensified approach and reiterated the importance of American leadership, like Obama, they were not prepared to deploy large numbers of ground forces to remove Bashar al-Assad or end the Syrian civil war militarily.

Senator Lindsey Graham was an exception, a leading proponent of a U.S. contingent as part of a regional force that would take back territory in Syria, but he suspended his campaign in late 2015 before any voting took place.[20] While Obama gave Graham credit for a proposal that involved more than "being louder or sounding tougher," he feared that large numbers of U.S. troops in Syria would obligate the United States to govern Syria for an indefinite period.[21]

Governor John Kasich supported the idea of troops to eliminate the Islamic State caliphate, but not to stabilize the country afterward. "I don't believe the United States should involve itself in civil wars," he said. "Civil wars are not in our direct interest."[22] Trump was even more explicit, saying "I don't think we should be nation building anymore. I think it's proven not to work."[23]

Senator Ted Cruz suggested that the campaign against the Islamic State should include "saturation bombing" along the lines of the Gulf War. Criticizing the Obama administration's cautious and incremental approach to Syria, Cruz failed to note that the Desert Storm air campaign attacked one of the world's largest standing armies, not a small insurgent force blended in with the civilian population. But Cruz seemed to echo the second Bush administration's initial expectations regarding Iraq, "We should use overwhelming force, kill the enemy and then get the heck out."[24]

But as the White House learned in 2003, interventions are never clearcut.

On the Democratic side, Hillary Clinton defended the existing Obama strategy, but signaled she would go further and establish a safe zone and add more special operations forces. But she too viewed combat troops as "off the table."[25] Instead, the United States should improve training and equipping of local forces, get "more Syrians to take on ISIS," and build the Iraqi National Army back "to fighting shape."[26]

Clinton viewed the Islamic State in terms of "three mutually-reinforcing dimensions," each of which needed to be targeted and defeated: its enclave in Syria and Iraq; its growing network of affiliates across the region and around the world; and the ideology of "radical jihadism" that it propagates.[27]

For his part, Senator Bernie Sanders called the conflict a "quagmire within a quagmire" given the dual challenge of Assad and the Islamic State. To a large degree, Sanders started his presidential campaign where Obama started his presidency, a desire to learn the lessons of Iraq and avoid "never-ending, perpetual warfare."[28]

Obama bristled at the campaign criticism of his strategy. He labeled many of the proposals from the campaign trail as "mumbo jumbo."[29]

And yet, even as the campaign was unfolding, there was an understanding that the threat was once again evolving as the Islamic State expanded its reach into more countries, potentially opening up new fronts for the next adminis-tration. That expansion includes Libya, which now serves as a base for thou-sands of Islamic State fighters.[30] The Pentagon began an air campaign against the new Islamic State outpost in Libya in early 2016.

Clinton defended the Libya intervention, arguing that Qaddafi's demise led to far fewer deaths than in Syria, where the civil war is driven by Assad's refusal to step down. While some Republican candidates believed Qaddafi's removal was a mistake, Clinton assumed the mantle of Ronald Reagan, who launched air strikes against Qaddafi and Libya following a terrorist bombing at a Berlin discotheque.[31]

Rubio suggested in hindsight that the United States should have been more engaged in Libya from the outset to prevent it from becoming a failed state and extremist haven. Cruz was far more categorical.

"Assad is a bad man. Qaddafi was a bad man. Mubarak had a terrible human rights record," said Cruz. "But they were assisting us—at least Qaddafi and Mubarak—in fighting radical Islamic terrorists."[32] Cruz believed that over-throwing dictators to promote democracy "ends up undermining our national security."[33] That view was largely shared by Sanders.[34]

WHO OR WHAT IS THE ENEMY?

The campaign debate surrounding the Islamic State was almost as much about what to call it as what to do about it. Republican candidates criticized Obama for his unwillingness to employ the term "radical Islamic terrorism," a label that is self-evident at first blush, yet can be misleading.

"Look, we are having a tremendous problem with radical Islamic terror-ism," suggested Donald Trump on *Face the Nation* four days after the San Ber-nardino attack. Speaking of Obama, he suggested, "Until he admits that this is a problem, we're never going to solve the problem."[35]

Having launched his campaign for the presidency by calling for a new and improved wall between the United States and Mexico, one that somehow Mexico would be expected to fund, Trump advocated a temporary suspension of visas for Muslims to travel to the United States, profiling of Muslims in the country, and surveillance of mosques. The Islamic State seized on the rhetoric as proof of a fundamental divide with the West. America's closest ally consid-ered it "divisive, stupid and wrong."[36]

Trump, having tapped into an isolationist vein of the Republican elector-ate that was skeptical of international engagement and attracted to the concept of Fortress America, doubled down on this line of attack after Orlando.

"We cannot continue to allow thousands upon thousands of people to pour into our country, many of whom have the same thought process as this savage killer," Trump said in a speech linking the challenges of terrorism and immigration while ignoring the fact that the perpetrator was an American citizen.[37]

Trump's rhetoric generated a sharp presidential rebuke, that such "yapping" had dangerous strategic implications.

"So there's no magic to the phrase 'radical Islam.' It's a political talking point; it's not a strategy," said Obama. "And if we fall into the trap of painting all Muslims with a broad brush and imply that we are at war with an entire religion—then we're doing the terrorists' work for them."[38]

Lumping divergent groups in a single bucket, as the United States did with communism during the Cold War, can mask important differences. The assumption that all communists threatened the United States in the same way caused successive administrations to overlook the role played by nationalism in Vietnam. The conflict there was a civil war and tangential to the larger existential struggle with the Soviet Union.

Hillary Clinton, while saying "we're at war with jihadists," cautioned that a sweeping label like radical Islamic terrorism risked creating perceptions of a renewed "war with Islam," which is how the war on terror was viewed in the Middle East after the American invasion of Iraq.[39] She called Trump's proposed ban "un-American."[40]

DEBATE OVER THE 9/11 ERA STILL UNRESOLVED

Fifteen years into the war on terror, there remains a significant political divide regarding the American government's response, whether the government has not done enough to protect the country, or has compromised liberty and privacy in the interest of security. This divide was clearly visible during the 2016 campaign.

The first narrative emerged from the 9/11 Commission Report. At its heart, the 9/11 Commission concluded that the attack was preventable, although there was no single point of failure. Its report highlighted three systemic failures: a failure of intelligence—there were warnings, but they were not specific enough; a failure to connect the dots—the government was hampered by a bureaucratic mind-set of protecting rather than sharing information;

and a failure of imagination—that the government underestimated what a network like al Qaeda was capable of doing.

The political blame game that ensued included two misleading lines of criticism: that the Bush administration ignored repeated warnings in the weeks leading up to the attacks, including the infamous Presidential Daily Briefing item regarding the possibility that al Qaeda might employ aircraft as a weapon; and that the Clinton administration failed to mount an adequate response to the al Qaeda threat and failed to pull the trigger when it had bin Laden in its sights.

The dominant political narrative was "never again," that with the right policies, strategy, structures, and tools, terrorism attacks could and should be prevented.[41]

The Bush administration launched a global war on terror and a range of programs and practices, some of which may or may not have comported with domestic and international law, based on an urgent imperative that terrorists would be confronted over there to minimize the chances of more attacks back here. Congress undertook a major restructuring of the U.S. government based on the belief that the security system that existed on September 11 had failed.

Both the Bush and Obama administrations, working with Congress and within the courts, did much to correct perceived excesses, terminating some programs and adapting others. Arguably, changes made in counterterrorism programs and practices were greater between the first and second Bush terms than between the second Bush and first Obama terms, even though the idea of continuity in counterterrorism efforts is politically toxic.[42]

In 2013, Edward Snowden delivered a powerful counternarrative. Rather than not doing enough, the government, particularly the National Security Agency, had gone too far in its response to the terrorist threat, consistently acting beyond its authorities in its surveillance of information networks, violating the Fourth Amendment, and consciously compromising the privacy of American citizens while accumulating information regarding foreign persons.

Snowden's revelations, which included the fact the United States tapped the cell phone of the German chancellor, had a serious impact in relations with Europe, which has a much stricter definition of privacy. However, in light of the intelligence failings related to a string of attacks in Paris and Brussels, and the uncertainty surrounding the conflict in Syria, the political pendulum may well turn back in the direction of greater government action to detect and prevent future attacks.

But the debate over lessons learned from the 9/11 era remains unresolved regarding security, intelligence, detention, interrogation, and judicial practices launched and reformed during the Bush administration and further refined under Obama.

The most notable partisan disagreement continues to regard the military prison at Guantanamo Bay, Cuba. Presidents Bush and Obama both expressed publicly a desire to close the prison—Obama committed to doing so in his first year in office, but underestimated its political complexity.

During his first term, confronted with unanticipated opposition to bringing several Uighurs (Muslims who posed no threat but could not be returned to China) from Guantanamo to northern Virginia, the White House caved, which emboldened Congress to place more hurdles in Obama's path, including restrictions on funding an alternative prison, transferring detainees to the United States, and a requirement to certify that any detainee transferred to another country poses an acceptable security risk.[43]

With the prospects of transfers blocked, a number of detainees went on a hunger strike, which exacerbated the prison's impact on America's reputation. Over time, the Obama administration worked to at least make the problem smaller. In 2014, the White House directed the Pentagon to accelerate the pace of transfers, accepting some risk that any detainee could return to the fight.[44]

Under Obama, all new terrorist detainees were tried in civilian courts, which have proven to be more effective than military tribunals. A total of 779 detainees have been held at Guantanamo since it opened. As of February 2016 when the Obama administration submitted a plan to Congress to close Guantanamo, only 91 remained. That number was steadily reduced through the remainder of Obama's tenure.

In his final State of the Union address, Obama stressed the prison "does not advance our national security—it undermines it."[45] There are legitimate strategic concerns that Guantanamo remains a recruiting tool for al Qaeda. The Islamic State's use of orange jumpsuits in its brutal videos revealing the beheadings of Americans and other Western hostages suggests it retains resonance within the Islamic world. For former detainees resettled in other countries, the recidivism rate is not zero. Some have returned to the fight.[46]

Acknowledging that the politics surrounding Guantanamo are tough, he nonetheless encouraged Congress to "close this chapter in our history" and not pass the problem to the next president.[47] While he threatened to use his executive authority to close the facility, that would involve moving detainees who will never be released to American soil—including Khalid Sheikh Mohammed, the 9/11 attack mastermind—something Congress with considerable public support has specifically prohibited.[48]

All Republican candidates pledged not only to continue Guantanamo, but to expand its use. Senator Marco Rubio said in a debate in South Carolina that if any Islamic State operatives are captured, "they are getting a one-way ticket to Guantanamo Bay, Cuba, and we are going to find out everything they know."[49] He ignored strong evidence that interrogators can gain valuable information and then build a successful prosecution, a combination the military system has yet to demonstrate.

Donald Trump claimed, "I would bring back water boarding and I'd bring back a hell of a lot worse than water boarding."[50] When he was subsequently challenged about the prospect of ordering the military or intelligence services to ignore American law, he indicated that he would seek to expand the tools that would be available to interrogators, a step that would face a difficult political path through Congress.

Politics is an undeniable factor in the lingering disagreement over interrogation methods—whatever it takes to keep America safe has been a consistent mantra since September 11, and many voters in 2016 were drawn to a candidate like Trump who tells it like it is.

According to former Director of Central Intelligence Michael Hayden, the swing between the dueling narratives of not enough and too much government action was directly related to perception of the immediate sense of danger, most significantly felt following a successful attack and less so as time went on.[51] The politics of that aside, the balance between privacy and security or security and liberty should be dynamic, based on the understanding of the threat and informed decisions by the public through their elected representatives.

Even though the value of coercive techniques continues to be hotly debated, as former FBI agent and interrogator Ali Soufan wrote in *The Black Banners*, given how little is known about the typical detainee, "there is no way to know what is success and what is failure."[52]

Terrorist suspects such as Umar Farouk Abdulmutallab, the underwear bomber, provided valuable information to intelligence and law enforcement teams both before and after being given Miranda rights.[53]

In fairness, Hayden and other former top intelligence officials are adamant that enhanced techniques did yield valuable information that made a difference in the campaign against al Qaeda. But Hayden always understood that use of the techniques was a temporary response to an unprecedented emergency. He always envisioned the kind of "exit strategy" that Obama exercised by ending the practices by executive order (later codified in law by Congress) in the early days of his first term.[54]

The Obama administration built a hybrid model that balanced the security imperative to interrogate suspects within a legal structure that protected legal prerogatives for an eventual prosecution in a civilian courtroom.

In the case of a Somali associated with al Qaeda and captured at sea in 2011, Ahmed Abdulkadir Warsame, an interrogation team gained important intelligence regarding al Qaeda in the Arabian Peninsula and Anwar al-Awlaki over a two-month period on the *USS Boxer,* using a public safety exception to Miranda, before a separate FBI clean team read him his rights and began to build a legal case for trial. Warsame waived his rights, kept talking, and secretly pled guilty to the charges against him.[55]

For the first post-9/11 decade, the primary threat to the American homeland was from core al Qaeda and its main operational affiliate, al Qaeda in the Arabian Peninsula. They favored high-end and high-impact attacks—transportation systems and national landmarks—intended to make a major political statement and force a change in U.S. policy.

A handful of plots came dangerously close to fruition, including cases involving Abdulmutallab, the underwear bomber; Faisal Shahzad, the Times Square car bomber; and AQAP and the printer cartridge bombs. Several homegrown plots, including the Boston Marathon bombings and shootings at Fort Hood, Chattanooga, San Bernardino, and Orlando, were successful.

San Bernardino and Orlando, with attacks in Paris and Brussels in between, validated concerns among U.S. policy makers regarding the potency of the Islamic State's online appeals, either to entice followers to travel to Syria or encourage do-it-yourself terrorism in place. The sharpest disagreement was less about specific tactical steps on the battlefield, but what to do beyond it.

After San Bernardino, the FBI director raised concerns about the ability of law enforcement to monitor communications by radicalized individuals in order to stop attacks or access communications after the fact to better understand their path to radicalization. The question centers on valid and competing national security priorities. The dramatic shift in the telecommunications world toward ubiquitous encryption represents a response to the ongoing theft of intellectual property and personal data by international criminal syndicates and foreign governments (and surveillance by U.S. intelligence agencies) that arguably represents a far graver threat to American national and economic security over the long run.

After Orlando, Congress considered but did not act on proposals to delay or limit purchases by individuals on terrorist watch lists despite the support of Obama, Clinton, Trump, and a majority of lawful gun owners. Recent attacks directed or inspired by the Islamic State represent a clear shift in tactics—

attacking softer urban targets and attempting to kill as many people as possible—yet Congress appears incapable of making sensible and limited adjustments in response.

IRAQ SYNDROME

PBS anchor Gwen Ifill, referring to foreign policy insecurities, asked the two remaining Democratic candidates in a Milwaukee debate in February 2016 about America's role in the world. She alluded to exit polls from the New Hampshire primary, where two-thirds of Democratic voters expressed concerns about future terrorist attacks and the prospect of getting involved in another Middle East war that can't be won.

Senator Bernie Sanders talked about the "unintended consequences" of regime change that followed United States actions in Iraq, Libya, and even Iran. Like Obama eight years earlier, he criticized Hillary Clinton for her vote in favor of the Iraq war, a line of attack for which she was well prepared. "I do not believe a vote in 2002," she said, "is a plan to defeat ISIS in 2016."[56]

The exchange underscored how the intractable conflicts in Iraq and Syria and the political vacuum in Libya have only reinforced the prevailing public skepticism regarding military interventions even with the rise of the Islamic State.

Two days later, on a Republican debate stage in Greenville, South Carolina, on February 13, 2016, the tone was dramatically different, but not the bottom line. Once again taking on Republican orthodoxy that the Iraq War was worth waging, Trump provided a damning critique, calling it "a big, fat mistake" that "destabilized the Middle East."[57]

Trump accused President Bush and his senior national security advisors of lying. "They said there were weapons of mass destruction, there were none," said Trump. "And they knew there were none."[58] While many in the audience in the debate hall booed, Trump certainly reflected the view of a majority of Americans.

Four days later in another South Carolina debate, Trump pulled back from his accusation that Bush lied, but not his criticism of his decision to invade Iraq. He distinguished the strategy of George H. W. Bush, attacking Saddam Hussein to achieve a narrow purpose—"He didn't get into a quagmire"—from George W. Bush, whose invasion cost thousands of lives, two trillion dollars, and dramatically increased Iran's influence in the region.[59]

"Nobody really knows why we went into Iraq," Trump added, suggesting with characteristic overstatement that "going into Iraq may have been the worst decision anybody has made, any president has made in the history of this country."[60] In the end, the controversy didn't seem to hurt him politically. He became the Republican nominee.

Even then, he didn't let up. Calling Iraq the "Harvard of terrorism," Trump went so far as to praise Saddam Hussein for eliminating terrorists while ignoring his brutal human rights abuses and his presence on the state sponsor of terrorism list.[61]

Trump's broadside was in sharp contrast to conservative critiques that focused greater attention on the success of the Bush administration's surge. In May 2015, conservative columnist Charles Krauthammer wrote that by 2009 the Iraq War was won and was then squandered by the Obama administration. Retired Army General Jack Keane agreed that the Anbar Awakening constituted a win, "and now we are losing the peace." Keane placed that responsibility on the Maliki government.[62]

More than a dozen years after the U.S. invasion, Iraq is still politically divisive, with a significant majority of Democrats believing the war was not worth fighting but a slim majority of Republicans still believing it was.[63]

Just as the politically powerful narrative of the loss of China at the start of the Cold War skewed American foreign policy, strategy, and politics for decades, it would be just as destructive if the United States applies the wrong lessons learned from Iraq. Unlike Great Britain, which released a 2.6-million-word report detailing the flawed planning and execution of the Iraq war, an analysis that took seven years to compile, the United States has attempted nothing so comprehensive, at least not for public consumption. The Pentagon Papers served a similar purpose regarding Vietnam, although it was not intended for public release.

Notwithstanding the belief that generals consistently fight the last war, the lesson from Vietnam was actually the opposite. The Army wanted to avoid another Vietnam at all cost and abandoned counterinsurgency during the 1970s and 1980s in favor of conventional warfare. It is inclined to do the same after the inconclusive results in Afghanistan and Iraq.

The Obama administration came into office determined to end the lengthy and costly ground wars in Iraq and Afghanistan and avoid getting sucked into another open-ended military adventure in the Middle East. It largely followed that path until the virtual collapse of security forces in Iraq and effective governance in Syria led to the emergence of the Islamic State and a renewed threat of terrorism against the United States and the West.

In light of the widening conflicts across the Middle East, during the 2016 campaign but particularly on the Republican side, the political pendulum swung noticeably away from democracy promotion and toward tolerance of authoritarians who can effectively control territory and deny space to the likes of the Islamic State. The dilemma, as the United States learned in 2011 across the Middle East and North Africa, is that these governments are not as stable as they might appear.

THE CHALLENGE OF LIMITED WAR

During World War II, Winston Churchill famously declared that, with national survival at stake, there is only one acceptable outcome. "It is victory, victory at all costs."[64]

That said, this unconventional war against an unconventional adversary will not have a conventional ending, certainly not a complete surrender on the deck of a battleship or in a desert tent.

The United States has long had difficulty forming effective strategies and sustainable narratives around limited war. The tendency has been to view conflicts in predominantly military terms even when the objective is achieving a desirable political end state. The achievement of military objectives—even victory—come to be viewed as an end in itself rather than a means to an end—policy success at an acceptable cost.

While President Obama rightly warned of the dangers of perpetual war, the threat of extremism will remain for a lengthy period. A number of noted figures have compared the current conflict to the Thirty Years' War. It is conceivable we are still closer to the beginning of the war within Islam than the end.

As Obama's intelligence chief, James Clapper, points out, the underlying regional factors that enable extremism persist—a youth bulge with inadequate economic prospects, disaffected young males in particular; ungoverned or poorly governed territory; and lots of weapons—with no easy fixes in sight.

"The U.S. can't fix it," says Clapper, but neither can it "just leave town."[65]

The existing authorities under which the United States is engaged in various theaters are dated. In Obama's 2015 State of the Union speech, he called for Congress to provide explicit authority for the administration's interventions in Iraq and Syria. Even with Obama's perfunctory request for congressional action, the president believes he already has all the authority he needs to do whatever it takes for as long as it takes.

The Senate Foreign Relations Committee advanced a resolution that would authorize military action against the Islamic State, but it stalled over partisan disagreements. Republicans objected to restrictions such as limits on the numbers of ground forces that could be deployed. Democrats feared they would be authorizing another open-ended military campaign in the Middle East.[66]

It is important that Congress complete this effort so the American people understand and support what the United States needs to do in the Middle East over the next decade. If the United States is going to be effective, the authorization should allow the administration to deploy ground forces where and when needed.

A new authorization for the use of force should specify the countries that are being supported through the use of force, not only those involving combat forces but also those involving unmanned systems. The United States need not advertise every operation, but if the United States is dropping bombs on extremists in Pakistan, it is time to publicly explain what must be done and why.

The United States must be clearer regarding who it considers the enemy and where the military is operating; abide by international law; increase transparency regarding specific actions and the legal rationale behind them; update authorizations; and sunset them. The latter provision would ensure a periodic public debate about the nature of the conflict, shifts in the nature of our adversaries, and eventually termination when we believe that the threat can be managed at a level below the threshold of war.[67]

The Middle East is in the early stages of a generational transformation. There are local conflicts under way in Iraq, Syria, Yemen, Somalia, Libya, Afghanistan, Pakistan, and Nigeria that involve significant U.S. action, support, or interest. Within them, there are multilayered struggles rooted in history, sect, tribe, territory, power, money, and geopolitics. The demographic makeup of states is changing dramatically due to refugee flows and migration. The level of physical destruction, depth of religious and ethnic tension, and zero-sum regional politics call into question the viability of current sovereign states and existing borders.

The incoming administration must adopt the same kind of long view that the United States sustained during the latter stages of the Cold War. The threat from political extremism is not going to be solved in a single four- or eight-year presidential term of office. Yet it can be contained and effectively managed.

Obama came into office hoping to end America's wars and reduce the war on terror to a scale that would enable the United States to rescind the authorization of the use of force passed in 2001, end the state of emergency, and among other things close the military prison at Guantanamo. Instead, he left active military campaigns in Iraq, Syria, and Afghanistan to his successor.

Even if some of the existing conflicts are brought under control, the region will experience a lengthy and complex post-conflict period. Characteristic of the evolution of al Qaeda and the emergence of the Islamic State, given the current disillusionment throughout the region, some other entity will emerge as the new flavor of political extremism. "Turmoil is going to define the Middle East for the foreseeable future," predicts Dennis Ross.[68]

15

INCREDIBLE NATION

In the introduction to the popular version of the U.S. field manual on counterinsurgency operations, developed in the midst of the struggle in Iraq, Harvard professor Sarah Sewell (later an undersecretary of state) spoke of the "primacy of politics, seeing the largely undecided middle as the campaign's center of gravity."[1] The Gulf War in 1991 was the last war with a defined military battlefield. As General Rupert Smith suggests, war is now waged "amongst the people."[2]

If war in the twenty-first century is less about clashes of formal armies but rather clashes within civilizations, then war is ultimately about people. Success has to take into account what they think, what they expect, how they perceive government policies and the actions of some of their fellow citizens, and what they are willing to endure.

In the midst of global demonstrations against the pending U.S. invasion of Iraq in 2003, the *New York Times* labeled world public opinion as a "superpower."[3] Public opinion dictated the contours of the ongoing struggle. Public opinion in the United States viewed the war as a mistake. Public opinion in Iraq viewed the well-intentioned invasion as an occupation. The failure of the Baghdad government to cultivate cross-sectarian support opened the door for the Islamic State. The Islamic State will lose its caliphate when Muslims around the world see it as illegitimate, and no longer wish to join it or support it.

Carl von Clausewitz famously described war as "merely the continuation of politics by other means." Democratic governments, as Caspar Weinberger suggested in 1984, increase the odds of success when there is at least a reasonable assurance of support from the public and their elected representatives to wage war.

Because of Iraq, there are doubts at home about the efficacy of American power. According to Dominic Tierney, the United States confronts a "paradox of power." The types of interstate wars that the public has rallied behind in the past have largely disappeared. They have been replaced by civil wars that the United States has either fought to a stalemate or lost. But since such wars do not present an existential threat and yield outcomes that are inherently murky—it is difficult to sort out the good guys from the bad guys—public acceptance of the inherent costs is "dramatically reduced."[4]

But these are the very types of conflicts America now confronts. The public takes its cues from the partisan give-and-take of a functioning democracy and from expert elites that the public trusts. As Adam Berinsky has studied, "public opinion about war is shaped by the same attitudes and orientations that shape domestic politics."[5]

Walter Lippmann thought that "mass opinion" was unqualified to be a serious factor in the conduct of foreign policy.[6] George Kennan wondered if a democracy like the United States could ever develop a coherent foreign policy. Realists like Kennan preferred to work around public opinion, something that was feasible during the Cold War given government's dominant control over national security–related information.

Mobilizing public opinion in support of a particular policy or action is a function of politics. To get things done, governments need domestic support and international partners. Both depend on public opinion. But, according to Robert Kaplan, "politics in the mass media age will be more intense than anything we have experienced."[7]

In today's environment, the ability to control the flow of information is vastly diminished. More of what governments do, particularly related to war and diplomacy, is visible to more and more people. This requires leaders, regardless of the nature of the government, to pay more attention to what their "street" is thinking. Democrats focus on the next election; autocrats on the next color revolution.

The ability to move world opinion is a form of power. The crowd, suggests Kaplan, increasingly focused on the present, now possesses the ability to observe, react, communicate, and respond in real time.[8]

All wars in the twenty-first century are inherently political. They are less about military victory and more about political outcomes. Success in modern warfare still requires controlling territory, but it is also about developing credible narratives, shaping public perceptions, and undermining the influence of adversaries.

Should public opinion matter in the conduct of war and foreign policy? Yes, of course.[9] Any international commitment necessarily involves a domestic trade-off of some kind. Public opinion should never be a direct determinant of foreign policy, but Harvard's Joseph Nye believes politics do form "constraints, like dams or dikes" that create definite boundaries for its formulation and execution.[10]

What the people are willing to support, at what cost, and for how long will determine which side succeeds and which side fails. While a government can expect a spike in public support once engaged in hostilities—the so-called rally-round-the-flag effect—shifts in public opinion will depend on whether subsequent events fit with public expectations of what is at stake and the costs involved.

The Cold War was understood to be a long-term political, economic, and social challenge. The United States and its allies won the battle of narratives, in large part because it cared what the world thought, and acted accordingly. Most of the world saw clear differences between the United States and the Soviet Union and took sides. They did not approve of everything the United States did or represented, but consistently gave America and its allies the benefit of the doubt.

While there are significant differences to the present day—the threat posed by the Islamic State, al Qaeda, and other extremist groups is not existential—like the Cold War, the challenge is more about delegitimizing an ideology than defeating an opposing army. It's important to adopt a similar long-term perspective.

Thankfully, it would appear that the vast majority of Muslims do not want to live within a caliphate. They want to be integrated with the world, but on specific terms. The region needs to offer its citizens a more attractive alternative. This will not necessarily translate into greater support for the United States. People admire what America represents but retain concerns about U.S. policy. Thus, international support will be less carte blanche and more a la carte.

MARKET POWER

Moises Naim in his book *The End of Power* details the increasing challenge of employing power in a world that is more unstable and less cohesive. He advances the concept of "market power" to explain the new political dynamic. Market power is the ability to generate and sustain extra profits without ceding market share, to set a profitable market price without inviting rivals to under-cut your position.[11] In the foreign policy world, this means advocating a course of action that invites cooperation from key players and minimizes competition or resistance, both of which raise costs.

Notwithstanding rhetoric of America's decline, there is not another coun-try on earth that can supplant the United States, the world's only true global power. But a growing number of states—returning powers such as China and Russia and rising powers such as Brazil, India, and Turkey—have the ability to impact Washington's freedom of action. The world wants a say in how the United States exercises its power.

This is the rise of the rest.[12] It is not necessarily something to be feared. It is in fact the product of a deliberate U.S. policy of global integration pursued over several decades. The United States remains the bluest chip in the market-place, but it is now a more crowded exchange. This changes how the United States must exercise global leadership.

The information revolution has made it harder to manage foreign policy, even as global trends are evolving in directions that are favorable to American values over the long term.[13] Given the advent of integrated global networks, more of the world is now politically active, what former National Security Advisor Zbigniew Brzezinski calls a "global political awakening."[14]

Governments have lost the ability to set the global agenda. They are less able to conceal unpopular policies and actions from domestic and international audiences. World politics is no longer the sole province of governments.[15] More people are aware of more developments around the world, particularly the impact American foreign policy has on their lives. More issues are being pushed into the public realm.

This creates time and space for smaller players to have potentially dispro-portionate impact, whom Naim terms micropowers.[16] Terrorists are a good example.

Terrorism is violence as political theater intended to attract attention, deliberately polarize, create a following, and generate a political impact. Al Qaeda became the leading global terrorist brand in part because it was viewed as standing up to the United States. Its stock went up based on its success at pulling off spectacular attacks—and its stock declined steadily once Muslims recognized they were its primary victims.

As the Islamic State gained a foothold in the region, at the expense of unpopular governments in Iraq and Syria, it eclipsed al Qaeda as the terrorist flavor of the moment. There are strong indications already that its appeal has crested. As the Islamic State proves unable to defend its self-declared caliphate, its perceived legitimacy will decline further. That said, it has an adaptive structure and will likely survive in some form even after losing its caliphate in Iraq and Syria.

This is a perfect example of the market dynamic applied to regional geopolitics. Markets can fluctuate significantly, moved by actions, expectations, or fears. They go up and down. They surge and correct. What matters over time are trends, effectiveness, and value.

The information revolution has enhanced the role of markets.[17] It has also greatly complicated international affairs. Power is ultimately convincing others, whether leaders, governments, elites, or now broader publics, to support policies or actions that they may or may not like, particularly those that involve long-term gain but short-term costs.

This is not to suggest U.S. policy should be based on trying to win a popularity contest. All politics is local, and the impact of American power and influence will be felt and viewed in different ways in different places. Whatever America chooses to do, it will gain admirers and critics.

But in the conduct of American foreign policy, leaders must take into account how its words and more importantly its deeds will be perceived and factor those political effects into the policy-making process. Public opinion is becoming more dynamic. Governments need to understand how dramatic swings in public opinion can affect foreign policy. The 2016 Brexit vote, which shocked allies and roiled global markets, is a case in point. The Arab uprisings are another.

END OF PLAUSIBLE DENIABILITY

In an interview with Tim Russert on *Meet the Press* just after the September 11 attacks, Vice President Dick Cheney projected that much of the just-declared war on terror would be conducted on "the dark side" and "in the shadows," employing intelligence assets and special operations forces.[18]

The Bush administration took steps it did not intend for public consumption, such as expanded surveillance of global information networks and the establishment of black sites for detention and enhanced interrogation of terrorism suspects. They were controversial when revealed through government leaks and diligent news media reporting. Some of these practices may or may not have complied with domestic and international law. There were legitimate questions about their effectiveness and oversight.

The American people were split. Some conjured up worst-case scenarios of a ticking time bomb to justify whatever was required to prevent an attack. Others worried about the compromise of American values in the illusory pursuit of perfect security.

Around the world, many saw hypocrisy. The United States long championed human rights, the rule of law, and transparent justice but at a critical moment failed to practice what was preached. Such revelations undermined popular support for critical international partnerships and tarnished the American brand. Donald Trump's nativist campaign rhetoric about the wall and ban did as well.

The government responded to such leaks by stepping up its prosecution of government employees who violate the terms of their security clearances. This does not represent a war on leaks as some transparency advocates have alleged. The information revolution has increased both the number and volume of leaks, but technology also leaves digital fingerprints that enable law enforcement to more easily identify the culprit.

At the same time, the government cannot prosecute its way to better secrecy. Global forces are moving in the opposite direction. More of what the United States does is now visible to more people who can share what they see and what they think with others across a networked world.

There is no longer such a thing as plausible deniability.

Going forward, the United States must do a better job of explaining what it is doing to protect itself and its allies. It must assume that more of its actions will occur in the public realm. The United States cannot hide behind a veil of secrecy, particularly because its friends find transparency dangerous or inconvenient. Gaps between what we say and what we do have strategic consequences.

At the start of his administration, Obama pledged greater transparency, suggesting the era of secrecy is over.[19] But in a Google chat in 2013, the president acknowledged that his administration was less transparent than he hoped.[20] In a 2014 speech at West Point, Obama said that his administration needs to explain things better. He's right.

A good place to start would be ending the pseudosecrecy surrounding unmanned aerial vehicles or drones. In July 2016, the White House released a summary of the estimated number of combatants and noncombatants killed in drone strikes outside declared war zones, a welcome if belated step toward greater transparency. This needs to be a recurring practice, not just a one-time gesture.

Under Obama, the United States came to rely extensively on drones as the weapon of choice in this evolving conflict. It enabled the United States to significantly erode the capability of core al Qaeda while dramatically reducing the number of American boots on the ground in specific locations. In Obama's first year in office, between the military and CIA, there were more Predator drone strikes than in the entire Bush presidency.[21]

Drones enjoy strong bipartisan support. Drones are more precise. Even allowing for inevitable mistakes, the number of innocent civilians killed by drone operations numbers in the hundreds or perhaps low thousands, far less than a ground invasion.

But insufficient attention has been paid to the cost-benefit calculation of the employment of drones and its impact on the perceived legitimacy of American counterterrorism operations. In fact, more than a decade after the first use of drones, the CIA admitted it did not know what the strategic impact is.[22]

Until recently, the United States only viewed drone operations in terms of the number of bad guys eliminated. For a long time, the government refused to even acknowledge there were civilian casualties. Former CIA Director Michael Hayden argued in his book *Playing to the Edge* that civilian casualties are far fewer than alleged, but acknowledged that the failure to address the "second- and third-order effects" of such actions complicated the broader war of ideas, what he termed the "deep fight."[23]

The governments of Pakistan, Saudi Arabia, and Yemen have cooperated extensively with the United States in counterterrorism operations but decline to admit it publicly to their own people, undermining the very concept of accountable governance the United States freely acknowledges is missing across the Middle East.

In one of the more notable diplomatic cables released by WikiLeaks in late 2010, Yemeni President Ali Abdullah Saleh pledged to General David Petraeus that his government would "continue saying the bombs are ours, not yours," deliberately misleading his people (and by extension the American people) regarding the responsibility for attacks in his country against suspected militants.[24]

Despite claims Yemen developed as a model of counterterrorism cooperation with the United States, as the *New York Times*' Scott Shane wrote in *Objective Troy*, "after years of American strikes both Pakistan and Yemen were less stable and their people more hostile to the United States."[25]

The secrecy surrounding the program has left an open field for others to stir up anti-American sentiment and call into question America's commitment to international law. The United States is also setting precedents that other nations could follow as drone technology expands.

The reliance on secrecy may have been appropriate in the early phase of the conflict when the United States was still uncertain about what it confronted. But as former Director of National Intelligence Dennis Blair said, "Covert action that goes on for years doesn't generally stay covert."[26]

Such implicit international understandings—you can use our bases and airspace as long as no one talks about it—most be renegotiated. No one is being fooled. There is a global conversation under way about these missions and technologies. The secrecy is simply denying the United States the opportunity to inform it and generate necessary public support for what it is trying to do. The damage to American credibility and legitimacy is no longer acceptable.

There is a critical issue regarding democratic accountability at home as well.[27] President Obama confirmed the drone strike that eliminated Anwar al-Awlaki, a rising leader within Al Qaeda in the Arabian Peninsula but also an American citizen, but did not release a detailed analysis that justified the action absent due process.

Given Awlaki's participation in AQAP operational planning, not to mention his encouragement of further attacks against the United States, there was a strong legal basis to conclude he was a threat to the United States and a legitimate target. "Awlaki was both a strategist *and an operator,*" suggests Seth Jones of RAND (emphasis in the original).[28]

The Obama administration advanced a public narrative that drone strikes are approved only when there is near certainty that innocent civilians would not be harmed or killed in the process. But war by its very nature frequently defies that narrative. Intelligence is never perfect. The apparent accidental deaths of two hostages in Pakistan in January 2015, including an American citizen, Warren Weinstein, is a good example of the limits of intelligence in such remote areas.[29]

Mistakes are inevitable in war. The side judged to be most credible wins the information war. This was certainly the case in Kosovo, where NATO and its leading members—the United States, Great Britain, France, and Germany—created a real-time capability to publicly respond to what was happening in the air campaign, with particular emphasis on acknowledging collateral damage before President Slobodan Milosevic could exploit it for propaganda purposes.

The United States needs to factor public opinion—what might be termed information effects—more significantly into future decision making regarding counterterrorism efforts. The lack of even a robust public debate regarding drone operations represents a "hole in the middle" of U.S. strategy.[30]

The war on terror was conceived primarily as a battle of hearts and minds. For too long, secrecy has trumped politics. It's time to turn this table. This requires a far more open conversation with much of the world than occurred in the first fifteen years of this struggle. The United States should routinely and promptly reveal basic information about drone strikes, those targeted and the impact, both intended and inadvertent.[31]

As General Stanley McChrystal instructed his troops in Afghanistan, "The conflict will be won by persuading the population, not by destroying the enemy."[32]

The dramatic revelations by Edward Snowden are another case.

Snowden revealed details of a secret program that allegedly enabled the NSA to acquire user data from Internet companies, intercepting and storing vast amounts of communications from American citizens without a warrant or probable cause. He believed oversight and accountability of the NSA was inadequate for mass surveillance programs that did not in fact uncover terrorist plots.

Snowden claimed his actions were based on the public's right to "at least know the broad outlines of what our government's doing in our name."[33] He has a point—up to a point.

Shortly after 9/11, President Bush authorized the National Security Agency to expand its interception of international calls, one end of which might be in the United States, as an emergency exception to the normal requirements of the Foreign Intelligence Surveillance Act (FISA), which included a detailed, individualized warrant. The program, code-named Stellarwind, allowed the collection, retention, and interrogation of metadata associated with those calls. The exception to the normal FISA practice was based on the president's Article 2 powers as commander-in-chief and the AUMF, the de facto declaration of war against al Qaeda.

The Stellarwind program (later dubbed the Terrorist Surveillance Act) became controversial after its existence was leaked to the *New York Times* and revealed in an article in December 2005. Michael Hayden, while defending the legality and careful administration of the program, acknowledged later that more should have been done to ensure congressional and public support.[34] But the controversy resulted in adjustments to the law that brought the program within the boundaries of FISA.

In fact, well before the *New York Times* report, the FISA Court had been briefed on the program and agreed with the legal analysis that supported it. Congress in turn strengthened its legal foundation in subsequent legislation, including the Protect America Act in 2007 and FISA Amendments Act in 2008.[35]

For too long, political leaders and intelligence officials have been unwilling to engage in a public conversation regarding how this war was being waged on their behalf. Initially, the justification for excessive secrecy was not to reveal specific information that would benefit a potential adversary. While a legitimate concern, Snowden tipped the scales in favor of greater disclosure, although at a cost to legitimate security interests. It is notable that, whatever the damage, the director of the NSA, Admiral Mike Rogers, declined to say that "the sky was falling."[36]

But Snowden is wrong to claim that "the priorities of governments seem to be very distinct from the desires of the public."[37]

Given the political narrative that terrorist plots should be detected and intercepted, the bureaucratic response was understandable. The best way to connect more dots is to collect more dots. The response to Snowden's revelations was less about the fact of government surveillance of global information networks but shock at the sheer volume of personal information involved.

Snowden placed his finger on the essence of the challenge—will the American public accept occasional terrorist attacks in return for less intrusion, or do they want government to maximize tools available to it, yielding some privacy for better security?

The American public is torn between the security narrative of "whatever it takes" and the values narrative of "that's not who we are." That tension is always going to be present. In 2016, the candidates who ran for president represented all sides of this spectrum.

The truth is, there is no fixed line. In many respects, the American government went to war but left the American people behind. The balance between security and privacy should be continually debated and adjusted based on our understanding of the threat, but within the boundaries of American law and values.

Political leaders and intelligence officials operate on the assumption that secrecy can be maintained for an indefinite period. While there is information that needs to be protected, Snowden, Chelsea Manning, and Julian Assange employed modern information technology to compromise an unprecedented number of classified and sensitive documents. Government is improving its ability to detect leaks, but it can't stop them.

In an increasingly transparent and interconnected world, secrecy is no longer what it once was.

National security and foreign policy frequently require difficult decisions among less than optimal choices. Any choice will involve potential benefits and costs. What decision makers need to consider to a greater degree is the risk, perhaps even the likelihood, that specific actions, however well intentioned, will become public, and the potential strategic impact when revealed. When actions are viewed as inconsistent with existing laws, policies, or political narratives, potential costs rise dramatically.

If people are the "center of gravity" in foreign policy today, for it to be both politically viable and sustainable, government must carefully define the national interest at stake, whether vital or important; tailor a response according to the interest and within the boundaries of what the public and its representatives are likely to support; set the right expectations regarding the risk, duration, and anticipated costs; and work to meet those expectations to the degree possible. These are the keys to credibility, legitimacy, and sustainability. All depend on politics.[38]

CREDIBILITY

Credibility is a crucial area where the United States remains seriously challenged. Policy, strategy, and narratives must harmonize. Actions speak louder than words, but words matter as well. During the Cold War, propaganda was a prominent and effective tool. It was possible to communicate one message at home, a different one abroad, and remain credible. Not anymore.

The contest of ideas is a dimension of every major international challenge the United States confronts. Sustaining public support for policies and actions is "a core element of power, not merely an exercise in public relations."[39]

The information revolution has increased the potency of soft power, a concept advanced by Harvard's Joseph Nye. The idea is that the exercise of power is more successful and less costly when based on attraction rather than coercion. Soft power, says Nye, is "hard to use, easy to lose, and costly to reestablish."[40] Credibility (and legitimacy) creates conditions for deeper cooperation, since governments and leaders are more likely to accept the political risks of supporting American policy.

Public opinion can be a measure of whether a soft power strategy is working or likely to succeed. The goal is not always to get public support on every action. That is not realistic. As the most powerful country in the world, the United States is never going to please everyone. While it can be beneficial to be feared, it is better to be understood and respected. Most of the time, America will get the benefit of any doubt.

Narratives in turn are the "currency of soft power."[41] But in today's near continuous political campaign, the tendency to oversell a policy to gain public support and the political consequences of acknowledging mistakes have increased. Credibility rests in setting the right expectations and then achieving them. A gap between what a government says and what it does contributes to a perception of American unreliability.[42]

Social media can overturn carefully developed major power narratives. Facebook, Twitter, and YouTube now have as much impact as any government.[43]

An obscure film trailer that is perceived to insult the Prophet Muhammad sparked a protest in Cairo that became a presidential campaign issue. In all likelihood, there was a ripple effect in Benghazi; in the mayhem, four Americans were killed. A dramatic picture of a singed Koran was perceived as communicating disrespect for Islam and sparked violent protests in several countries. So did a YouTube video that depicted Marines desecrating the body of a dead Taliban fighter, and the decision by an obscure Florida pastor to put the Koran on trial.

The war on terror, now far more a war within Islam, is a battle of narratives. Bin Laden's strategy was to destroy American credibility in the Middle East, and the United States fell into that trap with its invasion of Iraq. Al Qaeda was perceived as holy warriors defending sacred lands in an American war against Islam.[44]

In this global political and information environment, communications strategies become more important. Outcomes are determined not merely by whose army wins, but also by whose story wins.[45]

Policy and narratives are now conflated to a significant degree.[46] There is a fair criticism that the Obama administration spent as much time thinking of what to say as what to do. Too often, the recommended solution to a foreign policy problem was to make a speech. But there was a persistent disconnect between speeches and actions.[47] For a leader with considerable oratorical skills—certainly in contrast to his immediate predecessor—the decline in public support for Obama's management of the threat of terrorism was less about a failure of policy and strategy and more about a failure of politics and narrative. Over time, a wide gap emerged between what he said, what he did, and how various conflicts unfolded.

Obama drew a red line regarding the use of chemical weapons in Syria, but hesitated to employ military force to defend it. Obama viewed the elimination of chemical weapons through coercive diplomacy as a foreign policy achievement—and it was. But the flawed process surrounding the red line damaged American credibility. The president preferred to see the issue through a domestic political lens—an enlightened White House moving beyond the traditional Washington playbook and foreign policy establishment. But there was a cost.

Obama listed the rebuilding of American alliances and partnerships as a part of his foreign policy legacy. But many key allies saw the red line as a critical error. Whether fair or not, "The global conventional wisdom has created its own reality."[48]

As *Washington Post* columnist David Ignatius suggests, to be strong, the United States must be credible. Credibility is the glue of the international system.[49] America's credibility challenge certainly did not originate with Obama. The Saudi king told Obama in 2009 that a critical responsibility was to restore American credibility around the world.[50] That remains a work in progress.

Employing bold words without a policy behind them is not cost free. Just sounding tough is not sufficient. The credibility of American power must be reinforced. This does not require the United States to jump into the first conflict that develops in 2017 or beyond. Leaping into a conflict and then figuring out a viable strategy is neither wise nor sustainable.

LEGITIMACY

There were good reasons to refocus on Iraq in the aftermath of the September 11 attacks, even if Saddam Hussein had no ties to al Qaeda. If the status quo in the region was viewed as undesirable and unsustainable, Iraq was a reasonable place to begin. There was a strong case against Saddam Hussein and his decade-long defiance of the United Nations and the United States.

But there was a rush to war. The threat posed by Saddam Hussein did not change after September 11, only the tolerance in Washington for the risk he posed to the region and a determination to eliminate it once and for all. The Bush administration decided that Saddam Hussein had to go, ironically a judgment shared by Osama bin Laden. But it was unwilling to allow time for the international community to reach the same conclusion.

The invasion of Iraq, controversial given the clear divide within the UN Security Council, was stunningly successful in the initial phase. But it steadily lost international legitimacy and public support with the failure to find the threatening stocks of weapons of mass destruction that were central to the American case for war. This was compounded by the lack of planning for the post-conflict phase and the inability of U.S. forces to stabilize the country.

While there were meaningful achievements—images of purple fingers as citizens in the Middle East got to vote and exercise self-determination—they were overwhelmed by a grinding civil war that turned a rogue state into a failed state. A campaign waged under the banner of a war on terror defeated a designated state sponsor, but in the process spawned far greater violent political extremism, with ripple effects that are still felt today.

The United States was responsible. Iraq devastated America's standing in the world. Obama was determined to learn and apply Iraq's lessons. Obama sought over eight years to reestablish common cause with the international community. America would play by established international rules.

Libya was a textbook case—a compelling situation as Qaddafi threatened to exterminate his political opponents; a request for intervention by the Arab League; and a United Nations Security Council resolution authorizing "all necessary means" to protect the Libyan people.

However, while George H. W. Bush made a strategic choice to pursue the limited goal that unified the international community—restoration of Kuwait's sovereignty and government—Barack Obama did not feel confined by the UN resolution regarding Libya and expanded the mission from a responsibility to protect to regime change.

In the aftermath of Qaddafi's demise, the Libyan government believed its legitimacy would be undermined by the presence of foreign troops. It was unable to consolidate its power, and the country fractured again. Even after restoring a government of national unity, Obama believed that ground troops in Libya "would send the wrong signal."[51]

To Bush, the use of force served a larger purpose—to protect the ability of the United States and Soviet Union to cooperate in the shaping of a new world order while enhancing America's standing in the Middle East. In 1991, it was not his objective to transform the region.

To Obama, the use of force served to preserve the potentially transformative dynamic under way across the Middle East and South Africa. But Libya became an obstacle to further cooperation regarding Syria. Russia and China blocked all attempts to legitimize any intervention in Syria through the United Nations.

When Obama confronted the prospect of military action in Syria following the Assad regime's use of chemical weapons, which crossed a presidential red line, the White House confronted a legal and political dilemma. Syria's actions violated at least one international treaty to which it was a party, but there was no specified enforcement mechanism to justify a military response. There was no plausible claim of self-defense. And since the atrocity had already taken place, it was difficult to argue as with Libya that an intervention would prevent a humanitarian disaster.[52]

Surprised by the unexpected negative vote by the British House of Commons that sidelined an anticipated ally, the administration then turned to a skeptical Congress, which was as leery of a slippery slope and deeper involvement as the public. The escalating crisis in Syria reminded many, including the president, of Iraq.

Obama's concern about the lack of a clear legitimating authority was appropriate. As Fareed Zakaria suggests, "Legitimacy is power."[53] But it is, says Richard Haass, "as much about perception as it is a legal concept."[54]

After Iraq, Obama's emphasis on international legitimacy was intended to help restore faith in American power. But given the degree to which domestic and global politics are more contested, gaining and sustaining legitimacy for international action is becoming more difficult.

That said, international legitimacy matters; it reduces the costs of American leadership. We saw in Iraq the consequences of a mind-set that places maximum value on freedom of American action. Acting as part of a coalition is more complex and takes longer to organize, but the benefits far outweigh the limitations.

The White House claimed victory after the United Nations passed a resolution ordering Syria to give up its chemical weapons, achieving a better result than was intended through the planned military strikes. But the choices presented—either military action or the removal of chemical weapons—were never properly linked.

The case Obama presented for defense of his red line was based on the notion of accountability, of justice. Assad had violated international norms and needed to pay a price. It should have been based on what the administration needed to achieve through military action—the removal of chemical weapons in order to deescalate the Syrian civil war.

Obama's failure was rooted in his disregard of the traditional Washington playbook, how to identify an appropriate military objective to achieve a desired political outcome. The White House could not generate the needed congressional support for military action because it did not make a case that the planned strikes would make a difference on the ground. A better case was available—threatening and if necessary employing military force not for reasons of accountability, but to impel Assad to yield his chemical weapons arsenal. Obama's fear that decisive military action would lead to responsibility for the Syrian civil war obscured what could be accomplished not to solve the crisis, but manage its regional impact.

As a result, Obama aimed too low and failed to gain public and congressional support for military action. Even though he achieved the objective through diplomatic means, the costs were significant. Not only did allies question American resolve, but many in the region believed that the United States had an opportunity to change the course of the Syrian tragedy and chose not to act.

Obama believes his caution regarding Syria will be redeemed over the long term. The problem is that when it comes to politics, judgments are rendered in weeks and months, not years. In the twenty-first century, as Steven Weber and Bruce Jentleson suggest, "political legitimacy is a function of performance, not just process."[55]

TRANSPARENCY

More than two decades ago, experts advanced the concept of the CNN Effect that suggested that governments would be impelled to respond to dramatic images portrayed on increasingly ubiquitous cable networks—in other words, to do something.

Somalia was its strongest argument, with the United States responding to dramatic images of people starving as a result of clan warfare that generated a humanitarian conflict in a country without a central government. A more sophisticated reading of the interaction between media and government was one of agenda setting—the media raised the urgency surrounding the situation and accelerated the decision-making process. But the ultimate course of action tracked with established interests and values.

When the Arab Spring broke out in Egypt, a corollary was the Al Jazeera Effect, which underscored the degree to which governments no longer control the flow of information.[56] President Hosni Mubarak presumed that he could contain the protests within a few days but failed. The information sphere around the demonstrations was too thick. The Egyptian government literally tried to disconnect the country from the Internet, but it could not change the dramatic picture in Tahrir Square. These were real revolutions, but the combination of old and new media gave the movements momentum and staying power.

Now there is the YouTube Effect, where any local event can instantly become global news thanks to the ability to transmit information through expanding global interconnections without cost. Or the Periscope or Facebook effect where an event can be viewed live as it happens. There is now a global culture of documenting and instantly sharing information—whether images of innocent selfies or brutal violence.

Images have enduring salience, as the Islamic State proved with the beheadings of captives dressed in Guantanamo-style orange jumpsuits, over-turning carefully crafted political narratives. Just as companies are required to work constantly to protect their brand from reputational risk, so too do countries, frequently reacting in real time.

To the extent that wars in the twenty-first century are waged far more within countries than between them, modern conflicts are inherently political. Narratives matter. Perceptions matter. As the Islamic State demonstrated, territory is important, but the high ground is virtual, not just physical.

As late as the first Gulf War, the United States maintained effective control of information emanating from the battlefield. To file coverage, the media relied on global satellite connections owned and operated by the government. That is no longer the case. Now there are thousands and thousands of combatants and spectators on the battlefield transmitting competing interpretations of what is happening. Governments can try to impose constraints on the Internet, but there will always be ways to circumvent censorship.

During the Iraq War, U.S. forces not only committed gross abuses of international law and human rights at Abu Ghraib, but they documented their actions and shared them with fellow soldiers. The compelling images found their way into the public sphere, reinforcing perceptions at home and abroad that the United States had lost its way.

A U.S. intelligence analyst viewed a video of an Apache helicopter crew firing on a Reuters film crew that it mistook for armed insurgents. While the helicopter crew felt it was acting in self-defense, the dramatic video depicted soldiers who had lost the ability to distinguish between civilians and combatants. The protection of the civilian population, central to success in counterinsurgency operations, no longer seemed to matter.

The intelligence analyst Private First Class Bradley (now Chelsea) Manning shared the video, intelligence logs from Iraq and Afghanistan, and diplomatic cables from posts around the world with a little-known website called WikiLeaks.*

On March 10, 2011, while speaking at MIT, I was asked why the government was "torturing" Private Manning. I responded that we were doing no such thing. But I acknowledged the controversy surrounding her incarceration, where Manning was effectively in solitary confinement and required to hand over clothing at night due to misguided military fears of suicide. I termed the situation "ridiculous, counterproductive, and stupid." I do not con-

During WikiLeaks, American credibility in some parts of the world actually went up. In the Middle East, there was validation of grievances that were deeply felt in countries undergoing transformations.[57] But there were costs as well, with real people intimidated, imprisoned, or worse in the aftermath of the compromise.

WikiLeaks made a dramatic reappearance on the global stage in 2016 with its release of internal emails from the Democratic National Committee. Assange was open regarding his objective to disrupt the Clinton campaign as it was poised to make history.

There have always been mistakes made on every battlefield—miscalculations of the adversary, weapons that hit the wrong target, and innocent civilians victimized by war. Some incidents, such as the 1968 massacre at My Lai, reinforced growing public doubts about the U.S. mission in Vietnam. Others, like the 1995 Serb massacre at Srebrenica, impelled more significant international action that led to the Dayton Accords that ended the brutal war in Bosnia.

---

sider Manning a whistleblower, nor a traitor. The leak was naïve, but still a serious violation of Manning's oath of service to the country. I could have dodged the question or answered off the record, but given the damage to America's reputation created by decisions surrounding the military prison at Guantanamo and actions at the military prison at Abu Ghraib, the last thing the United States needed was another controversy in a domestic military prison involving a U.S. soldier and citizen. My comments were not intended to create headlines, but they did. The following day, President Obama was asked about the issue during a press conference. He backed the Pentagon, believing that Manning's treatment met appropriate standards of care. But it was clear from the president's response that he was unhappy that an interagency disagreement had surfaced in public. The State and Defense Departments were at odds regarding how to approach a UN review of Manning's treatment. The Obama White House followed a "no drama" approach to policymaking, meaning agency disagreements should be resolved in the Situation Room and not through the media. Quite unintentionally, I had violated that rule. After the press conference, there were multiple high-level calls from the White House to the State Department complaining about what had occurred. I was giving a speech to WorldBoston regarding WikiLeaks at the time. When informed of the White House reaction—support for a planned but not yet announced nomination to be a U.S. ambassador was withdrawn—it was clear I had lost the confidence of the president and the White House staff. I immediately offered my resignation. In the aftermath, I stood by what I said. If the United States is to maintain its global leadership and be viewed as legitimate and credible, it must practice at home what it preaches abroad. Shortly after I resigned, the Pentagon transferred Manning to a different prison with very different conditions of confinement. The UN concluded that Manning's treatment violated her human rights. The trial judge considered the treatment excessive and modestly reduced Manning's sentence at trial. Unlike civilian jurisprudence, a key function of the military justice system is to reinforce good order and discipline. Manning's sentence of thirty-five years sent an appropriate message regarding the seriousness of her actions. At the same time, given the unique aspects of her case, the Army should consider an early parole.

The war in Iraq was perhaps the most intensively reported war in history, with a significant volume of information emanating from the battlefield through many sources no longer controlled by governments. To be sure, the government remained extremely active, with media imbedded with military units for all major operations, sponsored trips for military experts and talking heads, and regular media briefings from military commanders. Likewise, the insurgents spent a great deal of effort to undermine American narratives regarding security, progress, and victory.

Information warfare—or propaganda—is a growing dimension of modern warfare. The Assad regime has gone to great lengths to inhibit sustained coverage of the war within Syria. Traditional regional and war correspondents have covered the conflict from neighboring countries, with only sporadic access to various battle zones.

Various opposition groups have adapted, taking their story directly to the public through the use of social media. That was certainly the case with the video that revealed the use of chemical weapons in 2013.

The fact that combatants have the ability to communicate directly from the battlefield has changed perceptions of the traditional media's value and neutrality, creating unprecedented dangers. Reporters are viewed less as assets to explain the war from a particular point of view and more as targets or pawns, as the brutal beheadings of James Foley and Steven Sotloff by the Islamic State underscore.

The Islamic State is devoting as much effort to the virtual war as the physical one. The two dimensions seem to be of equal strategic importance. Media "emirs" were given equal rank as military commanders, and those engaged in the propaganda campaign received preferred status, pay, and living arrangements. One study calculated more than 1,100 distinct video and audio productions released in a single month, distributed through a network of media offices spread across the region, in multiple languages and tailored to specific audiences—internal, regional, and Western.[58]

Government agencies are finding it difficult to keep up, organize a cogent counternarrative, and respond in near-real time. But they need to be more forthcoming. As former CIA Director Michael Hayden fears, "American intelligence is losing both effectiveness (through leaks) *and* legitimacy (through its own reticence)." Hayden favors a policy of "translucence" that preserves essential operational details, but provides enough perspective to enable an informed debate that ensures needed public support.[59]

Information and communication technologies are not necessarily making the world more democratic. They are making the world more transparent.

They are raising the costs to government where there is a dramatic gap between words and actions. That gap has strategic significance.

When the Assad regime employed chemical weapons, YouTube videos caught the Obama administration undecided as to how to defend its red line. Russia denied any complicity regarding the shoot down of a civilian airliner over Ukraine, but an image released on Twitter suggested otherwise. When Moscow denied the presence of its forces within Syria, a social media trail followed them there.

In the United States, there is little appreciation of how closely the world follows what happens in America. Some still believe there is a moat between the United States and the rest of the world. One presidential candidate thought there should be a wall. But because of global media, the world has a front-row seat.

SUSTAINABILITY

There is a growing gap between how America views its role in the world and the burden it is willing to bear to sustain its global leadership. It is the flip side of the domestic political debate that, however much many Americans rail against government, the fact is most expect more from government than they want to support through tax dollars. There is significant support for American global leadership in the abstract, but buyer's remorse as costs grow.

Because of instantaneous communications, the political clock in today's world ticks faster, and it can have a profound impact on perceptions of war within a population that is by nature already impatient.[60] There is a narrower window where interventions must match expectations established beforehand.

Irrespective of what the intervention in Iraq accomplished, the actual U.S. experience diverged significantly from what Americans, Iraqis, and others were led to expect.

Americans were led to believe in the year prior to the U.S. invasion that the intervention was about weapons of mass destruction, would be accomplished in a straightforward manner at a relatively reasonable cost, and in the end would make the Middle East more stable and the United States safer.

When no weapons were found and the invasion turned into a lengthy occupation, insurgency, and civil war that exacerbated the terrorism threat to the United States and its allies, public support for the mission at home, in the region, and beyond evaporated.

The Bush administration found itself in a Catch-22 in Iraq, with a nation-building responsibility for which it did not plan and did not want. It equated the establishment of a new democracy with an election—a necessary process in a democracy—rather than with institution building that takes much longer.

On the one hand, growing public opposition did not prevent the Bush administration from continuing the mission and indeed surging forces in 2006 and 2007 in order to at least stabilize the country. But the lost legitimacy and credibility, given the severe gap between promise and reality, became an unsurmountable obstacle to the establishment of a long-term strategic partnership.

Given public skepticism for the efficacy of military interventions in light of Iraq and Afghanistan, Obama as a candidate pledged decisive but judicious use of military force when needed to defend the United States and its interests. Once in office, the Obama administration generally kept its military ambitions within the boundaries of available public support.

The United States and Iraq negotiated a new Status of Forces Agreement in good faith that would have enabled the kind of follow-on mission that exists with a number of American allies around the world, but the politics on both sides would not support it.

Only when the shocking videos of the beheadings of American citizens by the Islamic State emerged did the political boundaries broaden that enabled the reintroduction of forces into Iraq, although with little support for ground forces in a combat role.

The ability to gain and sustain public support is, as Weinberger suggested three decades ago, critical to military success. Going forward, future presidents must make more realistic assessments of what the public will support and for how long, and factor that as a core element of mission planning into what they hope to achieve through military action. It should be done before stepping up to a podium in the Rose Garden.

This will not be easy, given the deep political divisions at home and the complex international crises that the next president will inherit. The Trump administration in 2017, like the Obama administration in 2009, confronts the need to strengthen the credibility of American leadership once again and then sustain its legitimacy over time. But Trump's unconventional candidacy actually reflected many of the contradictions of America's current foreign policy and domestic politics: a strong belief in American power, represented in his campaign narratives of making America great again and helping the country win again, yet coupled with divisive rhetoric regarding border walls and travel bans, and skepticism regarding the value of alliances and trade that have long formed the supporting structure for American security and prosperity. Both Trump's improbable march to the White House and Great Britain's anticipated divorce from the European Union reflect the anti-establishment politics of the time that will only complicate the ability to reach a consensus for effective action.

16

A FOREIGN POLICY WITHIN THE POLITICAL LINES

George W. Bush was not elected as a war president, but became one on September 11. The American people gave the Bush administration wide latitude to define the suddenly tangible threat of terrorism and supported the aggressive policies shaped by expansive narratives of what was required.

During the 2000 campaign, Bush defined a more strategic role for the United States, believing the United States should conduct its international affairs from a position of strength. He was wary of humanitarian missions that placed American forces in the middle of conflicts that were not central to U.S. security.[1]

As Bush made clear, "I don't want to be the world's policeman."[2] The problem, of course, is there is no clear line between being indispensable and being the cop enforcing international norms on every global beat.

Bush's conception of the war on terror made that line even harder to draw. All countries had to make a choice. They were with us or against us. A war on terror did not distinguish between global terrorist organizations that threatened the United States, those that didn't, and those who supported them.

Early in his first term, Bush signaled to his leadership team that "I didn't take this job to play small ball."[3] After September 11, he crafted an expansive strategy to employ military power to reassert American global dominance, eliminate emerging threats, transform a vital yet unstable part of the world, and strengthen executive power.

Notwithstanding Bush's ties to the Texas Rangers, a baseball franchise for which he was a part owner, his approach to foreign policy embodied the New

York Yankees, the franchise with the most championships and biggest bankroll. There is an aura about the Yankees and an expectation of success. They are at the same time the most admired and hated team in baseball. Over the past century, they have been baseball's lone superpower, even though they now confront rising and returning competitors (most notably the Boston Red Sox).

Teams that rely on the big inning and the long ball, they tend to leave a lot of runners on base. In baseball, that is overlooked as long as the final result is a win. In foreign policy, however, such costs add up and jeopardize public support, particularly if the game goes beyond the anticipated nine innings. That's what happened in Iraq.

When Barack Obama became president, he substituted a bust of Martin Luther King in the Oval Office for one of Winston Churchill (Churchill was dispatched to the entrance to the White House Treaty Room on the second floor, a step that Senator Ted Cruz suggested was Obama's first mistake in office). Perhaps a better choice should have been Oakland A's General Manager Billy Beane, who on a different playing field employed similar contrarian strategies that diverged meaningfully from past practice.

Obama believed that American power was being squandered in Iraq and Afghanistan. In light of the global financial crisis and American recession, he did not believe that open-ended military adventures were strategically viable or economically affordable. By 2013, even a plurality of Republicans thought that the United States was doing too much around the world.

"Obama was determined that his foreign policy would always be broad-gauged and connected to what was affordable domestically, in both political and budgetary terms," wrote Jonathan Alter of his first year in office.[4]

Beane, guided by an array of sabermetrics that emphasize the sum of underappreciated elements of productivity, seeks players who bring discrete talents to the lineup and avoids high-priced alternatives that risk overpayment for past performance. He focuses on how to score more runs, yield fewer runs, and win more games at a more affordable cost. Under his leadership, Oakland, while a small market franchise, became more competitive.

After years of perceived excess, Obama brought a small-ball mentality to foreign policy. He said as much in a colloquy during a 2014 trip to Asia.

"You hit singles; you hit doubles. Every once in a while you may be able to hit a home run," he said in response to critics used to a very different style of play. "But we steadily advance the interests of the American people and our partnership with folks around the world."[5]

While acknowledging that such an approach is not "sexy," he tellingly added that a significant dimension of his strategy is to avoid errors, or what he described later to reporters as "Don't do stupid shit."[6]

Notably, Hillary Clinton, Obama's former secretary of state, did not believe this philosophy constituted an adequate "organizing principle" for U.S. foreign policy, suggesting it lent the appearance of an American withdrawal from the world stage.[7]

On the one hand, Obama was comfortable with incremental progress. But on the other hand, he frequently hesitated regarding options that he did not believe would solve the larger problem.

Obama, particularly compared with Bush, changed the way America exercised its global leadership. To a significant extent, it *was* "leading from behind," avoiding commitments that do not involve vital interests and ensuring that it had international partners and legitimacy for what it sought to accomplish. Solutions were assembled by America, but involved solutions that were rooted in the region, not imposed from the outside.

Most significantly, there was greater emphasis on return on investment and reestablishing America's "strategic solvency."[8] The United States, sobered by significant costs and modest returns in Afghanistan and Iraq, was under Obama unwilling to overpay based on past performance. This shift, while rational, was jarring to allies and friends around the world. More importantly, it called into question not so much how the United States plays the game as what it feels it needs to accomplish in the world.

Going forward, the next president will need to resolve the contradiction between America's outsized global ambition and the rational but more limited policies rooted in the politics of the moment. This will require a more realistic American national security narrative as well.

THE UNITED STATES: EXCEPTIONAL, GLOBAL, NOT INDISPENSABLE

Alexander Haig once wrote, "Of the many destructive effects of Vietnam and Watergate, none is worse than the tendency for a new administration to believe that history began on its inauguration day, and its predecessor was totally wrong about everything, and that all its acts must therefore be cancelled."[9]

For the past sixteen years, U.S. foreign policy has been excessively influenced by the negative hyperpartisanship of the time, encapsulated in the first decade of the twenty-first century as ABC and the second decade as ABB—Anything but Clinton and Anything but Bush. With the United States likely to remain engaged in an active conflict throughout the tenure of the new administration, U.S. foreign policy should be driven by realistic assessments of what the United States *needs* to do and what it *can* do in the world. Avoiding stupid stuff is not a strategy; neither is ABO—Anything but Obama.

In fact, there is much more continuity in foreign policy than either party wants to admit. Duke's Peter Feaver argues rightly that there has been significant bipartisan strategic consensus over the past two decades centered on maintaining U.S. military power, promoting democracy and free markets, preventing the spread of weapons of mass destruction to rogue states, and combating terrorist networks of global reach. Even agreeing on what is important has left plenty of room for political disagreements regarding how to use American power in particular circumstances.[10]

Since the end of the Cold War, four consecutive administrations have followed highly improvisational foreign policies, "largely making it up as they went along."[11] The United States has vacillated between realism and idealism, between action and reaction, between the world as it is and the world that should be, between wars viewed as good and bad. America can't seem to decide whether to transform the world or mind its own business. It relies on the president of the United States to resolve the contradiction.

Americans in recent polls want to see less military adventurism, although that is very different than advocating isolationism. Now the question is between unilateralism and multilateralism, or between internationalism and interventionism.[12]

The United States in an interconnected and interdependent world can't afford to mind its own business. With the world becoming more integrated and interdependent, isolationism is no longer a realistic option. Even the Islamic State, which wants to take the Middle East from the twenty-first century back to the seventh century, sells oil and antiquities on global black markets.

Comparisons among presidents and their foreign policies tend to focus on philosophies and actions in isolation, trying to discern a doctrine or label—realist, idealist, or pragmatist—to characterize what occurred over a four- or eight-year time span. They fail to fully account for the political boundaries of the time that influence what a president could actually achieve.

Barack Obama was a transformative political figure, invested by voters and supporters with high and perhaps unrealistic expectations. The Nobel

Peace Prize certainly reflected such global aspirations. To a very great extent, he pursued the agenda that he outlined during the 2008 campaign.

And yet, domestically, a substantial percentage of the electorate consistently rooted for the president to fail. His relations with the Republican-led Congress reflected this political reality. And internationally, a number of actors made it more difficult for Obama to achieve the lasting impact he sought.

Realism, two-time National Security Advisor Brent Scowcroft once said, is the recognition of the limits of what can be achieved.[13] By that definition, Barack Obama was a realist. He recognized the domestic political limits he confronted while in the White House and constructed a foreign policy accordingly.

Obama rejected both isolationism and unrestricted interventionism, the former as impractical in a more interconnected world and the latter as unaffordable in a more competitive world. He attempted to employ force more judiciously and in conjunction with others, making it more politically legitimate and strategically sustainable.

Laying out a kind of Obama doctrine, he suggested that the use of military force was appropriate when "core interests demand it"—a direct threat to the United States, its interests, and key allies. For crises that may be urgent, but represent less of a direct threat, "the threshold for military action must be higher. In such circumstances, we should not go it alone."[14]

He was a "limited interventionist."[15] As he reflected in remarks to the United Nations General Assembly in 2013, "the United States has a hard-earned humility when it comes to our ability to determine events inside other countries."[16] Obama delivered the foreign policy for which Americans elected him—advancing American interests "without boots on the ground, without breaking the Treasury, without repeating the mistakes of mission creep."[17]

But the Obama administration found it difficult to square two of its preferred political narratives: the need to retrench in the aftermath of Iraq and the global financial crisis, letting others deal with foreign monsters; and its belief in American exceptionalism, a perceived duty to enforce international norms and shape the world in ways consistent with American interests and values. Based on one narrative, the political watchword was to do less; based on the other, it was to do more, or at least do something.

There is tension between interventionism and stability, between change and the status quo. History argues for a world as it should be; politics reflects the world that is. Between the two, it is difficult to keep American interests and values in balance. The next president needs to square American policy, strategy, and rhetoric—what it wants to accomplish and what it is actually able to do given the politics of the time. They need to be in closer balance.

There is a disconnect between Obama's rhetoric and how he governed.[18] He acknowledged late in his second term that governing is far more complicated than campaign narratives would suggest. The world doesn't always cooperate with what we believe needs to be done. As *New York Times* columnist Ross Douthat wrote, even for the most powerful leader on the planet, the world is ultimately beyond the president's control.[19]

A rebalance among U.S. foreign policy, domestic politics, and strategic narratives is needed. We like the idea that the United States should be the most powerful. We get anxious when we are forced to prove it at considerable cost. The United States is the most influential country in the world, but we have flawed expectations regarding our actual ability to shape world events and in particular how long that takes. Time and time again in recent years, once we have committed to solve a problem, we have been surprised by the complexity and duration of that process. We shouldn't be.

What this rebalance requires is a new conception of America's role in the world and a more elastic horizon regarding what it will take to shape the world that is into the world as it should be. The good news is that we have done this before. During the Cold War, we gained confidence over time that we would succeed, but understood that the process would take decades. Playing the long game, as President Obama has rightly suggested, will not be easy in a world of instant messaging, constant news, and the never-ending political campaign.

More importantly, we have to understand ourselves and the difference between what we believe can be done, what should be done, what we are willing to support, at what cost, and for how long.

Americans, caught in a never-ending debate between big and small government, have lost sight of how effective (if not perfect) our government actually is and the appropriate burden that we need to shoulder to keep it that way. This is true at home and abroad. In terms of foreign policy, just as with domestic programs, you *do* ultimately get what you pay for. We have a foreign policy that is dominated by its military capability because politically that is how we interpret being strong and influential. We have a big stick, but recently we have discovered how expensive it is when we chose to wield it. We need to invest in a broader set of tools.

This is actually one of Obama's signature accomplishments. On the campaign trail in 2016, a number of candidates suggested that to defeat terrorism, we need to do whatever it takes. That's not quite right. We need to keep

America safe, while acknowledging that we can never eliminate all risk. But we need to take appropriate action at a cost that is sustainable and affordable. Obama carried out an effective foreign policy guided significantly by ROI—return on investment. As with any market, some investments didn't yield what was anticipated; others provided significant returns. The new administration should continue this prudent strategy.

On Wall Street, they call this value investing.

Obama ran into trouble when the rhetoric of indispensability and the expectations that flow from that diverged from what he viewed as his electoral mandate as a prudent steward of American power and influence. This manifested itself in Libya and Syria—the United States could not turn a blind eye to the prospect of horrific violence and took action in Libya, but long remained on the sidelines as millions were displaced and hundreds of thousands died in Syria. The former was a case of exceptionalism and smart power; the latter someone else's civil war. We made ourselves indispensable in Libya, but chose not to be the world's policeman in Syria.

These respective choices were rational—limited interventions with vastly different objectives—but the rhetoric surrounding both operations damaged the credibility of American power. The root problem is an outdated strategic narrative regarding America's role in the world.

America is exceptional. The world is a better place because of what America is and what it does: its ability to attract people from all corners of the world and assimilate them as Americans; and its willingness to shoulder the burden of global leadership. The attention given to walls and bans during the 2016 presidential debate is not a reflection of who we are, but such rhetoric did damage the American brand.

While the United States is exceptional, it is not indispensable. As it pursues its national interests, America can advance universal values as well. This does not mean, however, the United States should be expected to or has the ability to solve every major problem in the world. The world is too diverse and complex for that to be realistic.

The United States remains the most powerful and influential country in the world. The question is American power for what purpose. The United States is a *global power*, the only one with vital interests in every corner of the world. The ongoing challenge for America, one it has struggled with for seven decades, is to distinguish what is vital versus what is important; to understand its power, but also its limits; and to appreciate that the world can transform itself with America's help, but that process involves decades.

America needs to be strategic. America needs to be patient. America must solve problems in the world that is. America can be a beacon for the world as it should be. That is ultimately the work of generations.

Political cycles are sprints. Foreign policy is a marathon. The United States must continue to lead the world in solving the shared challenges that affect us all. But it must maintain a realistic understanding of what can be accomplished during four- or eight-year presidential terms. The world, ultimately, does get a vote.

ACKNOWLEDGMENTS

Writing a book is an ambitious undertaking, attempting to write something that will inform and interest people. One friend said, "Have you ever written a book? It's hard." He was right.

A book doesn't write itself—it would take a lot less time and energy if that were true—but it is the product of more than four decades of experience in the national security policy world, from that first day as a brand new Air Force second lieutenant, through various military assignments and operations, to positions at the Department of Defense, the National Security Council, the Center for American Progress, the Department of State, and The George Washington University. Many experiences, interactions, discussions, debates, and research sessions contributed in ways large and small to this work.

In particular, I am grateful to the staff and faculty of The George Washington University Institute of Public Diplomacy and Global Communication, supported by both the School of Media and Public Affairs and the Elliott School of International Affairs. GW has been my academic home for five years, and I am grateful in particular to Frank Sesno, director of the School of Media and Public Affairs; Dr. Sean Aday, director of the Institute for Public Diplomacy and Global Communication; Dr. Will Yeomans at SMPA; and Dr. Marc Lynch at the Elliott School. Chelsea Dreher made an enormous contribution with her early research that created the backbone of the book.

I spent three decades working in government. In fairly dramatic fashion in 2011, I left government service. As I pondered what to do next, I received a welcome call from Professor Amy Gaudion of the Penn State Dickinson School of Law and School of International Affairs, who was heading up the search effort for the General Omar N. Bradley Chair of Strategic Leadership, a joint academic fellowship with Penn State University, Dickinson College, and the Army War College. When I met with academic leaders from the three institutions, I asked, "What do you want me to teach?" Their response was, "That's up to you." After five months of intensive research, I stepped into a seminar room in Denny Hall and presented the first version of a hybrid course that combined elements of political science, history, international affairs, public diplomacy, strategic communication, and media studies. A lot of the research that informed that class and subsequent versions at Penn State and the Army War College informed this book.

This work emphasizes how the threat of violent political extremism—yes, it involves terrorism, but with the advent of the Islamic State has moved well beyond that label—has to be understood within a broader context. I was among those in the think tank world who believed that the emerging field of homeland security needed to be viewed as an integrated dimension of national security policy. The threat has evolved from al Qaeda as a terrorist movement into the Islamic State as an insurgency and proto-state that has at least for the moment changed the map of the Middle East. This analysis has been validated in the process.

In its initial conception, the Bush administration formed a parallel Homeland Security Council alongside the National Security Council. The Obama administration fused them to a significant degree. For five years, I was a Senior Fellow at the Center for American Progress, focused on the intersection between homeland and national security. I am enormously indebted to John Podesta, the first president of CAP and its inspiration; Bob Boorstin, Joe Cirincione, and Rudy DeLeon, who served successively as leaders of the national security team during my time there; and the many fellows, staff, and interns who helped make CAP a dynamic contributor to national policy in a remarkably short period. Working at a think tank, you are introduced to an extraordinarily rich network of people who try every day to help people better understand the world around them. I was fortunate to gain great insight from a number of friends and colleagues, including Michelle Dunn, Edmund Ghareeb, Jack Goldsmith, David Kramer, Doug Paal, Trita Parsi, General Colin Powell, Andrew Weiss, and Micah Zenko.

At the same time, thanks to Walter Isaacson and Clark Ervin of the Aspen Institute. For several years, the Aspen Institute's Homeland Security Group has served as a bipartisan forum to wrestle with the implications of the evolving threat of violent extremism and how governments, civil society, and the private sector need to respond more effectively to it. I am proud to continue to serve as part of this group, led by former Secretary of Homeland Security Mike

Chertoff and former Congresswoman and President of the Wilson Center Jane Harman. I have tapped into the rich network of "formers" for advice and perspective while writing this book and also have benefited greatly from the rich discussions as we meet twice a year to assess the latest developments related to this generational challenge and what they mean for U.S. national security policy. While a good number within the group are identified with one of the two political parties—a key premise of this book is about the confluence of national security policy and politics—there is a remarkable degree of bipartisanship in terms of how we see the challenge and what America needs to do to protect itself, reduce the threat, and remain faithful to its core values.

In 1997, I was nominated by the Department of Defense to serve on the White House staff. I could not have reached that point without the support of great leaders, bosses, and mentors, including two distinguished secretaries of defense, Bill Perry and Bill Cohen, and in particular the late Pentagon spokesman Ken Bacon. At the White House, the late Sandy Berger and Jim Steinberg ran an extraordinarily effective, creative, and impactful national security staff. Mike McCurry and Joe Lockhart are two of the best communicators to grace the podium in the White House Press Room, and they remain good friends to the present day. Over the years, a number of colleagues and friends from the Clinton White House were kind enough to provide insight for this project.

When you work at the White House, you become identified with an era of U.S. policy. It is an extraordinary honor to work on a presidential staff. When you are able to participate in the decision-making process at the highest level, you gain an appreciation for the intersection of public policy, domestic politics, and political narratives. It's a radical thing to say in the midst of the factious politics of this age, but presidents and their teams genuinely want to do what is best for the country. The easy decisions are made at or below the cabinet level. The issues that come to the Situation Room for deliberation, decision, and then execution are hard. There are no easy answers. Every option has an up and down side. I had the high privilege of working for President Bill Clinton. He greatly expanded the definition of national security, particularly elevating the importance of economic affairs, global public health, *and* terrorism. The president worked tirelessly to resolve intractable conflicts. He was successful in Northern Ireland, and came close with the Israeli-Palestinian peace process. He made a groundbreaking trip to China. He wrestled with the intractable challenge represented by Saddam Hussein and continued unrest in the Balkans. The issues play a significant role in this book.

Having worked with President Clinton, I was also privileged to work for Hillary Clinton as secretary of state for the first two-plus years of the Obama administration. During that time, the table was set for groundbreaking and transformative diplomatic initiatives with Iran and Burma. I watched Richard Holbrooke and his extraordinary team wrestle with the question of what could or needed to be accomplished in Afghanistan and Pakistan, respectively. Dennis Ross once said that nothing is static in the Middle East—events are either moving forward or backward. When the Arab uprisings began, it was impossible to tell which was which. Sitting in the Situation Room with Assistant Secretary Jeff Feltman, for example, there were no easy answers to how the United States should respond, given that everything we thought we understood about the region was suddenly subject to review. Many members I served with during my two years in the Obama administration were kind enough to share their insights and recollections of this tumultuous period, but in particular Admiral Dennis Blair, Kurt Campbell, Derek Chollet, Ivo Daalder, Robert Ford, Marc Grossman, Chris Hill, Fred Hof, Jim Jeffrey, Harold Koh, Mike McFaul, Vali Nasr, Bruce Riedel, Dennis Ross, Vikram Singh, Admiral and Dean James Stavridis, Jake Sullivan, and Tamara Wittes.

The book would not have happened without the intrepid support of Diane Nine, my agent, and Jonathan Sisk and his team at Rowman & Littlefield Publishers. A number of very good friends, in particular Jeff Barnett, Seth Center, Nanda Chitre, and Will Nelligan were kind enough to review early versions of the draft and provide great insight in how to make it better. Any errors that found their way into the final version are mine.

When you write a book, it becomes a family affair. My spouse and partner for more than four decades, Paula Kougeas, is a great editor in her own right and offered helpful suggestions throughout, as did our wonderful children Mary and Chris. Our dog Chester came into our lives at the midpoint of the project and from his study bed kept a watchful eye on its progress.

Alexandria, VA
September 2016

NOTES

FOREWORD

1. Vladimir V. Putin, A plea for caution from Russia, *The New York Times*, September 11, 2013, http://www.nytimes.com/2013/09/12/opinion/putin-plea-for-caution-from -russia-on-syria.html?_r=0.

2. The White House, Remarks by the President in Address to the Nation on Syria, September 10, 2013, https://www.whitehouse.gov/the-press-office/2013/09/10/remarks -president-address-nation-syria.

3. The White House, Remarks by the President in Commencement Address to the United States Air Force Academy, June 2, 2016, https://www.whitehouse.gov/the-press -office/2016/06/02/remarks-president-commencement-address-united-states-air-force -academy.

4. Richard Engel, *And Then All Hell Broke Loose*, p. 181.

5. Andrew J. Bacevich, *America's War for the Greater Middle East*, p. 109.

6. I. M. (Mac) Destler, How National Security Advisors See Their Role, in James M. McCormick, ed., *The Domestic Sources of American Foreign Policy*, p. 210.

7. Fred Hiatt, Obama's Syria achievement, *The Washington Post*, September 7, 2015, p. A17.

8. Steven Weber and Bruce W. Jentleson, *The End of Arrogance*, p. 154.

9. David Samuels, Through the looking glass with Ben Rhodes, *The New York Times Magazine*, May 13, 2016, http://www.nytimes.com/2016/05/12/magazine/through-the -looking-glass-with-ben-rhodes.html?_r=0.

10. Engel, *And Then All Hell Broke Loose*, p. 107.

INTRODUCTION

1. Jay Solomon, The Iran Wars, pp. 6–7.

2. The White House, Remarks by the President at the National Defense University, May 23, 2013, https://www.whitehouse.gov/the-press-office/2013/05/23/remarks -president-national-defense-university.

3. The White House, Remarks by the President on the Way Forward in Afghanistan, June 22, 2011, https://www.whitehouse.gov/the-press-office/2011/06/22/remarks-president-way-forward-afghanistan.

4. The White House, Statement by President Obama on the Situation in Syria, August 18, 2011, https://www.whitehouse.gov/the-press-office/2011/08/18/statement-president-obama-situation-syria.

5. Ibid.

6. The White House, Press Briefing by Senior Administration Officials on Syria, August 18, 2011, https://www.whitehouse.gov/the-press-office/2011/08/18/press-briefing-senior-administration-officials-syria.

7. The White House, Remarks by the President to the White House Press Corps, August 20, 2012, https://www.whitehouse.gov/the-press-office/2012/08/20/remarks-president-white-house-press-corps.

8. Charlie Savage, *Power Wars*, p. 628.

9. The White House, News Conference by the President, April 30, 2013, https://www.whitehouse.gov/the-press-office/2013/04/30/news-conference-president.

10. Derek Chollet, *The Long Game*, p. 4.

11. U.S. Department of State, John Kerry, Statement on Syria, August 30, 2013, http://www.state.gov/secretary/remarks/2013/08/213668.htm.

12. U.S. Department of State, John Kerry, Remarks with United Kingdom Foreign Secretary Hague, London, United Kingdom, September 9, 2013, http://www.state.gov/secretary/remarks/2013/09/213956.htm.

13. Jeffrey Goldberg, The Obama Doctrine, *The Atlantic*, April 2016, http://www.theatlantic.com/magazine/archive/2016/04/the-obama-doctrine/471525/.

14. Fifty individuals who had served Republican presidents back to Richard Nixon issued a rare public denunciation of Donald Trump in advance of the election, saying he lacks the temperament to be president. A copy of the letter is available at http://www.nytimes.com/interactive/2016/08/08/us/politics/national-security-letter-trump.html.

15. The White House, Press Conference by the President, July 15, 2015, https://www.whitehouse.gov/the-press-office/2015/07/15/press-conference-president.

16. Leon Panetta, *Worthy Fights*, p. 434.

17. David Ryan, Vietnam, Victory, Culture and Iraq, in John Dumbrell and David Ryan, *Vietnam in Iraq*, p. 114.

18. Ryan Lizza, The Consequentialist: How the Arab Spring Remade Obama's Foreign Policy, *The New Yorker*, May 2, 2011, http://www.newyorker.com/magazine/2011/05/02/the-consequentialist.

19. Quoted in Dennis Ross, *Doomed to Succeed*, p. 345.

CHAPTER 1

1. Caspar W. Weinberger, The Uses of Military Power, Speech at the National Press Club, Washington, D.C., November 28, 1984, www.pbs.org/wgbh/pages/frontline/shows/military/force/weinberger.html.

2. James Mann, *Rise of the Vulcans*, p. 119.

3. Weinberger, op. cit.

4. Marvin Kalb and Deborah Kalb, *Haunting Legacy*, p. 112.

5. Andrew J. Bacevich, *America's War for the Greater Middle East*, p. 68.

6. Id., p. 273.

7. Bin Laden's Fatwa, August 23, 1996, *PBS NewsHour*, http://www.pbs.org/newshour/updates/military-july-dec96-fatwa_1996/.

8. Weinberger, op cit.

9. David Halberstam, *The Best and the Brightest*, p. 333.

10. President Harry S. Truman, Address to Joint Session of Congress, March 12, 1947, http://www.trumanlibrary.org/whistlestop/study_collections/doctrine/large/documents/pdfs/5-9.pdf.

11. Evan Thomas, *Being Nixon*, p. 62.

12. Julian E. Zelizer, *Arsenal of Democracy*, p. 100.

13. General Douglas MacArthur, quoted in Zelizer, *Arsenal of Democracy*, p. 111.

14. Fredrik Logevall, *Choosing War*, p. 385.

15. Fredrik Logevall, *Embers of War*, p. 106.

16. Halberstam, *The Best and the Brightest*, p. 337.

17. Jean Edward Smith, *Eisenhower in War and Peace*, p. 509.

18. Dwight D. Eisenhower Presidential Library, Address by Dwight D. Eisenhower, Republican Nominee for President, Delivered at Detroit, Michigan, October 24, 1952, http://www.eisenhower.archives.gov/research/online_documents/korean_war/I_Shall_Go_To_Korea_1952_10_24.pdf.

19. Dwight D. Eisenhower, Campaign Speech, Champaign, Illinois, October 2, 1952, courtesy of the Eisenhower Presidential Library and Museum. Eisenhower was referring to Korea, but his thinking undoubtedly applied to Vietnam as well. Also Halberstam, *The Best and the Brightest*, p. 139.

20. David F. Schmitz, *The Tet Offensive*, p. 16.

21. Smith, *Eisenhower in War and Peace*, p. 612.

22. Marvin Kalb, *The Road to War*, p. 51.

23. Ray Takeyh and Steven Simon, *The Pragmatic Superpower*, p. 123.

24. Logevall, *Embers of War*, p. 630.

25. Id., p. 676.

26. Schmitz, *The Tet Offensive*, p. 23.

27. Id., p. 24.

28. John F. Kennedy, Inaugural Address, January 20, 1961, http://www.presidency.ucsb.edu/ws/?pid=8032.

29. Halberstam, *The Best and the Brightest*, p. 76.

30. Walter Cronkite, *A Reporter's Life*, p. 243.

31. Logevall, *Choosing War*, p. 22.

32. Henry Kissinger, *Diplomacy*, p. 646.

33. Halberstam, *The Best and the Brightest*, p. 298.

34. Kalb, *The Road to War*, p. 26.

35. Logevall, *Choosing War*, p. 304.

36. David Fromkin, Lyndon Johnson and Foreign Policy: What the New Documents Show, *Foreign Affairs*, Review Essay, January/February 1995, http://www.foreignaffairs.com/print/50594.

37. Logevall, *Choosing War*, p. 244.

38. George C. Herring, *America's Longest War*, p. 145.

39. President Lyndon B. Johnson, Remarks in Oklahoma at the Dedication of the Eufaula Dam, September 25, 1964, http://www.presidency.ucsb.edu/ws/?pid=26528.

40. Logevall, *Choosing War*, p. 347.

41. Id., p. 360.

42. Walter L. Hixson, *The Myth of American Diplomacy*, p. 241.

43. Gordon M. Goldstein, *Lessons in Disaster*, p. 183.

44. Logevall, *Choosing War*, p. 196.

45. Stephen Sestanovich, *Maximalist*, p. 148.

46. Don Oberdorfer, *Tet!*, p. 81.

47. Id., p. 83.

48. Herring, *America's Longest War*, p. 188.

49. Id., p. 244.

50. Oberdorfer, *Tet!*, p. 159.

51. Id., p. 184.

52. Id., p. xvi.

53. Id., pp. 269–70.

54. Andrew J. Polsky, *Elusive Victories*, p. 246.

55. Id., p. 273.

56. Herring, *America's Longest War*, p. 268.

57. Richard M. Nixon, Asia after Viet Nam, *Foreign Affairs*, October 1, 1967, http://www.foreignaffairs.com/print/1108784.

58. Id., p. 297.

59. Kalb, *The Road to War*, p. 175.

60. Herring, *America's Longest War*, p. 278.

61. Thomas, *Being Nixon*, pp. 239, 429.

62. Herring, *America's Longest War*, p. 56.

63. James T. Patterson, *Restless Giant*, p. 100.

64. James C. Thomson Jr., How Could Vietnam Happen?, in James M. McCormick, ed., *The Domestic Sources of American Foreign Policy*, p. 335.

65. Logevall, *Choosing War*, pp. xvi, 31.

66. George P. Shultz, *Turmoil and Triumph*, p. 650.

67. General Colin L. Powell, U.S. Forces: Challenges Ahead, *Foreign Affairs*, Winter 1992/93, www.cfr.org/world/us-forces-challenges-ahead/p7508.

68. Ivo H. Daalder and Michael E. O'Hanlon, *Winning Ugly*, p. 213.

69. Interview with General Colin Powell, February 19, 2013.

70. George C. Herring, The Impact of the Vietnam War on the U.S. Military, in Charles E. Neu, ed., *After Vietnam, Legacies of a Lost War*, p. 65.

71. Kalb and Kalb, *Haunting Legacy*, p. 6.

72. Charles E. Neu, The Vietnam War and the Transformation of America, in Neu, ed., *After Vietnam, Legacies of a Lost War*, p. 21.

73. Halberstam, *The Best and the Brightest*, p. 182.

74. Robert S. McNamara, Reflections on War in the Twenty-First Century, in Neu, ed., *After Vietnam, Legacies of a Lost War*, p. 113.

75. Singapore's Lee Kuan Yew believed that Vietnam successfully delayed the advance of communism through the region. See Mann, *Rise of the Vulcans*, p. 53.

76. James Mann, *The Obamians*, p. 71.

77. Id., p. 233.

CHAPTER 2

1. David E. Sanger, *Confront and Conceal*, p. 15.

2. Jonathan Alter, *The Promise*, p. 133.

3. Erika G. King, *Obama, the Media, and Framing the U.S. Exit from Iraq and Afghanistan*, p. 79.

4. George W. Bush, A Period of Consequences, The Citadel, South Carolina, September 23, 1999, http://www3.citadel.edu/pao/addresses/pres_bush.html.

5. Andrew J. Bacevich, *America's War for the Greater Middle East*, p. 205.

6. Steve Coll, *The Bin Ladens*, p. 470.

7. George Tenet, *At the Center of the Storm*, p. 119.

8. Bob Woodward, *Bush at War*, pp. 37–38.

9. George W. Bush, Remarks by the President after Two Planes Crash into World Trade Center, Emma Booker Elementary School, Sarasota, Florida, September 11, 2001, http://georgewbush-whitehouse.archives.gov/news/releases/2001/09/text/20010911.html.

10. George W. Bush, Remarks by the President upon Arrival at Barksdale Air Force Base, September 11, 2001, http://georgewbush-whitehouse.archives.gov/news/releases/2001/09/text/20010911-1.html.

11. Peter Baker, *Days of Fire*, p. 130.

12. Woodward, *Bush at War*, p. 37.

13. Id., p. 30.

14. George W. Bush, Statement by the President in His Address to the Nation, September 11, 2001, http://georgewbush-whitehouse.archives.gov/news/releases/2001/09/20010911-16.html.

15. Baker, *Days of Fire*, pp. 128–29.

16. George W. Bush, Address to a Joint Session of Congress and the American People, September 20, 2001, http://georgewbush-whitehouse.archives.gov/news/releases/2001/09/20010920-8.html.

17. Ibid.

18. Timothy Naftali, George W. Bush and the "War on Terror," in Julian Zelizer, ed., *The Presidency of George W. Bush*, p. 66.

19. Bush, Address to a Joint Session of Congress and the American People, September 20, 2001.

20. Ibid.

21. James Mann, *Rise of the Vulcans*, p. 298.

22. Robert L. Grenier, *88 Days to Kandahar*, p. 40.

23. Seth G. Jones, *In the Graveyard of Empires*, p. 89.

24. David E. Sanger, *The Inheritance*, p. xvii.

25. Richard N. Haass, *War of Necessity, War of Choice*, p. 189.

26. Walter Russell Mead, *Power, Terror, Peace, and War*, pp. 168–72.

27. Baker, *Days of Fire*, pp. 135–36.

28. Ivo H. Daalder and James M. Lindsay, *America Unbound*, p. 92.

29. Jones, *In the Graveyard of Empires*, p. 112.

30. Woodward, *Bush at War*, p. 192.

31. Condoleezza Rice, *No Higher Honor*, p. 86.

32. Woodward, *Bush at War*, p. 228.

33. Id., p. 315.

34. Grenier, *88 Days to Kandahar*, p. 8.

35. Rice, *No Higher Honor*, p. 99.

36. Baker, *Days of Fire*, p. 186.

37. Haass, *War of Necessity, War of Choice*, p. 204.

38. Baker, *Days of Fire*, p. 191.

39. Jones, *In the Graveyard of Empires*, p. 97.

40. Id., p. 128.

41. Bacevich, *America's War for the Greater Middle East*, p. 233.

42. Vali Nasr, *The Dispensable Nation*, p. 15.

43. Bob Woodward, *Obama's Wars*, p. 110.

44. Id., p. 81.

45. Id., p. 170.

46. Id., p. 52.

47. Fred Kaplan, *The Insurgents*, p. 297.

48. Sanger, *Confront and Conceal*, p. 19.

49. Scott Shane, *Objective Troy*, p. 130.

50. Leon Panetta, *Worthy Fights*, pp. 254–55.

51. Mann, *The Obamians*, p. 122. Woodward, *Obama's Wars*, p. 145.

52. Jonathan Alter, *The Promise*, p. 376.

53. Id., pp. 387–88.

54. Kaplan, *The Insurgents*, p. 313.

55. Woodward, *Obama's Wars*, p. 167.

56. Robert M. Gates, *Duty*, p. 299.

57. James Mann, *The Obamians*, pp. 138–39.

58. Alter, *The Promise*, p. 390.

59. President Barack Obama, *60 Minutes* Interview, December 7, 2009, http://www
.cbsnews.com/news/transcript-president-barack-obama-part-1-13-12-2009/.

60. The White House, Remarks by the President in Address to the Nation on the Way
Forward in Afghanistan and Pakistan, December 1, 2009, https://www.whitehouse.gov/
the-press-office/remarks-president-address-nation-way-forward-afghanistan-and-pakistan.

61. Ibid.

62. Ibid.

63. Ibid.

64. Ibid.

65. Obama, *60 Minutes* Interview, December 7, 2009.

66. Colin Dueck, *The Obama Doctrine*, pp. 132–33.

67. Obama, *60 Minutes* Interview, December 7, 2009.

68. Jones, *In the Graveyard of Empires*, p. 325.

69. Dominic Tierney, *The Right Way to Lose a War*, p. 311.

70. Shane, *Operation Troy*, p. 40.

71. Id., p. 87.

72. Id., p. 190.

CHAPTER 3

1. Barack Obama, My plan for Iraq, *The New York Times*, July 14, 2008, http://
www.nytimes.com/2008/07/14/opinion/14obama.html?_r=0.

2. Ibid.

3. Thomas L. Friedman, Schieffer Series: A Discussion on Syria, Center for Strategic
and International Studies, November 16, 2015, video available at http://csis.org/event/
schieffer-series-discussion-syria.

4. Robert M. Gates, *Duty*, p. 376.

5. Barack Obama, Floor Statement on Bush's Decision to Increase Troops in Iraq,
January 19, 2007, http://www.obamaspeeches.com/096-Floor-Statement-on-Presidents
-Decision-to-Increase-Troops-in-Iraq-Obama-Speech.htm.

6. Robert K. Brigham, ed., *The United States and Iraq Since 1990*, p. 8.

7. Quoted in Jon Meacham, *Destiny and Power*, p. 433.

8. Richard N. Haass, *War of Necessity, War of Choice*, p. 73.

9. Bartholomew Sparrow, *The Strategist*, pp. 481–83.

10. James A. Baker III, *The Politics of Diplomacy*, p. 333.

11. Zbigniew Brzezinski and Brent Scowcroft, *America and the World*, p. 6.

12. Sparrow, *The Strategist*, p. 425.

13. Haass, *War of Necessity, War of Choice*, p. 71.

14. Julian E. Zelizer, *Arsenal of Democracy*, p. 376.

15. Brzezinski and Scowcroft, *America and the World*, pp. 11–12.

16. Meacham, *Destiny and Power*, p. 459.

17. Dennis Ross, *Doomed to Succeed*, p. 236.

18. David Halberstam, *War in a Time of Peace*, p. 16.

19. Sparrow, *The Strategist*, p. 415.

20. James Mann, *Rise of the Vulcans*, p. 191.

21. Quoted in Ray Takeyh and Steven Simon, *The Pragmatic Superpower*, p. 323.

22. Mann, *Rise of the Vulcans*, pp. 190–91.

23. Takeyh and Simon, *The Pragmatic Superpower*, p. 327.

24. Sparrow, *The Strategist*, p. 418.

25. Andrew J. Bacevich, *The Limits of Power*, p. 54.

26. Michael Morell, *The Great War of Our Time*, pp. 13–14.

27. Brigham, ed., *The United States and Iraq Since 1990*, pp. 41–42.

28. Anthony Lake, From Containment to Enlargement, speech at Johns Hopkins University School of Advanced International Studies, Washington, D.C., September 21, 1993, quoted in Brigham, ed., *The United States and Iraq Since 1990*, pp. 75–76.

29. Haass, *War of Necessity, War of Choice*, p. 155.

30. Derek Chollet and James Goldgeier, *America Between the Wars*, p. 183.

31. Brigham, ed., *The United States and Iraq Since 1990*, p. 50.

32. Id., p. 88.

33. Haass, *War of Necessity, War of Choice*, p. 167.

34. President Bill Clinton, Address to Joint Chiefs and Pentagon Staff, February 17, 1998, http://www.cnn.com/ALLPOLITICS/1998/02/17/transcripts/clinton.iraq/.

35. PNAC statement of principles quoted in Brigham, ed., *The United States and Iraq Since 1990*, p. 91.

36. Quoted in Max Boot, What the Heck Is a 'Neocon'? Op-ed, Council on Foreign Relations, December 30, 2002, available at http://www.cfr.org/world/heck-neocon/p5343.

37. John Dumbrell and David Ryan, Introduction, *Vietnam in Iraq*, p. 3.

38. Fredrik Logevall, Anatomy of an Unnecessary War: The Iraq Invasion, in Zelizer, ed., *The Presidency of George W. Bush*, p. 91.

39. George Tenet, *At the Center of the Storm*, p. 305.

40. Id., p. 103.

41. Max Boot, quoted in Bacevich, *America's War for the Greater Middle East*, p. 241.

42. Haass, *War of Necessity, War of Choice*, p. 5.

43. Matthew A. Baum and Philip B. K. Potter, *War and Democratic Constraint*, p. 66.

44. Id., pp. 105–6.

45. Haass, op. cit., p. 225.

46. Donald Rumsfeld quoted in Bacevich, *America's War for the Greater Middle East*, p. 239.

47. Michael V. Hayden, *Playing to the Edge*, p. 49.

48. Baker, *Days of Fire*, p. 211.

49. Interview with Condoleezza Rice, *CNN Late Edition*, September 8, 2002.

50. Unclassified National Intelligence Estimate findings, quoted in Brigham, *The United States and Iraq Since 1990*, p. 136.

51. Michael Isikoff and David Corn, *Hubris*, p. 83.

52. Peter Baker, *Days of Fire*, pp. 245–46.

53. Joby Warrick, *Black Flags*, p. 95.

54. President George W. Bush, President Discusses the Future of Iraq, February 26, 2003, http://georgewbush-whitehouse.archives.gov/news/releases/2003/02/print/20030226-11.html.

55. Richard N. Haass, *The Opportunity*, pp. 185–89.

56. Haass, *War of Necessity, War of Choice*, p. 280.

57. Condoleezza Rice, *No Higher Honor*, p. 187.

58. Id., p. 187.

59. Morell, *The Great War of Our Time*, p. 99.

60. Tenet, *At the Center of the Storm*, p. 341.

61. Quoted in Dominic Tierney, *The Right Way to Lose a War*, p. 305.

62. Logevall in Zelizer, ed., *The Presidency of George W. Bush*, p. 113.

63. Barack Obama, Speech Against the Iraq War, Chicago, Illinois, October 2, 2002, http://www.npr.org/templates/story/story.php?storyId = 99591469.

64. Richard Sobel, Peter Furia, and Bethany Barratt, eds., *Public Opinion and International Intervention*, p. 25.

65. Arthur M. Schlesinger Jr., *War and the American Presidency*, p. 81.

66. Baker, *Days of Fire*, p. 240.

67. Id., p. 253.

68. President George W. Bush, President Bush Addresses the Nation, March 19, 2003, http://georgewbush-whitehouse.archives.gov/news/releases/2003/03/print/20030319-17.html.

69. Brigham, *The United States and Iraq Since 1990*, p. 114.

70. Kaplan, *The Insurgents*, p. 59.

71. Ken Adelman, quoted in Hendrik Hertzberg, Cakewalk, *The New Yorker*, April 14, 2003, http://www.newyorker.com/magazine/2003/04/14/cakewalk.

72. Tierney, *The Right Way to Lose a War*, p. 187.

73. Solomon, *The Iran Wars*, pp. 50–51.

74. Tenet, *At the Center of the Storm*, p. 424.

75. Bacevich, *America's War for the Greater Middle East*, p. 259.

76. Bacevich, *The Limits of Power*, p. 63.

77. President George W. Bush, quoted in Brigham, *The United States and Iraq Since 1990*, p. 151.

78. Bacevich, *America's War in the Greater Middle East*, p. 266.

79. Seth G. Jones, *In the Graveyard of Empires*, p. 129.

80. Steve Coll, *The Bin Ladens*, p. 569.

81. Osama bin Laden, Declaration of War against the Americans Occupying the Land of the Two Holy Places, Translated from Arabic and available at http://www.pbs.org/newshour/updates/military-july-dec96-fatwa_1996/.

82. Seth G. Jones, *Hunting in the Shadows*, p. 159.

83. Morell, *The Great War of Our Time*, p. 78.

84. Warrick, *Black Flags*, pp. 156–58.

85. Id., p. 98.

86. Id., p. 7.

87. Richard Engel, *And Then All Hell Broke Loose*, pp. 132–33.

88. William McCants, *The ISIS Apocalypse*, pp. 10–11.

89. Aki Peritz and Robin Simcox, Why is the Islamic State so intent on provoking the West?, *The Washington Post*, November 30, 2014, p. B1.

90. Warrick, *Black Flags*, p. 185.

91. McCants, *The ISIS Apocalypse*, p. 146.

92. Quoted in Brigham, ed., *The United States and Iraq Since 1990*, p. 187.

93. Tierney, *The Right Way to Lose a War*, p. 145.

94. Michael R. Gordon and General Bernard E. Trainor, *The Endgame*, p. 178.

95. President George W. Bush, quoted in Brigham, ed., *The United States and Iraq Since 1990*, p. 200.

96. Barack Obama, Interview with the *New York Times* on Senator Obama's Campaign Plane, September 20, 2008, http://www.presidency.ucsb.edu/ws/index.php?pid = 84931.

97. Ibid.

98. David Fitzgerald and David Ryan, *Obama, US Foreign Policy and the Dilemmas of Intervention*, p. 29.

99. Gordon and Trainor, *The Endgame*, pp. 532–39.

100. Warrick, *Black Flags*, p. 148.

CHAPTER 4

1. CNN/YouTube Democratic presidential debate transcript, July 23, 2007, Part I, http://www.cnn.com/2007/POLITICS/07/23/debate.transcript/.

2. The White House, President Barack Obama's Inaugural Address, January 20, 2009, https://www.whitehouse.gov/blog/2009/01/21/president-barack-obamas-inaugural -address.

3. Michael V. Hayden, *Playing to the Edge*, p. 320.

4. David E. Sanger, *Confront and Conceal*, p. 157.

5. President Jimmy Carter, quoted in Ray Takeyh and Steven Simon, *The Pragmatic Superpower*, p. 246.

6. Id., 260.

7. David Crist, *The Twilight War*, p. 29.

8. Ray Takeyh, *Guardians of the Revolution*, p. 58.

9. Andrew J. Bacevich, *America's War for the Greater Middle East*, p. 24.

10. Flynt Leverett and Hillary Mann Leverett, *Going to Tehran*, p. 49.

11. Crist, *The Twilight War*, p. 5.

12. Leverett and Leverett, *Going to Tehran*, pp. 30–31.

13. Seyed Hossein Mousavian, *Iran and the United States*, p. 59.

14. Takeyh and Simon, *The Pragmatic Superpower*, p. 82.

15. Ray Takeyh, *Hidden Iran*, p. 91.

16. Mousavian, *Iran and the United States*, p. 84.

17. Id., pp. 84–87.

18. Bacevich, *America's War for the Greater Middle East*, p. 97.

19. Takeyh and Simon, *The Pragmatic Superpower*, pp. 281–82.

20. Takeyh, *Hidden Iran*, p. 173.

21. Takeyh and Simon, *The Pragmatic Superpower*, p. 290.

22. Id., pp. 109–10.

23. Crist, *The Twilight War*, p. 388.

24. Trita Parsi, *Treacherous Alliance*, p. 153.

25. Crist, *The Twilight War*, p. 389.

26. Parsi, *Treacherous Alliance*, p. 133.

27. Leverett and Leverett, *Going to Tehran*, pp. 338–39.

28. Parsi, *Treacherous Alliance*, pp. 186–87.

29. Id., pp. 188–89.

30. Mousavian, *Iran and the United States*, p. 146.

31. Id., pp. 150–52.

32. Id., p. 158.

33. Crist, *The Twilight War*, p. 433.

34. Parsi, *Treacherous Alliance*, p. 230.

35. Takeyh, *Hidden Iran*, pp. 115–16.

36. Parsi, *Treacherous Alliance*, pp. 233–34.

37. Takeyh, *Hidden Iran*, p. 129.

38. Trita Parsi, *A Single Roll of the Dice*, p. 2.

39. Ibid.

40. Parsi, *A Single Roll of the Dice*, p. 3.

41. David E. Sanger, *The Inheritance*, pp. 48–49.

42. Takeyh, *Guardians of the Revolution*, pp. 217–18.

43. Leverett and Leverett, *Going to Tehran*, pp. 125–26.

44. Condoleezza Rice, *No Higher Honor*, pp. 626–27.

45. Leverett and Leverett, *Going to Tehran*, p. 129.

46. Iranian President Mahmoud Ahmadinejad letter to Barack Obama, November 6, 2008, translated by the *Washington Post*, http://www.washingtonpost.com/wp-dyn/content/article/2008/11/06/AR2008110603030_pf.html.

47. Parsi, *A Single Roll of the Dice*, p. 33.

48. Jonathan Alter, *The Promise*, p. 226.

49. The White House, Videotaped Remarks by the President in Celebration of Nowruz, March 20, 2009, https://www.whitehouse.gov/the-press-office/videotaped-remarks-president-celebration-nowruz.

50. Dennis Ross and David Makovsky, *Myths, Illusions, and Peace*, pp. 225–33.

51. Id., p. xiii.

52. Parsi, *A Single Roll of the Dice*, pp. 66–67.

53. The White House, Remarks by President Barack Obama in Prague As Delivered, April 5, 2009, https://www.whitehouse.gov/the-press-office/remarks-president-barack-obama-prague-delivered.

54. The White House, Remarks by Deputy National Security Advisor Ben Rhodes at the Arms Control Association, June 6, 2016, https://www.whitehouse.gov/the-press-office/2016/06/06/remarks-deputy-national-security-advisor-ben-rhodes-arms-control.

55. Ibid.

56. Hayden, *Playing to the Edge*, p. 303.

57. Ross and Makovsky, *Myths, Illusions, and Peace*, p. 194.

58. Parsi, *A Single Roll of the Dice*, pp. 86–87.

59. Id., pp. 88–89.

60. Alter, *The Promise*, p. 356.

61. Ryan Lizza, The Consequentialist: How the Arab Spring Remade Obama's Foreign Policy, *The New Yorker*, May 2, 2011, http://www.newyorker.com/magazine/2011/05/02/the-consequentialist.

62. Parsi, *A Single Roll of the Dice*, p. 95.

63. Id., p. 92.

64. Council on Foreign Relations, A Conversation with U.S. Secretary of State Hillary Rodham Clinton, July 15, 2009, http://www.cfr.org/diplomacy-and-statecraft/conversation-us-secretary-state-hillary-rodham-clinton/p34589.

65. Jeffrey A. Bader, *Obama and China's Rise*, p. 53.

66. Sanger, *Confront and Conceal*, p. 185.

67. Kim Ghattas, *The Secretary*, p. 148.

68. Parsi, *A Single Roll of the Dice*, p. 197.

69. Ross and Makovsky, *Myths, Illusions, and Peace*, p. 231.

70. Leverett and Leverett, *Going to Tehran*, p. 85.

CHAPTER 5

1. The White House, Remarks by President Obama to the Turkish Parliament, April 6, 2009, https://www.whitehouse.gov/the-press-office/remarks-president-obama-turkish-parliament.

2. Ibid.

3. James Mann, *The Obamians*, p. 144.

4. Ross Douthat, Obama the Theologian, *The New York Times*, February 8, 2011, p. SR8.

5. Dennis Ross, *Doomed to Succeed*, p. 353.

6. The White House, Remarks by the President on a New Beginning, Cairo University, June 4, 2009, https://www.whitehouse.gov/the-press-office/remarks-president-cairo-university-6-04-09.

7. James Traub, The Hillary Clinton Doctrine, *Foreign Policy*, November 6, 2015, http://foreignpolicy.com/2015/11/06/hillary-clinton-doctrine-obama-interventionist-tough-minded-president/.

8. Ross, *Doomed to Succeed*, p. 351.

9. Ibid.

10. The White House, On-the-Record Conference Call Previewing the Visit of Israeli Prime Minister Netanyahu, November 6, 2015, https://www.whitehouse.gov/the-press-office/2015/11/06/record-conference-call-previewing-visit-israeli-prime-minister-netanyahu.

11. Derek Chollet, *The Long Game*, p. 94.

12. Walter Russell Mead, *Power, Terror, Peace, and War*, p. 60.

13. Inaugural Address of President George W. Bush, January 20, 2005, http://www.inaugural.senate.gov/swearing-in/address/address-by-george-w-bush-2005.

14. Michael H. Hunt, *Ideology and U.S. Foreign Policy*, p. 20.

15. Id., p. 30.

16. Franklin Delano Roosevelt, quoted in Michael Hirsh, 9/11—and counting, *The Washington Post*, September 11, 2005, http://www.washingtonpost.com/wp-dyn/content/article/2005/09/09/AR2005090902473_pf.html.

17. Derek Chollet and James Goldgeier, *America Between the Wars*, p. 67.

18. President George W. Bush, Remarks at The National Cathedral, September 14, 2001, https://georgewbush-whitehouse.archives.gov/infocus/bushrecord/documents/Selected_Speeches_George_W_Bush.pdf.

19. Stephen Sestanovich, *Maximalist*, p. 286.

20. Peter Baker, *Days of Fire*, pp. 219–20.

21. Id., p. 301.

22. Michael Gordon and General Bernard E. Trainor, *The Endgame*, p. 131.

23. Baker, *Days of Fire*, p. 471.

24. James Mann, *Rise of the Vulcans*, pp. 326–27.

25. Condoleezza Rice, *No Higher Honor*, p. 419.

26. Discussion with the author, October 26, 2015.

27. Rice, *No Higher Honor*, p. 376.

28. Barack Obama, Moving Forward in Iraq, Speech to the Chicago Council on Foreign Relations, November 22, 2006, http://www.obamaspeeches.com/040-Moving-Forward-in-Iraq-Chicago-Council-on-Foreign-Relations-Obama-Speech.htm.

29. Ibid.

30. Dennis Ross and David Makovsky, *Myths, Illusions, and Peace*, p. 317.

31. Mann, *The Obamians*, pp. 257–58.

32. Ryan Lizza, The Consequentialist: How the Arab Spring Remade Obama's Foreign Policy, *The New Yorker*, May 2, 2011, http://www.newyorker.com/magazine/2011/05/02/the-consequentialist.

33. David E. Sanger, *Confront and Conceal*, p. 280.

34. Lizza, op. cit.

35. Hillary Rodham Clinton, *Hard Choices*, p. 337.

36. The White House, National Security Strategy, May 2010, p. 1, https://www.whitehouse.gov/sites/default/files/rss_viewer/national_security_strategy.pdf.

37. The White House, Remarks by the President on the Middle East and North Africa, May 19, 2011, https://www.whitehouse.gov/the-press-office/2011/05/19/remarks-president-middle-east-and-north-africa.

38. Marc Lynch, *The Arab Uprising*, pp. 10–11.

39. Sanger, *Confront and Conceal*, p. 286.

40. Mann, *The Obamians*, p. 263.

41. Id., pp. 161–63.

42. Ross, *Doomed to Succeed*, p. 354.

43. There are twenty-two countries in the Arab League.

44. David Fromkin, *Kosovo Crossing*, p. 156.

45. Sestanovich, *Maximalist*, p. 315.

46. Rice, *No Higher Honor*, pp. 376–77.

47. Lizza, op. cit.

48. The White House, Remarks by the President on the Situation in Egypt, January 28, 2011, https://www.whitehouse.gov/the-press-office/2011/01/28/remarks-president-situation-egypt.

49. Marc Lynch, *The New Arab Wars*, p. 147.

50. Clinton, *Hard Choices*, p. 341.

51. Mark Landler, *Alter Egos*, pp. 154–55.

52. Robert F. Worth, *A Rage for Order*, p. 24.

53. Sanger, *Confront and Conceal*, pp. 294–97.

54. The White House, Remarks by the President on the Situation in Egypt, February 1, 2011, https://www.whitehouse.gov/the-press-office/2011/02/01/remarks-president-situation-egypt.

55. Ross, *Doomed to Succeed*, p. 354.

56. Thanassis Cambanis, *Once Upon a Revolution*, p. 56.

57. Worth, *A Rage for Order*, pp. 30–31. See also Cambanis, *Once Upon a Revolution*, p. 69.

58. Josh Rogin, The Inside Story on the Exploding Egypt 'Envoy,' Frank Wisner, The Cable, *Foreign Policy*, February 7, 2011, http://foreignpolicy.com/2011/02/07/the-inside-story-on-the-exploding-egypt-envoy-frank-wisner/.

59. The White House, Statement by President Barack Obama on Egypt, February 10, 2011, https://www.whitehouse.gov/the-press-office/2011/02/10/statement-president-barack-obama-egypt.

60. Cambanis, *Once Upon a Revolution*, p. 74.

61. The White House, Remarks by the President to Parliament in London, United Kingdom, May 25, 2011, https://www.whitehouse.gov/the-press-office/2011/05/25/remarks-president-parliament-london-united-kingdom.

62. Lynch, *The New Arab Wars*, p. 55.

63. Vali Nasr, *The Dispensable Nation*, pp. 172–75.

64. Lynch, *The New Arab Wars*, p. 155.

65. Cambanis, *Once Upon a Revolution*, p. 185.

66. Id., p. 156.

67. Charlie Savage, *Power Wars*, p. 676.

68. The U.S. Department of State, Daily Press Briefing, July 26, 2013, http://www.state.gov/r/pa/prs/dpb/2013/07/212484.htm.

69. Michael Crowley, The Obama Issue: 'We Caved,' *Politico*, January 6, 2016, http://www.politico.com/magazine/story/2016/01/we-caved-obama-foreign-policy-legacy-213495.

70. Sanger, *Confront and Conceal*, p. 315.

71. Jackson Diehl, Fulfilling the Arab Spring, *The Washington Post*, April 27, 2015, p. A15.

72. John Kerry, quoted in *The Washington Post* Editorial, Don't reward Egypt for torturing innocents, March 18, 2016, p. A20, https://www.washingtonpost.com/opinions/dont-reward-egypt-for-torturing-innocents/2016/03/17/f49d1dc4-eb9f-11e5-b0fd-073d5930a7b7_story.html.

73. Ibid.

74. Sanger, *Confront and Conceal*, p. 301.

75. Lynch, *The New Arab Wars*, p. 222.

CHAPTER 6

1. Remarks by the President on Libya, Brasilia, Brazil, March 19, 2011, https://www.whitehouse.gov/the-press-office/2011/03/19/remarks-president-libya.

2. Derek Chollet, *The Long Game*, p. 107.

3. James Mann, *The Obamians*, p. 170.

4. The White House, Remarks by the President in Address to the Nation on Libya, March 28, 2011, https://www.whitehouse.gov/photos-and-video/video/2011/03/28/president-obama-s-speech-libya.

5. Mann, *The Obamians*, p. 153.

6. David Rothkopf, *National Insecurity: American Leadership in an Age of Fear*, p. 280.

7. Baker quoted in Richard Holbrooke, *To End a War*, p. 27.

8. James A. Baker III, *The Politics of Diplomacy*, p. 651.

9. Jon Meacham, *Destiny and Power*, p. 529.

10. Marvin Kalb and Deborah Kalb, *Haunting Legacy*, p. 172.

11. Bill Clinton, *My Life*, p. 593.

12. Quoted in Stephen Sestanovich, *Maximalist*, p. 260.

13. David Halberstam, *War in a Time of Peace*, p. 317.

14. Holbrooke, *To End a War*, p. 316.

15. Id., p. 211.

16. Id., p. 320.

17. Halberstam, *War in a Time of Peace*, p. 390.

18. Holbrooke, *To End a War*, pp. 21–26.

19. William J. Clinton, Inaugural Address, January 20, 1997, http://www.presidency.ucsb.edu/ws/?pid=54183.

20. *Spiegel* Online International, Interview with Madeleine Albright, November 5, 2012, http://www.spiegel.de/international/world/interview-with-former-us-secretary-of-state-madeleine-albright-a-865308.html.

21. David Fromkin, *Kosovo Crossing*, p. 161.

22. Bartholomew Sparrow, *The Strategist*, p. 455.

23. Ivo H. Daalder and Michael E. O'Hanlon, *Winning Ugly*, pp. 108–9.

24. Id., p. 75.

25. Christopher R. Hill, *Outpost*, p. 166.

26. Michael Mandelbaum, *Mission Failure*, pp. 123–24.

27. Derek Chollet and James Goldgeier, *America Between the Wars*, p. 216.

28. Id., p. 106.

29. Mann, *The Obamians*, p. xi.

30. Baker, *Days of Fire*, p. 620.

31. Condoleezza Rice, *No Higher Honor*, p. 703.

32. The White House, Remarks by President Obama and President Calderon of Mexico at Joint Press Conference, March 3, 2011, https://www.whitehouse.gov/the-press-office/2011/03/03/remarks-president-obama-and-president-calder-n-mexico-joint-press-confer.

33. Samantha Power, *A Problem from Hell*, quoted in Ryan Lizza, The Consequentialist: How the Arab Spring remade Obama's foreign policy, *The New Yorker*, May 2, 2011, http://www.newyorker.com/magazine/2011/05/02/the-consequentialist.

34. Jo Becker and Scott Shane, Clinton, 'smart power' and a dictator's fall, *The New York Times*, February 28, 2016, p. 1, http://www.nytimes.com/2016/02/28/us/politics/hillary-clinton-libya.html.

35. Mann, *The Obamians*, p. 289.

36. Lizza, op. cit.

37. Robert M. Gates, *Duty*, p. 519.

38. Kevin Sullivan, A tough call on Libya that still haunts, *The Washington Post*, February 3, 2016, http://www.washingtonpost.com/sf/national/2016/02/03/a-tough-call-on-libya-that-still-haunts/.

39. *The New York Times*, Transcript of the Democratic Presidential Debate in Miami, March 10, 2016, http://www.nytimes.com/2016/03/10/us/politics/transcript-democratic-presidential-debate.html?_r=0.

40. Donald Trump speech on fighting terrorism, Youngstown, OH, August 15, 2016, available at http://www.politico.com/story/2016/08/donald-trump-terrorism-speech-227025.

41. Charlie Savage, *Power Wars*, p. 643.

42. Remarks by the President in Address to the Nation on Syria, East Room, September 10, 2013, https://www.whitehouse.gov/the-press-office/2013/09/10/remarks-president-address-nation-syria.

43. The White House, Remarks by the President on Libya, March 19, 2011.

44. Ibid.

45. Mann, *The Obamians*, p. xiv.

46. Remarks by the President in Address to the Nation on Libya, National Defense University, March 28, 2011.

47. Savage, *Power Wars*, p. 645.

48. Lizza, op. cit.

49. Michael Hastings, Inside Obama's War Room, *Rolling Stone*, October 13, 2011, http://www.rollingstone.com/politics/news/inside-obamas-war-room-20111013.

50. Steven Mufson, Italy's Renzi points finger at post-Gaddafi turmoil, Libya Debrief, *The Washington Post*, April 23, 2015, p. A8.

51. Becker and Shane, op. cit.

52. Hillary Clinton, *Hard Choices*, p. 364.

53. United Nations Security Council, Resolution 1970, February 26, 2011, http://www.un.org/en/ga/search/view_doc.asp?symbol=S/RES/1970 (2011).

54. North Atlantic Treaty Organization, Statement on Libya, April 14, 2011, http://www.nato.int/cps/en/natohq/official_texts_72544.htm.

55. Barack Obama, David Cameron, and Nicolas Sarkozy, Libya's Pathway to Peace, *International Herald Tribune* Op-Ed Contributors, http://www.nytimes.com/2011/04/15/opinion/15iht-edlibya15.html?_r=2&ref=global.

56. The White House, Remarks by President Obama and President Sebastian Pinera of Chile at Joint Press Conference, March 21, 2011, https://www.whitehouse.gov/the-press-office/2011/03/21/remarks-president-obama-and-president-sebastian-pinera-chile-join-press-.

57. Mann, *The Obamians*, p. 299.

58. David E. Sanger, *Confront and Conceal*, p. 346.

59. Michael Morell, *The Great War of Our Time*, p. 192.

60. NPR, Transcript of Third Presidential Debate, October 22, 2012, http://www.npr.org/2012/10/22/163436694/transcript-3rd-obama-romney-presidential-debate.

61. Becker and Shane, op. cit.

62. Peter Baker, U.S.-Russian ties still fall short of 'reset' goal, *The New York Times*, September 3, 2013, p. A8.

63. Steven Lee Myers, In Putin's Syria intervention, fear of a weak government hand, News Analysis, *The New York Times*, October 4, 2015, p. A1, http://www.nytimes.com/2015/10/04/world/europe/in-putins-syria-intervention-fear-of-a-weak-government-hand.html?_r=0.

64. Michael Hastings, Inside Obama's War Room, *Rolling Stone*, October 13, 2011, http://www.rollingstone.com/politics/news/inside-obamas-war-room-20111013?print=true.

65. Thomas L. Friedman, Obama on the world, *The New York Times*, August 8, 2014, http://www.nytimes.com/2014/08/09/opinion/president-obama-thomas-l-friedman-iraq-and-world-affairs.html?_r=0.

66. Ibid.

67. Robert F. Worth, *A Rage for Order*, p. 38.

68. Scott Shane and Jo Becker, 'A new Libya, with very little time left,' *The New York Times*, February 29, 2016, p. 1, http://www.nytimes.com/2016/02/28/us/politics/libya-isis-hillary-clinton.html.

69. Chollet, *The Long Game*, p. 110.

70. *The Washington Post*, Transcript: Clinton testifies before House committee on Benghazi, October 22, 2015, https://www.washingtonpost.com/news/post-politics/wp/2015/10/22/transcript-clinton-testifies-before-house-committee-on-benghazi/.

71. Shane and Becker, op. cit.

72. *The New York Times*, Transcript of the Democratic Presidential Debate in Miami, March 10, 2016, http://www.nytimes.com/2016/03/10/us/politics/transcript-democratic-presidential-debate.html?_r=0.

73. Morell, *The Great War of Our Time*, pp. 206, 228.

74. Robert F. Worth and Eric Schmitt, Caustic light on response to a threat of terrorism, *The New York Times*, August 8, 2013, p. A4.

75. Ross Douthat, Prisoners of the Saudis, *The New York Times*, January 25, 2015, p. SR13.

76. Colin Dueck, *The Obama Doctrine*, p. 83.

77. Karen DeYoung, Fight against ISIS in Libya must wait for a government there, Egypt says, *The Washington Post*, February 9, 2016, p. A9, https://www.washingtonpost.com/world/national-security/egyptian-foreign-minister-libya-intervention-should-wait/2016/02/08/50864bd0-ceb6-11e5-b2bc-988409ee911b_story.html.

78. James Traub, The Hillary Clinton Doctrine, *Foreign Policy*, November 6, 2015.

79. Ibid.

80. Marc Lynch, *The New Arab Wars*, p. xi.

CHAPTER 7

1. Donald Trump speech on terrorism, Youngstown, OH, August 15, 2016.

2. Bob Woodward, *Obama's Wars*, p. 336.

3. Colin Dueck, *The Obama Doctrine*, pp. 141–42.

4. The White House, Remarks by the President on the Way Forward in Afghanistan, June 22, 2011.

5. The White House, Remarks by the President on the Middle East and North Africa, May 19, 2011.

6. Ibid.

7. Ibid.

8. Barack Obama, Speech at the Woodrow Wilson Center for International Scholars, Washington, D.C., August 1, 2007, http://www.cfr.org/elections/obamas-speech-woodrow-wilson-center/p13974.

9. The White House, Remarks by the President at the National Defense University, May 23, 2013.

10. The White House, Remarks by the President at the Acceptance of the Nobel Peace Prize, December 10, 2009, https://www.whitehouse.gov/the-press-office/remarks-president-acceptance-nobel-peace-prize.

11. Ibid.

12. Leon Panetta, *Worthy Fights*, p. 326.

13. Michael Morell, *The Great War of Our Time*, p. 169.

14. Robert M. Gates, *Duty*, pp. 544–45.

15. David E. Sanger, *Confront and Conceal*, p. 102.

16. The White House, Remarks by Vice President Joe Biden on Foreign Policy at a Camapaign (sic) Event, April 26, 2012, https://www.whitehouse.gov/the-press-office/2012/04/26/remarks-vice-president-joe-biden-foreign-policy-camapaign-event.

17. David Kilcullen, *Blood Year*, pp. 72–74.

18. Obama, Moving Forward in Iraq, Speech to the Chicago Council on Foreign Relations, November 22, 2006.

19. Ibid.

20. The White House, Remarks by the President on Ending the War in Iraq, October 21, 2011, https://www.whitehouse.gov/the-press-office/2011/10/21/remarks-president-ending-war-iraq.

21. Erika G. King, *Obama, the Media, and Framing the U.S. Exit from Iraq and Afghanistan*, p. 119.

22. Gordon and Trainor, *The Endgame*, pp. 562–63.

23. Author interview with former U.S. Ambassador to Iraq James Jeffrey, February 19, 2016.

24. Michael R. Gordon and General Bernard E. Trainor, *The Endgame*, p. 670.

25. Author interview with Jeffrey, February 19, 2016.

26. Quoted in Dominic Tierney, *The Right Way to Lose a War*, p. 101.

27. The White House, Remarks by the President on Ending the War in Iraq, October 21, 2011.

28. Ibid.

29. The White House, Remarks by President Obama and Prime Minister al-Maliki of Iraq in a Joint Press Conference, December 12, 2011, https://www.whitehouse.gov/the-press-office/2011/12/12/remarks-president-obama-and-prime-minister-al-maliki-iraq-joint-press-co.

30. Christopher R. Hill, *Outpost*, p. 370.

31. Ibid.

32. Liz Sly, Petraeus: 'What happened in Iraq is a tragedy,' *The Washington Post*, March 22, 2015, p. A12.

33. Jeh Charles Johnson, The Conflict against Al Qaeda and Its Affiliates: How Will It End?, Oxford Union, November 30, 2012, https://www.lawfareblog.com/jeh-johnson-speech-oxford-union.

34. The White House, Remarks by the president at National Defense University, May 23, 2013.

35. Thomas L. Friedman, Schieffer Series: A Discussion on Syria, Center for Strategic and International Studies, November 16, 2015.

36. Derek Chollet, *The Long Game*, p. 90.

37. The White House, Remarks by the President and First Lady on the End of the War in Iraq, December 14, 2011, https://www.whitehouse.gov/the-press-office/2011/12/14/remarks-president-and-first-lady-end-war-iraq.

CHAPTER 8

1. Hillary Clinton, America's Pacific Century, *Foreign Policy*, October 11, 2011, http://foreignpolicy.com/2011/10/11/americas-pacific-century/.

2. Kurt M. Campbell, *The Pivot*, p. 1.

3. Clinton, America's Pacific Century, *Foreign Policy*.

4. Campbell, *The Pivot*, p. 338.

5. The White House, Remarks by President Obama to the Australian Parliament, November 17, 2011, https://www.whitehouse.gov/the-press-office/2011/11/17/remarks-president-obama-australian-parliament.

6. The White House, Remarks by Tom Donilon, National Security Advisor to the President: "The United States and the Asia-Pacific in 2013," The Asia Society, March 11, 2013, https://www.whitehouse.gov/the-press-office/2013/03/11/remarks-tom-donilon-national-security-advisor-president-united-states-an.

7. Campbell, *The Pivot*, p. 146.

8. The White House, Remarks by President Obama and President Xi of the People's Republic of China in joint press conference, September 25, 2015, available at http://

www.whitehouse.gov/the-press-office/2015/09/25/remarks-president-obama-and
-president-xi-peoples-republic-joint.

9. James Mann, Changing the rules of 'engagement,' *The Washington Post*, September 18, 2015, p. A19, https://www.washingtonpost.com/opinions/changing-the-rules-of
-engagement/2015/09/17/d96c955a-5bd2-11e5-b38e-06883aacba64_story.html.

10. David Shambaugh, *China Goes Global*, p. 21.

11. Mandelbaum, *Mission Failure*, p. 4.

12. Bartholomew Sparrow, *The Strategist*, p. 365.

13. Mandelbaum, *Mission Failure*, p. 25.

14. Id., p. 38.

15. Jeffrey A. Bader, *Obama and China's Rise*, p. 147.

16. Henry Kissinger, *World Order*, p. 226.

17. Douglas H. Paal, China's Counterbalance to the American Rebalance, Op Ed, *Strategic Review*, November 1, 2015, http://carnegieendowment.org/2015/11/01/china-s
-counterbalance-to-american-rebalance/ikv8.

18. Campbell, *The Pivot*, p. 235.

19. James Steinberg and Michael E. O'Hanlon, *Strategic Reassurance and Resolve*, p. 22.

20. Id., p. 25.

21. Shambaugh, *China Goes Global*, p. 317.

22. Campbell, *The Pivot*, p. 161.

23. Hillary Clinton, *Hard Choices*, p. 66.

24. The White House, Remarks by Deputy National Security Advisor Ben Rhodes on Burma Policy at the Center for New American Security, May 18, 2016, https://
www.whitehouse.gov/the-press-office/2016/05/18/remarks-de puty-national -security
-advisor-ben-rhodes-burma-policy-center.

25. Bader, *Obama and China's Rise*, pp. 69–70.

26. Department of State, Hillary Rodham Clinton, Remarks at the U.S. Institute of Peace China Conference, March 7, 2012, http://www.state.gov/secretary/
20092013clinton/rm/2012/03/185402.htm.

27. Donilon, The Asia Society, March 11, 2013.

28. Traub, The Hillary Clinton Doctrine, *Foreign Policy*, November 6, 2015.

29. Bader, *Obama and China's Rise*, p. 110.

30. Simon Denyer, Storm clouds gather over South China Sea ahead of U.N. ruling, *The Washington Post*, April 28, 2016, p. A10, https://www.washingtonpost.com/world/
storm-clouds-gather-over-south-china-sea-ahead-of-key-un-ruling/2016/04/27/
fd5d1c7b-d425-567-b225-21c7ee1ffba_story.html.

31. Ibid.

32. Campbell, *The Pivot*, pp. 235–36.

33. Shambaugh, *China Goes Global*, pp. 130–31.

34. Henry Kissinger quoted in Shambaugh, *China Goes Global*, p. 1.

35. Matthew Spence, China's model for Syria, *The Washington Post*, October 30, 2015, p. A19, https://www.washingtonpost.com/opinions/the-china-model-for-syria/2015/10/
29/af7b4892-79c1-11e5-b9c1-f03c48c96ac2_story.html.

36. Thomas J. Christensen, *The China Challenge*, pp. 308–9.

37. Steinberg and O'Hanlon, *Strategic Reassurance and Resolve*, p. 203.

38. Lawrence Summers, The reality of China's rise, *The Washington Post*, November 9, 2015, p. A19, https://www.washingtonpost.com/opinions/the-world--including-china
--is-unprepared-for-the-rise-of-china/2015/11/08/70aa6c70-84ab-11e5-8ba6
-cec48b74b2a7_story.html.

39. David Ignatius, A looming 'red line' with China, *The Washington Post*, March 16, 2016, p. A23, https://www.washingtonpost.com/opinions/the-us-is-heading-toward-a

-dangerous-showdown-with-china/2016/03/15/c835a1b4-eaf2-11e5-b0fd
-073d5930a7b7_story.html.

40. Simon Denyer, Beijing woos others in South China Sea dispute, *The Washington Post*, June 20, 2016, p. A8, https://www.washingtonpost.com/world/asia_pacific/us
-hypocrisy-and-chinese-cash-strengthen-beijings-hand-in-south-china-sea/2016/06/18/
6907943a-330a-11e6-ab9d-1da2b0f24f93_story.html.

41. Henry M. Paulson Jr., Why China's reforms matter, *The Washington Post*, September 20, 2015, p. A19, https://www.washingtonpost.com/opinions/why-chinas-economic
-reforms-are-critical-to-the-united-states/2015/09/18/b2227c9c-5bc5-11e5-b38e
-06883a acba64_story.html?tid = a_inl.

42. Shambaugh, *China Goes Global*, p. 7.

43. Christensen, *The China Challenge*, p. 63.

44. Id., p. 115.

45. Meacham, *Destiny and Power*, p. 373.

46. *The New York Times*, Transcript of the Republican Presidential Debate in Florida, March 11, 2016, http://www.nytimes.com/2016/03/11/us/politics/transcript-of-the
-republican-presidential-debate-in-florida.html?_r = 1.

47. Ibid.

48. *The New York Times*, Transcript: Donald Trump at the G.O.P.'s Convention, July 22, 2016, available at http://www.nytimes.com/2016/07/22/us/politics/trump-transcript
-rnc-address.html?_r = 0.

49. David Ignatius, President Trump would hand the world to China, *The Washington Post*, June 1, 2016, p. A19, https://www.washingtonpost.com/opinions/president-trump
-would-hand-china-the-world/2016/05/31/e4d1b1f8-2771-11e6-ae4a
-3cdd5fe74204_story.html.

50. *The New York Times*, Transcript: Donald Trump at the G.O.P. Convention, July 22, 2016.

51. Barack Obama, America, not China, should call the shots on trade, *The Washington Post*, May 3, 2016, p. A15, https://www.washingtonpost.com/opinions/president-obama
-the-tpp-would-let-america-not-china-lead-the-way-on-global-trade/2016/05/02/
680540e4-0fd0-11e6-93ae-50921721165d_story.html.

52. Ibid.

53. *The New York Times*, Transcript of the Republican Presidential Debate in New Hampshire, February 6, 2016, http://www.nytimes.com/2016/02/07/us/politics/
transcript-of-the-republican-presidential-debate-in-new-hampshire.html?_r = 1.

54. Christensen, *The China Challenge*, p. 126.

55. Victor Cha, *The Impossible State*, p. 317.

56. Anna Fifield, Japan, S. Korea stunned by Trump's comments on nuclear weapons, *The Washington Post*, March 29, 2016, p. A2, https://www.washingtonpost.com/world/
asia_pacific/in-japan-and-south-korea-bewilderment-at-trumps-suggestion-they-build
-nukes/2016/03/28/03eb2ace-f50e-11e5-958d-d038dac6e718_story.html.

57. Adam Taylor, North Korean state media offers support for 'wise politician' Donald Trump, *The Washington Post*, May 31, 2016, https://www.washingtonpost.com/news/
worldviews/wp/2016/05/31/north-korean-state-media-offers-support-for-wise
-politician-donald-trump/.

CHAPTER 9

1. The White House, National Security Strategy, February 2015, https://
www.whitehouse.gov/sites/default/files/docs/2015_national_security_strategy.pdf.

2. The White House, Remarks by the President at the United States Military Academy Commencement Ceremony, May 28, 2014, https://www.whitehouse.gov/the-press -office/2014/05/28/remarks-president-united-states-military-academy-commencement -ceremony.

3. Solomon, *The Iran Wars*, p. 105.

4. Thomas L. Friedman, Schieffer Series: A Discussion on Syria, Center for Strategic and International Studies, November 16, 2015.

5. Joby Warrick, *Black Flags*, p. 234.

6. Secretary of State Hillary Clinton, Remarks with European Union High Representative for Foreign Affairs Catherine Ashton after Their Meeting, July 11, 2011, http://www.state.gov/secretary/20092013clinton/rm/2011/07/168027.htm.

7. Warrick, *Black Flags*, p. 237.

8. Dennis Ross, Washington and the World: How Obama Created a Middle East Vacuum, *Politico*, January 10, 2016, http://www.politico.com/magazine/story/2016/01/obama-mideast-vacuum-213513.

9. Ibid.

10. Fred Hof, Primary Source: I Got Syria So Wrong, *Politico*, October 14, 2015, http://www.politico.com/magazine/story/2015/10/syria-civil-war-213242.

11. The White House, Press Briefing by Press Secretary Robert Gibbs, February 2, 2011, https://www.whitehouse.gov/the-press-office/2011/02/02/press-briefing-press-secretary -robert-gibbs-222011.

12. The White House, National Security Strategy, February 2015, p. 22.

13. U.S. Department of State, John Kerry, Solo Press Availability at the Geneva II International Conference on Syria, January 22, 2014, http://www.state.gov/secretary/remarks/2014/01/220524.htm.

14. Hillary Rodham Clinton, *Hard Choices*, pp. 463–64.

15. Traub, The Hillary Clinton Doctrine, *Foreign Policy*, November 6, 2015.

16. Warrick, *Black Flags*, p. 279.

17. U.S. Department of State, John Kerry, Statement on Syria, August 30, 2013, http://www.state.gov/secretary/remarks/2013/08/213668.htm.

18. Ibid.

19. Ibid.

20. Charlie Savage, *Power Wars*, pp. 651–52.

21. Id., p. 631.

22. Id., pp. 652–53.

23. Id., p. 650.

24. Derek Chollet, *The Long Game*, p. 5.

25. The White House, Statement by the President on Syria, August 31, 2013, https://www.whitehouse.gov/the-press-office/2013/08/31/statement-president-syria.

26. U.S. Department of State, John Kerry, Opening Remarks Before the United States Senate Committee on Foreign Relations, September 3, 2013, http://www.state.gov/secretary/remarks/2013/09/212603.htm.

27. The U.S. Department of State, John Kerry, Interview with Chris Hayes of MSNBC, September 5, 2013, http://www.state.gov/secretary/remarks/2013/09/213861.htm.

28. The U.S. Department of State, John Kerry, Remarks with United Kingdom Foreign Secretary Hague, London, September 9, 2013, http://www.state.gov/secretary/remarks/2013/09/213956.htm.

29. The White House, Remarks by President Obama and Prime Minister Reinfeldt of Sweden in Joint Press Conference, September 4, 2013, https://www.whitehouse.gov/the -press-office/2013/09/04/remarks-president-obama-and-prime-minister-reinfeldt -sweden-joint-press-.

30. The White House, Remarks by President Obama in a Press Conference at the G20, September 6, 2013, https://www.whitehouse.gov/the-press-office/2013/09/06/remarks-president-obama-press-conference-g20.

31. Putin, A plea for caution from Russia, *The New York Times*, September 11, 2013.

32. Dennis Ross, *Doomed to Succeed*, p. 359.

33. Background discussion with the author and a former Obama administration official.

34. Solomon, *The Iran Wars*, p. 229.

35. Panetta, *Worthy Fights*, p. 450.

36. U.S. Department of State, John Kerry, Remarks with Saudi Arabian Foreign Minister Saud al-Faisal, November 4, 2013, http://www.state.gov/secretary/remarks/2013/11/216236.htm.

37. The White House, Remarks by the President in Address to the Nation on Syria, September 10, 2013, https://www.whitehouse.gov/the-press-office/2013/09/10/remarks-president-address-nation-syria.

38. The White House, Press Conference by the President, October 2, 2015, https://www.whitehouse.gov/the-press-office/2015/10/02/press-conference-president.

39. Stephen Sestanovich, *Maximalist*, p. 319.

40. Michael Gerson, With a hands-off approach, Syria will continue to burn, *The Washington Post*, May 27, 2016, p. A17, https://www.washingtonpost.com/opinions/with-obamas-hands-off-approach-the-syrian-fire-will-continue-to-burn/2016/05/26/b7ec74c4-2362-11e6-9e7f-57890b612299_story.html.

41. Walter Russell Mead, The End of History Ends, *The American Interest*, December 2, 2013, http://www.the-american-interest.com/2013/12/02/2013-the-end-of-history-ends-2/.

42. David Kilcullen, *Blood Year*, pp. 3, 85.

43. The White House, Statement by the President on Iraq, June 13, 2014, https://www.whitehouse.gov/the-press-office/2014/06/13/statement-president-iraq.

44. Thomas L. Friedman, Obama on the world, *The New York Times*, August 8, 2014, http://www.nytimes.com/2014/08/09/opinion/president-obama-thomas-l-friedman-iraq-and-world-affairs.html?_r = 0.

45. Peter Baker and Eric Schmitt, Discordant verdicts on U.S. forces in Syria: Too much or too little, *The New York Times*, November 1, 2015, p. 6, http://www.nytimes.com/2015/11/01/world/middleeast/discordant-verdicts-on-us-forces-in-syria-too-much-or-too-little.html?_r = 0.

46. Friedman, op. cit.

47. The White House, Statement by the President, August 28, 2014, https://www.whitehouse.gov/the-press-office/2014/08/28/statement-president.

48. David Ignatius, The Islamic State is still on the rise, *The Washington Post*, February 5, 2016, p. A19, https://www.washingtonpost.com/opinions/the-islamic-state-is-still-on-the-rise/2016/02/04/e631bdea-cb82-11e5-88ff-e2d1b4289c2f_story.html.

49. Peter Baker and Eric Schmitt, Rampage has U.S. rethinking how to stop attacks, *The New York Times*, December 6, 2015, p. A1, http://www.nytimes.com/2015/12/06/us/politics/california-attack-has-us-rethinking-strategy-on-homegrown-terror.html.

50. Rukmini Callimachi, ISIS says 'soldiers of caliphate' carried out rampage, *The New York Times*, December 6, 2015, p. A31, http://www.nytimes.com/2015/12/06/world/middleeast/islamic-state-san-bernardino-massacre.html.

51. Peter Bergen, *United States of Jihad*, p. 262.

52. Interview with John Miller, Deputy Commissioner of Intelligence & Counter-terrorism, New York Police Department, July 25, 2016.

53. Bergen, *United States of Jihad*, p. 58.

54. Id., p. 272.

55. Richard Engel, *And Then All Hell Broke Loose*, p. 193.

56. William McCants, *ISIS Apocalypse*, p. 93.

57. The White House, Statement by the President, August 20, 2014, https://www.whitehouse.gov/photos-and-video/video/2014/08/20/president-obama-delivers-statement-murder-james-foley#transcript.

58. The White House, Statement by the President on ISIL, September 10, 2014, https://www.whitehouse.gov/the-press-office/2014/09/10/statement-president-isil-1.

59. The White House, Statement by the President on Airstrikes in Syria, September 23, 2014, https://www.whitehouse.gov/the-press-office/2014/09/23/statement-president-airstrikes-syria.

60. Karen DeYoung, U.S.-trained force in Syria gives equipment to al-Qaeda branch, *The Washington Post*, September 26, 2015, p. A20.

61. Marc Lynch, *The New Arab Wars*, p. 246.

62. CBS News, *60 Minutes*, Interview with President Obama, October 11, 2015, http://www.cbsnews.com/news/president-obama-60-minutes-syria-isis-2016-presidential-race/.

63. Ibid.

64. Secretary of Defense Ash Carter, quoted in Dana Milbank, No 'urgency' in this timid approach to Islamic State, *The Washington Post*, December 10, 2015, p. A2, https://www.washingtonpost.com/opinions/on-syria-us-military-leaders-offer-only-timidity/2015/12/09/f1dd2b9e-9eb8-11e5-8728-1af6af208198_story.html.

CHAPTER 10

1. See John Ikenberry's analysis, cited in Robert Legvold, *Return to Cold War*, pp. 18–19.

2. Thomas L. Friedman, Who's playing marbles now?, *The New York Times*, December 21, 2014, p. SR9.

3. Jeffrey Goldberg, The Obama Doctrine, *Atlantic Magazine*, April 2016.

4. George F. Kennan ("X"), The Sources of Soviet Conduct, Essay, *Foreign Affairs*, July 1947, https://www.foreignaffairs.com/articles/russian-federation/1947-07-01/sources-soviet-conduct.

5. Ibid.

6. Ibid.

7. Legvold, *Return to Cold War*, pp. 65–66.

8. John Lewis Gaddis, *The Cold War: A New History*, p. 10.

9. Id., p. 84.

10. George Crile, *Charlie Wilson's War*, p. 219.

11. James Mann, *The Rebellion of Ronald Reagan*, p. 29.

12. Id., p. 23.

13. Id., pp. 121–22.

14. Id., p. 202.

15. Id., p. 251.

16. Marvin Kalb, *Imperial Gamble*, p. 119.

17. William J. Perry, *My Journey at the Nuclear Brink*, pp. 86–87.

18. Ibid.

19. Derek Chollet and James Goldgeier, *America Between the Wars*, p. 120.

20. Henry Kissinger, *World Order*, p. 90.

21. Strobe Talbott, *The Great Experiment*, p. 287.

22. Steven Lee Myers, *The New Tsar*, p. 143.

23. Fyodor Lukyanov, Putin's Foreign Policy, *Foreign Affairs*, May/June 2016, https://www.foreignaffairs.com/articles/russia-fsu/2016-04-18/putins-foreign-policy.

24. Chollet and Goldgeier, *America Between the Wars*, p. 231.

25. James Mann, *Rise of the Vulcans*, pp. 244–45.

26. Condoleezza Rice, *No Higher Honor*, p. 63.

27. Id., p. 62.

28. Myers, *The New Tsar*, p. 204.

29. Legvold, *Return to Cold War*, p. 103.

30. Peter Baker and Susan Glasser, *Kremlin Rising*, pp. 215–29.

31. Rice, *No Higher Honor*, p. 360.

32. Baker and Glasser, *Kremlin Rising*, pp. 12, 37.

33. Myers, *The New Tsar*, p. 202.

34. Andrei Soldatov and Irina Borogan, In Russia, political engagement is blossoming online, *The Washington Post*, January 1, 2016, p. A19, https://www.washingtonpost.com/opinions/in-russia-political-engagement-is-blossoming-online/2015/12/31/b5bfbd8c-aef5-11e5-b820-eea4d64be2a1_story.html.

35. Robert M. Gates, *Duty*, pp. 157, 168.

36. Myers, *The New Tsar*, p. 350.

37. James Mann, *The Obamians*, p. 187.

38. Hillary Rodham Clinton, *Hard Choices*, pp. 230–31.

39. Kathryn Stoner and Michael McFaul, Who Lost Russia (This Time)? Vladimir Putin, *The Washington Quarterly*, Summer 2015, pp. 170–72.

40. Myers, *The New Tsar*, p. 384.

41. Colin Dueck, *The Obama Doctrine*, p. 69.

42. Ibid.

43. NPR, Transcript of the Third Presidential Debate, October 22, 2012.

44. Legvold, *Return to Cold War*, p. 108.

45. Myers, *The New Tsar*, p. 278.

46. Id., p. 436.

47. Id., p. 454.

48. Christopher Walker and Robert Orttung, Propping up Putin in the polls, *The Washington Post*, February 1, 2015, p. A17.

49. Chollet, *The Long Game*, p. 176.

50. The White House, Remarks by President Obama in Press Conference after G7 Summit, June 8, 2015, https://www.whitehouse.gov/the-press-office/2015/06/08/remarks-president-obama-press-conference-after-g7-summit.

51. Oleksandr Turchynov, A devil's bargain in Syria, *The Washington Post*, December 4, 2015, p. A21, https://www.washingtonpost.com/opinions/allying-with-putin-against-the-islamic-state-would-be-a-devils-bargain/2015/12/03/c0deeaca-9871-11e5-b499-76cbec161973_story.html.

52. Vladimir Putin, Interview with *60 Minutes*, aired on September 27, 2015, http://www.cbsnews.com/news/vladimir-putin-russian-president-60-minutes-charlie-rose/.

53. Greg Miller, Russian airstrikes changed 'calculus completely' in Syria, officials say, *The Washington Post*, February 10, 2016, p. A21, https://www.washingtonpost.com/world/national-security/spy-chief-warns-that-us-could-face-attacks-inspired-by-terrorism-in-paris/2016/02/09/29f172c8-cf2f-11e5-b2bc-988409ee911b_story.html.

54. Condoleezza Rice and Robert M. Gates, Countering Putin, *The Washington Post*, October 9, 2015, p. A23, https://www.washingtonpost.com/opinions/how-to-counter-putin-in-syria/2015/10/08/128fade2-6c66-11e5-b31c-d80d62b53e28_story.html.

55. Kareem Fahim, Sectarian leaders fan flames in Middle East, *The New York Times*, October 18, 2015, p. 14, http://www.nytimes.com/2015/10/18/world/middleeast/as -conflicts-flare-up-leaders-fan-sectarian-flames-in-middle-east.html.

56. Karen DeYoung, Putin's actions may force a choice on Obama: Act or yield, *The Washington Post*, October 8, 2015, p. A1, https://www.washingtonpost.com/world/ national-security/russias-syria-intervention-may-force-choice-on-obama-act-or-yield/ 2015/10/07/a88f9996-6d16-11e5-9bfe-e59f5e244f92_story.html.

57. Deputy Secretary of State Anthony Blinken, quoted in John Davison, Syrian rebel alliance launches offensive against Islamic State, *The Washington Post*, November 1, 2015, p. A1, https://www.washingtonpost.com/world/new-us-backed-syrian-rebel-alliance -launches-offensive-against-isis/2015/10/31/c6eeac0a-800e-11e5-afce-2af d1d3eb896_story.html.

58. Steven Mufson, Russia Debrief: Syria offensive is killing fragile hopes for diplomacy, *The Washington Post*, October 9, 2015, p. A14, https://www.washingtonpost.com/national/ russian-bombs-in-syria-killing-fragile-hopes-for-diplomacy-far-beyond/2015/10/08/ ed49f0e2-6d00-11e5-b31c-d80d62b53e28_story.html.

59. Fred Hof, Plan B for Syria, *Huffington Post*, February 16, 2016, http:// www.huffingtonpost.com/ambassador-frederic-c-hof/plan-b-fo r-syria_b_9242536.html.

60. Myers, *The New Tsar*, p. 462.

61. Micah Zenko, Hail to the Hugely Classy Commander-in-Chief, *Foreign Policy*, February 3, 2016, http://foreignpolicy.com/2016/02/03/hail-to-the-hugely-classy -commander-in-chief/.

62. Ludmilla Alexeeva, Help Russia's human rights activists, *The Washington Post*, February 25, 2016, p. A17, https://www.washingtonpost.com/opinions/in-russia-human -rights-groups-need-western-aid-more-than-ever/2016/02/24/b8e934d2-d1c0-11e5 -b2bc-988409 ee911b_story.html.

63. Gates, *Duty*, p. 532.

64. Myers, *The New Tsar*, p. 332.

65. Author interview, Washington, D.C., October 16, 2015.

66. Stoner and McFaul, Who Lost Russia (This Time)? Vladimir Putin, pp. 181–84.

67. *The New York Times*, Republican Presidential Debate Transcript, November 10, 2015.

68. Ibid.

69. *The New York Times*, Transcript of the Democratic Presidential Debate, January 17, 2016, http://www.nytimes.com/2016/01/18/us/politics/transcript-of-the-democratic -presidential-debate.html?_r = 0.

70. Sam Nunn, How to avoid nuclear catastrophe, *The Washington Post*, May 27, 2016, p. A17, https://www.washingtonpost.com/opinions/on-nuclear-weapons-nation s-must -cooperate-to-avoid-catastrophe/2016/05/26/f5af4c4c-21e0-11e6-9e7f-57890b 612299_story.html.

71. Pew Research Center, Public Uncertain, Divided Over America's Place in the World, April 2016, http://www.people-press.org/2016/05/05/3-international-threats -defense-spending/.

72. Legvold, *Return to Cold War*, p. 164.

CHAPTER 11

1. Roger Cohen, The Making of an Iran Policy, *The New York Times Magazine*, July 30, 2009, http://www.nytimes.com/2009/08/02/magazine/02Iran-t.html?_r = 0.

2. Solomon, *The Iron Wars*, pp. 198–204.

3. David E. Sanger, *The Inheritance*, p. xxv.

4. The White House, Remarks by President Obama in Address to the United Nations General Assembly, September 24, 2013, https://www.whitehouse.gov/the-press-office/2013/09/24/remarks-president-obama-address-united-nations-general-assembly.

5. Author interview with Trita Parsi, Washington, D.C., December 17, 2015.

6. The White House, Press Conference by the President, July 15, 2015, available at http://www.whitehouse.gov/the-press-office/2015/07/15/press-conference-president.

7. Dennis Ross, *Doomed to Succeed*, p. 365.

8. *The Washington Post*, Israeli Prime Minister Benjamin Netanyahu, Address to Congress, March 3, 2015, https://www.washingtonpost.com/news/post-politics/wp/2015/03/03/full-text-netanyahus-address-to-congress/.

9. Ibid.

10. Ibid.

11. *The New York Times*, United States Senate, An Open Letter to the Leaders of the Islamic Republic of Iran, March 9, 2015, http://www.nytimes.com/interactive/2015/03/09/world/middleeast/document-the-letter-senate-republicans-addressed-to-the-leaders-of-iran.html.

12. Ibid.

13. James Mann, *The Obamians*, p. 163.

14. The White House, Statement by the President on Iran, July 14, 2015, https://www.whitehouse.gov/the-press-office/2015/07/14/statement-president-iran.

15. The White House, Remarks by the President on the Iran Nuclear Deal, American University, August 5, 2015, https://www.whitehouse.gov/the-press-office/2015/08/05/remarks-president-iran-nuclear-deal.

16. Carol Morello, Retired generals and admirals urge Congress to reject Iran nuclear deal, *The Washington Post*, August 26, 2015, https://www.washingtonpost.com/world/national-security/retired-generals-and-admirals-urge-congress-to-reject-iran-deal/2015/08/26/8912d9c6-4bf5-11e5-84df-923b3ef1a64b_story.html.

17. David Ignatius, How the Iran deal became the most strategic success of Obama's presidency, *The Washington Post*, September 15, 2015, https://www.washingtonpost.com/opinions/the-obama-bet-that-paid-off/2015/09/15/e46b80f6-5be6-11e5-8e9e-dce8a2a2a679_story.html.

18. Thomas L. Friedman, Obama makes his case on Iran nuclear deal, *The New York Times*, July 15, 2015, http://www.nytimes.com/2015/07/15/opinion/thomas-friedman-obama-makes-his-case-on-iran-nuclear-deal.html?_r = 0.

19. Ibid.

20. Ibid.

21. David Sanger, Bet for Obama on Iran nuclear deal may take years to pay off, *The New York Times*, July 14, 2015, http://www.nytimes.com/2015/07/15/world/middleeast/iran-nuclear-deal-us.html.

22. David E. Sanger and William J. Broad, Now the hardest part: Making the Iran deal work, News Analysis, *The New York Times*, October 18, 2015, p. 10, http://www.nytimes.com/2015/10/18/world/middleeast/iran-nuclear-deal-sanctions.html?_r = 0.

23. Senator Lindsey Graham, *CBS This Morning*, July 21, 2015, http://www.cbsnews.com/news/sen-lindsey-graham-to-donald-trump-stop-being-a-jackass/.

24. The White House, Remarks by the President on the Iran Nuclear Deal, American University, August 5, 2015.

25. *The New York Times*, Transcript of the Republican Presidential Debate in Florida, March 11, 2016.

26. *The New York Times*, Transcript of the Republican Presidential Debate in New Hampshire, February 6, 2016, http://www.nytimes.com/2016/02/07/us/politics/transcript-of-the-republican-presidential-debate-in-new-hampshire.html?_r = 1.

27. Glenn Kessler, Do Americans really have 'strong support' for the Iran deal?, Fact Checker, *The Washington Post*, September 20, 2015, p. A4, https://www.washingtonpost.com/news/fact-checker/wp/2015/09/14/obamas-claim-that-the-iran-deal-has-strong-support-from-lawmakers-and-citizens/.

28. *The New York Times*, Transcript of the Main Republican Presidential Debate, January 28, 2016, http://www.nytimes.com/2016/01/29/us/politics/republican-presidential-debate-transcript.html.

29. Ben Cardin, A vote of conscience on Iran, *The Washington Post*, September 6, 2015, p. A21.

30. *CNN,* Reagan Library Debate, September 16, 2015, http://cnnpressroom.blogs.cnn.com/2015/09/16/cnn-reagan-library-debate-later-debate-full-transcript/.

31. Brent Scowcroft, An epochal moment: The Iran deal meets the key U.S. objective to curb Tehran's nuclear program, *The Washington Post*, August 23, 2015, p. A23.

32. Ibid.

33. The White House, Remarks by the President on the Iran Nuclear Deal, American University, August 5, 2015.

34. John Kerry, Remarks on Nuclear Agreement with Iran, Philadelphia, Pennsylvania, September 2, 2015, http://www.state.gov/secretary/remarks/2015/09/246574.htm.

35. Karoun Demirjian, Senate Democrats block bid to derail Iran deal, *The Washington Post*, September 11, 2015, p. A6.

36. The Brookings Institution, Hillary Clinton Addresses the Iran Nuclear Deal, September 9, 2015, http://www.brookings.edu/~/media/events/2015/09/09-clinton-iran/20150909_clinton_iran_transcript.pdf.

37. *The New York Times*, Transcript of the Democratic Presidential Debate, January 17, 2016, http://www.nytimes.com/2016/01/18/us/politics/transcript-of-the-democratic-presidential-debate.html?_r = 0.

38. *NBC News*, Transcript: MSNBC Democratic Candidates Debate, February 4, 2016, available at http://www.nbcnews.com/politics/2016-election/transcript-msnbc-democratic-candidates-debate-n511036.

39. *The New York Times*, Transcript of the Democratic Presidential Debate in Milwaukee, February 11, 2016, http://www.nytimes.com/2016/02/12/us/politics/transcript-of-the-democratic-presidential-debate-in-milwaukee.html?_r = 0.

40. CBS News, *60 Minutes* Interview Transcript, Steve Kroft and President Hassan Rouhani, September 20, 2015, http://www.cbsnews.com/news/iran-president-hassan-rouhani-nuclear-deal-60-minutes/.

41. Ibid.

42. Remarks by the President on the Iran Nuclear Deal, American University, August 5, 2015.

43. *The New York Times*, Transcript of Republican Presidential Debate, January 15, 2016, http://www.nytimes.com/2016/01/15/us/politics/transcript-of-republican-presidential-debate.html.

44. Barack Obama, The next steps in nuclear security, *The Washington Post*, March 31, 2016, p. A17, https://www.washingtonpost.com/opinions/obama-how-we-can-make-our-vision-of-a-world-without-nuclear-weapons-a-reality/2016/03/30/3e156e2c-f693-11e5-9804-537defcc3cf6_story.html.

CHAPTER 12

1. Barack Obama, Renewing American Leadership, *Foreign Affairs*, July/August 2007, available at http://www.foreignaffairs.com/articles/2007-07-01/renewing-american -leadership.

2. President Barack Obama, *60 Minutes* Interview, December 7, 2009 (aired on December 13), Transcript Part 1 available at http://www.cbsnews.com/news/transcript -president-barack-obama-part-1-13-12-2009/.

3. Ibid.

4. Ibid.

5. Peter Tomsen, The Good War?, *Foreign Affairs*, October 19, 2014, https:// www.foreignaffairs.com/articles/afghanistan/2014-10-19/good-war.

6. James Traub, When Did Obama Give Up?, *Foreign Policy*, February 26, 2015, http:// foreignpolicy.com/2015/02/26/when-did-obama-give-up-speeches/.

7. James Dobbins and Carter Malkasian, Time to Negotiate in Afghanistan: How to Talk to the Taliban, *Foreign Affairs*, July/August 2015, pp. 53–54.

8. Id., pp. 54–55.

9. Vali Nasr, *The Dispensable Nation*, p. 20.

10. Quoted in Dominic Tierney, *The Right Way to Lose a War*, p. 86.

11. The U.S. State Department, Remarks at the Launch of the Asia Society's Series of Richard C. Holbrooke Memorial Series, February 18, 2011, available at http://www.state .gov/sectetary/20092013clinton/rm/2011/02/156815.htm.

12. The White House, Remarks by the President on the Way Forward in Afghanistan, June 22, 2011.

13. David E. Sanger, *Confront and Conceal*, pp. 127–28.

14. Bob Woodward, *Obama's Wars*, p. 379.

15. Fred Kaplan, *The Insurgents*, p. 353.

16. Robert L. Grenier, *88 Days to Kandahar*, p. 411.

17. Nasr, *The Dispensable Nation*, p. 56.

18. Sanger, *Confront and Conceal*, p. 123.

19. Grenier, *88 Days to Kandahar*, p. 360.

20. Michael Morell, *The Great War of Our Time*, p. 74.

21. Quoted in Paul D. Shrinkman, Pakistani Ambassador: U.S. Drone Strikes Cross a 'Red Line,' *U.S. News & World Report*, February 5, 2013, http://www.usnews.com/news/ articles/2013/02/05/pakistani-ambassador-us-drone-strikes-cross-a-red-line.

22. Sanger, *Confront and Conceal*, p. 136.

23. Id., p. 250.

24. Husain Haqqani, *Magnificent Delusions*, p. 313.

25. Woodward, *Obama's Wars*, p. 26.

26. Haqqani, *Magnificent Delusions*, p. 327.

27. Id., p. 311.

28. George Tenet, *At the Center of the Storm*, p. 252.

29. Michael V. Hayden, *Playing to the Edge*, p. 345.

30. Fareed Zakaria, The key to solving Afghanistan, *The Washington Post*, October 9, 2015, p. A21, https://www.washingtonpost.com/opinions/the-key-to-solving-the -puzzle-of-afghanistan/2015/10/08/1ebfa63a-6df1-11e5-aa5b-f78a98956699_story.html.

31. Grenier, *88 Days to Kandahar*, p. 351.

32. Sanger, *Confront and Conceal*, p. 7.

33. James Mann, *The Obamians*, pp. 314–15.

34. Haqqani, *Magnificent Delusions*, p. 346.

35. Sanger, *Confront and Conceal*, p. 88.

36. Editorial, In praise of drones, *The Washington Post*, May 2, 2015, p. A14.

37. Pew Research Center, Pakistani Public Opinion Ever More Critical of U.S., June 27, 2012, http://www.pewglobal.org/2012/06/27/pakistani-public-opinion-ever-more-critical-of-u-s/.

38. Tim Craig, Anti-U.S. attitudes lessen in Pakistan, *The Washington Post*, May 5, 2015, p. 1.

39. Aqil Shah, Drone strikes aren't turning Pakistanis into radicals, *The Washington Post*, May 22, 2016, p. B3, https://www.washingtonpost.com/news/monkey-cage/wp/2016/05/17/drone-blow-back-in-pakistan-is-a-myth-heres-why/.

40. Peter Tomsen, The Good War?, *Foreign Affairs*, October 19, 2014, https://www.foreignaffairs.com/articles/afghanistan/2014-10-19/good-war.

41. Tim Craig, Islamic State seems to lack foothold in Pakistan, *The Washington Post*, December 6, 2015, p. A23, https://www.washingtonpost.com/world/asia_pacific/islamic-state-is-having-a-hard-time-taking-root-in-pakistan/2015/12/05/2fa548b0-8e2b-11e5-934c-a369c80822c2_story.html.

42. David Rothkopf, In Search of the Real Barack Obama, *Foreign Policy*, June 1, 2015, http://foreignpolicy.com/2015/06/01/in-search-of-the-real-barack-obama-jewish-president-jeffrey-goldberg/.

43. The White House, Statement by the President on Afghanistan, May 27, 2014, https://www.whitehouse.gov/the-press-office/2014/05/27/statement-president-afghanistan.

44. Robert K. Brigham, *The United States and Iraq Since 1990*, p. 234.

45. Ibid.

46. Greg Jaffe, Afghan decision tests Obama, *The Washington Post*, October 13, 2015, p. A1, https://www.washingtonpost.com/politics/hope-fades-on-obamas-vow-to-bring-troops-home-before-presidency-ends/2015/10/12/cc0daaec-6781-11e5-9ef3-fde182507eac_story.html.

47. Dan Lamothe, U.S. and Afghan troops destroy huge al-Qaeda training camp, *The Washington Post*, October 31, 2015, p. A9, https://www.washingtonpost.com/news/checkpoint/wp/2015/10/30/probably-the-largest-al-qaeda-training-camp-ever-destroyed-in-afghanistan/.

48. Carlotta Gall, Pakistan's hand in the rise of international jihad, *The New York Times*, February 7, 2016, pp. SR6-7, http://www.nytimes.com/2016/02/07/opinion/sunday/pakistans-hand-in-the-rise-of-international-jihad.html.

49. Tim Craig and Greg Miller, U.S. strike crossed Pakistani 'red line,' *The Washington Post*, May 24, 2016, p. A10, https://www.washingtonpost.com/world/asia_pacific/pakistan-expresses-concern-over-us-airstrike-against-taliban-leader/2016/05/23/14eff94a-20e6-11e6-b944-52f7b1793dae_story.html.

50. The White House, Statement by the President on Afghanistan, July 6, 2016, https://www.whitehouse.gov/the-press-office/2016/07/06/statement-president-afghanistan.

51. Missy Ryan, General urges more 'pressure' on Taliban, *The Washington Post*, March 12, 2016, p. A13, https://www.washingtonpost.com/news/checkpoint/wp/2016/03/11/former-commander-the-u-s-military-needs-to-do-more-in-afghanistan/.

52. Missy Ryan and Greg Jaffe, General: Resume striking Taliban, *The Washington Post*, March 15, 2016, p. 1, https://www.washingtonpost.com/world/national-security/top-us-general-wants-to-start-striking-the-taliban-again/2016/03/14/2f347c18-e9eb-11e5-b0fd-073d5930a7b7_story.html.

53. Vanda Felbab-Brown, Ronald Neumann, and David Sedney, What Afghanistan needs now, *The Washington Post*, October 18, 2015, p. A19, https://

www.washingtonpost.com/opinions/dont-abandon-afghanistan-too-soon/2015/10/16/
7a48eb4c-71e3-11e5-8248-98e0f5a2e830_story.html.

54. Greg Jaffe and Missy Ryan, The U.S. was supposed to leave Afghanistan by 2017.
Now it might take decades, *The Washington Post*, January 26, 2016, https://
www.washingtonpost.com/news/checkpoint/wp/2016/01/26/the-u-s-was-supposed-to
-leave-afghanistan-by-2017-now-it-might-take-decades/.

CHAPTER 13

1. Greg Miller, San Bernardino attack linked to al-Qaeda cleric, *The Washington Post*,
December 19, 2015, p. A9, https://www.washingtonpost.com/world/national-security/al
-qaeda-figure-seen-as-key-inspiration-for-san-bernardino-attacker/2015/12/18/f0e00
d80-a5a0-11e5-9c4e-be37f66848bb_story.html.

2. Jessica Stern and J. M. Berger, *ISIS: The State of Terror*, p. 187.

3. Scott Shane, *Objective Troy*, p. 316.

4. Fareed Zakaria, How not to stop jihadis, *The Washington Post*, January 16, 2015,
p. A19.

5. Quoted in Richard N. Haass, *The Opportunity*, p. 61.

6. Seth G. Jones, *In the Graveyard of Empires*, pp. 82–83.

7. Fareed Zakaria, *The Post-American World*, p. 12.

8. Shane, *Objective Troy*, pp. 9–10.

9. Zakaria, *The Post-American World*, p. 13.

10. Anthony H. Cordesman, Broad Patterns of Global Terrorism in 2014, Center for
Strategic and International Studies, June 19, 2015, http://csis.org/publication/broad
-patterns-global-terrorism-2014. See also Engel, op. cit., p. 132.

11. Rukmini Callimachi, Alissa J. Rubin, and Laure Fouquet, Paris attackers refined
tactics to inflict harm, *The New York Times*, March 20, 2016, p. 1, http://
www.nytimes.com/2016/03/20/world/europe/a-view-of-isiss-evolution-in-new-details
-of-paris-attacks.html?_r=0.

12. Rukmini Callimachi, Appealing to its base, ISIS tempers its violence in Muslim
countries, *The New York Times*, July 3, 2016, http://www.nytimes.com/2016/07/03/
world/middleeast/isis-muslim-countries-bangladesh.html?_r=0.

13. CBS *Face the Nation*, December 6, 2015, http://www.cbsnews.com/news/face-the
-nation-transcripts-december-6-2015-trump-christie-sanders/.

14. Quoted in David Ignatius, The Islamic State is still on the rise, *The Washington Post*,
February 5, 2016, p. A19, https://www.washingtonpost.com/opinions/the-islamic-state
-is-still-on
-the-rise/2016/02/04/e631bdea-cb82-11e5-88ff-e2d1b4289c2f_story.html.

15. Miller, Russian airstrikes changed 'calculus completely' in Syria, officials say, *The
Washington Post*, February 10, 2016, p. A21.

16. Mark Berman, Report: Domestic extremism took a deadly turn in 2015, *The
Washington Post*, January 6, 2016, p. A3, https://www.washingtonpost.com/news/post
-nation/wp/2016/01/05/2015-was-deadliest-year-for-domestic-extremist-violence-in
-two-decades-report-says/.

17. Robert L. Grenier, *88 Days to Kandahar*, p. 381.

18. Anthony H. Cordesman, Saudi Arabia, Iran, and the 'Clash within a Civilization',
Center for Strategic and International Studies, February 3, 2014, http://csis.org/
publication/saudi-arabia-iran-and-clash-within-civilization.

19. Memo from Secretary of Defense Donald Rumsfeld, Global War on Terrorism, October 16, 2003, reprinted in *USA Today*, May 20, 2005, http://usatoday30 .usatoday.com/news/washington/executive/rumsfeld-memo.htm.

20. The White House, Remarks by the President at the United States Military Academy Commencement, May 28, 2015.

21. Charles Krauthammer, Obama: Charlie who?, *The Washington Post*, January 16, 2015, p. A19.

22. David Motadel, 'Defending the faith' in the Middle East, *The New York Times*, May 24, 2015, p. SR6.

23. Peter Bergen, *United States of Jihad*, p. 29.

24. Missy Ryan, U.S. envoy: 'Long ways to go' in fight against the Islamic State, *The Washington Post*, February 11, 2016, p. A9, https://www.washingtonpost.com/world/ national-security/us-envoy-a-long-way-to-go-in-fight-against-the-islamic-state/2016/02/ 10/eb6458de-d007-11e5-b2bc-988409ee911b_story.html.

25. Hugh Naylor, Withering budget emerges as the Achilles' heel for ISIS, *The Washington Post*, February 7, 2016, p. A15, https://www.washingtonpost.com/world/ middle_east/islamic-state-is-no-longer-so-formidable-on-the-battlefield/2016/02/06/ 26d6c8e4-c6a7-11e5-b933-31c93021392a_story.html.

26. Joby Warrick, Senior Islamic State commander said to be killed in U.S. operation, *The Washington Post*, March 25, 2016, https://www.washingtonpost.com/news/ checkpoint/wp/2016/03/25/top-islamic-state-commander-killed-pentagon-official-says/ ?hpid = hp_rhp-top-table-main_isisdeath-1045a%3Ahomepage%2Fstory.

27. William McCants, *The ISIS Apocalypse*, p. 153.

28. David Ignatius, How the U.S. fights the Islamic State, *The Washington Post*, May 22, 2016, p. A19, https://www.washingtonpost.com/opinions/the-uss-show-of-power -against-the-islamic-state/2016/05/20/02096de6-1ecc-11e6-b6e0 -c53b7ef63b45_story.html.

29. U.S. Department of State, Press Availability with Iraqi Prime Minister Haider al-Abadi and French Foreign Minister Laurent Fabius, Paris, France, June 2, 2015, http:// www.state.gov/s/d/2015/243095.htm.

30. U.S. Department of State, Remarks, John Allen, Special Presidential Envoy for the Global Coalition to Counter ISIL, Doha, Qatar, June 3, 2015, http://www.state.gov/s/ seci/243115.htm.

31. Peter Bergen and David Sterman, Who Are ISIS' American Recruits, CNN, May 6, 2015, http://www.cnn.com/2015/05/06/opinions/bergen-isis-american-recruits/ ?utm_source = Sailthru&utm_medium = email&utm_term = %2ASituation%20Report& utm_campaign = SitRep0507.

32. Congressman Michael McCaul, Remarks at the Aspen Security Forum, July 25, 2015.

33. Stern and Berger, *ISIS: The State of Terror*, p. 118.

34. Quoted in David Ignatius, The Internet isn't to blame for radicalization, *The Washington Post*, January 15, 2015, https://www.washingtonpost.com/opinions/david -ignatius-the-roots-of-radicalization/2015/01/15/83cdffcc-9cf0-11e4-96cc -e858eba91ced_story.html.

35. John Hudson, Growth of Islamic State Forces State Department Overhaul, *Foreign Policy*, February 1, 2016, http://foreignpolicy.com/2016/02/01/growth-of-islamic-state -forces-state-department-overhaul/.

36. Greg Miller, Panel questions U.S. propaganda war against Islamic State, *The Washington Post*, December 3, 2015, p. A1, https://www.washingtonpost.com/world/ national-security/panel-casts-doubt-on-us-propaganda-efforts-against-isis/2015/12/02/ ab7f9a14-9851-11e5-94f0-9eeaff906ef3_story.html.

37. *CNN*, Fareed Zakaria GPS, Interview with President Barack Obama, Aired February 1, 2015.

38. Thomas L. Friedman, How ISIS drives Muslims from Islam, *The New York Times*, December 7, 2014, p. ST11.

39. Bergen, *United States of Jihad*, p. 27.

40. Kishore Mahbubani and Lawrence H. Summers, The Fusion of Civilizations, *Foreign Affairs*, May/June 2016, https://www.foreignaffairs.com/articles/2016-04-18/fusion -civilizations.

41. Nicholas Kristof, The terror the Saudis foment, *The New York Times*, July 3, 2016, http://www.nytimes.com/2016/07/03/opinion/sunday/the-terrorists-the-saudis -cultivate-in-peaceful-countries.html.

42. David Ignatius, Paranoia as a weapon, *The Washington Post*, December 3, 2014, p. A21.

43. Marlise Simons, Veteran U.S. lawyer foresees war crimes trials for ISIS, *The New York Times*, December 27, 2015, p. 14, http://www.nytimes.com/2015/12/27/world/ europe/veteran-international-prosecutor-foresees-war-crimes-trials-for-isis.html?_r=0.

44. Quoted in Kareem Fahim, Sectarian leaders fan flames in Middle East, *The New York Times*, October 18, 2015, p. 14, http://www.nytimes.com/2015/10/18/world/ middleeast/as-conflicts-flare-up-leaders-fan-sectarian-flames-in-middle-east.html.

45. Gideon Rose, *How Wars End*, p. 3.

46. Max Boot, More Small Wars: Counterinsurgency Is Here to Stay, *Foreign Affairs*, November/December 2014, p. 6, https://www.foreignaffairs.com/articles/libya/more -small-wars.

47. Quoted in Kareem Fahim, Sectarian leaders fan flames in Middle East, *The New York Times*, October 18, 2015, p. 14, http://www.nytimes.com/2015/10/18/world/ middleeast/as-conflicts-flare-up-leaders-fan-sectarian-flames-in-middle-east.html.

48. Liz Sly, Kurds declare their own region in northern Syria, *The Washington Post*, March 18, 2016, p. A17, https://www.washingtonpost.com/world/middle_east/syrian -kurds-declare-their-own-region-raising-tensions/2016/03/17/db762950-ec4c-11e5-a9ce -681055c7a05f_story.html.

49. Liz Sly, War against ISIS redrawing borders, *The Washington Post*, December 31, 2015, p. A1, https://www.washingtonpost.com/world/on-the-front-lines-of-the-war -against-the-islamic-state-a-tangled-web/2015/12/30/d944925a-9244-11e5-befa -99ceebcbb272_story.html.

50. Masrour Barzani, Kurds deserve a divorce from Baghdad, *The Washington Post*, May 6, 2016, p. A19, https://www.washingtonpost.com/opinions/kurdistan-deserves-an -amicable-divorce-from-baghdad/2016/05/05/b1d5218c-1221-11e6-81b4 -581a5c4c42df_story.html.

51. Ibid.

52. Missy Ryan and Greg Jaffe, Wider U.S. role vs. ISIS on table, *The Washington Post*, October 27, 2015, p. A1, https://www.washingtonpost.com/world/national-security/ obama-weighs-moving-us-troops-closer-to-front-lines-in-syria-iraq/2015/10/26/ 4ae2f36c-7bec-11e5-b575-d8dcfedb4ea1_story.html.

53. Lally Weymouth, Lebanon is 'heading toward a breakdown,' *The Washington Post*, September 20, 2015, p. B1, https://www.washingtonpost.com/opinions/lebanons-prime -minister-we-are-heading-toward-a-breakdown/2015/09/18/6c743c94-5c97-11e5-9757 -e49273f05f65_story.html.

54. Richard K. Betts, Pick Your Battles: Ending America's Era of Permanent War, *Foreign Affairs*, November/December 2014, p. 15, https://www.foreignaffairs.com/articles/ united-states/2014-10-20/pick-your-battles.

55. Dominic Tierney, *The Right Way to Lose a War*, p. 307.

56. Democracy in retreat, Editorial, *The Washington Post*, March 14, 2016, p. A16, https://www.washingtonpost.com/opinions/democracy-in-retreat/2016/03/13/dd2e5eba-e798-11e5-a6f3-21ccdbc5f74e_story.html.

57. Discussion with the author, October 26, 2015.

58. Author phone interview with Ambassador Chris Hill, January 15, 2016.

59. Matthew Yglesias, Barack Obama: The *Vox* Conversation, Part two: Foreign policy.

60. General David H. Petraeus, U.S. Army (Ret.), Testimony Prepared for the Senate Armed Services Committee on the U.S. Policy in the Middle East, September 22, 2015, http://www.armed-services.senate.gov/imo/media/doc/Petraeus_09-22-15.pdf.

61. Rukmini Callimachi, U.S. seeks to avoid ground war welcomed by Islamic State, *The New York Times*, December 7, 2015, http://www.nytimes.com/2015/12/08/world/middleeast/us-strategy-seeks-to-avoid-isis-prophecy.html.

62. The White House, Remarks by the President in Address to the United Nations General Assembly, September 24, 2013.

63. Nancy Youssef, Schieffer Series: A Discussion on Syria, Center for Strategic and International Studies, November 16, 2015.

64. James Dobbins, Philip Gordon, and Jeffrey Martini, A Peace Plan for Syria II, Rand Corporation Perspective, http://www.rand.org/pubs/perspectives/PE202.html.

65. Karen DeYoung, U.S. offers to share Syria intelligence on terrorists with Russia, *The Washington Post*, June 30, 2016, https://www.washingtonpost.com/world/national-security/us-offers-to-share-syria-intelligence-on-terrorists-with-russia/2016/06/30/483a2afe-3eec-11e6-84e8-1580c7db5275_story.html.

66. Adel Abdel Ghafar, Five years later, lessons of the uprisings in North Africa, The Brookings Institution, Middle East Politics and Policy, February 5, 2016, http://www.brookings.edu/blogs/markaz/posts/2016/02/05-lessons-of-arab-spring-abdelghafar?hs_u = crowley44@gmail.com&utm_campaign = Brookings + Brief&utm_source = hs_email&utm_medium = email&utm_content = 25987012&_hsenc = p2ANqtz-_tVoV5GOKoiPu8lYq2lAzi6RXDwok572iG19wrFiLgm1YH0FAzxWVYHTQGjqF-eSIGYP2qaxCJJ8bl3IuZhLnxiNnt3A&_hsmi = 25987012.

67. Ibid.

68. Souad Mekhennet, Tunisia's first freely elected president: The 'Arab Spring' is a European creation, WorldViews, *The Washington Post*, March 20, 2016, p. A20, https://www.washingtonpost.com/news/worldviews/wp/2016/03/19/tunisias-president-the-arab-spring-is-a-european-creation/.

69. Stern and Berger, *ISIS: The State of Terror*, p. 240.

70. Thomas L. Friedman, Schieffer Series: A Discussion on Syria, Center for Strategic and International Studies, November 16, 2015.

CHAPTER 14

1. David Weigel, In debate, can policy top the pizazz?, *The Washington Post*, September 16, 2015, p. A5, http://www.washingtonpost.com/politics/will-wednesdays-gop-debate-move-the-discourse-from-flash-to-substance/2015/09/15/44d2105a-5b2d-11e5-9757-e49273f05f65_story.html.

2. Pew Research Center, Public Uncertain, Divided over America's Place in the World, May 5, 2016, http://www.people-press.org/2016/05/05/public-uncertain-divided-over-americas-place-in-the-world/.

3. *The New York Times*, Transcript: Republican Presidential Debate, December 15, 2015, available at http://222.nytimes.com/2015/12/16/us/politics/transcript-main -republican-presidential-debate.html.

4. Donald J. Trump Foreign Policy Speech, April 27, 2016, https:// www.donaldjtrump.com/press-releases/donald-j.-trump-foreign-policy-speech.

5. David E. Sanger and Maggie Haberman, Foreign policy, in Trump's view, is about deals, *The New York Times*, March 27, 2016, p. 1, http://www.nytimes.com/2016/03/27/ us/politics/donald-trump-foreign-policy.html?hp&action = click&pgtype = Homepage& clickSource = story-heading&module = first-column-region&region = top-news& WT.nav = top-news&_r = 0.

6. Trump Foreign Policy Speech, April 27, 2016.

7. CNN Reagan Library Debate, September 16, 2015, http:// cnnpressroom.blogs.cnn.com/2015/09/16/cnn-reagan-library-debate-later-debate-full -transcript/.

8. G. John Ikenberry, *Liberal Leviathan*, p. 2.

9. Michael Mandelbaum, *The Case for Goliath*, p. 18.

10. The White House, Remarks by the President at the United States Military Academy Commencement Ceremony, May 28, 2014.

11. Senator Lindsey Graham, *CNBC*'s 'Your Money, Your Vote: The Republican Presidential Debate' Part I, October 28, 2015, http://www.cnbc.com/2015/10/29/cnbc -full-transcript-cnbcs-your-money-your-vote-the-republican-presidential-debate-part -1.html.

12. Robert Kagan, *The World America Made*, p. 110.

13. Dan Balz, The take: Trump worldview is a huge break from GOP line, *The Washington Post*, March 22, 2016, p. A1, https://www.washingtonpost.com/politics/ trumps-foreign-policy-views-a-sharp-departure-from-gop-orthodoxy/2016/03/21/ 6ef0d9f6-efa3-11e5-89c3-a647fcce95e0_story.html.

14. Micah Zenko, Hail to the Hugely Classy Commander-in-Chief, *Foreign Policy*, February 3, 2016, http://foreignpolicy.com/2016/02/03/hail-to-the-hugely-classy -commander-in-chief/.

15. *The New York Times*, Transcript of the Republican Presidential Debate in Florida, March 11, 2016.

16. Mead, The End of History Ends, *The American Interest*, December 2, 2013.

17. *The New York Times*, Transcript: Hillary Clinton's Speech at the Democratic Convention, July 28, 2016, available at http://www.nytimes.com/2016/07/28/us/politics/ hillary-clinton-dnc-transcript.html?_r = 0.

18. Colin Dueck, quoted in Karen Tumulty and David Weigel, What would the GOP candidates actually do about ISIS?, *The Washington Post*, December 10, 2015, p. A10, https://www.washingtonpost.com/politics/after-san-bernardino-how-the-foreign-policy -debate-may-be-shifting-for-gop-candidates/2015/12/07/64a96da2-9a9c-11e5-8917 -653b65c809eb_story.html.

19. David Ignatius, Lifting the 'fog of policy,' *The Washington Post*, September 11, 2015, p. A17.

20. Donald Trump on the Hugh Hewitt Show, quoted in Jacob Heilbrunn, The Neocons vs. Donald Trump, *The New York Times*, March 13, 2016, p. SR2, http:// www.nytimes.com/2016/03/13/opinion/sunday/the-neocons-vs-donald-trump.html.

21. David A. Fahrenthold, The long shots: Graham calls for sacrifice, with a smile, *The Washington Post*, September 11, 2015, p. A1.

22. *NPR*, Interview with President Obama, December 21, 2015, http://www.npr.org/ 2015/12/21/460030344/video-and-transcript-nprs-interview-with-president-obama.

23. *The New York Times*, Transcript of the Republican Presidential Debate, February 13, 2016, http://www.nytimes.com/2016/02/14/us/politics/transcript-of-the-republican-presidential-debate.html.

24. *The Washington Post*, A transcript to Donald Trump's meeting with *The Washington Post* editorial board, March 21, 2016, https://www.washingtonpost.com/blogs/post-partisan/wp/2016/03/21/a-transcript-of-donald-trumps-meeting-with-the-washington-post-editorial-board/.

25. *The New York Times*, Transcript of the Republican Presidential Debate in New Hampshire, February 6, 2016, http://www.nytimes.com/2016/02/07/us/politics/transcript-of-the-republican-presidential-debate-in-new-hampshire.html?_r=1.

26. Ibid.

27. Ibid.

28. Ibid.

29. Council on Foreign Relations, A Conversation with Hillary Clinton, November 19, 2015, http://www.cfr.org/radicalization-and-extremism/hillary-clinton-national-security-islamic-state/p37266.

30. *NBC News*, Transcript: MSNBC Democratic Candidates Debate, February 4, 2016.

31. Ibid.

32. *The Washington Post*, In Libya, it's time to act, Editorial, February 18, 2016, p. A16, https://www.washingtonpost.com/opinions/the-us-must-act-in-libya-before-the-islamic-state-grabs-more-territory/2016/02/17/a0d35382-d4ea-11e5-b195-2e29a4e13425_story.html.

33. Transcript of the *Fox News* Democratic presidential town hall, March 7, 2016, http://www.foxnews.com/politics/2016/03/07/transcript-fox-news-democratic-presidential-town-hall.print.html.

34. *The New York Times*, Republican Presidential Debate Transcript, November 10, 2015.

35. *The New York Times*, Transcript of the Republican Presidential Debate, February 13, 2016.

36. *The New York Times*, Transcript of the Democratic Presidential Debate in Milwaukee, February 11, 2016.

37. Ibid.

38. Karla Adam, GOP presidential debate, through the eyes of the world, *The Washington Post*, December 17, 2015, p. A7, https://www.washingtonpost.com/world/world-dissects-debate-macho-threats-border-fears-and-hint-of-bromance/2015/12/16/f5a2b42e-a372-11e5-8318-bd8caed8c588_story.html.

39. Donald J. Trump Addresses Terrorism, Immigration, and National Security, June 13, 2016, Text As Prepared, https://www.donaldjtrump.com/press-releases/donald-j.-trump-addresses-terrorism-immigration-and-national-security.

40. The White House, Remarks by the President After Counter-ISIL Meeting, June 14, 2016, https://www.whitehouse.gov/the-press-office/2016/06/14/remarks-president-after-counter-isil-meeting.

41. *CBS News*, Democratic debate transcript: Clinton, Sanders, O'Malley in Iowa, November 14, 2015, http://www.cbsnews.com/news/democratic-debate-transcript-clinton-sanders-omalley-in-iowa/.

42. *The New York Times*, Transcript of the Democratic Presidential Debate in Miami, March 10, 2016, http://www.nytimes.com/2016/03/10/us/politics/transcript-democratic-presidential-debate.html?_r=0.

43. Peter Baker, *Days of Fire*, p. 145.

44. Background discussion with a former senior government official, Aspen, Colorado, July 23, 2015.

45. Charlie Savage, *Power Wars*, p. 130.

46. Charlie Savage, Guantanamo is leaving Obama with choices, neither of them simple, *The New York Times*, November 1, 2015, p. 15, http://www.nytimes.com/2015/11/01/us/politics/guantanamo-is-leaving-obama-with-choices-neither-of-them-simple.html?_r = 0.

47. The White House, Remarks by the President on Plan to Close the Prison at Guantanamo Bay, February 23, 2016, https://www.whitehouse.gov/the-press-office/2016/02/23/remarks-president-plan-close-prison-guantanamo-bay.

48. Adam Goldman and Missy Ryan, Attacks on U.S. by men set free, *The Washington Post*, June 9, 2016, p. A1, https://www.washingtonpost.com/world/national-security/about-12-released-guantanamo-detainees-implicated-in-deadly-attacks-on-americans/2016/06/08/004d038e-2776-11e6-b989–4e5479715b54_story.html.

49. Ibid.

50. Jim Sensenbrenner, Congress can't be ignored on Guantanamo, *The Washington Post*, November 22, 2015, p. A29, https://www.washingtonpost.com/opinions/obama-must-avoid-a-constitutional-crisis-on-guantanamo/2015/11/20/70d44ce0-8d69-11e5-ae1f-af46b7df8483_story.html.

51. *The New York Times*, Transcript of Republican Presidential Debate, January 15, 2016.

52. *The New York Times*, Transcript of the Republican Presidential Debate in New Hampshire, February 6, 2016.

53. Michael V. Hayden, *Playing to the Edge*, pp. 34–35.

54. Ali H. Soufan, *The Black Banners*, p. 463.

55. Savage, *Power Wars*, pp. 88–91.

56. Hayden, *Playing to the Edge*, p. 382.

57. Savage, *Power Wars*, pp. 339–49.

58. *The New York Times*, Transcript of the Democratic Presidential Debate in Milwaukee, February 11, 2016.

59. *The New York Times*, Transcript of the Republican Presidential Debate, February 14, 2016.

60. Ibid.

61. Transcript: Donald Trump, *CNN* Republican Town Hall, Columbia, S.C., February 18, 2016, http://cnnpressroom.blogs.cnn.com/2016/02/18/rush-transcript-donald-trump-cnn-republican-presidential-town-hall-columbia-sc/.

62. Ibid.

63. Jose A. DelReal, Trump pays compliments to dictators, sowing discomfort within his party, *The Washington Post*, July 7, 2016, p. A6, https://www.washingtonpost.com/politics/trumps-favorite-dictators-in-reviled-tyrants-gop-nominee-finds-traits-to-praise/2016/07/06/8debf792-4385-11e6-bc99-7d269f8719b1_story.html.

64. Robert K. Brigham, ed., *The United States and Iraq Since 1990*, p. 234.

65. Anne Gearan and Ed O'Keefe, In both parties, the war in Iraq remains a divisive issue, *The Washington Post*, February 17, 2016, p. A5, https://www.washingtonpost.com/politics/the-war-in-iraq-haunts-the-2016-presidential-contest/2016/02/16/f29b8686-d44e-11e5-b195-2e29a4e13425_story.html.

66. Quoted in Dominic Tierney, *The Right Way to Lose a War*, p. 40.

67. David Ignatius, A spy chief's hardened perspective, *The Washington Post*, May 11, 2016, p. A17, https://www.washingtonpost.com/opinions/the-us-cant-fix-it-james-clapper-on-americas-role-in-the-middle-east/2016/05/10/377666a8-16ea-11e6-9e16-2e5a123aac62_story.html.

68. James Hohmann, The Daily 202: Kaine wants a vote on war against ISIS, *The Washington Post*, December 16, 2015, p. A19, https://www.washingtonpost.com/news/

powerpost/wp/2015/12/14/the-daily-202-tim-kaine-possible-hillary-running-mate-is
-madder-than-ever-congress-hasnt-declared-war-on-isis/.

69. Jack Goldsmith, Ryan Goodman, and Steve Vladeck, Reaching consensus on a war authorization, *The Washington Post*, November 16, 2014, p. A21.

70. Dennis Ross, *Doomed to Succeed*, p. 407.

CHAPTER 15

1. Sarah Sewell, Introduction to the University of Chicago Press Edition; A Radical Field Manual, in *The U.S. Army-Marine Corps Field Manual*, p. xliii.

2. General Rupert Smith, *The Utility of Force*, p. xiii.

3. Andrew J. Bacevich, *America's War for the Greater Middle East*, p. 249.

4. Dominic Tierney, *The Right Way to Lose a War*, p. 29.

5. Adam J. Berinsky, *In Time of War*, p. 2.

6. Arthur M. Schlesinger Jr., *The Imperial Presidency*, p. 279.

7. Robert D. Kaplan, *The Revenge of Geography*, pp. 122–24.

8. Ibid.

9. Vice President Dick Cheney was interviewed by ABC's Martha Raddatz on the fifth anniversary of the invasion of Iraq. When she mentioned that two-thirds of Americans felt the war was not worth fighting, he responded, "So?" By that time, the Bush administration was beyond its last election and Vice President Cheney was not seeking another high-level office. See Peter Baker, *Days of Fire*, p. 583.

10. Joseph S. Nye Jr., *The Paradox of American Power*, p. 136.

11. Moises Naim, *The End of Power*, p. 168.

12. Fareed Zakaria, *The Post-American World*, p. 204.

13. Nye, *The Paradox of American Power*, p. 41.

14. Zbigniew Brzezinski and Brent Scowcroft, *America and the World*, p. 2.

15. Joseph S. Nye Jr., *The Future of Power*, p. 116.

16. Naim, *The End of Power*, p. 51.

17. Nye, *The Paradox of American Power*, p. 50.

18. Baker, *Days of Fire*, p. 146.

19. Charlie Savage, *Power Wars*, p. 419.

20. Id., p. 458.

21. Jonathan Alter, *The Promise*, pp. 347–48.

22. Michael Morell, *The Great War of Our Time*, p. 140.

23. Michael V. Hayden, *Playing to the Edge*, p. 220.

24. Savage, *Power Wars*, p. 233.

25. Scott Shane, *Objective Troy*, p. 306.

26. David E. Sanger, *Confront and Conceal*, p. 260.

27. Savage, *Power Wars*, p. 439.

28. Seth G. Jones, *Hunting in the Shadows*, p. 343.

29. Greg Miller, Drone rules: Is 'near certainty' enough to pull the trigger?, *The Washington Post*, April 24, 2015, p. 1.

30. Sanger, *Confront and Conceal*, p. 245.

31. Rosa Brooks, Obama: The Last Year and the Legacy, Part I, *Foreign Policy*, January 13, 2016, http://foreignpolicy.com/2016/01/13/obama-the-last-year-legacy-guantanamo
-drones/.

32. General Stanley McChrystal, quoted in David Ignatius, The Middle Way on Afghanistan?, *The Washington Post*, September 2, 2009, http://www.washingtonpost.com/wp-dyn/content/article/2009/09/01/AR2009090103429_pf.html.

33. Alan Rusbridger and Ewen MacAskill, Edward Snowden interview—the edited transcript, *The Guardian*, July 18, 2014, http://www.theguardian.com/world/2014/jul/18/-sp-edward-snowden-nsa-whistleblower-interview-transcript.

34. Hayden, *Playing to the Edge*, p. 80.

35. Id., p. 90.

36. Admiral Michael Rogers, quoted in James Bamford, The Most Wanted Man in the World, *Wired*, June 13, 2014, http://www.wired.com/2014/08/edward-snowden/.

37. Ibid.

38. Joseph S. Nye Jr., *Soft Power*, p. 31.

39. Zakaria, *The Post-American World*, p. 248.

40. Nye, *The Future of Power*, p. 83.

41. Id., p. 104.

42. Richard N. Haass, *The Unraveling*: How to Respond to a Disordered World, *Foreign Affairs*, October 20, 2014, available at http://www.foreignaffairs.com/print/1113286.

43. Steven Weber and Bruce W. Jentleson, *The End of Arrogance*, p. 159.

44. Ian Shapiro, *Containment*, p. 13.

45. Nye, *The Future of Power*, p. 19.

46. James C. Thomson, Jr., How Could Vietnam Happen?, in James M. McCormick, ed., *The Domestic Sources of American Foreign Policy*, pp. 340–41.

47. James Mann, *The Obamians*, p. 156.

48. Jackson Diehl, Obama's Syria blinders, *The Washington Post*, March 21, 2016, p. A17, https://www.washingtonpost.com/opinions/the-costs-of-obamas-2013-syria-decision-are-apparent-to-everyone-but-him/2016/03/20/e526f614-ec56-11e5-a6f3-21ccdbc5f74e_story.html.

49. David Ignatius, Damage to Obama's foreign policy has been largely self-inflicted, The *Washington Post*, May 6, 2014, available at https://www.washiingtonpost.com/opinions/david-ignatius-damage-to-obamas-foreign-policy-has-been-largely-self-inflicted/2014/05/06/d3e7665a-d550-11e3-aae8/02d44bd79778_story.html:utm_term=01794e788859.

50. Ghattas, *The Secretary*, p. 126.

51. The White House, Remarks by the President Obama and Prime Minister Cameron in Joint Press Conference , April 22, 2016, https://www.whitehouse.gov/the-press-office/2016/04/22/remarks-president-obama-and-prime-minister-cameron-joint-press.

52. Savage, *Power Wars*, pp. 628–29.

53. Zakaria, *The Post-American World*, p. 247.

54. Richard N. Haass, *The Opportunity*, p. 177.

55. Weber and Jentleson, *The End of Arrogance*, p. 5.

56. See Philip Seib, *The Al-Jazeera Effect: How the Global Media are Shaping World Politics* (Washington, DC: Potomac Books, 2008).

57. Mann, *The Obamians*, p. 257.

58. Greg Miller and Souad Mekhennet, ISIS's army of propagandists: Confronting the 'Caliphate,' *The Washington Post*, November 22, 2015, p. A1, https://www.washingtonpost.com/world/national-security/inside-the-islamic-states-propaganda-machine/2015/11/20/051e997a-8ce6-11e5-acff-673ae92ddd2b_story.html.

59. Hayden, *Playing to the Edge*, pp. 423–24.

60. David Halberstam, *War in a Time of Peace*, p. 36.

CHAPTER 16

1. James Mann, *Rise of the Vulcans*, p. 257.

2. Id., p. 256.

3. Quoted in Jon Meacham, *Destiny and Power*, p. 566.

4. Jonathan Alter, *The Promise*, p. 227.

5. The White House, Remarks by the President and President Benigno Aquino III of the Philippines in Joint Press Conference, April 28, 2014, https://www.whitehouse.gov/the-press-office/2014/04/28/remarks-president-obama-and-president-benigno-aquino-iii-philippines-joi.

6. Christi Parsons, Kathleen Hennessy, and Paul Richter, Obama argues against use of force to solve global problems, *Los Angeles Times*, April 28, 2014, http://www.latimes.com/world/asia/la-fg-obama-military-20140429-story.html.

7. Quoted in Jeffrey Goldberg, Hillary Clinton: 'Failure' to Help Syrian Rebels Let to the Rise of ISIS, *The Atlantic*, August 10, 2014, available at http://theatlantic.com/international/archive/2014/08/hillary-clinton-failure-to-help-syrian-rebals-led-to-the-rise-of-isis/375832/.

8. Derek Chollet, *The Long Game*, p. 229.

9. Richard N. Haass, *War of Necessity, War of Choice*, p. 24.

10. Peter Feaver, 8 Myths about American Grand Strategy, *Foreign Policy*, November 23, 2011, http://foreignpolicy.com/2011/11/23/8-myths-about-american-grand-strategy/.

11. Derek Chollet and James Goldgeier, *America Between the Wars*, p. 8.

12. Joseph S. Nye Jr., *The Paradox of American Power*, p. xiv.

13. Zbigniew Brzezinski and Brent Scowcroft, *America and the World*, p. 243.

14. Ibid.

15. Nancy Youssef, Schieffer Series: A Discussion on Syria, Center for Strategic and International Studies, November 16, 2015.

16. The White House, Remarks by the President in Address to the United Nations General Assembly, September 24, 2013.

17. David E. Sanger, *Confront and Conceal*, p. 150.

18. Charlie Savage, *Power Wars*, p. 108.

19. Ross Douthat, Grading Obama's foreign policy, *The New York Times*, May 17, 2014, http://www.nytimes.com/2014/05/18/opinion/sunday/douthat-grading-obamas-foreign-policy.html?_r=0.

SELECTED BIBLIOGRAPHY

Christian Alfonsi, *Circle in the Sand: Why We Went Back to Iraq* (New York, Doubleday, 2006).

Jonathan Alter, *The Promise: President Obama, Year One* (New York, Simon & Schuster, 2010).

Andrew J. Bacevich, *America's War for the Greater Middle East* (New York, Random House, 2016).

Andrew J. Bacevich, *The Limits of Power: The End of American Exceptionalism* (New York, Metropolitan Books, 2008).

Jeffrey A. Bader, *Obama and China's Rise: An Insider's Account of America's Asia Strategy* (Washington, D.C., Brookings Institution Press, 2012).

James A. Baker III with Thomas M. DeFrank, *The Politics of Diplomacy: Revolution, War & Peace, 1989–1992* (New York, G.P. Putnam's Sons, 1995).

Peter Baker, *Days of Fire: Bush and Cheney in the White House* (New York, Doubleday, 2013).

Peter Baker and Susan Glasser, *Kremlin Rising: Vladimir Putin's Russia and the End of Revolution* (New York, Scribner, 2005).

Matthew A. Baum and Philip B. K. Potter, *War and Democratic Constraint: How the Public Influences Foreign Policy* (Princeton, NJ, Princeton University Press, 2015).

Daniel Benjamin and Steven Simon, *The Next Attack: The Failure of the War on Terror and a Strategy for Getting It Right* (New York, Times Books, 2005).

Daniel Benjamin and Steven Simon, *The Age of Sacred Terror* (New York, Random House, 2002).

Peter Bergen, *United States of Jihad: Investigating America's Homegrown Terrorists* (New York, Crown Publishers, 2016).

Peter L. Bergen, *Manhunt: The Ten-Year Search for Bin Laden from 9/11 to Abbottabad* (New York, Crown Publishers, 2012).

Adam J. Berinsky, *In Time of War: Understanding American Public Opinion from World War II to Iraq* (Chicago, University of Chicago Press, 2009).

Philip Bobbitt, *Terror and Consent: The Wars for the Twenty-First Century* (New York, Alfred A. Knopf, 2008).

Max Boot, *Invisible Armies: An Epic History of Guerrilla Warfare from Ancient Times to the Present* (New York, Liveright Publishing, 2013).

Ian Bremmer, *Superpower: Three Choices for America's Role in the World* (New York, Portfolio/Penguin, 2015).

Robert K. Brigham, ed., *The United States and Iraq Since 1990: A Brief History with Documents* (West Sussex, UK, Wiley-Blackwell, 2014).

Zbigniew Brzezinski, *Strategic Vision: America and the Crisis of Global Power* (New York, Basic Books, 2012).

Zbigniew Brzezinski, *Second Chance: Three Presidents and the Crisis of American Superpower* (New York, Basic Books, 2007).

Zbigniew Brzezinski, *The Choice: Global Domination or Global Leadership* (New York, Basic Books, 2004).

Zbigniew Brzezinski and Brent Scowcroft, *America and the World: Conversations on the Future of American Foreign Policy* (New York, Basic Books, 2008).

Daniel Byman, *The Five Front War: The Better Way to Fight Global Jihad* (New York, John Wiley & Sons, 2008).

Thanassis Cambanis, *Once Upon a Revolution: An Egyptian Story* (New York, Simon & Schuster, 2015).

Kurt M. Campbell, *The Pivot: The Future of American Statecraft in Asia* (New York, Twelve, 2016).

Victor Cha, *The Impossible State: North Korea, Past and Future* (New York, CCC, An Imprint of HarperCollins, 2012).

Thomas J. Christensen, *The China Challenge: Shaping the Choices of a Rising Power* (New York, W.W. Norton & Company, 2015).

Derek Chollet, *The Long Game: How Obama Defied Washington and Redefined America's Role in the World* (New York, PublicAffairs, 2016).

Derek Chollet and James Goldgeier, *America Between the Wars from 11/9 to 9/11: The Misunderstood Years between the Fall of the Berlin Wall and the Start of the War on Terror* (New York, PublicAffairs, 2008).

Wesley K. Clark, *Don't Wait for the Next War: A Strategy for American Growth and Global Leadership* (New York, PublicAffairs, 2014).

Richard A. Clarke, *Against All Enemies: Inside America's War on Terror* (New York, Free Press, 2004).

Bill Clinton, *My Life* (New York, Alfred A. Knopf, 2004).

Hillary Rodham Clinton, *Hard Choices* (New York, Simon & Schuster, 2014).

Steve Coll, *The Bin Ladens: An Arabian Family in the American Century* (New York, Penguin Books, 2008).

George Crile, *Charlie Wilson's War* (New York, Atlantic Monthly Press, 2003).

David Crist, *The Twilight War: The Secret History of America's Thirty-Year Conflict with Iran* (New York, Penguin Press, 2012).

Walter Cronkite, *A Reporter's Life* (New York, Alfred A. Knopf, 1996).

Ivo H. Daalder and James M. Lindsay, *America Unbound: The Bush Revolution in Foreign Policy* (Washington, D.C., Brookings Institution Press, 2003).

Ivo H. Daalder and Michael E. O'Hanlon, *Winning Ugly: NATO's War to Save Kosovo* (Washington, D.C., Brookings Press, 2000).

Mary L. Dudziak, *War Time: An Idea, Its History, Its Consequences* (New York, Oxford University Press, 2012).

Colin Dueck, *The Obama Doctrine: American Grand Strategy Today* (New York, Oxford University Press, 2015).

John Dumbrell and David Ryan, ed., *Vietnam in Iraq* (New York, Routledge, 2007).

Richard Engel, *And Then All Hell Broke Loose: Two Decades in the Middle East* (New York, Simon & Schuster, 2016).

Dexter Filkins, *The Forever War* (New York, Alfred A. Knopf, 2008).

David Fitzgerald and David Ryan, *Obama, US Foreign Policy and the Dilemmas of Intervention* (New York, Palgrave Macmillan, 2014).

Thomas L. Friedman and Michael Mandelbaum, *That Used to Be Us: How America Fell Behind in the World It Invented and How We Can Come Back* (New York, Farrar, Straus and Giroux, 2011).

David Fromkin, *Kosovo Crossing: American Ideals Meet Reality on the Balkan Battlefields* (New York, The Free Press, 1999).

John Lewis Gaddis, *The Cold War: A New History* (New York, Penguin Press, 2005).

John Lewis Gaddis, *Surprise, Security, and the American Experience* (Cambridge, MA, Harvard University Press, 2004).

Carlotta Gall, *The Wrong Enemy: America in Afghanistan, 2001–2014* (New York, Houghton Mifflin Harcourt, 2014).

Robert M. Gates, *Duty: Memoirs of a Secretary at War* (New York, Alfred A. Knopf, 2014).

Leslie H. Gelb, *Power Rules: How Common Sense Can Rescue American Foreign Policy* (New York, HarperCollins, 2009).

Barton Gellman, *Angler: The Cheney Vice Presidency* (New York, Penguin Press, 2008).

Kim Ghattas, *The Secretary: A Journey with Hillary Clinton from Beirut to the Heart of American Power* (New York, Times Books, 2013).

Jack Goldsmith, *Power and Constraint: The Accountable Presidency after 9/11* (New York, W.W. Norton & Company, 2012).

Gordon M. Goldstein, *Lessons in Disaster: McGeorge Bundy and the Path to War in Vietnam* (New York, Times Books, 2008).

Michael R. Gordon and General Bernard E. Trainor, *The Endgame: The Inside Story of the Struggle for Iraq, from George W. Bush to Barack Obama* (New York, Pantheon Books, 2012).

Michael R. Gordon and General Bernard E. Trainor, *Cobra II: The Inside Story of the Invasion and Occupation of Iraq* (New York, Pantheon Books, 2006).

Michael R. Gordon and General Bernard E. Trainor, *The General's War* (Boston, Little, Brown and Company, 1995).

Philip H. Gordon, *Winning the Right Way: The Path for America and the World* (New York, Times Books, 2007).

Bradley Graham, *By His Own Rules: The Ambitions, Successes, and Ultimate Failures of Donald Rumsfeld* (New York, PublicAffairs, 2009).

Robert L. Grenier, *88 Days to Kandahar: A CIA Diary* (New York, Simon & Schuster, 2015).

Richard N. Haass, *War of Necessity, War of Choice: A Memoir of Two Iraq Wars* (New York, Simon & Schuster, 2009).

Richard N. Haass, *The Opportunity: America's Moment to Alter History's Course* (New York, PublicAffairs, 2005).

David Halberstam, *The Making of a Quagmire: America and Vietnam during the Kennedy Era* (Revised Edition) (New York, Rowman & Littlefield Publishers, 2008).

David Halberstam, *War in a Time of Peace: Bush, Clinton and the Generals* (New York, Scribner, 2001).

David Halberstam, *The Best and the Brightest* (New York, Ballantine Books, 1992).

Daniel C. Hallin, *The Uncensored War: The Media and Vietnam* (New York, Oxford University Press, 1986).

Husain Haqqani, *Magnificent Delusions: Pakistan, the United States, and an Epic History of Misunderstanding* (New York, PublicAffairs, 2013).

Michael V. Hayden, *Playing to the Edge: American Intelligence in the Age of Terror* (New York, Penguin Press, 2016).

John Heilemann and Mark Halperin, *Game Change: Obama and the Clintons, McCain and Palin, and the Race of a Lifetime* (New York, Harper Collins Publishers, 2010).

George C. Herring, *America's Longest War: The United States and Vietnam, 1950–1975,* (Fourth Edition) (New York, McGraw-Hill, 2002).

Gary R. Hess, *Presidential Decisions for War: Korea, Vietnam, the Persian Gulf and Iraq* (Second Edition) (Baltimore, MD, Johns Hopkins University Press, 2009).

Gary R. Hess, *Vietnam: Explaining America's Lost War* (Oxford, UK, Blackwell Publishing, 2009).

Christopher R. Hill, *Outpost: Life on the Frontlines of American Diplomacy* (New York, Simon & Schuster, 2014).

Walter L. Hixson, *The Myth of American Diplomacy: National Identity and U.S. Foreign Policy* (New Haven, CT, Yale University Press, 2008).

Richard Holbrooke, *To End a War* (New York, Random House, 1998).

Michael H. Hunt, *Ideology and U.S. Foreign Policy* (New Haven, CT, Yale University Press, 2009).

G. John Ikenberry, *Liberal Leviathan: The Origins, Crisis, and Transformation of the American World Order* (Princeton, NJ, Princeton University Press, 2011).

Martin Indyk, *Innocent Abroad: An Intimate Account of American Peace Diplomacy in the Middle East* (New York, Simon & Schuster, 2009).

Martin Indyk, Kenneth G. Lieberthal, and Michael E. O'Hanlon, *Bending History: Barack Obama's Foreign Policy* (Washington, D.C., Brookings Institution Press, 2012).

Walter Isaacson and Evan Thomas, *The Wise Men: Six Friends and the World They Made* (New York, Simon & Schuster, 1986).

Michael Isikoff and David Corn, *Hubris: The Inside Story of Spin, Scandal, and the Selling of the Iraq War* (New York, Crown Publishers, 2006).

Seth G. Jones, *Hunting in the Shadows: The Pursuit of Al Qa'ida Since 9/11* (New York, W.W. Norton & Company, 2012).

Seth G. Jones, *In the Graveyard of Empires: America's War in Afghanistan* (New York, W.W. Norton & Company, 2009).

Robert Kagan, *The World America Made* (New York, Alfred A. Knopf, 2012).

Marvin Kalb, *Imperial Gamble: Putin, Ukraine, and the New Cold War* (Washington, D.C., Brookings Institution Press, 2015).

Marvin Kalb, *The Road to War: Presidential Commitments Honored and Betrayed* (Washington, D.C., Brookings Institution Press, 2013).

Marvin Kalb and Deborah Kalb, *Haunting Legacy: Vietnam and the American Presidency from Ford to Obama* (Washington, D.C., Brookings Institution Press, 2011).

Fred Kaplan, *The Insurgents: David Petraeus and the Plot to Change the American Way of War* (New York, Simon & Schuster, 2013).

Robert D. Kaplan, *The Revenge of Geography: What the Map Tells Us about Coming Conflicts and the Battle against Fate* (New York, Random House, 2012).

David Kilcullen, *Blood Year* (New York, Oxford University Press, 2017).

Erika G. King, *Obama, the Media, and Framing the U.S. Exit from Iraq and Afghanistan* (Burlington, VT, Ashgate, 2014).

Henry Kissinger, *World Order* (New York, Penguin Press, 2014).

Henry Kissinger, *Diplomacy* (New York, Simon & Schuster, 1994).

Daniel Klaidman, *Kill or Capture: The War on Terror and the Soul of the Obama Presidency* (Boston, Houghton, Mifflin Harcourt, 2012).

Charles A. Kupchan, *No One's World: The West, the Rising Rest, and the Coming Global Turn* (New York, Oxford University Press, 2012).

Daniel C. Kurtzer, Scott B. Lasensky, William B. Quant, Steven L. Spiegel, and Shibley Z. Telhami, *The Peace Puzzle: America's Quest for Arab-Israeli Peace, 1989–2011* (Ithaca, NY, Cornell University Press, 2013).

Mark Landler, *Alter Egos: Hillary Clinton, Barack Obama, and the Twilight Struggle over American Power* (New York, Random House, 2016).

Flynt Leverett and Hillary Mann Leverett, *Going to Tehran: Why the United States Must Come to Terms with the Islamic Republic of Iran* (New York, Metropolitan Books, 2013).

Robert Legvold, *Return to Cold War* (Malden, MA, Polity, 2016).

Charles R. Lister, *The Syrian Jihad: Al-Qaeda, the Islamic State and the Evolution of an Insurgency* (New York, Oxford University Press, 2015).

Fredrik Logevall, *Embers of War: The Fall of an Empire and the Making of America's Vietnam* (New York, Random House, 2012).

Fredrik Logevall, *Choosing War: The Lost Chance for Peace and the Escalation of War in Vietnam* (Berkeley, University of California Press, 1999).

Marc Lynch, *The New Arab Wars: Uprisings and Anarchy in the Middle East* (New York, PublicAffairs, 2016).

Marc Lynch, *The Arab Uprising: The Unfinished Revolutions of the New Middle East* (New York, PublicAffairs, 2012).

Michael Mandelbaum, *Mission Failure: America and the World in the Post-Cold War Era* (New York, Oxford University Press, 2016).

Michael Mandelbaum, *The Frugal Superpower: America's Global Leadership in a Cash-Strapped Era* (New York, PublicAffairs, 2010).

Michael Mandelbaum, *The Case for Goliath: How America Acts as the World's Government in the 21st Century* (New York, PublicAffairs, 2005).

James Mann, *George W. Bush* (New York, Times Books, 2015).

James Mann, *The Obamians: The Struggle Inside the White House to Redefine American Power* (New York, Viking, 2012).

James Mann, *The Rebellion of Ronald Reagan: The History of the End of the Cold War* (New York, Viking, 2009).

James Mann, *Rise of the Vulcans: The History of Bush's War Cabinet* (New York, Viking, 2004).

Mark Mazzetti, *The Way of the Knife: The CIA, a Secret Army, and a War at the Ends of the Earth* (New York, Penguin Press, 2013).

William McCants, *The ISIS Apocalypse: The History, Strategy, and Doomsday Vision of the Islamic State* (New York, St. Martin's Press, 2015).

Jon Meacham, *Destiny and Power: The American Odyssey of George Herbert Walker Bush* (New York, Random House, 2015).

Walter Russell Mead, *Power, Terror, Peace, and War* (New York, Alfred A. Knopf, 2005).

Michael Morell with Bill Harlow, *The Great War of Our Time: The CIA's Fight against Terrorism from Al Qa'ida to ISIS* (New York, Twelve, 2015).

Seyed Hossein Mousavian, *Iran and the United States: An Insider's View of the Failed Past and the Road to Peace* (New York, Bloomsbury Academic, 2014).

Steven Lee Myers, *The New Tsar: The Rise and Reign of Vladimir Putin* (New York, Alfred A. Knopf, 2015).

John A. Nagl, *Knife Fights: A Memoir of Modern War in Theory and Practice* (New York, Penguin Press, 2014).

Moises Naim, *The End of Power: From Boardrooms to Battlefields and Churches to States, Why Being in Charge Isn't What It Used to Be* (New York, Basic Books, 2013).

Vali Nasr, *The Dispensable Nation: American Foreign Policy in Retreat* (New York, Doubleday, 2013).

Vali Nasr, *The Shia Revival: How Conflicts within Islam Will Shape the Future* (New York, W.W. Norton & Company, 2006).

Charles E. Neu, ed., *After Vietnam: Legacies of a Lost War* (Baltimore, MD, Johns Hopkins University Press, 2000).

Joseph S. Nye Jr., *Is the American Century Over?* (Cambridge, UK, Polity Press, 2015).

Joseph S. Nye Jr., *Presidential Leadership and the Creation of the American Era* (Princeton, NJ, Princeton University Press, 2013).

Joseph S. Nye Jr., *The Future of Power* (New York, PublicAffairs, 2011).

Joseph S. Nye Jr., *Soft Power: The Means to Succeed in World Politics* (New York, PublicAffairs, 2004).

Joseph S. Nye Jr., *The Paradox of American Power: Why the World's Only Superpower Can't Go It Alone* (New York, Oxford University Press, 2002).

Don Oberdorfer, *Tet! The Turning Point in the Vietnam War* (Baltimore, MD, Johns Hopkins University Press, 2001).

Leon Panetta, *Worthy Fights* (New York, Penguin Press, 2014).

Trita Parsi, *A Single Roll of the Dice: Obama's Diplomacy with Iran* (New Haven, Yale University Press, 2012).

Trita Parsi, *Treacherous Alliance: The Secret Dealings of Israel, Iran, and the U.S.* (New Haven, Yale University Press, 2007).

James T. Patterson, *Restless Giant: The United States from Watergate to Bush v. Gore* (New York, Oxford University Press, 2005).

William J. Perry, *My Journey at the Nuclear Brink* (Stanford, CA, Stanford University Press, 2015).

Andrew J. Polsky, *Elusive Victories: The American Presidency at War* (New York, Oxford University Press, 2012).

Colin Powell with Tony Klotz, *It Worked for Me: In Life and Leadership* (New York, HarperCollins, 2012).

Ahmed Rashid, *Pakistan on the Brink: The Future of America, Pakistan, and Afghanistan* (New York, Viking, 2012).

Condoleezza Rice, *No Higher Honor: A Memoir of My Years in Washington* (New York, Crown Publishers, 2011).

Thomas E. Ricks, *The Generals: American Military Command from World War II to Today* (New York, Penguin Press, 2012).

Thomas E. Ricks, *Fiasco: The American Military Adventure in Iraq* (New York, Penguin Press, 2006).

Bruce Riedel, *The Search for Al Qaeda: Its Leadership, Ideology, and Future* (Washington, D.C., Brookings Institution Press, 2008).

Gideon Rose, *How Wars End: Why We Always Fight the Last Battle* (New York, Simon & Schuster, 2010).

Dennis Ross, *Doomed to Succeed: The U.S.-Israeli Relationship from Truman to Obama* (New York, Farrar, Straus and Giroux, 2015).

Dennis Ross and David Makovsky, *Myths, Illusions, and Peace: Finding a New Direction for America in the Middle East* (New York, Viking, 2009).

Dennis Ross, *Statecraft and How to Restore America's Standing in the World* (New York, Farrar, Straus and Giroux, 2007).

David Rothkopf, *National Insecurity: American Leadership in an Age of Fear* (New York, Public Affairs, 2014).

David E. Sanger, *Confront and Conceal: Obama's Secret Wars and Surprising Use of American Power* (New York, Crown Publishers, 2012).

David E. Sanger, *The Inheritance: The World Obama Confronts and the Challenge to American Power* (New York, Harmony Books, 2009).

Charlie Savage, *Power Wars: Inside Obama's Post-9/11 Presidency* (New York, Little, Brown and Company, 2015).

Arthur M. Schlesinger Jr., *War and the American Presidency* (New York, W.W. Norton & Company, 2004).

Arthur M. Schlesinger Jr., *The Imperial Presidency* (Boston, Mariner Books, 1973 with new introduction in 2004).

Eric Schmidt and Jared Cohen, *The New Digital Age: Reshaping the Future of People, Nations and Business* (New York, Alfred A. Knopf, 2013).

Eric Schmitt and Thom Shanker, *Counterstrike: The Untold Story of America's Secret Campaign against Al Qaeda* (New York, Times Books, 2011).

David F. Schmitz, *The Tet Offensive: Politics, War, and Public Opinion* (Lanham, MD, Rowman & Littlefield, 2005).

Gabriel Schoenfeld, *Necessary Secrets: National Security, the Media, and the Rule of Law* (New York, W.W. Norton & Company, 2010).

Philip Seib, *Real-Time Diplomacy: Politics and Power in the Social Media Era* (New York, Palgrave Macmillan, 2012).

Philip Seib, *The Al-Jazeera Effect: How the New Global Media Are Reshaping World Politics* (Washington, D.C., Potomac Books, 2008).

Stephen Sestanovich, *Maximalist: America in the World from Truman to Obama* (New York, Alfred A. Knopf, 2014).

David Shambaugh, *China Goes Global: The Partial Power* (New York, Oxford University Press, 2013).

Scott Shane, *Objective Troy: A Terrorist, a President, and the Rise of the Drone* (New York, Tim Duggan Books, 2015).

Ian Shapiro, *Containment: Rebuilding a Strategy Against Global Terror* (Princeton, NJ, Princeton University Press, 2007).

George P. Shultz, *Turmoil and Triumph: My Years as Secretary of State* (New York, Charles Scribner's Sons).

Jean Edward Smith, *Eisenhower in War and Peace* (New York, Random House, 2012).

General Rupert Smith, *The Utility of Force: The Art of War in the Modern World* (New York, Alfred A. Knopf, 2007).

Richard Sobel, *The Impact of Public Opinion on U.S. Foreign Policy Since Vietnam* (New York, Oxford University Press, 2001).

Richard Sobel, Peter Furia, and Bethany Barratt, eds., *Public Opinion and International Intervention: Lessons from the Iraq War* (Washington, D.C., Potomac Books, 2012).

Jay Solomon, *The Iran Wars: Spy Games, Bank Battles, and the Secret Deals that Shaped the Middle East* (New York: Random House, 2016).

Ali H. Soufan, *The Black Banners: The Inside Story of 9/11 and the War Against al-Qaeda* (New York, W.W. Norton & Company, 2011).

Bartholomew Sparrow, *The Strategist: Brent Scowcroft and the Call of National Security* (New York, PublicAffairs, 2015).

James Steinberg and Michael E. O'Hanlon, *Strategic Reassurance and Resolve: U.S.-China Relations in the Twenty-First Century* (Princeton, NJ, Princeton University Press, 2014).

Jessica Stern, and J. H. Berger, *ISIS: The State of Terror* (New York: CCC, 2015).

Ray Takeyh and Steven Simon, *The Pragmatic Superpower: Winning the Cold War in the Middle East* (New York, W.W. Norton & Company, 2016).

Ray Takeyh, *Guardians of the Revolution: Iran and the World in the Age of the Ayatollahs* (New York, Oxford University Press, 2009).

Ray Takeyh, *Hidden Iran: Paradox and Power in the Islamic Republic* (New York, Times Books, 2006).

Strobe Talbott, *The Great Experiment: The Story of Ancient Empires, Modern States, and the Quest for a Global Nation* (New York, Simon & Schuster, 2008).

Shibley Telhami, *The World through Arab Eyes: Arab Public Opinion and the Reshaping of the Middle East* (New York, Basic Books, 2013).

George Tenet, *At the Center of the Storm: My Years at the CIA* (New York, HarperCollins, 2007).

Evan Thomas, *Being Nixon: A Man Divided* (New York, Random House, 2015).

Evan Thomas, *Ike's Bluff: President Eisenhower's Secret Battle to Save the World* (New York, Little, Brown and Company, 2012).

Dominic Tierney, *The Right Way to Lose a War: America in an Age of Unwinnable Conflicts* (New York, Little, Brown and Company, 2015).

Chuck Todd, *The Stranger: Barack Obama in the White House* (New York, Little, Brown and Company, 2014).

U.S. Army and Marine Corps, *Counterinsurgency Field Manual*, U.S. Army Field Manual No. 3-24 and Marine Corps Warfighting Publication No. 3-33.5 (Chicago: University of Chicago Press, 2007).

Joby Warrick, *Black Flags: The Rise of ISIS* (New York, Doubleday, 2015).

Steven Weber and Bruce W. Jentleson, *The End of Arrogance: America in the Global Competition of Ideas* (Cambridge, MA, Harvard University Press, 2010).

Tim Weiner, *One Man against the World: The Tragedy of Richard Nixon* (New York, Henry Holt and Company, 2015).

Bob Woodward, *Obama's Wars: The Inside Story* (New York, Simon & Schuster, 2010).

Bob Woodward, *The War Within: A Secret White House History 2006–2008* (New York, Simon & Schuster, 2008).

Bob Woodward, *State of Denial: Bush at War, Part III* (New York, Simon & Schuster, 2006).

Bob Woodward, *Plan of Attack* (New York, Simon & Schuster, 2004).

Bob Woodward, *Bush at War* (New York, Simon & Schuster, 2002).

Robert F. Worth, *A Rage for Order: The Middle East in Turmoil, from Tahrir Square to ISIS* (New York, Farrar, Straus and Giroux, 2016).

Lawrence Wright, *Al-Qaeda and the Road to 9/11* (New York, Alfred A. Knopf, 2006).

Robin Wright, *Dreams and Shadows: The Future of the Middle East* (New York, Penguin Press, 2008).

Fareed Zakaria, *The Post-American World* (New York, W.W. Norton & Company, 2008).

Fareed Zakaria, *The Future of Freedom: Illiberal Democracy at Home and Abroad* (New York, W.W. Norton & Company, 2003).

Julian E. Zelizer, ed., *The Presidency of George W. Bush: A First Historical Assessment* (Princeton, NJ, Princeton University Press, 2010).

Julian E. Zelizer, *Arsenal of Democracy: The Politics of National Security—From World War II to the War on Terrorism* (New York, Basic Books, 2010).

Micah Zenko, *Between Threats and War: U.S. Discrete Military Operations in the Post-Cold War World* (Stanford, CA, Stanford University Press, 2010).

Index

ABOUT THE AUTHOR

Philip J. (P. J.) Crowley served as a spokesperson for the U.S. government for thirty years. He is a Professor of Practice and Distinguished Fellow at the Institute for Public Diplomacy and Global Communication at The George Washington University and a member of the Aspen Institute Homeland Security Group.

He served as the assistant secretary for public affairs and spokesman for the U.S. Department of State between 2009 and 2011 and was the primary U.S. government interlocutor with major media regarding WikiLeaks. He resigned after making public comments critical of the government's pretrial treatment of Private First Class Bradley (now Chelsea) Manning. *Atlantic* magazine named him as one of 21 Brave Thinkers in 2011.

P. J. is a retired Air Force colonel and veteran of Operations Desert Shield and Desert Storm. He served on the National Security Council staff at the White House as a special assistant to President Clinton and deputy press secretary. He deployed to NATO Headquarters in Brussels during the 1999 Kosovo crisis.

Between 2002 and 2009, P. J. was a senior fellow at the Center for American Progress and authored several studies on national and homeland security issues. He appears frequently as a national security commentator on national and global television networks, including BBC and Al Jazeera.

P. J. is a graduate of the College of the Holy Cross. He and his spouse, Paula Kougeas, also a retired Air Force colonel, have two children and live in Alexandria, Virginia.